DISTURBED GROUND

Also by Carla Norton

Perfect Victim

DISTURBED GROUND

The True Story of a Diabolical Female Serial Killer

· · · · · · ·

CARLA NORTON

William Morrow and Company, Inc.
New York

It is the policy of William Morrow and Company, Inc., and its imprints and affiliates, recognizing the importance of preserving what has been written, to print the books we publish on acid-free paper, and we exert our best efforts to that end.

    Norton, Carla.
       Disturbed ground : the true story of a diabolical female serial killer / by Carla Norton.
       p. cm.
     ISBN 0-688-09704-9
       1. Puente, Dorothea. 2. Murder—California—Sacramento—Case studies.
3. Socially handicapped—California—Sacramento—Crimes against—Case studies. 4. Welfare recipients—California—Sacramento—Crimes against—Case studies. I. Title.
     HV6534.S16N67   1994
     364.1'523'0979454—dc20   94-6212
                                        CIP

Printed in the United States of America

First Edition

1 2 3 4 5 6 7 8 9 10

BOOK DESIGN BY LISA STOKES

Dedicated to the memory of
"Bert"
Alvaro José Rafael Gonzáles Montoya,
the innocent catalyst for all that followed

AUTHOR'S NOTE

Writing nonfiction crime, one is continually struck by how subjective the "truth" can be. Like those proverbial blind men describing the elephant, each person has a singular version of reality. The writer's task, in my view, is to distill the facts down to the essential truth, presenting the reader with an account that flows with authenticity, leaving behind the flotsam and jetsam.

Over the years of researching and writing this book, countless people have shared information, and I owe them all a debt of thanks. Any errors in this text are doubtless due to my own misunderstanding of the elephantine "truth," for, as with my last book, this account is subject to the fallible judgment of the author.

ACKNOWLEDGMENTS

First and foremost, my deep appreciation to Judy Moise, whose personal thoughts and feelings about this case, and most especially about Bert Montoya, not only helped shape the manuscript, but compelled me to undertake this story.

Warmest thanks to Reba Nicklous, to William Clausen and the entire Clausen family, and to Jerry Hobbs for sharing their views, feelings, and sometimes painful memories.

I owe special thanks to the attorneys, who were kind enough to share their time and insights with me: the always illuminating prosecutors, George Williamson, and Assistant Chief Deputy District Attorney John O'Mara; and the unfailingly gracious defense attorneys, Kevin Clymo, and Supervising Assistant Public Defender Peter Vlautin.

Special thanks also to the Honorable Michael J. Virga and to his able court clerk, Barbara Beddow, for their unmatched kindness and strong coffee.

Recognition is also due the many saintly souls in social services, most particularly: Bill Johnson and J. D. Ridgley at the Volunteers of America; Mary Ellen Howard at the Department of Welfare; Lucy

Acknowledgments

Yokota at the Chest Clinic; and Michael Coonan, whose comprehensive report, "Sins of Omission," was an early compass for this project.

At the Sutter County Sheriff's Department, many thanks to Lieutenant Wilbur Terry, Lieutenant Steve Sizelove, and Sergeant Loren Felts for their time, honesty, and refreshing openness.

At the Sacramento County Coroner's Office, my thanks to Coroner James A. Moore; to Deputy Coroners Edward Smith and Laura Synhorst; to forensic toxicologist James Beede; and most especially to forensic pathologists Dr. Robert Anthony and Dr. Gary Stuart.

At the California Department of Justice, a nod of thanks to Supervising Toxicologist William Phillips, and to Senior Document Examiner David Moore.

Long-distance thanks to Dr. Janet Warren of the Institute of Law, Psychiatry & Public Policy at the University of Virginia, and to Roy Hazelwood of the FBI's Behavioral Sciences Unit in Quantico.

Thanks also to Deputy District Attorney Janice Hayes; to former Deputy District Attorney Bill Wood; to Parole Officer Jim Wilson; to Deputy Pete James at the Sacramento County Main Jail; to court reporter Mary Corbitt; and to bartender Marjorie Harper. And special gratitude to the aptly named Mr. John Sharp.

A bow to my many colleagues in the news media, always a source of inspiration, including Mike Boyd, Sharon Chin, Mark Schumacher, Gene Silver, Dana Spurrier, and Jim Wieder, as well as photographers Glen Korengold, David Morris, and Paul Sakuda. And highest respects to print journalists Tracie Cone of the *San Jose Mercury News;* John Enders of the Associated Press; Richard Paddock of the *Los Angeles Times;* and most particularly ace reporter Wayne Wilson of *The Sacramento Bee.*

Thanks also to the long-suffering, hardworking jurors for understanding that this book differs from the accounts presented at trial, since some things simply didn't make it through the legal filter into the courtroom.

Profound thanks to my family and friends, who stood by me during more than four years of work and personal "challenges," never once suggesting that I switch careers; and especially to my sister, Dianne Jurgensen, and *tomodachi* Lisa Ellenberg, for their invaluable help with the manuscript.

A thousand thanks to my excellent agent, Richard Pine, for taking me on long before any whispers of the best-seller list. And deepest

Acknowledgments

appreciation to Liza Dawson, my astute editor, who believed in me from the start and expertly guided me through the writing of this book, as with *Perfect Victim.*

And my most heartfelt gratitude to my superb photographer and sweet husband, George Fardell, for his patience, help, and understanding, and for spicing my life with complications.

PROLOGUE

The morning of January 1, 1986, dawned with the usual promise of hangovers, parades, and football games. But in Sutter County, a rural stretch in Northern California, this particular New Year's Day was less memorable for any holiday reverie than for the excitement surrounding a discovery down on the banks of the Sacramento River.

There was a damp chill in the early-morning air, but local fisherman Roy Beals was flushed when he burst into the Verona General Store and Restaurant. "Hey! Hey! You gotta come out and take a look," he cried between gasps. "I found a dead body! No kiddin'! At least I think so. It's in a box, down by the river, 'bout a mile or two."

Startled, Marge and Marvin Horstman, the owners of the store, stared at their stocky friend. Before they could respond, he was tugging at Marvin's sleeve. "You gotta come with me," Beals implored. "I ain't for sure. It's wrapped up in plastic. You gotta come an' see. I'll show ya I ain't jokin'."

A few minutes later the two scurried down the steep embankment, coming to a stop next to a large rectangular wood box resting just a few feet from the water.

"There's a body in there, I'm pretty sure," Beals whispered. "I just took a peek."

The two men drew closer and stared inside at something suspiciously large wrapped in plastic. "Well, let's take a look," Horstman said, squatting down next to it.

Abruptly, Horstman stood back up. "I don't want to touch it," he said bluntly. "Have you got anything in your car? Some pliers maybe?"

Beals hurried back up the embankment to fetch them. Then, with his heart in his throat, Horstman pulled away enough of the plastic to discover what was inside.

Their call to the Sutter County Sheriff's Department sent a jolt through the office on what should have been a sleepy holiday. Detective Sergeant Wilbur Terry handled all homicide investigations, so he drew the grim duty of going out to tiny Verona to investigate the report.

Two patrol deputies in the area were also sent to take a look, and by the time Detective Sergeant Terry arrived, the deputies had already interviewed Beals and Horstman. One deputy had carefully made his way down the riverbank to ascertain that, indeed, there was a corpse in that box. One deputy: one extra set of footprints. Henceforth, Terry mandated, they would all share that single trail, stepping on as little evidence as possible.

More backup arrived shortly, transforming this quiet fishing spot into a bustling crime scene. The deputies approached the perimeter of the scene cautiously, careful not to disturb possible evidence. Leaves had fallen into the box, so it had been there for some time. Photographs were taken, tire tracks and footprints lifted. Cigarette butts, bottle tops, odd scraps of material were carefully removed from the site.

Detective Sergeant Terry believed in taking his time, in scrutinizing every detail. You never know what you're looking for, he thought, just something that doesn't belong. Morning had long yielded to afternoon by the time he wrapped things up.

A hearse was called to take the body into Yuba City, the county seat, where the putrefied corpse was X-rayed. This was done not only for possible identification, but also to determine whether bullets, broken knife blades, or other lethal objects were lodged within. There were none.

It was discovered, however, that in a curiously fastidious gesture, more than a dozen mothballs and a room deodorizer had been placed in the box with the corpse.

Big cities have fancy morgues for conducting autopsies; in Sutter County any possible homicide victims are taken to Ullrey's Memorial Chapel. There, Dr. Frederick Hanf did the honors, unwrapping the remains like some ominous gift.

The body was in a fetal position, wrapped in a bed sheet and layers of plastic, secured with tape. Additionally, the head and hands had been bagged in black plastic garbage bags. Uncovering the body, Dr. Hanf found a bloated, decomposed white male with white hair and a mustache, dressed only in a T-shirt and undershorts, wearing a wrist-watch. He couldn't estimate the time of death beyond saying that a couple of weeks or months might be "fair." And he could not deter-mine the cause of death.

During the autopsy, Dr. Hanf took a blood sample from the heart that would be sent to the Department of Justice (DOJ) crime lab in Sacramento for toxicological testing. There, the sample was found to be so decomposed as to be "unsuitable" for a number of tests.

The body's fingertips were snipped from the hands and also sent to the DOJ in Sacramento, where they were prepared and rolled for prints. No matching prints were found, but it was noted that the man was missing the tip of his right thumb.

Meanwhile, Detective Loren Felts had the odious task of examining the slimy plastic for fingerprints. (The stench was so sickening that his partner finally told him to take the work outside.) After many hours of painstaking examination, Felts found only a few disappointing partial prints.

With no ID, no missing person's report, no matching prints, and no hint to who this fellow might be, the name on the case filed remained "John Doe." Rather than file unsolved cases in a drawer, Detective Sergeant Terry believed it best to keep them out in the open, on his desk, as a constant reminder that there were answers yet to be found. He plopped this slim "John Doe" file down on top of his desk.

By now the detective had arrived at his own name for the old fellow. Having pondered the case for a while, he'd developed a theory. The autopsy had revealed no cause of death, so it seemed the old man had died of natural causes. Why hadn't he been buried? Why had he been so quietly deposited at the riverbank? Because, Terry surmised, the family simply hadn't wanted a death certificate. "That's somebody's old Uncle Harry," the detective concluded, "and somebody's still collecting old Uncle Harry's Social Security checks."

His guess was better than most, but if the case had seemed more sensational, if the mostly nude victim found down by the river had been young and female, law enforcement may have guessed something closer to the truth. They may have at least considered that this was the work of a mad lover, might have even wondered whether this could be their first hard look at the work of a serial killer.

But only a fraction of all murders—3 or 4 percent—are committed by serial killers, so this seemed highly unlikely. Besides, there was no pattern to guide them.

For now, the method and identity of the killer would remain as mysterious as the name of the victim. So elusive was this killer that even a long criminal history would not invite scrutiny, for this crafty individual possessed the most extraordinarily convenient of disguises, beyond the ken of even the FBI's most sophisticated profilers.

Over years of intense forensic study the FBI has fine-tuned the art of "profiling," time and again divining the age, build, behavior, even the type of residence of a serial killer long before it has narrowed its investigation to individual suspects. It has distilled a formula. Serial murders, done secretly and systematically over a period of time, are virtually by definition sexually motivated, the victims random strangers. Typically, serial killers are white, in their late twenties to early forties, and almost exclusively male.

Almost.

INTRODUCTION

It rarely snows in Sacramento, California, making it a much more amenable place for the homeless than, say, Kansas City or Detroit. A few winter days might turn brutally frigid, but the blistering heat of summer warrants more complaint than the cold of winter.

In any case, street people are virtually never found frozen to death on Sacramento's park benches.

They die in other ways.

Not that many notice. In death as in life, anonymity cloaks them like grimy overcoats. Strangers who have seen their faces soon forget. Even their families may have been trying to forget them for a very long time.

When Sacramento's itinerants die, the county buries them by the cheapest means possible. No one comes to their funerals; no one visits their graves.

As in other American cities, the citizens of Sacramento perceive a large and growing "homeless problem." They can't help but notice the clusters of vagrants loitering around town; and they're pained to spot the occasional bag lady on the curb tending not just small parcels, but also small children.

Still, this is a city rich in distractions, with more to recommend it than the infrequency of days when the mercury dips below freezing. While it lacks the glamour of Hollywood or the charm of San Francisco, Sacramento basks in a growing reputation as a desirable place to live, with two universities, a plethora of fine shops and cafés, and its providential location at the confluence of two glistening rivers (the Sacramento and American). The snow-capped Sierras rise to the east, fields of orchards and sunflowers stretch across the valley, and a bustle of new developments, belted together with a rush of freeways, girds the city. Old-fashioned Victorian homes endow the downtown with a sense of style and tradition. And the streets are flanked with a deciduous lushness that dies each autumn with a shout of crimson.

At the city's heart, past a clot of government buildings, the magnificently restored state capitol dome gleams above Capitol Park. Here, tasteful dark suits stream along sidewalks and heels click down hallways as ideas are delivered to the state's legislators. Outside, buses deposit tour groups who have come for a government pilgrimage.

Yet even this capital city of "the world's sixth largest economy" has not been immune to the toxic side effects of "Reaganomics," and small, dirty caravans of overburdened shopping carts also clatter along these sidewalks.

Though Sacramento's weather is kind and its charities busy, life on the street is a wearisome limbo of waiting and walking, of stubborn rules, of being hungry, of making do. The well-traveled route from shelter to soup kitchen and back is called, simply, "the Walk."

Benefit checks—veterans' benefits, disability, Social Security, SSI (Supplemental Security Income), Medicaid, pensions—are the slow heartbeat that feeds this flow of society. The money comes in spurts: a wealth of food, alcohol, and cigarettes for a few days that trickles to nothing by the end of the month. Some budget, some splurge, others have it stolen. Street people, with little to lose but less for protection, make easy targets for con artists and thugs.

Those with physical handicaps are hard to begrudge our tax dollars to, but those with mental handicaps meet more often with incomprehension than compassion. They are "the crazies," "the ranters," and they suffer a gamut of mental afflictions: schizophrenia, manic depression, Down syndrome, organic and inorganic brain damage. For many, internal distractions loom larger than mundane matters such as shaving or brushing their teeth. The voices they hear, the paranoias

18

that mold their behavior are as real to them as any tree or building, and far more demanding than mere social graces. No one pretends they could get work but for a failure of will.

With the number of public mental hospital beds dwindling to a fraction of what they were a generation ago,° and with "deinstitution-alization" the prevailing ethic, housing the mentally ill is a formidable task. Those recognized as ill—not merely discounted as obnoxious—may be rescued from the street by mental health workers who then try to place them in appropriate facilities. (Ironically, those "lucky" enough to be tagged "5150"—law enforcement lingo for "a danger to themselves or others"—often get the most comprehensive care.)

If the mentally ill can simply remember to take their own medications (or "meds," in the parlance of mental health workers), they've crossed a major hurdle: They can live on their own rather than in a licensed facility, where a supervisor administers their meds to them.

Surely, some who could manage to take their meds on their own don't, simply because the prospect of greater freedom is too frightening.

It could be, there's good reason to be scared.

° In 1955, public mental institutions offered 559,000 beds; by 1990, that number had shrunk to 110,000.

19

Part I

CANARY

There's no loneliness on the street—there's a million of us out here.

—Vietnam veteran MIKE BAILEY,
in *Red Heart*

CHAPTER 1

A T FIRST BLUSH, BERT MONTOYA WASN'T A PARTICULARLY APPEAL-
ing fellow. His grooming habits were poor, his big stomach pushed
out over his trousers, and a mean case of psoriasis assailed his scalp.
With his thick gray-white hair, unruly beard, full lips, and soft dark
eyes, he had an unkempt yet benevolent look. He rarely spoke, even
with others who spoke his native Spanish. And at his most articulate
he mumbled so badly that he was hard to understand, perhaps because he had so few teeth. Shy and acquiescent, he usually watched
from the sidelines, appearing isolated, remote . . . yet somehow
irresistible.

Bert talked to trees. Wagging one thick finger skyward, shuffling
down the street in ill-fitting boots and rumpled clothes, he conversed
with people only he could hear. When more fleshly beings interrupted, he fell silent.

While Bert Montoya had many problems, alcohol wasn't among
them. Other than the infrequent beer, he simply didn't drink. Call
him simple, call him mentally retarded, call him delusional, but he
didn't really belong here in this metal warehouse, sleeping every night

23

on a vinyl mat on the concrete floor, surrounded by fifty-nine drunks in various stages of inebriation. It was rather chance that had put him here and inertia that had kept him, since the early 1980s, at Detox.

"Detox," short for "detoxification," is a misnomer, actually, for the Volunteers of America (VOA) Central Reception Center on Front Street. This long metal structure, tucked unobtrusively into a corner of Sacramento, is really just a no-fuss drunk tank, a money-saving alternative to jailing those who commit the misdemeanor of public inebriation. But unlike the down-and-out drunks who arrive at Detox in paddy wagons, stay a couple of nights, then leave, Bert was a regular here.

Though Bert was reclusive and communicated mostly in grunts, he had such a gentle, unassuming manner that the staffers at Detox took a liking to him. They gave special vigilance to assuring that Bert got to sleep on his customary mat, B-11. (Characteristically, he slept with his head and feet pointed in directions opposite everyone else's.)

Though he was quietly friendly, he remained an enigma. No one ever mistook him for an idiot savant, but perhaps he understood more than he let on. A staffer recalled: "He spoke Spanish to us for three years. Then one day he came into the office and spoke English. Nobody knew he could."

Besides keeping a protective eye on Bert, the VOA staff gave him food, cigarettes, clothes, even an occasional buck. Noticing Bert's penchant for cigars, a few employees (and even the odd cop) would make a point of bringing him a stogie from time to time. One staffer observed, "He'd rear back like he was worth a million and smoke 'em."

Bill Johnson, who at age thirty was already a five-year veteran at Detox, was particularly intrigued by this misfit who preferred coffee or tobacco to whiskey or wine. A blue-eyed fellow with a compassionate smile hidden in thick whiskers, Johnson was a man who had seen a world of hurt, but also a sprinkling of miracles. He approached his work with hope, in a quiet, understated way. And he deliberately mingled with the most solitary, asocial fellows at Detox—especially the shy one who was always mumbling to himself.

Johnson could manage only the simplest Spanish, so he stuck to English. When he first asked the man's name, he'd heard Alberto— thus, the nickname Bert.

Over time, Bert began to spend a good deal of time in Johnson's company, and the two established a singular bond. Though Bert never became loquacious, he told Johnson that he was originally from Costa

Rica, and that he used to work as a mechanic. Eventually, Bert synchronized his schedule so that when Bill Johnson drove up at 7:30 each morning, he was standing there, waiting with a smile.

Johnson always made sure that Bert got a cup of coffee and something to eat. He reminded him when it was time to take a shower. And Bert even let him cut his hair. "Bert was special," Johnson mused, "and we always treated him special."

More than special, Bert was honest. Once he found more than two hundred dollars in the parking lot. Did he pocket it? No, he turned it in to the office. When no one claimed it, the staff rewarded him with a few dollars each day until the money was gone.

Bert also liked to help with chores. Working mostly for smokes, he helped the seventy-four-year-old maintenance man paint picnic tables, wash cars, pick up trash, and sweep floors. He became such a permanent fixture around the grounds that someone dubbed Bert the Detox "mascot."

Perhaps due to Bill Johnson's soft-spoken, religious influence, Bert also went to church "like clockwork." Boarding the Glory Bound Ministries bus every Sunday, he would ride to the modest church, take a seat, and listen to the service. Here, Bert and others from Detox took comfort in one of the few places where indigents were truly welcome.

But no matter how regularly Bert went to church, religious faith wasn't going to cure his most pernicious affliction. Bert heard voices.

Psychologists would say he suffered "auditory hallucinations," but Bert insisted he was talking to "spirits." They were always with him—around the grounds at Detox, and especially down the street near the cemetery—carrying on a running commentary to which Bert responded with gestures in the air, admonitions and protest, even smiles and laughter.

When Judy Moise first noticed the big, clumsy man who would become her obsession, he was standing in front of the graveyard, muttering.

Moise had started working as a "street counselor" with the Volunteers of America Courtesy Outreach Program, and Detox was her base, her "office," if you will. Each day, she'd go to the corrugated metal structure on Front Street, and after greeting the staff and punching in, she'd leave her car in the dusty parking lot and head out in the VOA van.

One day shortly after starting work in the spring of 1986, Judy saw

Bert on the sidewalk. It was hard to understand his words, but he seemed to be arguing with himself, saying, "Get out of here! Keep away from me!"

She stopped and asked, "Who are you talking to?"

He turned his deep brown eyes on her. "Those people," he explained, waving an arm in the air. "Spirits. In the graveyard."

"Oh, I see." Auditory hallucinations were nothing new to Judy Moise. She understood that the voices were real to Bert, so she simply asked what the spirits were like. With effort, she discerned that one "bad spirit" had first come to Bert when he was nineteen.

"Have the voices ever gone away?" she asked.

He shook his head.

"What about medicine? Maybe medicine will make them go away."

"No." He frowned. "Won't work."

Apparently, Bert's demons were permanent. In any case, Judy observed, he conversed with these ephemeral citizens more than with anyone else.

It disturbed Judy Moise to see Bert here, where he seemed the most sadly displaced of displaced persons. He wasn't an alcoholic, yet he spent his nights in a long, narrow, locked room, surrounded by inebriates snoring on vinyl mats. The perpetual buzz of fluorescent lights. Benevolent but constant surveillance. Not the best environment for someone with mental problems.

Other walk-in shelters might offer more commodious accommodations, such as bunk beds, but all except Detox required, as a minimum, identification and sobriety.

At Detox, even skid-row alcoholics could get help. The slightest interest in getting sober was met with ready support. Clients could be transferred to a true detoxification clinic, and the Detox staff kept close ties with Alcoholics Anonymous. (Bill Johnson declared earnestly that he'd "seen too many miracles happen" to believe that even the most hard-core drunk was beyond redemption.)

But what about Bert? He wasn't an alcoholic. He was only at Detox because he had nowhere else to go. What could they offer someone with mental problems?

It was impossible to move Bert elsewhere, Judy learned, because he didn't have any money. And he didn't have any money because he didn't have a Social Security number. As Judy put it, "He had an identity problem."

Worse, rumors of imminent closure were always afloat. Neither pretty nor profitable, Detox wasn't a very popular place. Even many skid-row alcoholics thought it uncomfortable and déclassé.

But where else could Bert go?

It was hard to imagine him surviving well on the streets. While Bert's vulnerability tended to draw out the best impulses in some, others saw him as a target; he was easily taken advantage of. Bert often went without a shirt at least partly because every time someone would bring him one from a charity bin, he would give it away to the first guy who coveted it. He was too well-meaning even to look out for his own best interests.

Early on, Judy Moise decided to make Bert a priority. She resolved to track down his identification and his Social Security number so that he could receive the benefit checks to which he was entitled, then find a real home for him, a safe place with a real bed to sleep in and a light he could turn out at night.

It was a simple enough wish, born of a generous impulse. And years later, it should have been a source of pride.

CHAPTER 2

As peculiar as Bert was, Judy found his eccentricities endearing, his vulnerability disarming. Her relationship with him deepened over the summer. And when she decided to undertake a video project on homeless persons, she asked Bert if he would mind doing an interview.

Rumpled, dirty, with his large belly protruding from beneath a plaid shirt, Bert wasn't the most photogenic subject, but he agreed. Judy hoisted her videocamera and Bert followed her to a side of the building, where they started taping. But it was a false start: It was getting late, and after just a few questions they agreed to resume the next day.

When Judy arrived at Detox the next morning, she was stunned by Bert's transformation: He was clean, his hair was nicely combed, and he was wearing a neat khaki shirt. Judy realized that it was easy to underestimate someone like Bert.

During the interview, she learned a bit more about her puzzling friend. When she asked whether he would rather live in the city or in the country, Bert said he preferred the city—a trivial exchange that only later gained significance.

When Bert murmured that he had "no place to live," Judy asked, "Which is better, Detox or a boarding home?"

"Boarding home," he replied.

"If we could find you one, would you rather live in a boarding home?"

"Yeah."

The interview was marred by Bert's nearly unintelligible mumbling,* but it heightened Judy's commitment to helping him. In a way, Judy made herself Bert's private guardian. As one observer put it, Judy not only befriended Bert, "she adopted him."

With her wide smile and graying, sandy-blond hair, Judy Moise had the sunny good looks of a plump, middle-aged Doris Day; she looked like she'd be more at home at a school board meeting than on the front lines in the losing battle against homelessness. And she hadn't arrived at this job through carefully planned career goals, nor through some pious calling. It was rather a way to purge her personal demons, for behind those lively eyes lay a private pool of pain.

Divorced in 1978, self-described as having been "privileged" and "somewhat unrealistic," Judy had at first felt liberated by the fresh opportunities facing her after eighteen years as a housewife. With her children nearly grown, she felt her life accelerating toward new horizons. So, she was caught utterly off-balance when, just six months later, schizophrenia hit her family with double punches. First her twenty-seven-year-old stepson, who'd been depressed since college and had complained of hearing voices, committed suicide. Two weeks later, her seventeen-year-old son, Todd, had a psychotic break, succumbing to delusions Judy could neither understand nor penetrate.

Her first clear impulse was to get Todd into the best private hospital she could find. But even with her ex-husband's help, she could scarcely stretch her income to cover the bills. Working first in a sandwich shop, then selling hearing aids, she struggled to maintain a modest home for herself and her fourteen-year-old daughter, Britt. And she worried constantly that Britt was getting shortchanged, her ordinary emotional needs eclipsed by her brother's extraordinary ones.

Meanwhile, Judy's visits to Todd's hospital left her increasingly disturbed over his treatment. After a year, he seemed to be getting

---

*The footage of Bert Montoya proved unusable. Later, Judy Moise and a colleague, Russ Parker, completed an award-winning video documentary entitled *Red Heart,* based on a homeless Vietnam veteran.

worse, not better. She took him out of the hospital, determined to find better treatment within the mental health services offered in Sacramento, but was again slapped by reality. Her son ended up house in "sleazy hotels"—a big step down from his upper-middle-class youth. When Judy complained, she was informed that this was unfortunately the only placement available.

Unconvinced, Judy clung to the belief that if she could only find the right agency, the right administrator, the right doctor, the right medication, she could turn things around and help Todd recover. "There's *got* to be something out there that can help my son," she insisted.

She spent hours in the library, poring over all she could find on schizophrenia and its treatments. She sent letters, made phone calls, nagged anyone she thought could help. But she met mostly with indifference, even hostility. Just trying to get her son's medication changed was tougher than getting a credit card company to admit a billing error. Apparently, mothers weren't supposed to take such an active interest in their children's treatment.

Finally, Judy realized there was nothing left but to relent, stop fighting, and enter the jaws of the beast. She joined volunteer groups, such as the California Alliance of Mental Illness (CAMI), a support group for families of the mentally ill, and the California Planning Council of Mental Health. Only then did she understand that she wasn't fighting an irrational, malevolent system, but rather one crippled by insufficient funds and conflicting policies.

At the same time, Judy was being drawn into her son's friends' problems. One might ask her to help him find a better doctor, another to file a complaint with a caseworker. Applying herself with characteristic energy, she became an advocate without meaning to. She fell into it. It suited her.

Now sensitized to the problems of the mentally ill, Judy was troubled to see so many unkempt people walking the streets, muttering to themselves. "These people clearly can't cope," she mused, "but they're not getting any help."

It seemed obvious to Judy that rather than waiting for such bewildered souls to locate their offices, mental health workers ought to go directly to the streets. So, when Judy heard that the Volunteers of America was opening two positions for "street counselors" who would do exactly that, she snapped up an application. Never mind that she was only a paraprofessional, not a credentialed social worker; that's what they were looking for.

By May 1986, Judy Moise was working with a partner, driving around in a VOA van, and, as she put it, "rescuing" people. Spying a disheveled woman on a bench surrounded by bags of belongings, Judy might plop down beside her and offer assistance. Or the pager might send the VOA team to intercept a man who was ranting on a street corner and they would try to persuade him to come in for assessment and services.

Driving such people to hospitals, shelters, or social service agencies, Judy and her partner often had to roll down the van's windows, even on cold days, to dilute the stench of urine-soaked clothes and un-washed humanity.

The job was poorly paid and emotionally demanding, but Judy didn't moan about how hard it was. Instead, she concentrated on the rewards of the job. "I have a success story every week," she declared. "Yester-day, I found two missing people."

Few things pleased her more than seeing people she had helped off the streets living better lives: in apartments, cleaned up, taking better care of themselves. With the help of proper medication, they often regained clarity, judgment, and self-esteem.

And now she was determined to help Bert Montoya.

While Judy didn't usually place people—instead serving as an inter-mediary, getting unbalanced people off the street and into the care of other social workers who then found homes—her boss had given her permission recently to do "occasional placement" in just this sort of case.

One day, Judy learned from a Detox staffer that Bert had briefly lived in a boardinghouse called Altos House. She was elated; this meant Bert's Social Security number had to be on record! She dashed to the boardinghouse, and sure enough, the proprietor's books yielded a number. But when she took it up with the Social Security Adminis-tration, it didn't check out. It wasn't Bert's.

Help came in the fall of 1986, when Beth Valentine joined Judy at the Volunteers of America. Judy had known Beth for years: She was her best friend's daughter, and Judy had watched Beth grow from a child of promise to a woman of character. Now a tenacious thirty-year-old, Beth's more measured, no-nonsense style was a nice comple-ment to Judy's effervescence. Soon Judy and Beth were working together full-time, helping some two hundred people a month.

Best of all, Beth shared Judy's enthusiasm for helping Bert.

But trying to locate some record of him was like cracking open nutshells and finding nothing inside. Judy and Beth contacted an ever-lengthening list of people, querying some thirty agencies and individuals. Ultimately, they were rewarded with not one, but *two* Social Security numbers attributed to Bert. Neither turned out to be valid.

Having exhausted all other options, the VOA co-workers reluctantly took Bert to the Immigration Office. This was a calculated risk. Though originally from Costa Rica, Bert insisted that he was a U.S. citizen. Still, he had no proof of this, and contacting Immigration could easily backfire: If Bert proved to be here illegally, he could be deported. But it seemed their only option.

At the Immigration Office, Judy and Beth were told that Bert couldn't be issued an ID without fingerprints, so they should take him to the Department of Motor Vehicles to be fingerprinted. But the DMV refused to take Bert's fingerprints without official identification.

Catch-22.

Instead of gnashing their teeth and slamming doors when they hit a roadblock, Judy and Beth tried another approach. They prayed. They stopped at the St. Francis Assisi Catholic Church, a grand old sanctuary that offered the perfect place to kneel and pray. Parting at the doorway, each made her private rounds—lighting candles, gazing up at the luminous, stained-glass images—ending up at the foot of a beautiful, gilt-edged rendering of Our Lady of Guadalupe. The Dark Madonna. The patron saint of the downtrodden.

They'd long felt that their prayers for Bert were best directed to Our Lady, and her image was always with them, even in the van. When pressed for time, they sometimes prayed on the go, sending their prayers rolling up from the city streets. After so many months of frustrating dead ends, any smidgen of divine favor could only help. "Beth and I always prayed," Judy reflected, "and some door always opened."

In May 1987 came a turning point. Judy had tried and failed to compile a comprehensive history of Bert. Now, at an office specializing in advocacy services for Hispanics (called, appropriately, Central Guadalupe), a woman interviewed Bert in Spanish. For the first time, they learned that Bert's name wasn't Alberto, but Alvaro José Rafael Gonzáles Montoya. Born in Costa Rica on September 8, 1936, he'd come to New Orleans in 1962 with his mother, sister, niece, and nephew.

Armed with this new information, Judy Moise composed a letter to the U.S. Embassy in San José, Costa Rica, requesting confirmation of Bert's identification. Popping it into the mail, she turned and told Beth, "All we can do is hope and pray that he entered the country legally."

Months later, a letter from the consul general arrived, including the original birth certificate for Alvaro José Rafael González Montoya!

With a bit more paperwork and a few more dollars donated by friends, the digits of Bert's Social Security number finally rang into place like a row of cherries on a slot machine. More than a year of gambling with bureaucracies had finally won a smile from Lady Luck: Bert was a legal citizen, with a legal identity, and was therefore legally entitled to government benefits. Finally, he could leave his limbo at Detox.

But where could he go?

Bert balked at taking neuroleptics,* but most boardinghouse operators refused to accept tenants who heard voices *unless* they took medication, so finding a home for him would be doubly difficult.

After another quick appeal to Our Lady of Guadalupe, Judy and her colleague sought recommendations. Peggy Nickerson, a hardworking, compassionate soul, seemed a logical resource. As a "street counselor" with St. Paul's Senior Center, Nickerson assisted the elderly homeless, so her work often meshed with theirs. Nickerson suggested that Bert might be happy in a home run by a woman named Dorothea Puente.

Puente was that rare find, she said: a widow who ran a good clean boardinghouse yet didn't flinch at housing difficult types, such as alcoholics. "Puente has an edge," Nickerson told them. "She can work with street people. She doesn't freak out."

Judy and Beth decided to give Dorothea Puente a try, and they jotted down her address: 1426 F Street.

---

*Tranquilizers used in treating mental illness, particularly psychosis.

CHAPTER 3

O<small>N THE CLEAR, CRISP MORNING OF FEBRUARY</small> 1, 1988, <small>THE</small> VOA van pulled up in front of a blue-and-white two-story Victorian house on F Street. From the outside, it looked promising: clean and well-tended without being prim.

Judy and Beth climbed out of the van and mounted the stairs to the second-story porch, where an old woman in a print dress greeted them at the door. Her white hair was wound around curlers atop her head. With the translucent patina of age, her fine, pale skin stretched across her broad cheeks then shrunk in around her mouth: She had no teeth.

After a round of polite introductions, Dorothea Puente invited them inside. Judy and Beth inhaled savory aromas wafting in from the kitchen as they followed the grandmotherly woman into the parlor. Glancing about, Judy noticed the landlady showed a weakness for old-fashioned ceramic figurines, doilies, and dime-store religious pictures—kitschy, but inoffensive. A wide assortment of paperback novels bulged from a full bookcase. A few magazines were splayed across the lace tablecloth covering a low coffee table, and morning sun spilled through lace curtains, lending warmth to the clean but cluttered interior. Boardinghouses were never fancy, but this one had a homey feel to it.

"Can I get you some coffee?" the landlady offered.

The two visitors declined, "Oh, no thank you, Mrs. Puente."

The landlady quickly corrected them, "Please, call me Dorothea." And with that, she launched into conversation, first apologizing for her appearance; her new dentures weren't ready yet she explained, seeming vexed. Her toothlessness made her look every bit her age—"I'm seventy, you know"—but it didn't seem to inhibit her from talking.

As they could see, she was saying, this wasn't a particularly large house. The guests mostly roomed downstairs, she lived upstairs. She did the cooking up here and the guests came upstairs for meals. This sort of arrangement worked well, in her experience. "I've been in the boardinghouse business for a long time," she told them. "I used to run a much bigger house at 2100 F Street some years ago. But I'm not in this business for the money, you know. I don't need the money. It's just that life has been good to me, and this is my way of giving something back."

Judy didn't completely buy this—people didn't run these sorts of businesses strictly out of the goodness of their hearts—but guessed that the landlady was too proud to admit she needed extra income.

"I don't have any family living nearby," Puente went on, "so I need my boarders around me. They're like a substitute family for me—I'd be lonely without them. Besides, they keep me busy." She sat erect, her hands folded, and smiled at them with sealed lips, a toothless Cheshire cat.

Judy and Beth began telling her about Bert and his history. When they mentioned that he was from Costa Rica, with Spanish his native tongue, Puente chimed in, "Well, we'll get along fine then, because I'm Hispanic, too."

She explained that her large family, composed of many siblings, was still in Mexico. "I'm the light one, the baby of the family. They always used to tease me about being the *gringa*." She chuckled, seeming amused by distant memories.

Looking at her, no one would have guessed Dorothea Puente to be Mexican American, but hanging on the walls were framed awards given to her for contributing to Hispanic causes. And regardless of the woman's pale complexion, the general decor did seem to reflect Mexican tastes, Judy decided.

Turning the conversation back to Bert, Judy said that she wanted to make sure Dorothea understood that, even though he'd been staying at Detox for years, Bert Montoya wasn't an alcoholic. "He hears voices—he says they're spirits talking to him—and he answers them and gestures to them. But usually he's very quiet and very sweet. Physically, he's fine, except for a really bad case of psoriasis on his scalp that he's had for years."

"Well, I can clear that up for him," Dorothea announced. "I was an RN in World War Two, you know. Some people in the Hispanic community here even call me 'the Doctor,' " she added with apparent pleasure.

As Puente went on, laying out a few of the house rules, Judy appraised her. She had a humanitarian streak, but seemed streetwise, not saccharine. Ordinarily, Judy might have worried about a woman of Puente's age running a rooming house like this, but this little old lady had savvy, with a hint of the sort of toughness one needed in dealing with sometimes unruly house-guests. She made eye contact, which invited confidence. And even with a bandanna tied over her curlers, even without her dentures, she communicated dignity. She certainly didn't seem out to impress them—perhaps that's what impressed Judy most.

"Well, how would you like to look around?" Puente offered, standing.

First, they followed her into the kitchen, where Judy and Beth discovered the source of the delicious aroma that permeated the house. They stood and watched as the apron-clad woman took a spatula and turned several fat hamburgers sizzling on the stove. Not skimpy burgers. Not macaroni and cheese. But big, hearty, half-pound burgers. This was considerably better than typical room-and-board fare; too often, the operators prepared minimal meals and pocketed the profits.

And Bert liked to eat.

"I cook in the morning," Dorothea was explaining. "We have an early breakfast and early dinner. The tenants take care of their own lunch. I'm always up by five, so I like to get started right away. Lots of times I do my gardening first thing in the morning."

From the kitchen, Dorothea stepped out on the back-stair landing and pulled some cat food from a shelf. "I know some people hate cats," she said while filling a small bowl, "but I have a weakness for strays. My mama cat just had kittens."

Dorothea set the bowl in a corner, and Judy watched mewing little balls of fur squirming in a cardboard box. How kindhearted of this woman to take in strays, she thought.

The tour continued. Besides the parlor and kitchen, the upstairs included a dining room, the landlady's bedroom, a guest bedroom, and a bathroom. Downstairs, where the boarders mainly stayed, cheap paneling covered the walls, but the furnishings were sturdy and clean. It was far from luxurious, yet there were plenty of televisions and even a downstairs refrigerator for the boarders to use.

Outside, they saw that the yard was remarkably well kept, with flowering plants and shrubs, even a small vegetable garden. Here was an ornamental cherub, there a small windmill, and in the front, a religious figurine—almost a shrine.

The threesome was soon back in the parlor, and when the conversation drifted to chitchat, Judy asked to use the phone. Leaving Beth and Dorothea, she used this opportunity to take another look around. Magazines and a big stack of mail, mostly bills, sat near the phone. Normal enough. She noticed the liquor cabinet was unusually well stocked . . . but this somehow made the place seem homey. Overall, the house was remarkably clean and well cared for, more than sufficient.

The two VOA co-workers were soon saying their good-byes. Judy waited until they were back in the van before venturing, "Well, Beth, what do you think?"

Without hesitation, Beth answered, "I think Bert would really like it here."

"Oh good," Judy said, flashing her wide smile. "I'm glad it's not just me."

After so much delay, Judy and Beth felt the system was finally working for Bert. There seemed no reason to wait, so they decided to bring him by that very afternoon.

If Bert Montoya had any reservations about meeting this stranger, they melted within minutes of his arrival. He spoke little, his reactions always filtered through his innate shyness, but Mrs. Puente was thoroughly disarming, speaking Spanish with him, showing him around, patting him as if he were a son.

"You know, if you move in here, I like cooking Mexican meals," Dorothea told him. "At the moment, no one here is Mexican, but I like Mexican food, and I would be real happy to cook some for you. Wouldn't you like that?"

Bert probably couldn't remember the last time someone had offered to cook a meal especially for him. A blush of pleasure showed on his face.

Dorothea showed him the room that could be his if he decided to move in. It was small and tidy, with just the essentials, really, but private, and with his very own TV. To anyone accustomed to first-class treatment, it would seem a dump; but to someone used to a vinyl mat on a concrete floor, it was a palace.

By the time they were ready to leave, Bert seemed utterly enamored of his Hispanic landlady with the big house. He let them know that he was ready to move in that same day.

But, knowing how easily he was swayed, Judy and Beth cautioned him to take a couple of days to think about it. This was the first place he'd seen, after all, and he might like another boardinghouse even better.

This was Monday. On Wednesday, February 3, Bert Montoya moved into 1426 F Street. Leaving behind the corrugated metal warehouse on Front Street and saying good-bye to his friends at Detox, he moved to a cozy, storybook house of blue and white near the heart of downtown. After years of living in a shelter meant as a last resort for the woefully down-and-out, Bert finally had a home. That night, for the first time in years, he would lay his head on a real pillow and sleep in a real bed.

Part II

F IS FOR FATAL

Dorothea was a woman you just didn't question.... She was Dr. Jekyll and Mrs. Hyde as far as I could tell.

—JOHN SHARP, tenant

CHAPTER 4

FROM THE MOMENT BERT MOVED INTO DOROTHEA PUENTE'S boardinghouse, the texture of his life changed. He was no longer ignored, isolated, an outcast among outcasts. Rather, he became an important consideration within Dorothea's busy arena. From now on, what he wore, whom he spoke with, and how he spent his time were matters worthy of interest, even scrutiny.

Dorothea was constantly patting down his unruly hair, straightening his clothes, tucking in his shirts. In Spanish, she was always instructing him: "Don't forget to shave, Bert," or "Go and wash your hands," or "Give me your laundry, and I'll make sure you have some clean shirts."

Within two weeks, Dorothea had managed to eradicate Bert's chronic psoriasis—an accomplishment so swift and complete that Judy and Beth blinked with amazement at the sudden improvement in his appearance. His hair was clean; the mantle of flakes had disappeared from his shoulders. And this proved only the beginning.

During their visits over the next several weeks, Judy and Beth were delighted to see how Bert thrived under Puente's care. It seemed that

41

every time they came by, Bert had undergone yet another transformation. The man who had wandered barefoot in summer, or clomped about in ill-fitting boots in winter, now wore snappy new shoes—Dorothea had given him two new pairs. His hair was combed, his nails were clean. And Dorothea made sure he had fresh clothes, making a present of six new shirts, a couple pairs of slacks, and a jacket.

Besides improving his grooming habits, Dorothea seemed to help him psychologically. She curtailed Bert's discourse with the spirits, openly scolding him for "talking to the devil." She even managed to get him to again start taking his antipsychotic medication, Mellaril (though he continued to murmur protests; he never did like the drug).

Over the weeks, Bert seemed more aware, more grounded, more confident. He even started speaking more clearly. One afternoon when she came by the F Street boardinghouse, Judy was startled when Bert came out to greet her, asking, "How are you?"

"Oh, I'm fine," she answered, stunned that, for the first time, Bert had initiated a conversation.

"Beth said you were sick," he mumbled, but Judy was impressed by Bert's improved pronunciation.

"I was sick this morning but now I'm better," she replied with a nonchalance that masked her astonishment. His former grunts, his monosyllabic "yeah" and "nah" answers had given way to complete sentences!

Judy and Beth, who felt a special responsibility for Bert, were elated. After such a frustrating struggle with his "identity problem," they felt doubly gratified that Bert now had his own room, his own wardrobe. And more than the big meals, more than the creature comforts, they saw that Dorothea Puente offered Bert dignity, reviving in him a connection with his long-neglected Hispanic roots. His self-esteem seemed to soar under her tutelage as they never would have dared hope.

Whatever Dorothea was doing, everyone noticed the near-miraculous improvements in Bert's appearance and demeanor. And Dorothea clearly enjoyed reaping credit for this, seeming to derive personal satisfaction from Bert's progress.

But Bill Johnson, Bert's bearded friend from Detox, viewed the move to Puente's residence with some skepticism. Time and again, Johnson had watched people leave the humble sanctuary of Detox for better accommodations, only to end up having their benefit checks snatched up by greedy landlords. One day while visiting Bert, he even said as much to Mrs. Puente. "All board-and-care operators are in it for the money," he muttered.

Not one to sit back and take insults, the landlady shot back, "If I was, I would have kept the other place," referring to the grand house at 2100 F Street that she'd operated years before.

Johnson knew little and cared less about places she'd managed in the past; he cared about Bert, who he believed was due a large retroactive payment from SSI,* and he harbored a festering suspicion that this sly old cat "was going to snag it."

It didn't set well with Dorothea Puente that her favorite tenant's buddy didn't trust her.

The next time Bill Johnson stopped by for a visit, Bert wasn't there, so Mrs. Puente seized this opportunity to give him a tour of the premises. She slowly led him through the house, room to room, purring with fondness for Bert. She showed him the thriving vegetable garden, gushing about how Bert so enjoyed helping with the gardening, and was *so* helpful with the weeding and planting. She steered Johnson downstairs, pointing out that a downstairs refrigerator was stocked with sodas so that her tenants could help themselves (unusual for this sort of establishment), and showed him that most of the tidy rooms had televisions.

Bert's room, Johnson noticed, was spotless. But as they wandered in and out, what lodged in Johnson's mind was not the domestic touches, the quilts and paperbacks, the cleanliness and comfort of the house, but the delectable aroma streaming from the oven. Pot roast: mouth-watering and savory.

Later, with that tantalizing fragrance still in his nostrils, Johnson grudgingly admitted to himself that such hearty fare set Puente's place above others. Bert was lucky to be living here. Few former Detox dwellers had it so good.

With time, Johnson learned that Dorothea Puente did much more than the ordinary boardinghouse operator, and took special care of Bert. She cooked him Mexican meals, and Johnson knew how Bert loved Mexican food. And she made sure Bert went to church every Sunday, a fact that the devout Mr. Johnson found heartening, since he'd assumed a similar role for Bert back at Detox.

Still, Johnson wasn't as thrilled as some about the changes in Bert.

---

*Supplemental Security Income, formerly called Aid to the Totally Disabled, is a need-based program directing cash benefits to those who qualify, such as blind or aged persons with extremely low incomes.

It seemed to him that the landlady "hovered over him, put too much emphasis on his appearance." She was always straightening his collar or flicking lint off his shoulders, and she made him wear a sports coat even in hot weather. In retrospect, Johnson perceived that Mrs. Puente wielded excessive control over his docile friend. "She manipulated him," he decided.

But that's hindsight.

Dorothea Puente was taking such good care of Bert that the other tenants were jealous. They complained that she babied him and granted him special favors. And it was true. She made lunches for him, while everyone else was offered only breakfast and dinner. She gave him spending money, and even ran a tab for Bert across the street at Joe's Corner Bar, supporting what became Bert's daily pilgrimage to the darkened tavern for burritos and beer.

Moreover, it was uncommonly generous of Dorothea to agree to take in Bert even before his entitlement checks started coming. He wouldn't start receiving food stamps until early March, his first SSI check wouldn't come until June, and in the meantime he was living at 1426 F Street, for $175 per month, more or less on credit. Dorothea had said that if Bert's benefit checks were at first a little slow in coming, that was all right. This was typical of the extraordinarily kind Dorothea Puente.

Various charities—from the Policemen's Association to Mexican-American groups—benefited from her checkbook. On occasion, she even made it to the hundred-dollar-a-plate political fund-raisers. Sometimes she would pop into the Camellia Senior Center to donate a box or two of clothes—sometimes men's, sometimes women's. She made sure that workers collected her recyclables every Friday, which contributed a little extra cash to the work furlough center. And every Thanksgiving she donated a turkey to some needy group.

John Sharp, a tall, thin man with keen blue eyes and a bald pate rimmed with white hair, had nothing but praise for his new landlady. Sharp had moved in about a month before Bert. Just out of the hospital after back surgery, the sixty-four-year-old retired cook had no place to sleep. But Puente had a room for him under the stairway landing at the rear of the house for $160 per month, plus another $87 in food stamps.

To him, she seemed a whirlwind of activity, constantly cooking and cleaning. Super-landlady. And Sharp appreciated Puente's thought-fulness. "She had cable TV wired into my room at no cost to me, and she bought me a recliner chair because of my bad back," Sharp crowed. "She also bought a three-wheel bicycle for another guy who was crippled."

Some other tenants were less coherent or less reputable than the sober Mr. Sharp. John McCauley, a bearded, truculent fellow who lived upstairs, was such a mean drunk that people generally stayed out of his way, though Dorothea seemed to like him. Homer Myers, a lumbering, white-haired old guy who was hard of hearing, tended to shy away from strangers, smiling vaguely at comments he probably didn't catch. And Ben Fink, a wiry man in his late fifties who walked with a cane, would characteristically drink up his benefit check as soon as it came each month, floating through the first few days, then drying out until his next check arrived.

Besides these men—five including Bert—other men and women occasionally stayed at Dorothea's. A week, a month, they were a transient population. But in the midst of this flux, Dorothea carved out a routine and stuck to it.

She was up before dawn, and the first light of day usually found her in the yard, gardening, watering, sweeping, and raking. Breakfast was on the table at 5:30. Though not everyone fancied the idea of such an early meal, Dorothea treated the early risers to a hearty spread of eggs, bacon, pancakes—the works.

It was Dorothea's daily habit to remind her tenants to take their medications. Each had individual health problems, and it wasn't strange to see pill bottles sharing the table with the salt and pepper shakers. On a kitchen calendar Dorothea noted appointments with dentists, social workers, and doctors, reminding her tenants of the dates, even making sure they arranged for transportation. The woman was organized.

And she was busy. She took care of chores, laundry, and shopping herself, and by early afternoon she was usually dressed and ready to go out.

At home, she was just an old hausfrau in an apron, but when she went out, she was always the lady. She favored bright dresses and, ever-conscious of her appearance, put on a touch of makeup and a mist of her favorite perfume before leaving.

Dorothea Puente didn't mind walking to nearby destinations, such as McAnaw's Pharmacy, where she routinely picked up a variety of cigarettes, cosmetics, over-the-counter drugs, scandal sheets, greeting cards, and monthly prescriptions. Or, just down the street, she'd stop in on a Mexican friend who had a magic touch for making tamales. Dorothea might buy a dozen or two at a time, carrying the heavy bags back up the street and upstairs into her kitchen, where she would serve them for dinner.

The Clarion Hotel, also just a short walk away, was another favorite stopping spot. With its plushness and polish, the Clarion offered a pleasant reprieve from the coarse habits of her tenants, and Dorothea's pale, pretty face was often seen here at the bar. She befriended one bartender in particular, whom she surprised on her birthday with a dozen roses and a big bouquet of balloons.

This was Dorothea's way: the big display, the lavish gesture. After all, she was a retired doctor; she had the money, didn't she? Hadn't she come in here one morning looking dog-tired, complaining that the hospital had called her in on some emergency and she'd been up all night in surgery?

Another reason for visiting the Clarion Hotel was that Dorothea Puente's "nephew," Ricardo Ordorica, worked there. A gnomish man of a child's size, Ordorica had worked as a gardener at the Clarion for many, many years. When Ordorica saw her come into view, his sad, droopy face would break into smiles. Dorothea was more than a good friend, she was his *tía* (aunt). When she'd been in prison, he and his wife had stood by her; now that she was back, everything was fine again.

Dorothea had a special fondness for this little man. She greeted him warmly in Spanish, patting his shoulder, asking about his family. He beamed up at her.

Few people knew that Ordorica was not really her nephew but her landlord. For a time, Dorothea Puente had rented just the top floor of 1426 F Street, with the Ordoricas downstairs, and they'd lived there almost as kin. The children loved her like a grandmother, for Dorothea baked them cakes, took them on trips, and surprised them with gifts.

Now that the Ordoricas had moved into their new home, Dorothea was renting the entire house on F Street, and the children didn't see her as often. But she frequently came to see her "nephew" at the Clarion Hotel, and he regularly stopped by the house to see his *tía*.

But more than friends, more than "family," they were business associates.

Often when she saw him she would open her purse and, murmuring a few words, take out some checks and hand them to him. Ordorica would nod his head of black hair, fold the checks in his tiny hands, and put them into his pocket.

Dorothea didn't drive, and if she were venturing many blocks from home she always called a cab. These days, her favorite cabbie was Patty Casey, a trusting woman who enjoyed Puente's company and was pleased to oblige whenever Dorothea called. Besides, Dorothea was a good tipper.

When Casey pulled up in front, Dorothea was usually waiting. And, as she hurried out the gate, Casey noticed that she always dressed impeccably, her shoes and handbag matching.

During the week, the landlady often called Patty Casey to take her on errands, to appointments, to the bank, or to shop at nurseries, where she indulged what Casey considered a "fanatical" love of gardening. The cabbie would drop her off at Lumberjack, a huge place, and pick her up when she called a couple of hours later, laden with landscaping supplies.

Back at the house, Dorothea would insist, "Now, I don't want you lifting a thing, Patty, with that bad back of yours. Promise me you'll sit right there. I'll get Bert to come help me." And right away, Bert would come out to hoist the heavy stuff into the house or under the stairs, wherever Dorothea directed him.

(Casey thought Bert such a sweet, likable person that, spying him in the neighborhood, she would sometimes pick him up and treat him to a short ride. She noticed that he loved to "watch the little digits go around" on her meter.)

Casey thought it touching that Bert called Dorothea "Mama," and she considered it bighearted of Dorothea to take Bert in and care for him the way she did. In fact, Dorothea was one of the kindest, most considerate people Patty Casey had ever met.

Dorothea also had a vain streak, Casey noticed, but whatever her faults, she was the anchor of 1426 F Street. A houseful of people relied on her, and week after week, Casey saw how hard Dorothea worked to run the household and care for her marginal boarders.

All this despite Dorothea's own health problems.

On the way to a doctor's appointment one day, Dorothea sadly revealed that she was battling cancer. "Imagine that," she sighed. "I don't even smoke, and I'll probably die of lung cancer."

Casey clucked with genuine concern. With a personality as plain and sturdy as her build, Casey was becoming Dorothea's loyal confidante.

One day early in March, the landlady invited her into the house to pick out a kitten. She carried the mewing little thing home, nursing it like a warm, fuzzy token of their friendship.

On Sundays, dressed with her finest jewelry, Dorothea Puente would ride to the lovely old Catholic church, the Cathedral of the Blessed Sacrament, at Eleventh and K streets. But more often, whether or not she admitted it to Patty Casey, her destination would be a bar.

Henry's Lounge, Joe's, 501, Round Corner—she was probably too old to be called a barfly even though she patronized several bars around town. They were simply part of her routine: up before dawn, breakfast at 5:30, housekeeping, errands, then a favorite bar before returning home to put dinner on the table. It was a pattern that she repeated day after day, almost with the regularity of a job.

Henry's Lounge was a dimly lit, smoky place on Ninth Street that Dorothea frequented. Marjorie Harper, a stocky, no-nonsense bar-tender who knew all the regulars, said Dorothea was hard to miss: She was always dressed "fit to kill." She always took the same seat at the bar—second from the end, where she could watch everyone—and she'd order a vodka and grapefruit juice. In no time she'd have an audience, and then she'd be off on some "fabulous story," perhaps about being a survivor of the Bataan Death March, or about how she used to be in movies with Rita Hayworth.

One day, a pharmaceuticals salesman sat down next to her. "They discussed drugs for over an hour," Harper recalled. "She had him convinced that she was a retired surgeon."

Dorothea Puente was loquacious, a good storyteller, and a colorful character. If she tended to embroider her tales, well, who could begrudge the old lady's fantasies? Her eccentricity was part of her charm. At least she was entertaining; let her have her little white lies.

Thriving on attention, she stoked a reputation for generosity. Doro-thea was quick to give gifts, frequently left five-dollar tips, and on a good day might buy rounds for the house, or even order pizza. "She wanted to do nice things for everybody," according to Harper. "She even said she wanted to buy me my own bar."

With the Camellia Center for Seniors just next door, a lot of elderly folks stopped in at Henry's every day. These were people who didn't sleep much, who might be standing out on the sidewalk, waiting for the bar to open at 6:00 A.M. They really didn't have much of anywhere else to go. True to character, Dorothea would invite a few of them to come to her place for Thanksgiving dinner, or even to move into her boardinghouse.

To the old gents she met in bars, she was an aged angel, a wrinkled coquette. But, as Harper saw it, "Her thing was elderly men with checks."

It seemed that Bert Montoya had struck a maternal chord with Dorothea Puente. She fawned over him and shepherded him so closely that one wouldn't think of accusing her of anything more sinister than of being overprotective. So on Thursday, March 31, 1988, when she dressed nicely as always and took Bert Montoya out, no one thought much about it.

She took him to a redbrick government building on the corner of Fifteenth and L streets, where she took a number and waited. When her number was finally called, Dorothea politely explained to the Social Security Administration representative, "I'm here with Mr. Montoya. He's mentally retarded, you see, and can't really manage his money, so he'd like me to be the payee for his SSI checks."

Not an unusual request. People with mental or physical handicaps that may cause "fiscal irresponsibility" are often encouraged to have their benefit checks handled by someone more competent, usually a relative. (This person serves as a "representative payee" in the Social Security vernacular.)

The elderly woman was handed a form to fill out. In the blank asking her relationship to the applicant, she wrote "I am cousin." When she was finished, she handed back the form, and the process was under way.

Later, the Social Security Administration would contact Bert's psychiatrist, who confirmed that Bert suffered from "psychosis, a degree of mental retardation, and abnormal behavior." Further, the doctor reported, Bert was "nonparticipative in society . . . withdrawn . . . generally needing someone to watch out for him." Yes, Social Security would be careful to establish medical evidence of Bert Montoya's mental disability. In that area, it was thorough. Yet no one would check even the most basic elements of Dorothea Puente's background. The Federal Privacy Act prohibited that.

In time, the application was approved, and checks of $637 per month—intended for Bert Montoya but made payable to Dorothea Puente—were being sent to 1426 F Street.

And at this address, there was one hard-and-fast rule: Only Dorothea could collect the mail.

CHAPTER 5

Tending the private details of her life as fastidiously as she tended her garden, Dorothea Puente enjoyed her secrets. She cultivated contacts, nurtured confidences. And she revealed only what she chose, vigilantly keeping certain segments of her life discrete, which she'd done for so many years now that it was second nature.

Some knew her as a retired doctor, some as a retired nurse, yet she'd had no formal medical training. Virtually everyone believed she was a widow, yet all four of her ex-husbands were still alive. And she'd come very close to marrying a fifth. But such things were nobody's business.

To most who met her, Dorothea Puente was a widowed landlady with a generous streak. They knew her to be a hard-nosed business-woman with a soft heart, a civic-minded matron who donated money and clothing to charities. She had certain rules, certain standards, but she was willing to grant broad favors to her friends, even to lend some extra cash in a pinch. And she could always be counted on for a fresh cup of coffee and a chat on the porch.

But Mrs. Puente had her weaknesses. For one, she had a little trouble with consistency, being the sort who advised against drinking alcohol one day, then offered to spot a few rounds at the bar the next. And then, of course, there was her temper. When it came to certain things that were important to her, she could be downright testy. And Bert was important to her.

Unlike most of Dorothea Puente's tenants, Bert Montoya had a handful of regular visitors, including a couple of nurses. Known collectively as "the two Lucys," Lucy Yokota and Lucy Aquitania had treated Bert along with other tuberculosis patients at Detox.* Now one or both of them would stop by the house twice a week to check on Bert's dormant TB.

Naturally, Lucy Yokota couldn't help but notice how dramatically Bert's appearance improved after moving into 1426 F Street. He was clearly thriving in his new environment, thanks to the kind attentions of Dorothea Puente, who said she always stocked cookies for Bert and prepared steak for him every day.

So Lucy Yokota was startled one day to hear the landlady's angry voice on the phone. "Just stay away from Bert," she hissed. "Stop visiting. You make him nervous. He doesn't want you coming by all the time." Yokota started to protest, but Puente cut her off, saying she didn't want the nurses coming by to see Bert anymore or he'd "have to be sent back to Detox." With that, she hung up.

Bewildered, Yokota sat and stared at the phone, wondering what to do. Finally, she picked it up and dialed Mrs. Puente's number. When Dorothea answered, the soft-spoken nurse diplomatically offered, "I think we were disconnected."

"We weren't disconnected!" Puente declared. "I hung up on you!" Then she laughed abruptly and switched to an entirely different tone.

Yokota thought this "a very strange mood swing, from very angry, to all sweetness."

The next time she saw Bert, she came out and asked him, "Do we make you nervous? Do you want us to keep away?"

He innocently told her no.

Yokota didn't quite know what to think of the mercurial Mrs. Puente. She certainly wasn't going to alter Bert's treatment because of her. But after this, she definitely didn't trust her.

---

*TB patients often end up living on the street because staying in a hospital is too expensive and board-and-care operators, fearing contagion, refuse to house them.

DISTURBED GROUND

※ ※ ※

When Judy Moise and Beth Valentine came over, Mrs. Puente would crow about Bert's latest deeds, saying, "Let me tell you what he did!" She even boasted with a chuckle that Bert wanted to change his last name to Puente.

One day the VOA co-workers ended up in her kitchen, watching her bustle about as they talked. She pressed them to take home some food. "I made all these tamales this morning," Dorothea said, wiping her hands on her apron and looking around for something to wrap them in. "And I just have more than we can eat. Please. Won't you take some home? You do like tamales, don't you?"

Judy, who had a weakness for all things Mexican, from the artifacts that decorated her home to the dream vacations that lay just out of reach, accepted with thanks.

"You know," Dorothea was saying, "I'm planning on taking everyone to Mexico with me the next time I go down for a visit."

This was a surprise. "Everyone? You mean everyone in the boarding-house? The entire household?"

"Uh-huh. Everyone. Bert and everyone else. We'll all go down and visit my family. They live just outside of Guadalajara, you know, and I think we'd all have a good time."

"I see," said Judy, trying to digest this. "Well, how would you be getting down there?"

"Oh, John Sharp will drive us down," Dorothea replied airily.

Beth thought this was wonderful. But Judy gave the landlady a quizzical look. She could scarcely imagine Bert as a tourist. Surely it was unrealistic to expect him to navigate in a foreign city. He could get lost.

It was a brief exchange—a bit peculiar, even eccentric—but nothing ominous. Judy didn't really take it seriously. She let the subject drop.

Now that Bert was doing so well, Judy felt that she and Beth could back off a bit. His condition had miraculously improved, and now she had other, more pressing problems.

And so did Dorothea Puente. If she was unpredictable, she was also clever. Watching, waiting, she methodically wove together elements of a plan that stretched into the months ahead. It was an intricate web, pleasing in its complexity.

This spring, the white-haired landlady had big plans for her yard. On several occasions she called her favorite cabdriver, Patty Casey, and asked that she drive her to landscape supply stores, where she purchased building materials, plants, seeds, and ready-mix concrete.

Of course, this little old lady, hardy though she was, didn't plan on doing all the yard work herself. Much as she enjoyed gardening in the cool morning air, for any heavy labor she always called the Sacramento Valley Correctional Center (SVCC). A halfway house for convicts with just a few months left on parole, it would send out work crews of nonviolent offenders, and Dorothea paid them each twenty dollars a day for doing odd jobs around her house.

Not many private individuals were even aware that a halfway house could supply laborers. But Dorothea Puente was conversant with ex-cons; she knew about parolees and work furlough. In fact, she knew many things that others did not.

Parolees worked at the F Street house off and on during the months of April, May, and June. As the air grew hot and the season turned the dry corner toward summer, the grounds were transformed. Sinewy workers arrived early and left late, sweating over their labors. Mrs. Puente directed them and John McCauley supervised as they continued painting, cleaning, digging trenches, mixing and laying cement, even building a shed in the yard.

At noon, the landlady always invited the young men upstairs for a midday meal—an unnecessary but highly welcome gesture. And over lunch, she revealed a secret side of herself. "I know what it's like, being an ex-con," she confided, "because I've been in prison myself."

To these men who'd endured hard times and were hoping for better, Mrs. Puente was a kind soul who didn't condemn them for past mistakes. She gave them a chance. One wiry young fellow named Don Anthony even said she was "like a mother."

Some may have found it refreshing that the old landlady was investing so much effort in her yard (this wasn't one of the nicest neighborhoods after all, and few on the block seemed to sweat much over their property), but the landlord next door, forty-eight-year-old Will McIntyre, wasn't thrilled about his neighbor's noisy projects. It seemed endless, he thought. For nearly two years now he and his tenants had put up with Puente's racket. It seemed to him that she was always hammering, always improving. In fact, McIntyre was not at all enamored of little old Mrs. Puente. "She could be very nice," he admitted, but he'd seen her "turn in a minute," treating the object of her wrath to "a vocabulary that could make most sailors blush."

Some neighbors found her extraordinarily friendly, but others called her "weird" or "off the wall," noting that she was "always yelling at people if they put even a step onto her lawn."

That temper.

Eventually Dorothea brought up the subject of Mexico with John Sharp, the one tenant who had a car. She suggested that they might all travel down to Guadalajara after he got his SSI payments started and asked if he would drive.

The prospect of driving all the way from northern California into Mexico, shut inside a car for days with his dubious housemates, seemed about as appealing as self-flagellation. John Sharp was no martyr: He told her no.

Sharp didn't socialize much with the other boarders. He found Bert uncommunicative and childlike, sitting in the living room and watching cartoons. Sometimes, tormented by voices, Bert would stomp on the floor in frustration, "having a tantrum," in Sharp's view, until Dorothea would come and calm him, uttering motherly reassurances in Spanish.

John Sharp's vice was poker, not liquor, and the sober old gent didn't find much in common with the drinkers of the house either. But on a couple of occasions, he did enjoy standing outside and conversing with Ben Fink and his younger brother, Robert, who visited him there. Ben, who had moved into Dorothea's place in March, wasn't too bad a fellow, really. But it was mainly Robert, who looked like a rugged extra from a Clint Eastwood movie, who was sober and coherent enough to hold Sharp's attention.

Ben Fink never really bothered anybody, and though his room was just a thin wall away, Sharp didn't spend much time with him. He knew Fink was quite a drinker, and he could hear him moving about, coming and going. Each month, after receiving his benefit check, Ben would go on a major drinking binge until the money ran out.

In the spring of 1988, though, things were about to change.

Sharp heard Ben Fink come to the back door, heard him fumbling with his keys. Sharp's door was open, as usual. Ben staggered past, bleary-eyed, his hand wrapped around a bottle in a paper sack. In a minute, his neighbor's door closed, then he heard the familiar creak on the other side of the wall as the bed accepted Fink's weight.

John Sharp more or less forgot about Ben until later that evening when he bumped into the landlady in the hall. Dorothea promptly told him that Ben needed sobering up. "I'm going to take him upstairs," she announced, "and make him feel better."

Well, perhaps this particular bender had been going on a bit too long. Maybe Dorothea thought that, after three or four days of pathetic drunkenness, Ben was getting out of hand. But after that, Sharp noticed, he didn't hear or see Ben Fink around anymore. The room next door was dead still.

About four days later, John Sharp climbed the back stairs to use the telephone, and when he walked past the spare bedroom by the kitchen, he was hit by a distinct and terrible odor. He recoiled, his nose sniffing at a memory. Years before, he'd worked in a mortuary; he knew the awful stench of death.

Ben Fink's disappearance struck him with new clarity.

For hours afterward, Sharp puzzled over what he should do. Should he confront Dorothea? Should he contact the authorities? But what if he were wrong? He could imagine how angry Dorothea would be, and he sure didn't want to end up back on the street . . .

Dorothea Puente was soon fretting about the smell herself, telling John Sharp that the sewer had backed up, complaining that she didn't know how to get the smell out of the house. "It has ruined the carpet," she said. "I just don't know what to do."

Soon a noisy machine was rumbling back and forth, back and forth, above the heads of the downstairs tenants. The landlady had resorted to the obvious solution and rented a rug shampooer. But apparently even repeated shampooing proved futile, for it seemed to John Sharp that Dorothea must have shampooed that carpet at least a dozen times. Finally, she had workers tear the carpet out.

Then she called Patty Casey, the cab driver, and went shopping. On the way, Dorothea explained that she had to get new carpeting for one room in the house that "had a curse."

By late May Puente's next-door neighbor, Will McIntyre, was also grumbling loudly about the stench permeating the neighborhood. The tenants in his three apartments were complaining, he said. It got so bad that he couldn't even use his air conditioner because "it would suck the smell in, and you would have to go outside to get away from it."

When McIntyre confronted Mrs. Puente about the stink, she just clucked and agreed, "It sure is bad. I think it's coming from that

56

duplex out behind my house." Seemed like it must be the sewer, she said.

By then McIntyre had called public health officials to complain about the foul smell, and on June 1 they sent out an inspector, who couldn't find the source of the dreadful odor.

Weeks passed, the smell diminished, and Dorothea Puente continued to work early every morning in her garden. The plants and flowers flourished under the encouragement of her green thumb, and she was rightfully proud of the results. She even walked Ricardo Ordorica around the grounds as if she were the owner and he the guest, pointing out this or that improvement—the gazebo, the new flower bed, the rosebushes, the walkway—telling him how much she'd increased the value of his property.

Ben Fink wasn't the sort of man that many people would miss or come looking for, but Peggy Nickerson, the street counselor who had placed him at Puente's, later stopped by asking about him. Dorothea told her that he'd left. And Nickerson, who was used to dealing with transients who come and go without notice, didn't find this too peculiar.

Sometime later, John Sharp thought he saw a man on the street who looked like Ben, and he mentioned this to Dorothea.

"No, that can't be," she told him. "Ben has gone up north."

CHAPTER 6

A$_S$ SOON AS MARY ELLEN HOWARD CAME INTO VIEW, JUDY could sense tension. Her friend usually greeted everyone with a refreshing openness, but this time she wore gravity stamped across her brow. Polly Spring, who Judy knew less well, also seemed somber.

Judy and Beth had worked peripherally with the veteran social workers, Polly Spring at Adult Protective Services* and Mary Ellen at the welfare department, where she'd impressed them with her blend of competence and compassion. Usually clients brought them together; this request for a meeting seemed unusual. Judy's worried colleagues had called shortly after Will McIntyre started complaining about the stench wafting past his residence. They said they wanted to meet with the two VOA partners, and rather than discuss it on the phone, they wanted to talk in person.

With few preliminaries, Mary Ellen launched into an explanation of what had brought them here, and Judy and Beth listened, dumb-

---

*Adult Protective Services is a county agency responsible for investigating abuses against elderly and adult-dependent (such as mentally ill) people.

founded, to her confusing tale: A client, who wasn't really her client, had been temporarily placed at Dorothea Puente's boardinghouse. Dorothea had kicked him out—for no reason, he'd said; for good reason, she'd said—and now he was living someplace else. Anyway (though it wasn't technically her responsibility), Mary Ellen Howard had called the proprietor—Dorothea, he'd said her name was—to try to work things out. But when she'd called, Dorothea had unleashed an abusive tirade, then hung up.

The incident had set her thinking, Mary Ellen said, about another landlady by the name of Dorothea whom she'd known of years before. Her memory wasn't clear, but she was so disturbed by the idea that this might be the same person that she'd done some checking. She'd called Polly Spring, then Mildred Ballenger, another former co-worker from Adult Protective Services. Ballenger was now retired, Mary Ellen said, but it was she who'd alerted authorities to Dorothea Johansson and had her sent to prison in the early eighties for victimizing elderly tenants.

Whoa, whoa, whoa! Judy and Beth stared at Mary Ellen, flabbergasted. What was she talking about? Was she suggesting that softhearted Dorothea Puente—caretaker of stray cats and unwanted souls—could be this awful Johansson character? It seemed ludicrous!

Much as she liked and respected Mary Ellen, Judy just couldn't fathom what she was getting at. She cleared her throat and ventured diplomatically, "Well, this really doesn't sound at all like Dorothea Puente, you know. Um, what did Johansson look like?"

Mary Ellen Howard and Polly Spring glanced at each other and gave it their best. When they'd finished, it was hard to imagine anyone *less* like Dorothea Puente than the woman they described: over two hundred pounds, given to wearing muumuus, dark hair piled atop her head. This Johansson woman hardly resembled small, snowy-haired Dorothea Puente.

"And, well, about how old would she be?" Judy asked.

Howard and Spring figured that Johansson would be in her late fifties.

"Then she can't be Dorothea Puente," Judy said, shaking her head. "She's at least seventy!"

The two veteran social workers persisted. They still believed that Puente *could be* Dorothea Johansson. And, they insisted, the woman was *dangerous*. She'd been convicted of some sort of crime, she'd been in prison. Mary Ellen Howard went on to explain that *Sacramento* magazine had even done an article about how Mildred Ballenger had put a stop to Johansson's evil deeds.*

"I'd like to read that," Judy said, and Mary Ellen volunteered to get them a copy.

Still, Judy and Beth remained skeptical. How could Puente and Johansson be one and the same? Dorothea Puente's tenants thought the world of her. Some even said her boardinghouse was the best place they'd ever stayed. And Dorothea's results with Bert were so remarkable, so unequivocally positive, that Judy and Beth could only believe that Polly Spring and Mary Ellen Howard were sadly confused.

Judy shrugged. "This just doesn't mesh with our personal observations."

"That's right," Beth concurred. "It's amazing how well Bert Montoya has been doing since he moved there. He's improved in every way because Dorothea is such a good care provider."

"Well, if I were you," Spring advised in her throaty voice, "I wouldn't want my client staying in that woman's house."

"So where would you suggest Bert stay instead?" Judy wanted to know.

"The Gate House,"† Spring replied, referring to a local room-and-board operation.

This hit a sour note, for this was one establishment that had aggrieved Judy and Beth, even within the past few days. The manager had neglected one tenant to the point of abuse, compelling them to file a report with Sacramento's ombudsman for senior care. They could hardly imagine a worse placement for Bert. Puente's residence was clearly superior, and that Spring would even suggest dumping Bert at the odious Gate House seemed to cast doubt on her judgment.

They were polite enough to stifle a scoff, but given their firsthand experiences, the VOA partners just couldn't take Spring and Howard's suspicions seriously. Still, since their colleagues were so obviously concerned, they promised not to place any more clients in Puente's boardinghouse and to ask Dorothea a few questions.

But Spring and Howard weren't about to stop with just one conversation with a couple of VOA employees. They were so profoundly

---

*"Unsung Heroes," *Sacramento* magazine, February 1983, portrays Mildred Ballenger's role in Dorothea Johansson's arrest.

†This is a fictitious name.

distressed by the idea that Dorothea Johansson might be on the loose again that they decided to push the limits of their respective bureaucracies. And for an unlucky few, the unfolding dance of accusation and acquiescence played out like a Kafkaesque plot.

By chance, Polly Spring shortly learned that Peggy Nickerson was also making placements at Dorothea Puente's boardinghouse. "She's crazy as a hoot!" she exclaimed to Nickerson. "I remember something about her being in trouble with the law. If I were you, I'd avoid Puente in the future."

Nickerson, who didn't have the highest opinion of Polly Spring to begin with, reacted with incredulity. She'd never heard a single word of complaint against Dorothea Puente. Hadn't Dorothea been terrific with all of her clients? In Nickerson's mind, she was "the best the system had to offer."

But Spring was tenacious; she recounted some of what she knew of Puente's history, believing she was imparting a "warning" to Peggy Nickerson.

Again, these allegations were so contrary to Nickerson's personal experience that she, like Judy Moise and Beth Valentine, simply couldn't swallow them.

Having her suspicions meet only with skepticism put Polly Spring in an exasperated funk. Finally, she was moved to send a memo to her supervisor, Phil Goldvarg.

Re: Dorothea Johansen [sic] AKA: Dorothea Puente
Date: June 9, 1988

Ms. Puente has surfaced again in the community, furnishing housing and tender-loving, but street-wise, care to vulnerable clients. She is used by Case Management Services and by Peggy Nickerson of the Elderly Homeless program.

Since neither referring agency is aware of Ms. Puente's history, each is enthusiastic about her not requiring money up front and running a good unlicensed facility. Ms. Puente, as this department is aware, poses some dangers to helpless clients, however, and I wonder what our responsibility is.

I knew Dorothea as Ms. Johansen [sic] in the '60s and the '70s, located at 21st & F St. Her facility was ultimately closed and she was sent to prison then for misusing clients' funds.

Subsequently, there was an allegation (later proved I think) of homicide against the lady, involving an elderly client. I don't know how to document this part of Ms. Johansen's [sic] history, except to ask Blanche Blizzard and Mildred Ballenger, who were instrumental in the case.

Informally, Judy Mollice [sic] of Case Management Services and Peggy Nickerson have been apprised of Ms. Johansen's [sic] history as far as I remember it.

Is anything more required?

When Goldvarg attempted to act on this memo he was hampered by simple errors, but he shortly spoke with his supervisor, Fran Alberghini, who then relayed these concerns to her supervisor, Charlene Silva. The upshot of their discussion was that they should do two things: First, report Puente to Community Care Licensing; second, ask county counsel whether they could legally share their suspicions about Puente with other agencies.

Good intentions, lousy follow-through.

Community Care Licensing sent a representative to check out Puente's establishment. For half an hour, she "toured" the upstairs quarters while Puente poured on her old-fashioned charm. Dorothea maintained that she didn't run a board-and-care facility, that she didn't really even have tenants. The downstairs residences, she said, were "separate and unconnected."

Before departing, the gullible representative asked Mrs. Puente to sign a licensing report indicating that complaints against the establishment were unsubstantiated and that no deficiencies were cited. With that, she handed Puente a copy of the report and bid good-bye.

To conclude her investigation, the representative phoned Peggy Nickerson about placements made to Puente's home. Afterward, she filled out a form, which read, in part:

Knickerson [sic] stated approx. 2 years ago Dorothea called her to offer her home as temporary shelter. A little less than once a month, Dorothea takes people in who have run out of money. They stay for 1 to 5 days. Dorothea provides food and shelter for free. The people she takes in are independent but have just run out of money.

Later that day, the representative phoned Goldvarg to report that Puente was not operating the type of facility that required licensing and that everything was "okay."

Step one was completed. As step two, Alberghini spoke with Deputy County Counsel Michelle Bach.

One of the county counsel's functions is to protect county agencies from litigation. Less politely, this job function might be summed up by those three inglorious little words: *Cover your ass.*

Bach asked, "Do you have any facts? Any indications that Dorothea Puente is doing something that she shouldn't be doing?"

No, actually, they didn't.

"Do you have a client staying at Puente's home?"

They did not.

No facts, no indications of abuse, and no client. Bach's advice was to avoid any appearance of being alarmist. Rather than risk infringing on Puente's rights, it would be better to keep mum.*

All in all, Polly Spring's memo had ignited a chain reaction like a lit string of firecrackers: much noise but little damage.

Mary Ellen Howard got similarly cautious advice when she approached Deputy Sharon Cadigan, stationed at the Department of Social Services, with questions about Dorothea Puente. Howard stood and watched as Cadigan pulled up information on the computer. But Deputy Cadigan didn't tell Howard what she wanted to hear: In essence, she said that Puente was on parole for writing bad checks and for property crimes, that she'd committed no offenses against people, and she had a right to have a business license.†

Knowing that she had no official reason for being concerned about the Puente home (since none of her clients resided there), Mary Ellen Howard didn't alert her supervisors. Even if she had, they admitted later, they would have informed Howard that she was venturing "beyond her jurisdiction."

So far, no one had detected any legal violations. No one had stopped Dorothea Puente from carrying on pretty much as she had been. And apparently, no one had even considered contacting the parole board. Everyone seemed unanimous about the wisest course of action: Do nothing.

---

*Ironically, county counsel had given similar advice years before. According to *Sacramento* magazine, when Mildred Ballenger first contacted the DA's office about Johansson's suspicious behavior, she got nowhere because "County Counsel said the Welfare Department 'could not interfere with her employment.'"

†Cadigan does not recall this conversation.

✿   ✿   ✿

Meanwhile, Judy Moise was awash in emergencies: battered women with broken bones, drunks brandishing firearms, hostile street people having delusional episodes right there in front of Woolworth's. If Dorothea Puente wanted to keep some portions of her life secret, Judy certainly wasn't left with much time to pry.

Still, she was troubled by that conversation with Mary Ellen Howard and Polly Spring. Howard had claimed that Dorothea had spitefully cursed her, yet Judy had never even heard Dorothea swear.

The whole story seemed outlandish, but Judy had promised to try to ascertain whether the landlady she and Beth so ardently defended could possibly be the vile character that Howard and Spring suspected her to be. So, quite deliberately, Judy and Beth went to Puente's to ask questions.

Ostensibly, they went to see Bert. Soon enough, however, they managed to end up chatting with Dorothea in the parlor. Ever so casually, Judy remarked, "You know, you're so fair-skinned, Dorothea, you sure don't look Mexican. What was your name before it was Puente?"

"Montalvo," she replied.

"But that was your previous husband's name, wasn't it?" Judy persisted. "I mean, what was your name before you were married?"

Dorothea paused, turning upon her a most peculiar look, as if weighing the question before replying. She finally spoke, "It was Johansson," and the words crackled through the air like static.

CHAPTER 7

Whispers of suspicion had breathed through the air, memos had ricocheted from office to office, but so far Dorothea Puente had no cause to worry. All the heat generated by Mary Ellen Howard and Polly Spring had amounted to only so much smoke. The landlady suffered no provocations, threats, or accusations. Her daily routine at 1426 F Street went on as unruffled as a cat's nap on a warm windowsill.

But Judy Moise had been knocked off-balance by the realization that Dorothea Puente was truly Dorothea Johansson. By nature a curious person—some would say just plain nosy—Judy wondered just what sorts of skeletons Dorothea Puente might have rattling about in her closet. Now the magazine article that Mary Ellen Howard had mentioned was nagging at her. She and Beth had agreed they ought to read this supposedly scandalous article, but Mary Ellen was in the process of moving, and they were having some trouble connecting.

Finally, arrangements were made. Mary Ellen would photocopy the article and leave it in her out box at work. They could come by and pick it up. Fine.

That day the VOA workers were in a rush, as usual, on their way to some emergency or other. Judy was driving, so Beth jumped out, fetched the article, and hopped back in. Popping the van into gear, Judy asked Beth to read the article aloud. While Judy wheeled through traffic, Beth skimmed the two photocopied pages.

It was confusing. The first page was apparently missing, and the first paragraph began in midsentence; "... son (not her real name) was sentenced to a maximum of five years in prison on charges of forgery, grand theft, and administering stupefying drugs. But she was never, some feel, convicted of her worst crimes."

Beth flipped from one page to the other. There was no photograph of Mildred Ballenger, Dorothea Johansson, or anyone they recognized. Instead, there was an American Indian pictured and quoted, as well as a heavy boy working in a kitchen, both apparently unrelated to the article. Odd.

Beth quickly skimmed until she came to parts she thought relevant.

> *Everybody trusted Eleanora Anderson, even Mildred Ballenger. A long-time Sacramento health care attendant, Eleanora had references that included some of the city's most prominent citizens and famous politicians ... About four years ago a client of Mildred's, a woman in her eighties, developed a mysterious illness and kept bouncing back and forth between her home and the hospital like a rubber ball. Her doctor was completely puzzled. Mildred was concerned. Only the woman's home attendant took the situation in stride. Her name was Eleanora Anderson, and when she visited her sick employer in the hospital she always made sure to bring a sandwich. "Here, eat this," she said. "I know you don't like the hospital food."*

The article went on to explain that Eleanora Anderson, the villain of this story, was apparently poisoning this elderly woman, then stealing from her. Beth continued:

> *Several more of Eleanora's victims came through Mildred's office reporting things missing ... Four other clients reported having health problems while under her care ...*

The story seemed so incredible that Judy and Beth couldn't help but punctuate the reading with exclamations: "Oh, isn't that ridiculous?" "That just seems absurd!" "This can't possibly be Dorothea!"

But Puente had already admitted that her name used to be Johansson. . . .

Judy mused, "If 'Eleanora Anderson' is really this same Johansson character that Mary Ellen is so worried about—"

"It's hard to believe," Beth interjected.

"That's just it. Dorothea seems so unlike that. . . . Maybe she's changed."

"Well, right. Even if she made a mistake once, don't we owe her another chance? Because now she's paid her debt to society."

"That's true. Besides, we don't really know the circumstances."

"Right. For one thing, she could have been desperate at the time. For another, she could have been framed."

Judy sighed. "It's really impossible for us to know exactly what did happen."

"Yeah. And you know how the press always sensationalizes anything having to do with social services."

Judy paused, mentally reviewing everything she knew about Dorothea Puente. Beyond those conversations with Mary Ellen Howard and Polly Spring, she'd neither seen nor heard anything negative about Dorothea. Nothing. On the contrary, Dorothea's boardinghouse was among the best in town, the tenants seemed utterly content, and Bert had flourished beyond all expectation since moving there in February.

"So what are we supposed to do?" Judy wondered aloud. "Even if Dorothea broke the law some years ago, she hasn't done anything wrong now. And Bert is the only one we've placed in her boardinghouse. What would be the point of moving him elsewhere?"

"Right. Dorothea absolutely dotes on Bert," Beth added.

"I just don't think he'd get that kind of attention anywhere else."

Beth agreed, and the VOA partners, who had worked so hard to find Bert a home in the first place, decided that even if Dorothea Puente was formerly this Dorothea Johansson person, that wasn't a legitimate reason for uprooting Bert and placing him in some less-desirable residence.

Before they could finish the article, the VOA street counselors had reached their destination. Judy told Beth she wanted to read the article later herself, and at the end of the day she took it home, stashing it with some other papers she meant to read just as soon as she had the time.

❖   ❖   ❖

While rumors about Dorothea Puente's past had sparked and fizzled within certain small circles, none reached the ears of Bill Johnson, back at Detox. He heard nothing of the suspicions raised by Mary Ellen Howard and had no reason to distrust Dorothea Puente. For the most part, Johnson's suspicions had been washed away by Puente's fluid charm. So, when she complained to him about Bert's never-ending string of visitors, he didn't give it much thought.

Dorothea was tired of "those girls" coming over all the time, she told him, meaning the "two Lucys" from the Chest Clinic, and the two VOA workers, Judy Moise and Beth Valentine. She peevishly told him that "all this interference has got to stop."

Bill Johnson listened noncommittally, but was apparently too nice a fellow to convey this admonition to the "girls" for whom it was intended.

Still, Puente had reason to believe that her words had been passed on and heeded. Because in mid-June, due to peculiar coincidences, the unwelcome visits ceased.

Bert's Tuesday and Thursday TB checkups came to a sudden end because, according to Lucy Yokota, "We considered him cured." During her final visit, Yokota told Bert that if he had any problems, he should call. Otherwise, they would check on him again in a year.

Coincidentally, visits from Judy and Beth also came to a halt in mid-June. It was nothing planned. It just happened that way. Call it a fluke. Call it fate.

As the summer heated up, so did things at the Volunteers of America headquarters. Everyone on the staff, every program, every dollar was to undergo review. Rumor had it that all the dead weight would be axed. So, for the next several weeks, besides the usual running around, handling emergencies, giving talks, and participating in support groups, the VOA street counselors spent a good deal of time enduring meetings, shuffling papers, and preparing presentations. Further, with more and more homeless on the streets whose cases demanded immediate attention, there simply wasn't time for a social call on Bert, who was, after all, doing extremely well.

No one had any reason to worry about Bert. In fact, wasn't he a shining example of how even a seemingly hopeless case could turn around, given enough care and the right environment?

So, with "those girls" out of the picture, gentle Bert was now left to the lingering affections of his friends back at Detox and the dominant influences of Dorothea Puente. No one guessed how precariously he was situated in that sweet old blue-and-white Victorian, imperiled as a canary in a mine shaft.

On a sweltering Saturday, July 30, Bert Montoya made his way across town to the converted warehouse on Front Street that he'd once called home and sought out his friend Bill Johnson. Bert was by nature amicable and uncomplaining, but Johnson could tell that something was troubling him. With a bit of gentle prodding, he learned what it was. Bert didn't want to stay at Dorothea's any longer, he told Johnson. He didn't want to "take meds."

This didn't seem especially alarming. Johnson knew that even though the antipsychotic drugs stopped Bert's auditory hallucinations, he disliked the side effects. And just a couple of weeks earlier, Bert had said that once he started receiving his SSI checks he wanted to leave Puente's and get a place of his own.

So now, if Bert wanted to come back to Detox and stop taking meds, that was fine with Johnson. He would drive him back to Dorothea's so they could pick up his things.

But once there, things got muddled.

At first, when Johnson told Dorothea that Bert wanted to leave, she replied flippantly, "He can leave any time he wants." But then she wanted to know why he wanted to go.

When Johnson explained that Bert wasn't happy because he didn't like having to take medication, she turned to Bert and demanded, "Then why did you wake me up at four in the morning the other day?"

Bert turned sheepish. It seemed he *had* woken her up early one morning, asking for his medication because he hadn't been able to sleep. Bert's resolve disintegrated. Well, yes, the meds weren't so bad. He would take them. Well, no, he didn't really want to leave. He would stay.

"My intention was to take him back to Detox," Bill Johnson mused later. "She changed his mind. . . . I could have told him to get in the van—I was his friend, he would have done what I told him—but all I could think was of him banging on the door [at Detox], and there'd be no mat for him."

Johnson knew that Detox would be getting full once the weather changed; at Dorothea's, at least Bert was assured of a place to sleep.

❀   ❀   ❀

Less than two weeks later, on Wednesday, August 10, Bert again inexplicably returned to Detox. He spent that night on a vinyl mat on the concrete floor. Uncomfortable, no doubt, but familiar. Safe.

The next morning, Bill Johnson again offered to take Bert back to 1426 F Street. Clearly, it was a better place for him. The food was better, he had his own room, his own TV. It made no sense for him to stay at Detox. He would be happier at Dorothea's. Really. He should go back.

And Bert relented.

When they got within three blocks of the house, Bert asked his friend to let him out at the corner. He didn't want Dorothea to know that Johnson had brought him back. He would walk the rest of the way so that she wouldn't get mad.

CHAPTER 8

Early in October, when summer's hot grip had loosened and Sacramento residents could walk unbowed by the pounding sun, Judy Moise returned from vacation and plunged back into work. She felt refreshed and enthusiastic, not least because the VOA review, which she'd so dreaded, had gone astonishingly well. On top of that, the Mental Health Association had recently named her "Mental Health Worker of the Year." Though she seemed to be earning more recognition than money, this wasn't too bad for a woman who had reentered the work force at forty-two, without benefit of a graduate degree, specific training, or even clear-cut career goals.

So midweek, when Judy popped in at Detox and peppered Bill Johnson with questions, eager to be brought up to date, she wasn't ready for the odd news he imparted.

In his unhurried way, Johnson spoke softly of Bert . . . his unexpected reappearance at Detox and how he'd returned to Dorothea's . . . what an uncommonly kind person Mrs. Puente was . . . cooking such fine meals, making sure Bert was going to church . . . she was even taking her tenants on a trip to Mexico—

"Mexico?" For a moment, the room went out of focus and Judy had a sinking feeling. Then she recalled Dorothea mentioning a trip to Mexico, and an idea surfaced. "Why don't you call Dorothea and see how Bert's doing?" she suggested.

Johnson placed the call while Judy stood waiting. When he hung up, he turned to her and announced, "Bert's in Mexico."

Judy frowned as some vague muttering commenced in the back of her mind. "Well, why isn't Dorothea in Mexico with him?" she asked.

"She *was*," he explained. "She took him down to visit her relatives in Guadalajara, and they stayed with her brother-in-law, who's a doctor down there. And you know what? Everyone liked Bert so much, they wanted him to stay longer. She says her brother-in-law has a nice home in the country, and Bert's really enjoying the country life— he's even stopped smoking—so she's letting him stay awhile."

Country life? Didn't Judy remember that Bert preferred the city? She didn't want to say anything to upset Bill, but there was something strange going on here.

Distantly, the muttering commenced again in her subconscious, a muffled rumble, like indigestion in her intellectual tract. She said good-bye to Bill Johnson and left, but the muttering followed her out the door and dogged her the rest of the day. It persisted through the week, greeting her in the mirror, following her during rounds at work, nagging through dinner. Finally, very early Saturday morning, it shook her awake.

She stared into the darkness, listening to her mind tick, wondering why this business about Mexico troubled her so much, debating whether she was being irrational. She looked at the clock and saw it was 5:00 A.M. Dorothea had said she was always up before five, that she liked to garden early in the morning. So she'd already be up. Very well. Judy would call her.

She dialed the number, and sure enough, Dorothea answered, clear and alert.

"Good morning, Dorothea, this is Judy Moise," she said, affecting a casual tone. Without even apologizing for phoning so early, she simply inquired, "I wondered, how's Bert doing?"

If Dorothea was startled, she didn't show it. "Oh, Bert's in Mexico," she said cheerily. In an effusive rush, she told Judy the same story she'd told Bill Johnson: her brother-in-law, the doctor, with the nice house in the country. The relatives who liked Bert so much that they'd insisted he stay. "They just love Bert," she cooed.

Judy didn't voice her doubts, but she was having a hard time believing that Dorothea's family would be so enamored of Bert that they'd welcome him into their home. He was sweet and even-tempered, true, but he was still mentally ill, and such people were hard to place even when the hosts were *paid* to take them in.

Now Dorothea was saying that he was just doing wonderfully. "He likes it down there so much, he's been calling me three times a week just to talk about what they've been doing."

Calling? Bert placing international calls? Judy tried to picture this, but it just wouldn't come. Maybe Dorothea's relatives were dialing for him.

Dorothea was volunteering more details about her family in Guadalajara, but Judy cut her off, saying, "You know, Dorothea, I'm kind of uncomfortable about Bert being down there without you. I mean, what if he gets lost? What if he wanders away from your sister's place and can't find his way back? He'd never be found again. And since he's Spanish-speaking, no one would believe that he's American. He'd never make it back across the border."

In truth, this was exactly what Judy feared had happened: Dorothea had taken Bert down there, he'd wandered off, and now she just couldn't admit that he was lost.

But Dorothea laughed this off. "That would never happen in that area, it's rural. Besides, now everyone down there knows him, and they'll keep an eye out for him. Please don't worry, Judy. Anyway, he'll be back next week."

"Next week?" a glimmer of hope.

"Well yes," Dorothea was saying. "You know that if he's out of the country more than two weeks, he'll lose his Social Security. So he'll be back by then."

So Dorothea knew it was illegal for Bert to be gone for more than two weeks! Judy took this as a good sign. She rang off, her apprehension lifting like an untethered balloon. Bert would be back in a week. Everything would be all right.

But when Judy called a week later, Bert still wasn't there.

"Oh, there was a fiesta that he wanted to stay for," Puente said breezily. She apologized, promising again that Bert would be back within a week.

Judy had little recourse but to implore Puente to have Bert call as soon as he returned. The landlady agreed, and Judy was left to wait.

But no call came.

By now Judy's muttering disquiet was a constant buzz in her head. Given the nasty rumors that had floated around about the old woman's past, she was beginning to worry that maybe Dorothea had intentionally "lost" Bert so that she could collect his checks.

Again, Judy called Dorothea. And again, Dorothea put her off with excuses.

Now it was approaching the end of October, and Judy was approaching the end of her patience. "Look," she said, "you're really putting me in jeopardy by having him out of the country this long." (This wasn't exactly true, but Judy hoped to sound weighty.)

Puente became repentant and less cavalier. "I'm really sorry that he's not here, but he'll be back next week. Really. Because I know I could get in a lot of trouble if he's not."

But Judy had heard this before. They were getting nowhere, and she couldn't put aside her fear that Dorothea had somehow lost Bert. Suddenly she asked, "Dorothea, don't you have something to tell me?"

"What do you mean?"

"I really feel like there's something that you need to tell me. This would be a good time, you know, if there's something you have to say."

Dorothea paused briefly, but responded, "No, no. There's nothing."

Judy sighed, back at square one, and tried to sound firm, "Okay. You'd just better have Bert back here by the first of November."

Dorothea gravely agreed. Bert would be back at the house by then. She promised.

Unannounced and with some trepidation, the VOA partners climbed out of their van and ascended the sun-dappled stairs at 1426 F Street. It was Tuesday, November 1, and Dorothea Puente's house was still festooned with Halloween decorations.

Puente met them at the door, alone, solemn, looking pale. Bert was still in Mexico, she conceded, her hands clasped together. She asked them to come sit with her out on the porch, and so the three sat down, not a smile among them.

"You said he'd be here today, Dorothea. What happened?" Judy asked.

"Well, I just don't know. He said he'd be here. I'm so sorry, but I really thought he'd be back by now." She sounded distressed, even embarrassed.

Judy didn't know what to say. Dorothea was their sole link to Bert and she didn't want to bully her, but so far the soft and sympathetic approach had gotten them nowhere. "Look," she said, assuming an assertive tone, "this is the third time you've said you'd have him here, and each time you've let us down. We don't really have any choice now but to contact the authorities."

"Well, Bert will be back," Puente insisted. "He'll definitely be back, there's no doubt about that. I just need a little more time."

"Dorothea, you know I'm responsible for him." (Judy was bluffing; she wasn't a caseworker and had no official responsibility for Bert, but now she was grasping for extra authority.) "Now you've violated the two-week deadline for his Social Security, and we're going to have to report that. And we're going to have to place him somewhere else when he gets back."

Dorothea's China-blue eyes glistened with tears. "Oh, dear, I'd really hate to lose him. I'd really miss having Bert here," she said, a catch in her voice. "And, oh, I've already gone out and got Christmas presents for him. I just, well, I was looking forward to sharing the holidays with him."

Moved by this sudden display of affection, Judy wondered how she could have been suspicious of this woman who cared so deeply for Bert. How could she doubt someone who had done so much for him? In a conciliatory tone she said, "When Bert gets back, it might be possible for him to stay through Christmas. We'll see what we can arrange."

Dorothea sighed heavily, wiped the tears from her cheeks, then stood suddenly and started pacing. "Well, this has just gone on too long," she pronounced. "I'm just going to have to go down to Mexico and bring him back myself."

Beth and Judy exchanged hopeful looks. "How are you going to do that?" Beth asked.

"I'll fly down."

"When?"

"Wednesday. I'll fly down on Wednesday and bring him back." Dorothea's whole countenance had changed. Her posture was erect, her voice resolute.

And somehow, her plan made sense. It was as if a light had been switched on. Of course! Bert was having trouble getting back because he was incapable of making the arrangements himself. He needed to have Dorothea go down and physically bring him back to Sacramento.

"So you'll have him back here when?"

"Oh, I'll have him back by Saturday. You can come by and see him then."

"Saturday is our day off," Judy said, "but we can come by next Monday. That would be the seventh."

"He'll be here," Dorothea promised.

Oddly, after leaving the F Street boardinghouse, Judy Moise and Beth Valentine settled back into work without discussing their conversation with Bert's landlady. Perhaps they had turned fate over to the power of positive thinking and didn't want to contaminate the air with negativity. Or perhaps their belief was too fragile to subject to much scrutiny. They *wanted* to believe that Dorothea would bring Bert back to them and everything would be fine.

But nighttime proved less hospitable to hope, and during these still hours Judy's worries festered. For the fourth time, the landlady had put them off with promises. A month of promises, and still no Bert.

She tried to remember the last time she'd seen him. Summertime, yes. June, probably. Now it seemed an awfully long time ago.

And she racked her brain: What *was* it that Mary Ellen Howard and Polly Spring had said last summer about Dorothea? It had seemed so ludicrous at the time, but what had they said? Something about Dorothea robbing some old guy, wasn't it?

She searched the house for the misplaced copy of the magazine article that Mary Ellen Howard had given her. She moved stacks of books, sifted through papers, flipped through files, shuffled her in and out boxes. Zip.

The next day, she virtually upended her desk at the office, but the article didn't surface. It seemed to have vanished.

Every night that week, deep into the small hours, Judy lay awake, pondering. If Dorothea didn't genuinely care for Bert, why would she have bought Christmas presents for him? Why would her eyes tear up when she talked about him? Surely she was trustworthy. Surely she would have Bert with her on Monday morning, as promised.

But Sunday night, again, Judy couldn't sleep. She kept telling herself that Bert was fine, that he would be there tomorrow. But still she wrestled with the nagging question: "What if he's not?"

CHAPTER 9

ONE MIGHT EXPECT THE SEVENTH DAY OF THE ELEVENTH month to dawn auspiciously. Not so. Even as Judy Moise was coming into her office that morning, events were veering off in unexpected directions.

As she came in the door, the phone was ringing. She rushed to answer it, and a man's voice said, "Hello, this is Michel Obregon."

"Michel?" An odd name for a man, Judy thought. A French given name with a Spanish surname?

"I mean Miguel," he corrected himself. "I'm Bert Montoya's brother-in-law. I'm calling from Shreveport, Utah, and I have Bert here with me."

Judy frowned. "Bert doesn't have a brother-in-law."

"Yeah, he does. We've been close for many years."

You sound much too young to be married to any sister of Bert's, Judy thought to herself. Incredulous, she responded, "I know about Bert's family, and I don't know about any brother-in-law."

"Well, you don't know everything," he snapped. "I came to California and picked Bert up on Saturday to bring him home with me. Now he's here with me and my wife. He's going to live with us in Utah. I'm calling because we want you to stop Bert's Social Security. We're a real proud family and we don't accept charity. So just please stop the checks."

"If Bert's there with you, let me talk to him."

"He can't come to the phone," the man said. "He's under the weather."

"What do you mean, 'He's under the weather'?"

"He's under the weather," the man repeated forcefully.

"I want to talk to him," Judy insisted. "Give me your number so I can call you back."

"No, uh, you can't," he said. "I'm calling from a pay phone at the side of the road."

"Then give me your home phone number and address. I'll call later."

"No, uh, we're moving and we don't have a phone yet. Anyway, my wife is sick. Uh, I have to go now. Good-bye." And he hung up.

While Judy had been on the phone, Beth had been checking messages left on their pager. Now, before Judy could absorb this strange conversation, Beth was bringing something equally odd to her attention: a message left earlier that morning by Mr. Obregon. They played the tape, and Judy again heard the man stumble over his alleged name. He said, "This is Don Anthony—I mean, Michel Obregon."

What kind of ridiculous charade was this supposed to be? Dorothea Puente had to be behind this, Judy decided, so she would just call her.

When Dorothea answered, Judy had just one question: "Who is Don Anthony?"

Puente said nothing. The silence turned elastic, stretching long moments before she responded, "I don't know what you're talking about."

Judy quickly explained about the phone call from "Michel" or "Miguel" Obregon, who claimed to have taken Bert to Utah.

Then Dorothea perked up. "Oh yeah, that's just what happened," she said.

"I have a hard time believing that."

"No, no, he's right. That's exactly what happened. I went down to Mexico and brought Bert back on Saturday, like I said I would. Then on Sunday his brother-in-law came while I was at church. It was very unexpected, but he just loaded up Bert's things in his truck and took him off to Utah."

"Dorothea, this is pretty farfetched," Judy chided. "I've never heard of Bert having a brother-in-law."

"Well, you know, I hadn't either, but Bert was so glad to see him and just seemed as pleased as anything to be invited to go live with him."

"Listen, this just doesn't seem right. There's something wrong here. I'm going to have to call the police and report Bert to Missing Persons."

Puente said hastily, "You know what? I can make a few phone calls, and if you want to get back to me later today, say around three o'clock, maybe I can have some new information for you."

"Like what?" Now thoroughly vexed, Judy cut Dorothea off, saying, "Never mind. I'm going to call the police."

And that's just what she did. Judy knew the number for Missing Persons by heart, she'd called it so many times for so many street people. The officer on the other end took Bert's name and other information, then promised to send someone over to talk to Judy later that morning.

With that, suspicions about Dorothea Puente had finally catapulted beyond private speculation into legal inquiry.

But the day was just beginning, and fears that Judy had fought to suppress were now blasting through her like hot vapor. *Where was Bert?* And what exactly had Dorothea Puente been accused of in the past?

Judy placed more calls. First, she phoned Peggy Nickerson to ascertain the last name of John, the thin, white-haired, hawk-eyed old fellow that Nickerson had placed at Dorothea's house back in January. Sharp, Nickerson told her. John Sharp.

Second, with self-reproach ringing in her ears for not having heeded warnings months earlier, Judy called Polly Spring to ask for Mildred Ballenger's phone number, and to ask just what sort of record Dorothea Puente had.

Spring didn't remember the precise details, but said that Ballenger would. Then she asked, "Why are you calling about this?"

To keep control of her emotions, Judy kept it brief. "A man is missing," she said simply.

While Judy Moise was busy with her calls, Dorothea Puente was busy with arrangements of her own. She rushed downstairs and found John Sharp, the loyal tenant for whom she'd bought a special chair when he'd moved into her boardinghouse after having had back surgery. She told him the police were coming to ask about Bert, and she implored him to tell them a specific story. "I'll make it worth your while," she promised.

When Officer Richard Ewing arrived at the Volunteers of America office at 10:30, Judy and Beth told him all they could about Bert Montoya's disappearance, Dorothea Puente's dance of broken promises and rash excuses, and the morning's weird phone calls. The earnest, good-looking officer filled out a report and promised to go by the house at 1426 F Street to investigate. Before he left, Judy urged him to be sure to talk to John Sharp. "He's a tenant there and he's reliable," she said. "He'll be a good source of information for you."

Mrs. Puente was composed and prepared when officer Ewing appeared at her door. She graciously invited the policeman inside, offered to show him around the house, and stuck to her story. Those social workers were just overreacting to Bert Montoya's trip to Utah, she said.

Officer Ewing found nothing amiss during his routine check of the Puente residence. The upstairs was quiet, as was the downstairs—which, Mrs. Puente hastened to point out, was separate from her own quarters.

When they encountered tall, skinny Mr. Sharp, the officer prodded him with questions, and Sharp mouthed his dull, reassuring answers. Detail for detail, he substantiated Puente's story that she'd gone down to Mexico for a couple of days, then had returned with Bert on Saturday. On Sunday, he said, Bert had gone away. "Yes," John Sharp told Ewing, "I saw Bert moving out. He and this other fellow were loading his things into a red pickup truck."

Satisfied, the officer and the landlady went back upstairs.

But once they'd gone, John Sharp scribbled a note on the back of an envelope: "She wants me to lie to you."

When Ewing came back downstairs, Sharp shoved the note into his hand. Thinking quickly, Ewing stepped into Sharp's room and turned up the television so they couldn't be heard. Sharp told him that they had to meet secretly so they could talk, and the two agreed to rendezvous outside on the corner of Sixteenth and E streets.

That afternoon, after Judy and Beth returned from the Social Security Administration, where they'd reported Dorothea Puente and asked that Bert Montoya's payments be stopped, Judy got a message from the VOA office on Bannon Street: "John Sharp is here and he wants to speak to you."

At Bannon Street, they found John Sharp looking agitated. He knew that Judy had specifically suggested that the cops seek him out, so he'd come to talk. Now he and she were bonded by their shared suspicions of Dorothea Puente.

Earnestness etched across his face, Sharp related the information he'd shared with Ewing after slipping him the note. There was something strange going on, he was saying, and he wasn't just talking about Bert. He was talking about another fellow, Ben Fink, who had suddenly disappeared last spring. He was talking about holes in the yard that Dorothea had ex-cons dig for her—several of them—holes that were empty one day and mysteriously covered over the next. And he was talking about a bad odor that came from a room upstairs and then settled over the house like a pestilence. He was talking about having worked in a mortuary back in Kansas City, and how he'd recognized that awful smell as the stink of death.

As Sharp's story poured out, the grim notion of homicide loomed like ugly weather. Judy shuddered. It seemed unreal. How could John Sharp believe that the little old women who had doted on Bert like a mother could be capable of murder?

Sharp went on, the deep creases in his face working to hold back an avalanche of emotion. He said he knew that ten or twelve Social Security checks arrived at the house every month—for people who weren't even living there.

If John Sharp had been a chronic drunk or a "mental," maybe Judy could have disregarded his words, but the concern in his voice hit not a false note. A damp chill passed over her as she understood for the first time that Bert might be dead.

Shaken by John Sharp's suspicions, Judy and Beth reported this new information directly to their boss, Leo MacFarland. They felt that, given the seriousness of Sharp's allegations, they ought to make sure the cops were giving the case their utmost attention.

MacFarland listened but was reluctant to interfere. "I think we ought to just let the police do their job," he said. Bringing their meeting to a close, he casually added, "It's been an interesting day, I'd say, with this on top of the break-in."

"What break-in?" Judy asked.

"Didn't anyone tell you? Someone broke into the office last night."

"Oh no! Did they take anything?"

"No, oddly enough, it doesn't seem that anything was stolen. But whoever it was ate something out of the refrigerator, used the phones, and left murder notes all around."

"Murder notes?" This was too much. The room was spinning.

Judy began asking questions, but MacFarland insisted there was nothing more to know. He dismissed Judy and Beth, saying, "There's no cause to worry; the police were already looking into it."

Driving home, reflecting on the roller-coaster events of the day, Judy worried that there could be some connection between the break-in, Dorothea Puente, and "Miguel Obregon." Nothing had been taken. . . . Could Puente and her friend have been looking for something? Could the murder notes have been aimed at Judy? Did Dorothea think she knew too much? The landlady didn't seem dangerous, but what if she'd somehow learned Judy's address?

Spooked, Judy rushed home and called her daughter, who had recently moved to her own apartment. When Britt finally answered, Judy related the wildly spiraling events of the day, saying she no longer felt safe at home. Britt told her to pack her things, and Judy went to stay with her daughter.

That same night, John Sharp was also wrestling with fears of what Dorothea Puente might do if she realized he was cooperating with the police. He listened to the house creak and pondered his options. Before retiring to bed, he adopted a precautionary measure of his own, wedging a chair tightly against his door.

CHAPTER 10

THE REVELATIONS OF NOVEMBER 7 PROFOUNDLY AFFECTED JUDY Moise. By her own admission, she became "kind of obsessed" with the shifting identities of the landlady on F Street. "Who is this Dorothea Puente?" she wondered aloud. "Now that I know who she's *not*, I have to find out who she *is*."

But Dorothea Montalvo Puente had confounded far more accomplished sleuths in the past, and wasn't about to stop.

Meanwhile, Judy's zeal for learning the truth about Puente and what had happened to Bert wasn't going to endear her to her co-workers. When Judy shared her rising fears with her partner, she was scoffed at. "What do you mean?" Beth chided. "You're really being paranoid."

"I'm just going to call the police to find out what's happening," Judy explained.

Beth quietly insisted that they should follow their boss's instructions and "let the police do their job."

"You don't realize the import of this," Judy protested. "I think it's big! I think it's a very dangerous situation."

But Beth was incredulous: "I can't believe you think that way."

"I can't believe you don't."

Clearly, Judy wasn't going to get much support from her partner, but it seemed understandable: She felt personally endangered in a way that Beth did not. So, while Beth was concerned about following the boss's orders, Judy felt that something was so seriously wrong, she just couldn't let it go. She had to do something.

With tension rising, the longtime partners set off in different directions, working independently.

Judy went to the Social Security Administration, where she hoped to stop the numerous checks that John Sharp had said were going to Dorothea Puente's residence. Instead, she heard that sad old song of a huge bureaucracy overloaded with cases; with so many checks being processed, there was no way to zero in on exactly which checks were going to whom. And Judy Moise was about to hear a similar tune from the police.

Back at the office, she called Officer Ewing, who told her the case had been transferred to Detective John Cabrera, Missing Persons and Homicide. Before ringing off, Ewing offered ominously, "It's probably even worse than you thought."

Feeling a queasy urgency, Judy phoned Detective Cabrera. At first he seemed well informed, volunteering that the police had "been watching the [Puente] house for a year." He implied that Judy's fears were no news to them, and they had things under control. But when she asked for a case number, Cabrera admitted they "didn't have one yet," and when she asked if he'd been out to the house, he told her he had not.

Some investigation, she thought.

In the end, Cabrera tried to reassure her that they were doing all they could, but she had to understand that they had several thousand cases to investigate. . . .

On Tuesday, November 8, George Bush was elected President of the United States. Meanwhile, as far as Judy could tell, the police were doing nothing about finding Bert Montoya or investigating Dorothea Puente.

By Wednesday it was conventional wisdom around the office that Judy had gone off the deep end over her missing client. At one point, her boss openly laughed at her, calling her suspicions of homicide "absurd."

Still, she couldn't stop worrying. She placed repeated calls to Detective Cabrera to find out how and if the investigation was progressing, but he was always out. When he didn't call back, she called his superior, Sergeant Jim Jorgensen, and was even threatening to call Congressman Matsui if something wasn't done. Whether as a result of her pushiness or not, Detective Cabrera finally returned her calls on Thursday and asked her to come to police headquarters the next morning.

By now Judy was particularly anxious to come in because she'd just received a disturbing letter, posted from Reno, Nevada. It read:

Mrs. Moise,

As I told you on the phone Alvaro, "Bert" as you know him Jose as we in the family call him. Until he was told he was going to have to move again after the holidays and he did not want. He liked Dorothea and she took care of him like a "mom." As you know she has had difficulty with the law which she also told us about. What Jose did not tell you was he had called here at our home for the last 3½ years. When we get settled we will send you photos and will let him call you about Thanksgiving if he wants to.

Yours truly,
Michel Miguel Obregon

P.S. As you know Jose does not write English. I will also be writing to Mrs. Puente. Also he has been wanting to go to Costa Rica for the Navidad period.

Judy was convinced that the mysterious Don Anthony had penned this clumsy letter, and she cynically noted how he'd tried to cover his blunders on the phone by signing both Michel and Miguel. It was almost laughable. But the implication concealed in the last line made her wince: Bert would be gone for Christmas; she shouldn't expect to see him again.

By the time her Friday, November 11, appointment with Detective Cabrera arrived, alarm was buzzing through Judy like too much caffeine. She and Beth shared a few tense moments out in the van as Judy tried to persuade her co-worker to come inside and lend emotional support. Reluctantly, Beth agreed, and the two marched solemnly into police headquarters.

Inside, they were greeted by Detective John Cabrera, a compact man with a fresh, boyish face, who directed them to a small room and asked them to wait. They perched on their chairs, discussing Bert's disappearance in worried tones, speculating about what Dorothea had done with him, declaring that the police had better *do something*, because if they didn't, Judy was going to call Congressman Matsui and newspaper columnist Pete Dexter.

Cabrera meanwhile tape-recorded their conversation, listening to their intense whispers and gauging their sincerity. About half an hour of eavesdropping apparently eased his skepticism, for the detective finally invited them into his office, and they settled down to business.

Cabrera read Judy's letter from "Miguel" and listened to her fret about Don Anthony, whom she feared was working as Puente's accomplice. But Cabrera didn't seem to think Anthony was much to worry about; he was more interested in Dorothea Puente. He disclosed that Puente had a substantial criminal record. Forgery. Theft. Drugging and robbing elderly victims. (He didn't mention that Sacramento police had received complaints about Puente some months earlier—theft of Social Security checks, even allegations of murder—but since the source of those complaints had been an ex-con, they hadn't given them much credence.)

"What I'm most worried about is Alberto," Judy was saying. "He might still be in Mexico, just lost, so I hope you can find him. Here's a written description of him," she said, passing him a sheet of paper with a description that she and others at Detox had labored over. Then, handing him a videotape, she added, "This might help, too. It's a video I made of Bert and some other homeless people. It's not the best, but I thought maybe you could take a picture off this and make posters." Her voice hopeful. "You know, missing person posters? So you can distribute them?"

Detective Cabrera accepted these without voicing his misgivings. Having handled missing persons and homicides since 1982, he knew that transients sometimes just wandered off, and he wouldn't have ordinarily bothered much with a stray like Bert Montoya . . . but this time, things were shaping up differently. Now there was not only a missing person, but the "holes" in the yard that John Sharp had described.

A tall, bespectacled man appeared in the doorway. Federal Parole Agent James Wilson introduced himself and took a seat, explaining that he'd been assigned to Puente's case only a couple of weeks earlier. Wilson had brought along Puente's file, including reports, newspaper clippings, and various notes. As he pulled out papers, Judy Moise squinted at someone's handwritten entry: "I went over to see Dorothea and she was planting about twenty tomato plants." It gave her the creeps.

Wilson admitted with apparent chagrin that Dorothea Puente—or Montalvo, as she was known—was violating the conditions of her parole by running a boardinghouse.

Puente had made a point of seeming extremely conscientious about staying on the right side of the law—calling her parole agents often, seeking permission for the least little out-of-town trip—and they'd believed she was genuinely repentant about her past offenses. Her sweet little old lady routine had lulled their vigilance. Though parole agents had visited the house more than a dozen times since her release from prison in the fall of 1985, none had discerned that she was anything but a boarder at 1426 F Street.

Cabrera explained that Jim Wilson would be accompanying him and his partner, Detective Terry Brown, to investigate Puente's residence. The men stood to go and Cabrera turned to the VOA partners, "Would you like to come along?"

Startled, they declined.

Out in the hallway, they encountered a jarring air of gaiety. In contrast to their mood, the two detectives seemed in jovial spirits as they prepared to requisition shovels. Their supervisor, Lieutenant Joe Enloe, was even wearing a humorous button, something like "I *Dig* Sacramento" (an allusion to Sacramento's biggest mass murder to date, the Solomon case, in which several women were found buried around town the previous year*). Apparently, the idea that anyone thought bodies were buried in Dorothea Puente's yard struck them as funny.

It was about 11:00 A.M when police arrived at the neat blue-and-white house on F Street. Grandmotherly Dorothea Montalvo Puente politely greeted Detectives Cabrera and Brown and Federal Parole Agent Jim Wilson at the door.

"Sorry to bother you, Mrs. Puente. We're here to talk to you about Bert Montoya," Cabrera said.

The police officers had no warrant, but Puente didn't ask for one.

---

*Morris Solomon was convicted in 1991 on six murder counts and other felonies.

Instead, the landlady welcomed them inside and offered them candy, which they courteously declined.

In his most disarming manner, Cabrera conversed with Puente about Bert. The pale old woman seemed a bit flustered by all this bother, but she steadfastly maintained that Bert had left for Utah with his brother-in-law, and her boarders could verify this. In fact, Bert had phoned her just recently, she told them.

Oddly, Puente also raised the subject of another former tenant, Benjamin Fink. She volunteered that he'd left during the summer and had gone back to Marysville. Cabrera noted this, but saw little connection between Fink and the man he was seeking.

At one point, Jim Wilson let Puente know that she was violating parole by running a boardinghouse and by failing to disclose this source of income. She solemnly acknowledged this, and when he informed her that he would have to revoke parole, she only nodded, offering not a word of protest.

Within her rights, Puente could have balked at any time and expelled her "guests," yet she maintained a calm, cooperative attitude. When the officers said they wished to speak to some of her tenants, she said, "Certainly, yes, by all means," and the officers went off to question those they could find.

Cabrera, who later admitted he had "no idea what we were looking for," also requested permission to search her upstairs residence. Again, Puente consented.

In a bedroom, he spied an empty medicine vial, picked it up, and read the name on the prescription. "Who's Dorothy Miller?" he asked.

"She's a relative," Puente said. "She stayed with me not too long ago."

Cabrera accepted this, took the vial, and went on with his search.

When they'd finished with the house, one large, unexamined area remained: the yard. The group quietly assembled on the back porch, pulled outside as if by some magnetic apprehension. As delicately as one could, Cabrera broached the outlandish subject of possible graves and asked permission to do a little digging.

They had no warrant—Puente could have refused—but she granted permission. With a wave of her hand, this woman who had spent so much time and effort on her garden offered airily, "I don't know what's back there."

With that, the two detectives hurried out to their unmarked car and returned in coveralls, carrying two short-handled shovels. Puente stood by and watched as they selected a likely-looking spot and started to dig. A chilly wind was blowing in with a promise of rain, but the men soon began to sweat from their labor. They took turns with the digging, one hole, then another.

Eventually, they had dug three exploratory holes in the backyard, but had found nothing but dark soil. It began to seem a bit ridiculous, even rude, gouging up this old lady's well-kept garden on the basis of some lame suspicions about "holes" in her yard.

Jim Wilson was having serious second thoughts when, shortly after starting on a fourth hole in a corner of the yard, his shovel found something peculiar. About eighteen inches down, the dirt yielded a white powder. He reached down, touched it, then sniffed his white fingertips. Lime.

If the digging had begun to seem routine, this broke the spell. Wilson began to dig with fresh intensity. Then he hit something. Calling over Brown and Cabrera, he prodded the thing with his shovel, pushing earth away from a dirty cloth object, steadily scooping out dirt until they could make out ... what looked like material wrapped around a tree root.

They exchanged looks. Wilson scraped away more dirt, trying to dislodge it, but it wouldn't budge.

Finally Cabrera climbed down into the hole, wrapped his hands around the root, braced his feet, and yanked. It suddenly broke loose, and he pulled out what they all recognized as a leg bone.

CHAPTER 11

WITH THE DISCOVERY OF HUMAN REMAINS IN HER YARD, DORO-
thea Puente's impassivity yielded to apparent shock. "Oh my Lord!"
she said, unlocking her crossed arms and pressing her palms to her
milky-white cheeks.

The grim-faced officers meanwhile stood around the gaping hole,
assessing the situation. Besides the bone, they'd identified a small,
white tennis shoe, with the remains of a foot inside. Having discovered a grave site, they concurred that they should cease digging
and report to their superiors before further disturbing any potential evidence.

Detective Brown hurried to the car and radioed headquarters. He
reported what they'd unearthed and requested backup. City workers
and some heavy equipment would be dispatched to the house. It was
clear they were going to need more than mere muscle and a couple
of shovels to excavate Puente's well-cultivated grounds.

And they were going to need more than a couple of gumshoes
and a parole agent—with nary a warrant among them—to handle the
technicalities, delicacies, and mechanics of the site. The coroner's office

was notified and both a forensic pathologist and a coroner's deputy promptly headed for F Street. Crime scene investigators were on their way. The district attorney's office was informed, and first one and then two forensic anthropologists were summoned to Sacramento to oversee the exhumation and help identify the skeletal remains.

In a few minutes police cars would start arriving, and the November stillness would be trampled underfoot along with Puente's flower beds. In the midst of this temporary calm Detective John Cabrera shifted uneasily from foot to foot. They'd found human bones . . . but they were looking for Bert Montoya, and that tennis shoe seemed much too small for a man. Also, Montoya had been missing only since August—surely not enough time for such extreme decomposition, lime or no lime. Whose skeletal remains had they found?

Cabrera scrutinized the proper-looking landlady, who hovered nearby, distress playing across her porcelain features. Despite her criminal record, it was hard to believe this elderly lady could be involved in something so brutal as murder. Nonetheless, he determined to take her down to police headquarters for questioning.

Parole Agent Jim Wilson watched quietly as Detective Cabrera escorted Mrs. Puente to the unmarked car, put her in the passenger seat, and headed off toward the Hall of Justice. Wilson knew enough about this crafty old con to realize that she wasn't what she seemed, and after the morning's grisly discovery, he was relieved to see that the police had the situation in hand, that she was being taken into custody. He'd have his report in first thing Monday morning, and by then the legal machinery would be up and humming.

Sitting alone in interview room number 5, Dorothea Puente looked small, old, and vulnerable. Her snow-white hair had been hastily combed, and before leaving the house she'd changed into a small-print dress with lace trim on the sleeves—not the tough sort of person usually positioned at the table in front of the secret videocamera concealed behind the air vent.

Now Detective Cabrera entered and bustled around solicitously, making sure she had water, asking if she were comfortable, speaking clearly so that his voice was easily picked up by the hidden microphone. He went over a few preliminaries for the record, then turned softly to the missing Mr. Montoya. "I need all the truth from you," he coaxed. "Now, his disappearance is very suspicious, I can tell you that." He started mildly, "There are a lot of inconsistencies in your statement."

Mrs. Puente answered each question, never balked or flinched, but she was not going to budge on her story. With elbows propped on the table, she looked straight across at Detective Cabrera and maintained that Bert's brother-in-law had taken him to Utah.

Cabrera turned contentious. "Now, Mr. Sharp says he hasn't seen him for three months. And the social worker hasn't seen him. So who is lying to me? Who is lying to me, Dorothea?"

"Well, I'm not," she insisted. "He [Bert] was here Saturday and Sunday."

Cabrera was not to be deterred. He kept after her, phrasing things this way and that, trying to trick her into a contradiction, and finally stating baldly, "Mr. Montoya's dead."

Puente scoffed, "No he's not," as if this were a ridiculous suggestion.

Cabrera vigorously queried and quizzed, yet Puente maintained her soft-spoken calm. Throughout a barrage of questions, she stuck to her story, appearing somewhat distraught, yet eager to help. She didn't know why John Sharp had cooked up that story about her making him lie, but supposed it was because he was mad at her because she'd asked him to move. And she certainly knew nothing about the bones they'd unearthed. In fact, she suggested, once they found out how old the bones were, they'd find that she had nothing to do with it.

Frustrated, Cabrera told Mrs. Puente that he held her accountable for the bones they'd found. He tried a bluff. "Dorothea, I know if we dig, we're going to find more," he said ominously. "I know that, I know that."

"Well, I didn't put 'em there," she replied. "I couldn't drag a body any place."

No one had said anything about "dragging" bodies.

"I believe that," he conceded, "but I believe there's somebody else involved here. Somebody else. Because here's people that are still getting checks and they haven't even been seen, hide nor hair, Dorothea. You have to look at it from my view, dear. I look at it, and I think, *nothing makes sense*."

"Sir," she interjected with dignity, "I have not killed anybody."

This seemed to be going nowhere, but Cabrera pressed on, raising questions about the whereabouts of Ben Fink.

Dorothea maintained that she'd kicked him out of the house, and he'd gone up to Marysville. "I told him not to ever come back on the property," she explained.

She looked awfully old and small to be a killer. And with each of Cabrera's questions, she'd blink uncomprehendingly, blameless as a house cat, then offer up some semi-plausible reply. Asked about finding in her yard a curious amount of corrosive lime (a substance used in treating sewage, which might also be used to dissolve human tissue), Puente explained that she was using the lime to "soften the dirt."

She also made extravagant proposals. They could tap her phone, she suggested, so they could monitor any incoming calls from Bert. Or, she offered, she could hire a contractor to dig up the yard, so they could see she had nothing to hide. And of course she had no problem with taking a polygraph examination, though she thought it might be better to wait until Monday, to give her nerves a chance to settle.

At times, Cabrera goaded her about her criminal record. He even claimed that they'd known about bodies in her yard for a whole year, which seemed to startle Mrs. Puente.

Finally, the interview wound down, Dorothea seeming tired. "Well," she said wistfully, "I wish Mr. Montoya would show up right now."

"I just don't think he's going to," Cabrera replied.

"He is. He is," she insisted. "I believe in God, and I know he's going to show up."

Cabrera remembered something else. "Okay, one thing I need to ask you is, ah, we'd like to dig some more. Okay?"

She nodded.

"And that might entail, ah, digging up that concrete where those flowers are."

"That's okay."

"Okay, do you have any problem with us digging, or—"

"No."

"None whatsoever?"

"No."

"Because you don't have to let us."

"Look, I want to get this over with."

Meanwhile, the investigation at 1426 F Street was becoming something of a spectacle. Bright yellow police tape cordoned off the crime scene, announcing to all who drove past on busy F Street that something was up. Now crime scene investigators had arrived, and other officers stepped aside as they methodically examined the site, plotting diagrams, taking photographs, measuring and marking locations. City workers had arrived, and since rain was on the way, a protective canopy was quickly erected over the grave site.

Of course, a body cannot be discovered within a mile of the state capitol without the press showing up. Damp reporters strained against the police tape, calling across to various people at the scene who looked to be in the know. They queried and scribbled, working for the facts, hoping for a scoop, while brazen cameramen stomped about, looking for the best angles.

Next-door neighbor Will McIntyre meanwhile titillated the media with the choice bit of news that he had contacted health officials, complaining about a foul stench coming from Puente's yard in May and September. "It was a rancid, sweet, nauseous odor—almost like a dead body," he told them, adding, "I smelled them in 'Nam, unfortunately, so I know what a dead body smells like."

The police were less forthcoming, but Lieutenant Joe Enloe, supervisor of the homicide field unit, finally relented and briefed reporters on what was going on. At one point he told them, "We don't think the body found is the one we're looking for," volunteering a quote for the first brief reports.

All agreed that Puente seemed the key suspect. By now, everyone knew that police had swept the old woman away to police headquarters for questioning, which only fueled suspicions of her guilt. But speculation was brought to an abrupt halt when a car rolled up, the door opened, and Dorothea Puente stepped out onto the sidewalk.

Released after more than two hours of questioning, the landlady looked somber but unshaken. Having no comment for the hungry press, she moved through the crowd, reentered her house, and shut the door behind her.

What a surprise.

Though floodlights had been brought in, work outdoors ceased as the early November darkness fell. Still, some police work continued. An all-night watch was ordered, and police continued to question boarders.

John Sharp, who had been taken to headquarters for about an hour of questioning, was returned to the house. A lone officer stood by and watched while he gathered up his belongings. When he came out a reporter called to him, "Are you moving out?"

The reply was immediate: "You bet."

❖   ❖   ❖

It's impossible to say what Dorothea Puente might have done during those long, quiet hours of the night while she was left unattended in her home on F Street. She could have paced the floor, occasionally stopping to pull back her lace curtains and spy on the officer beneath her window. She could have sorted through papers, carried a neat pile to the kitchen sink, and burned them, washing ashes down the drain. She could have emptied the contents of vials, bottles, and jars into the toilet bowl, flushing them away. She could have poured herself several stiff drinks. She could have fumed and planned. Or, exhausted after such a trying day, she may have simply curled up in bed and fallen asleep.

The next day dawned gray and drizzly, but any neighbors hoping to sleep in that Saturday found the morning stillness shattered by the hard growl of heavy equipment. Homicide detectives were back at 1426 F Street, along with a small crowd of coroner's deputies, crime scene investigators, and others.

Forensic anthropologist Dr. Rodger Heglar presided over the recovery of the skeletal remains, which were slowly exposed as the hole was enlarged around them. Using shovels and then hand trowels, the diggers sunk a circle around the body to a depth of about three and a half feet, sifting the dirt for evidence. Final layers of soil were swept away with brushes, the body being photographed at every stage of exhumation.

The remains, which were wrapped in a sheet of some sort, now rested on a pedestal of dirt. Eventually, a sheet of plywood would be slipped beneath the strange bundle, and the body, which weighed very little, would then be slipped into a zippered plastic body bag. An unmarked van waited to take the remains to the coroner's office, where they would be examined. For now, Dr. Heglar surmised that they'd uncovered "the entire skeletal remains of a gray-haired, rather petite, elderly female."

Now the police were gearing up for some major excavations: If there were more bodies to be found, they were going to find them. They selected a site at the side of the house—a concrete slab of about six-by-eight feet—and moved the back-hoe into place. The pounding backhoe easily broke through the rectangular slab and moved it aside, ready to dig up the ground beneath.

Now it was shortly after 8:30 A.M., and Dorothea Puente was poised to make her move.

Grizzled ol' John McCauley, Puente's tenant and confidant, stepped out onto the porch and beckoned Detective Cabrera. Calling through a beard of gray bristles, McCauley said that Dorothea wanted to talk to him.

Cabrera climbed the stairs and found Mrs. Puente wearing a smart pink dress and purple pumps—the very antithesis of understatement.

"Mister Cabrera, am I under arrest?" she asked.

He told her no, and the little landlady then asked if he would mind if she and her friend John McCauley went to the nearby Clarion Hotel to meet her nephew for a cup of coffee. She promised to be back soon.

Dorothea Puente had been so cooperative, there was no reason not to let her go, was there? Cabrera quickly consulted with his superiors, who said they lacked enough evidence to arrest the woman; she was free to go.

Cabrera returned with this news, and Mrs. Puente went to get her coat.

Stepping back into the room in her red wool coat, she suddenly remembered, "Oh, my soup!" and spun off toward the kitchen, Cabrera at her heels. A big pot was simmering on her stove, and she took up a spoon to stir the bubbling liquid. Glancing shyly at Cabrera, she asked, "Would you mind very much, while I'm out, keeping an eye on my soup?"

An amicable fellow, the detective agreed. Then, peering out the window at the gathering crowd, thinking that Puente might be intimidated by the press, Cabrera chivalrously volunteered to escort her out.

Puente hastily grabbed her umbrella, then the threesome went outside and down the steps into the chill morning air. Cabrera lifted the yellow police tape, then shepherded his charges past the throngs of reporters and onlookers. After a couple of blocks, he stopped and watched as Dorothea Puente and John McCauley walked away.

No one followed.

Minutes later, back at the house, this error in judgment became painfully clear. Just fifteen inches underground, Cabrera's shovel uncovered a second body. And the sky, which had been threatening rain all morning, now wept upon the disturbed ground of Dorothea Puente's yard.

CHAPTER 12

SATURDAY, NOVEMBER 12, 1988, WOULD NOT BE A GOOD DAY for Sacramento's police department. They'd discovered graves— plural—in the yard of a downtown Sacramento residence, they'd just let their primary suspect walk away, and TV vans with satellite dishes were sprouting like mushrooms around the crime scene. While microphones hungered for sound bites, the most natural spokesperson in such a serious situation, Police Chief John Kearns, was away at a convention in southern California—"golfing," as one cynic put it.

With the body count hovering at two and Dorothea Puente nowhere to be found, the unsavory job of facing an indignant press fell to Lieutenant Joe Enloe. He composed himself, took a breath, and floated out the official explanations. He declared that there hadn't been enough evidence to arrest Dorothea Puente that morning, and that following Puente would have violated her rights.

But as reporters badgered him for details, Enloe's excuses fell like blasted skeet. It could hardly have looked worse: Their primary suspect had been escorted past police lines in broad daylight, *despite* growing suspicions that her well-tended backyard was a well-planted graveyard, *despite* her criminal record, and *despite* the fact that she was in obvious violation of parole. Clearly, it was best to keep these encounters with the media brief.

Officers meanwhile searched Sacramento's airport, bus and train stations, where they spotted many little old ladies . . . but not a single snowy-white hair of Dorothea Puente's head.

She was elsewhere.

At 9:45 that morning, Dorothea Puente called a cab, which took her and John McCauley to Tiny's, a bar in West Sacramento. While McCauley sipped a lone beer, Dorothea thirsted for more potent fortification: She downed three screwdrivers in a row.

By 11:00, courage bolstered, she was ready. Correctly figuring that she was by now being sought at Sacramento's transportation centers, she called a cab and asked to be driven to the nearby town of Stockton. A fifty-mile drive, a sixty-dollar fare plus a generous ten-dollar tip, and she was clear of Sacramento's tightening net of law enforcement.

The taxi driver deposited her at Stockton's Greyhound bus terminal, where she bought a ticket and boarded a bus. Sitting back and making herself comfortable for the long, anonymous ride to Los Angeles, she could breathe a little easier now. She'd escaped as cleanly as she had back at the age of nineteen . . .

Dorothea stared out the window at the familiar streets of Stockton as the bus turned onto the freeway on-ramp and gathered speed, leaving behind a trail of exhaust and a cloud of confusion.

Few people anywhere, in Sacramento, Stockton, or deeper in her past, could say they truly knew the white-haired passenger staring boozily out at the fleeting landscape. Johansson, Montalvo, Puente—they were all just temporary tags on a slippery identity. Enmeshed as she was in so much deception, Dorothea seemed to have lost herself somewhere along the way. The thread of truth had gotten tangled with lies long ago, before she'd become the landlady on F Street, even before her four failed marriages . . . But this was no time to try to sort it all out.

She knew from where Cabrera had been digging that at least two of the bodies had been found by now, and worried about whether they would find them all. Still, even if they missed one or two, it made no difference. No one was going to understand. No matter what the numbers, it added up to the same thing: She was running for her life.

Dorothea must have secretly scolded herself for not having been smarter about this. Things had been going along pretty smoothly, but then she'd made some bad judgments, some mistakes, and that Judy Moise woman had gone and called the cops. She should have seen that coming. She'd had a feeling that Judy was going to be trouble, the way she was sniffing around all the time. Just like Mildred Ballenger back in 1982. Nosy, trouble-making social workers, both of 'em! Dorothea surely scowled at the memory.

In 1982, she hadn't acted fast enough. If she'd only been quicker, she could have used that ticket to Mexico. That time, she'd dawdled, and the cops had picked her up.

But not this time.

While the police were struggling with their investigation, the press was busy with its own, and by the next morning those who love the Sunday papers were being treated to hefty doses of this sensational case. Big, colorful, front-page photos of the scene on F Street grabbed attention, and Dorothea Montalvo Puente, the primary suspect, was given a liberal share of the paper's column inches.

Many in the Mexican-American community practically spat out their coffee when they read that *la doctora* was suspected of murder! And those who had known Dorothea Puente as a kindly, seventy-year-old grandmother were shocked that she was really a fifty-nine-year-old ex-con, a woman with a nefarious past and an elusive identity. She had glided through aliases like a fun seeker at Mardi Gras, her personal history shifting with each turn of her identity, details blurring and contradicting each other.

The hard facts of Dorothea's history could be found, mostly, in court documents. Criminal charges, dates of arrest, terms of parole—these sorts of things made up the loose weave of her past. Highlights from her criminal record were there in black and white: Toward the end of 1978 she'd been caught and convicted of illegally cashing thirty-four federal checks, filching benefit checks intended for her tenants. But apparently these thefts hadn't impressed the judge as especially serious—her sentence had been light: five years' probation.

She emerged as a woman prone to aliases, with a weakness for grand lies. She'd lied about being a survivor of the Bataan Death March in 1942, about having cancer, about making movies with Rita Hayworth, about being the ex-lover of this or that star. And she'd lied

99

about being a doctor, or nurse, or health care worker—whatever she could get away with.

One of her past victims, Malcolm McKenzie, described Dorothea Puente as a slick con artist. "She was a sharp dresser, sharp in her ways," he recalled. "She knew what she was doing. She could have fooled you or anybody."

One afternoon in January 1982, she'd walked into a midtown bar called the Zebra Club, shed her coat, and slid into conversation with a group of oldsters who were meeting over drinks. In particular, she'd befriended the seventy-four-year-old McKenzie, a retiree and a regular at the bar.

McKenzie recalled for the press how he'd become ill after just a couple of drinks. Dorothea had offered to escort the old gent home, then had rifled through his belongings. Stricken by some sort of temporary paralysis, he'd watched helplessly as she stole checks, cash, even a ring which she brazenly slipped off his limp finger. "She could have killed me," he reflected.

When McKenzie recovered, it seemed obvious to him that Dorothea had slipped a Mickey into his drink, and that's just what he told the police later on. A detective looked into the matter, and even interviewed "Miss Montalvo," but she apparently worked her little old lady charm, denying everything, claiming that McKenzie was just a drunken old fool.

Even back in 1982, it took Sacramento police a while to put two and two together. Not until April, when Dorothea Montalvo was in court for a preliminary hearing for having drugged and robbed Malcolm McKenzie in January, was she arrested on a forgery warrant for having robbed someone back in 1981.

Frail and ailing, seventy-nine-year-old Esther Busby had needed a live-in health care attendant. An energetic and caring woman named Dorothea Montalvo had seemed perfect for the job. But soon after hiring her, Busby had become repeatedly and mysteriously ill.

At the hospital, Dorothea had dazzled all onlookers with her solicitous ways. She was so kind and attentive that even nurses had been impressed. But eventually, Busby's doctor got suspicious. He guessed that Dorothea Montalvo was over-medicating, perhaps even poisoning this elderly patient. And he told her social worker, Mildred Ballenger, that he suspected Montalvo was "ripping Mrs. Busby off."

Alarmed, Ballenger had checked and discovered that Busby's latest Social Security check had indeed been cashed, the signature forged.

Ballenger had itched to hand Dorothea Montalvo over to police. But luckily for Dorothea, Esther Busby simply wasn't up to pressing criminal charges; instead, she'd merely fired her.

Like Busby, eighty-three-year-old Dorothy Gosling was also old and ill. And like Busby, Gosling hired Dorothea Montalvo as a night nurse, then ended up at Sutter General Hospital suffering repeated bouts of inexplicable illness. But Gosling had a healthy skepticism and plenty of fight left in her. When her case attracted the attention of Mildred Ballenger, she acted on the social worker's recommendations. She checked her belongings, then reported to police that Dorothea Montalvo had stolen her jewelry, a rare gold coin, and some blank checks (later forged and made payable to—no surprise—Dorothea Montalvo).

On November 18, 1981, Sacramento police dutifully recorded Gosling's complaint. But it wasn't until 1982, after Malcolm McKenzie's charges, that Dorothea's illegal activities finally attracted some heat.

Still, she wasn't jailed. And, Teflon criminal that she was, Dorothea slid right back into action. She pulled off two robberies in quick succession.

Just a month after the McKenzie preliminary hearing, Dorothea slipped into a secured apartment complex and knocked at the door of eighty-two-year-old Irene Gregory. Introducing herself as Betty Peterson of the Sacramento Medical Association, Dorothea talked her way into Gregory's apartment, saying she'd been sent to check on the elderly woman's medications. Gregory obediently showed the "nurse" to her medicine cabinet, then was handed two pills and instructed to lie down and close her eyes.

The "nurse" said she was going to take Gregory's blood pressure, but when Gregory awakened, she found that the "nurse" had instead taken two valuable rings and a bottle of sleeping pills. Only after she received a bill for $730 would she discover that a credit card was missing too.

Even then, Dorothea had time to escape. But apparently she needed just a little more money.

So, late one morning, Dorothea unexpectedly dropped in on a neighbor, eighty-three-year-old Dorothy Osborne. She came bearing gifts—a bottle of brandy and a bottle of vodka—and prepared a concoction for her friend. Osborne hardly sipped the foul-tasting drink, but didn't awaken until about eight that evening. Only later did she realize that some keys, her Visa card, a checkbook, an unemployment check, an ID card, and some rolled coins had been stolen.

Two days later, Dorothea Montalvo Puente was arrested, charged with assorted crimes, and ordered held without bail. Police confiscated the ticket to Mexico in her purse.

By the time readers had finished the back page of Sunday's paper, many were wondering how police could have let this disreputable woman slip through their fingers.

Part III
THE SPECTACLE

You always have questions about whether a placement is the best . . .
But we have to put them somewhere. We have to take what society
provides us, and it's not always the best.
—PEGGY NICKERSON

The focus in this tragedy has been on the spectacle of mass murder.
I work constantly, however, with people who live in the continuing
jeopardy of homelessness, poverty, and mental illness. I think we
should all focus even more intently on these people whose daily lives
are a tragic exercise in futility and abandonment. We have a national
tragedy ongoing that we must deal with.
—JUDY MOISE

CHAPTER 13

A<small>T ABOUT THE SAME TIME DOROTHEA PUENTE WAS CATCHING</small> her taxi to Stockton, a forensic anthropologist was applying his craft in the back corner of her yard. With a practiced eye, Dr. Heglar had identified areas where slight changes in the color and texture of the soil indicated recent digging. Plants had been uprooted, and here and there topsoil had been removed. There had been a momentary stir over some suspicious discoveries, but they turned out to be only trash.

Now he was scooping dirt away from a dubious patch of fabric. Crouched at the base of a newly planted tree, he next used a metal probe, testing the surrounding area for resistance. Then, with meticulous care, he began flicking soil away with his brush.

Heglar enlisted the help of a coroner's investigator and others, and now this spot became the focus of a controlled commotion. Shovels scooped a broad ring of earth away from the bundle, then small hand trowels were employed. It became obvious that this was yet another body. Dr. Heglar and the coroner's investigator stood knee-deep in the hole, whisking away dirt from the encircled form, watching as the cloth took on human dimensions. Like the others, it had been wrapped in layers of material before burial.

The body would not be tampered with here at the site. In accordance with protocol, it was tagged, photographed, sealed in a white plastic body bag, and removed to the morgue to await the necessary indignities of autopsy. For now, it would be known only by the impersonal designation, coroner's case #88–3381.

Police found it hard to imagine little old Dorothea Puente maneuvering dead bodies into the ground by herself. "We're making the assumption that it would be pretty hard for a woman of her small size to carry those bodies," Lieutenant Enloe disclosed to the press. So, with Puente off to parts unknown, finding an accomplice became a top priority.

When Puente's tenant and morning's escort, John McCauley, arrived back at the house, he was first confronted by voracious reporters. He loyally defended his landlady, saying, "She's helped people out. She's taken them in. She has let them stay there for a couple days without paying."

But as soon as the police learned that McCauley had returned, they challenged him, demanding to know where Puente was. McCauley claimed that she was still at the Clarion Hotel, and the police rushed over to search, but of course found nothing. (In the meantime, Puente allegedly phoned McCauley and advised him to flee.) Police then arrested the cantankerous fifty-nine-year-old McCauley as an accessory to homicide. Puente had slipped past them, but now at least they'd arrested *somebody*.

With McCauley in jail, his arrest a welcome offering to on-the-spot news reports, the digging on F Street continued. News of the exhumations seeped through the community like a stain, and the crowd of spectators who gaped and endured the drizzle swelled to more than a hundred. They came on foot and on bicycles. They perched in trees and atop cars.

Early on, they joked nervously about the number of bodies that might be found in the little old lady's yard, but when an actual body bag was loaded into the coroner's van, reality set in, and the titters fell to hushed exclamations, looks of naughty inquisitiveness tightening to shock and concern.

Initial reaction to the spectacle on F Street quickly moved into a phase of disbelief. Surely that sweet little old lady couldn't be responsible for such atrocities. No one in his right mind could believe that a fragile old grandmother could have murdered those people and then buried them in her own backyard! Right here in downtown Sacramento! It had to be some kind of mistake.

When the broadcast images spewing from F Street became too ugly, many found relief in detachment—that primordial numbness that clamps over our nervous systems to shield us from true horror. But eventually another sort of ugliness would begin. Minds and tongues would thaw, and then the conjecture would begin, the speculation and I-told-you-sos that spin off into accusation and rumor.

Police meanwhile hustled to contact those who might somehow shed light on the case. And some who had information to share made the effort to contact them.

One who came to the scene and asked to speak to an investigator was Patty Casey, Dorothea Puente's favorite taxi driver. Stunned by the discovery of bodies on F Street, Casey stood on the corner with Detective Terry Brown, telling of her fourteen-month friendship with Puente. She was rocked by the ramifications of incidents that had previously seemed innocent, recalling for the officer that she'd taken Dorothea to buy plants and flowers, to buy cement.

And she remembered that Dorothea had replaced her carpets—twice—saying that one of her rooms "had a curse" and that people were "constantly dying in there." It stuck in her mind that the grandmotherly passenger had moaned, "Everyone who has lived there has had something happen to them. . . . There's always blood in there." Through tears, Casey whispered, "I'm sorry my friend might have done something so horrible."

And Patty Casey wasn't the only one to whom events now seemed more sinister than mere coincidence. Puente's next-door neighbor, Will McIntyre, also made a point of talking to the police that Saturday. He, too, remembered Puente's problem with carpets: She'd offered to give him one, but he'd declined—it was stained.

And now he'd found some things out in his backyard, he said, that he believed had been tossed over the fence the night before: a handful of gold teeth, a bullet, and a piece of gold jewelry. They couldn't have been there yesterday, McIntyre insisted, because he would have noticed them during his daily cleanup after his dog. It seemed obvious to McIntyre that Puente had tossed them there to get rid of evidence, and he was disgruntled when the police seemed unmoved by his assertions.

Peggy Nickerson also came forth, innocent of the trouble she was about to wade into. She introduced herself to Detective Cabrera as the street counselor who had spoken earlier with Sergeant Jorgensen about clients of hers who had roomed with Dorothea Puente. She handed Cabrera a list of people she'd placed with her during the past eighteen months. As he read it over, one name stopped him. "Is Dorothy Miller related to Puente in any way?" he asked.

"No, she was just rooming with her," she replied. "Dorothea was the payee for her benefits." Nickerson added that Miller had "disappeared sometime around January."

Cabrera mentally flashed to the vial of pills he'd confiscated from Puente's bedroom. The name on the prescription: Dorothy Miller.

The next day, as law enforcement's search for Puente spread, earth-moving equipment continued to rip through her yard, heaving through concrete, uprooting bushes, breaking small trees. Topsoil was shoved away, and when some odd-looking buried scrap aroused suspicions, forensic anthropologists, police, and coroner's investigators cooperated in the more delicate removal of underlayers of earth.

By now, neighbors had come to resent the noise, the confusion, the TV crews, the police blocks, and especially the growing crowd. The block was closed to traffic, and from curb to curb curiosity seekers gathered behind the yellow police line, craning to get some glimpse of this strange excavation. They gathered early and continued to multiply, drawn to the magnetic tragedy unfolding at Puente's boardinghouse as to some gala civic event. Some carried cameras. Others brought children, carrying them on their shoulders for a better look. Tourists and townspeople alike stood transfixed, watching with the interest of theatergoers while the excavations continued.

And their vigilance did not go unrewarded: Two more bodies were unearthed that Sunday.

Investigators discovered the fourth corpse in the morning, buried just in front of a metal shed standing in the side yard. Now a second forensic anthropologist, Dr. Chuck Cecil, oversaw the exhumation. Using a technique that had by now become familiar, the workers "pedestaled" the body, circumscribing the earth around it until it rested on a preserved pedestal of dirt. All evidence was carefully labeled and photographed. Then, using hand trowels and brushes, they removed the last blanket of soil.

This individual had been wrapped not in cloth but in plastic, carefully sealed with duct tape. While this hid the corpse's features, it only slightly diminished its stench. Even after the body was zipped into a body bag, death hung in the air.

The forensic team grimly carried the corpse from the landlady's garden, the morgue its destination. Excitement rippled through the crowd and television cameras sparked to life as the body was loaded into a waiting van.

The work continued—taking some toll on those who had drawn this awful duty. Muscles ached, and stomachs wrestled with impending nausea. (One police clerk, Joy Underwood, was so sickened that she later claimed disability. Handling the evidence, including body bags and victims' clothing, triggered violent nightmares and vomiting. "I still have the taste of death in my mouth," the police clerk said. "I can't eat vegetables grown in the ground because they have dirt around them, like the people dug up" from Puente's yard.)

At midday a decorative gazebo, dismantled and removed, turned out to be an apparent attempt to conceal yet another unmarked grave. The concrete beneath the structure was shattered, shovels bit into the ground below, and a fifth body soon yielded to the search. Coroner's case #88–3384 was tagged and photographed. It, too, had been wrapped for burial, this time in bed sheets.

"We're still digging," Police Sergeant Bob Burns assured the gathered media. "We'll continue to dig, and we won't stop digging until we've dug up every square inch of this yard."

Long and narrow, the side yard was now pocked with freshly overturned earth. It almost seemed the bodies had been planted in an uneven row, from the end of the driveway all the way to the back fence.

The systematic digging continued late into the afternoon, but the gashes in Puente's once-lovely garden yielded nothing further. The day's work came to a close, a tractor shoving soil and broken branches into piles of debris, the crowd dispersing into the chilling air before darkness fell.

CHAPTER 14

FIVE BODIES AWAITED IDENTIFICATION AT THE MORGUE. THE coroner's office revealed little except that it would be difficult to determine rates of decomposition because of the way the bodies had been wrapped and buried.

With the corpses thus far unidentifiable, no one could say whether Bert Montoya's body had been unearthed from Puente's yard. Yet it seemed unlikely that someone dead only two months could be among such extremely decomposed remains. People began to wonder just how many bodies could possibly be buried in the innocent-looking grounds of that gingerbread house. The long silences of itinerant siblings, alcoholic uncles, and absentminded aunts became suddenly less a source of relief than of alarm, spurring some to do a quick check on the well-being of vagrant friends and family members. Some made contact and were reassured. Others drew blanks, swallowed, and contemplated the news stories about disinterred remains, wondering what to do.

One woman in Sweet Home, Oregon, had already decided on a course of action. On Monday, November 14, for the second time in three years, Reba Nicklous found herself contacting the Sacramento Police Department. On Saturday, she'd received a phone call from her daughter in California who had asked, "What was the name of the woman in Sacramento that Everson went to live with?" When she'd replied, "Puente," her daughter had gasped and spilled fears about the ominous reports coming out of Sacramento.

Now Reba Nicklous waited "on hold," a cold dread coursing through her veins. When an officer picked up the line, she wrestled her facts into order. "My brother Everson went to live with Dorothea Puente in September 1985. I haven't heard from him in three years." She explained that she felt there might be "some connection" between his disappearance and the graves being discovered at Puente's residence. The last thing she'd known for certain, Everson had been intent on marrying Dorothea Puente.

He'd started writing to Dorothea Puente while she was in prison. The family hadn't approved of this correspondence, but the lonely, trusting widower found comfort in two primary pastimes: crafting elaborate wood carvings and writing to various women.

Puente wasn't the only prison inmate to whom he wrote, but only she had captured the man's heart, bewitching the septuagenarian Gillmouth so that he was deaf to criticism. He insisted he'd found "a good woman," discounting the objections of one family member who countered, "Everson, they don't put good women in prison."

In August 1985, Everson Gillmouth had packed up his red pickup truck and new trailer and bade good-bye to his family in Oregon. He'd told Reba that he was going down to California to meet Dorothea, "and if things worked out all right, they planned on getting married."

Since Everson had lived with Reba and her husband for two years after his wife's death, she'd assumed he'd send word as soon as he got settled. When no word came after a few weeks, she wrote the Sacramento police, asking that they check on her older brother.

This had brought results from 1426 F Street, for Everson promptly phoned his sister.

"Were the police there?" Reba had asked him.

"They just left," he'd replied, sounding ruffled. But contrition soon crept into his voice, and he'd apologized for his silence. "I should have written," he said over and over.

That was the last time Reba Nicklous had heard from her brother.

Later, Dorothea Puente had written on Everson's behalf, but Reba thought the letters—where had she put those letters?—were a pack of lies.

Now Reba gave police all the pertinent information she could muster. By the time she hung up, assured she would get a call back sometime soon, she was hopeful of learning some answers, of gaining some sense of closure, perhaps even of seeing justice done.

Reba Nicklous wasn't the only one worrying about a missing brother. Back in California, Robert Fink had been following the news emanating from F Street with the gloomiest of expectations. He'd already spoken with police. Questions had been asked and answered. Reports had been filed. Now there wasn't much to do but wait, fret, and remember.

Benjamin Fink was the black sheep in his family—the one who couldn't quite pull his life together, who made promises he couldn't keep, and borrowed money he couldn't repay. From the time he was a teenager, he had a thirst for alcohol he could never quite quench. By the time he was fifty-six, he'd spent plenty of time on the street; hard times had left their imprint on his face and had taken a toll on his body. He'd lost part of his left foot to frostbite, and when he'd staggered out in front of a car from between two trash bins, both legs had been shattered. After that, he'd walked with a cane, drank to senseless inebriation, smoked two packs of cigarettes a day, and gave up all hopes of changing.

Not that he hadn't tried. "He went to every [treatment facility] he could think of," said Robert, "and as soon as he got out he would walk by a bar, and if he smelled alcohol, that was it, he turned and went."

In March 1988, when Peggy Nickerson introduced Ben to Dorothea Puente's boardinghouse on F Street, Robert had hoped that perhaps this time his ne'er-do-well brother had found a stable home. When he came to visit, Robert noticed the garden full of tomatoes, cucumbers, and cabbages, and the homey atmosphere at the blue-and-white Victorian impressed him. He never actually spoke with the landlady, who lived upstairs, but he sure thought her boardinghouse was a nice place, and he'd been relieved to see his brother settle there.

Still, with Thanksgiving coming up, the Finks expected Ben to join them so they could all share in a traditional family meal. It was only recently that Robert's wife had said, "We ought to be hearing from Ben any day."

Now, while they waited to hear word from the police, it seemed that it had been an extremely long time since they'd last heard from Ben.

Back on F Street, the weather had cleared, the crowd numbered in the hundreds, and the atmosphere was almost festive, with some voyeurs skipping work to watch the grisly spectacle.

Determined to search every square foot of Puente's property, the police pulled down a shed that stood in the middle of the side yard, then shoveled through the moist earth beneath. It seemed almost routine when they discovered a sixth grave just inches below the surface.

A pattern had emerged. Like the others, this body had been wrapped "mummylike," and was lodged in the ground in a fetal position. They were like huge larvae—curled up, spun into cocoons of plastic and cloth, then deposited into the dark soil. Now they were lifted out, zippered into body bags, loaded onto gurneys, and removed to laboratories, where they would be dissected and examined.

One gray-haired woman who watched had more than a passing interest in these discoveries. She was moved to strike up a conversation with the stranger standing next to her. "I had a friend who lived with Dorothea Puente back in 1982," the woman confided, "and she died suddenly."

Sandy Lang, distracted by the commotion around her, turned half her attention toward the woman speaking to her. "Your friend died?"

"Yes. In the spring of 1982. They ruled it a suicide, but I never believed that. They said she'd died of an allergic reaction to codeine, but Ruth—that was her name, Ruth Munroe—she used to work in a pharmacy, so she was familiar with medications, and she wouldn't have knowingly taken that."

"Well, did you go to the police?"

"I did, yes, I sure did. And I told her family they should, too. But nothing was ever done about it, so far as I know."

Later, Sandy Lang wished she'd asked more questions of the woman. She recounted as much of the conversation as she could recall to her boss, Michael Coonan, who was preparing to do what he did best: stir up controversy. (As Sacramento's ombudsman for senior care, Coonan had a distinct interest in the discoveries at Puente's boardinghouse, and he was preparing to pen a long, provocative report on the subject.) Now he phoned the police and reported the possible connection between Dorothea Puente and Ruth Munroe's death.

But Ruth Munroe's family was way ahead of him.

William Clausen, a no-nonsense family man in cowboy boots, had already been on the phone with his siblings, rehashing the bizarre circumstances of their mother's death, rekindling old suspicions. The police had already been notified. They would check into it, they said . . . just like they'd said back in 1982.

Later that Monday, the police removed a flower bed and a religious shrine from the small front yard, just to the right of the stairs leading up to Dorothea Puente's entrance. There, eighteen inches below the surface and within just a few feet of the front sidewalk, they discovered another curled, wrapped bundle.

Even given Puente's well-known penchant for predawn gardening, it was hard to imagine how she could have managed to plant seven bodies in her yard without drawing a single neighbor's notice. The neighbors murmured about this among themselves, and when their turns came, they individually assured police that, odd as it seemed, none of them had observed any burials. As one longtime resident put it, "I don't know how this could have been going on."

CHAPTER 15

THE WORD IN CERTAIN CIRCLES AROUND SACRAMENTO WAS that if you had to be murdered, it was better that the deed be done outside city limits, because the county sheriff's homicide squad would do a better job of finding your killer than the city cops would. With its handling of the Puente case, the police department did little to dispel this reputation.

Between Friday morning, November 11, and Monday afternoon, November 14, Dorothea Puente had vanished and seven bodies had been dug out of her yard. Though the "on-call judge" can issue warrants during the weekend—even during long three-day weekends such as this Veterans Day holiday—Sacramento's police department didn't manage until late Monday to obtain a search warrant. Granted, obtaining a search warrant can be time-consuming. But this delay added to an impression that the police were less afraid evidence might be flushed or tampered with than with the possibility that a corpse or two might get away.

So it was on Tuesday, November 15, that police officers finally got around to their first thorough search of 1426 F Street. Rumor had it that by then various people with "legitimate" reasons for being there had rifled through the house. Some even claimed that Puente's friend and landlord, Ricardo Ordorica, had removed boxes full of stuff (including murder mysteries and demonology texts) over the weekend. But others said this seemed unlikely, given the twenty-four-hour surveillance of Puente's boardinghouse.

If evidence had been removed, some extremely interesting items had been overlooked. Police seized several paper bags filled with, among other things, a Folgers coffee can with "Lye" printed on the lid; several bottles of pills; some stained linens; and two books with catchy titles, *The Smell of Evil* and *150 Commonly Prescribed Drugs.*

In her dining room, officers found the landlady's cheerful Christmas cards, preprinted from "Dr. Dorothea Puente" and ready for mailing.

Additionally, they seized a plastic floor runner with duct tape at both ends, which prompted speculation that it "may have been used to slide heavy loads down the stairs."

All evidence was channeled into the "chain of custody" pipeline—booked, bagged, marked or tagged—so that police officers could correctly identify it on the witness stand years hence. Some items were sent on to the crime lab at the coroner's office, where certain substances would be analyzed. And, if the integrity of some material had to be maintained, it would be frozen. The bulk was sent on to the great, locked police department property warehouse where most evidence awaits trial.

Also on Tuesday, the FBI was finally put on Puente's rather cold trail. It was an accident of timing that the FBI hadn't been enlisted in the search earlier. If Puente had disappeared during the workweek, a fugitive warrant could have been approved sooner, but since that requires a court hearing by a federal magistrate, little could be done over the weekend. Time had been on her side, and the all-points bulletin (APB) didn't go out over FBI teletypes until late Tuesday.

The popular guess was that Puente had escaped to Mexico. Not only was her Spanish fluent, but court records revealed that she had fourteen siblings in Mexico; in 1986 she'd asked parole agents for permission to travel to Mexico; and she'd had an airline ticket to Mexico in her purse when arrested in 1982.

In the meantime, police were tracking an airline passenger with the name of Puente to Las Vegas. While Las Vegas Metropolitan Police issued an APB of their own, one officer bluntly complained that they'd received conflicting reports from Sacramento: "We got one wire from there that says she's en route to Mexico, another one says she's en route to here, and another one said she's been spotted in Reno. I didn't look who signed them because I thought they were all bullshit anyway."

He wasn't far wrong. The search for Puente in Las Vegas soon lurched to a halt. Puente, the consummate con, had apparently booked a seat on a USAir flight bound for Vegas, then a "close relative" had tipped the police to Puente's morning flight. But Puente hadn't boarded the plane, and the "relative"—perhaps the lamster herself—never materialized.

While the police claimed that photos of Puente had been circulated at the airport, an investigative reporter spoke with two security guards, a USAir flight attendant, and even two Sacramento County Sheriff's Deputies who stated that no such photos has been provided. This heaped more humiliation on the Sacramento police, amplified the impression they were bungling the case, and increased the heat they were taking from the media.*

Meanwhile, the sole person being held in connection with the Puente case was about to be released. John McCauley had been hauled down to police headquarters with great hopes, but their interrogation hadn't yielded the ripe facts they'd hoped for. They'd lamely accused him of such things as lying about when the concrete had been poured and denying that he'd received a phone call from Puente after her escape. But McCauley's main revelation was that Dorothea had decided to "rabbit" because she believed the police were going to go after her "no matter what."

Investigators finally determined they had insufficient evidence to hold McCauley, who came across as such a bumbling drunk that it was hard to believe he'd be capable of anything more diabolical than rude behavior and bad language. Police Lieutenant Joe Enloe gamely explained to the media, "He was a confidant of hers, but we do not believe he was involved in the hands-on work involving the bodies." Having been arrested on charges of being an accessory to homicide on Saturday, McCauley was set free late Tuesday.

Now they had no one.

---

*While Puente's flight was outrageous in itself, it was even worse in context. As *The Sacramento Bee* was quick to point out, this was all too similar to a case a year before in which the Sacramento police, after finding bodies in and around homes renovated by Morris Solomon, Jr., maintained for some time that they had insufficient evidence to arrest the ex-con, who had a history of violent crimes. Solomon was eventually convicted on six counts of murder.

McCauley had been suspected of helping Puente bury the bodies, but now Sergeant Burns volunteered a new theory: "We have pictures that show at one time she was a very big woman." So they were reconsidering the possibility that Puente had buried the bodies herself.

It seemed indefensible that their primary suspect had been escorted past police lines, past throngs of reporters and spectators, and allowed to escape. Detective John Cabrera didn't help matters with his cha- grined confession: "I thought she was a nice, warm, gentle person. She fooled me, too."

During two press conferences on Tuesday, Sergeant Bob Burns, as the designated spokesperson, found himself in the hot seat. "At the time we found the first body, the lady was very cooperative. She stood over the grave as we dug. There was no need at this point to follow her. You can't harass people. We didn't have enough information to arrest her at that time."

Legal experts publicly disagreed, and the finger pointing continued.

In their defense, the police department had tried to follow protocol, consulting closely with the district attorney's office. While Puente was at the police station, they had called Deputy DA Tim Frawley and asked if they needed a search warrant to continue digging. He advised that they did not so long as consent was freely given. According to Frawley, it was "agreed at that point they didn't have probable cause to arrest her ... We were digging on her property pursuant to her consent, and if she was in custody, an argument could be raised later that her consent had been coerced."

Deputy DA Frawley asserted that the police were only trying to preserve the legality of their search. He pointed out that the second body was discovered less than an hour after Puente walked. "That was her window of opportunity, and she made her getaway ... It was a confusing situation and I can understand how it happened the way it did."

Still, he conceded that Puente had "conned [police] into thinking she wasn't going anywhere. The detective on the scene felt he had a good rapport with her and he wanted to preserve that. He didn't want to back her into a corner where she might invoke her Miranda rights."

Despite Frawley's legalistic protestations, it sounded as if the police had failed to arrest Puente simply because she was being so nice. They hadn't wanted to hurt her feelings.

Through this whole ordeal, relations between the news media and the police department sunk in a downward spiral of accusations and hostilities. No matter how hard they back-pedaled, the police couldn't slacken criticisms stemming from their gaffe of having let Puente walk.

In a trenchant moment, Police Sergeant Burns, standing out in the middle of F Street, found himself surrounded by reporters demanding to know why the police had let Puente go. Burns finally turned tight-lipped. "I've already answered that," he said, staring at the ground.

One reporter sniped, "Have the police made *any* mistakes at all?" and Burns turned away, asking, "Any other questions?"

Just before darkness fell Tuesday evening, the police called the digging on F Street to a halt. "There are no more bodies at this site," Police Sergeant Jim Jorgensen announced.

For now, the body count would hold at seven.

CHAPTER 16

W

ITH SO MUCH ATTENTION FOCUSED ON THE SEARCH FOR
Puente, the bodies plucked from her yard slipped out of the media's
limelight toward another sort of scrutiny. One by one, whisked from
the curious gaze of onlookers and loaded into the waiting van, they
were sped through Sacramento's shady streets to the Sacramento
County Coroner's Office where they were logged in and parked in
the "cold room." Unlike the TV image of a morgue—a room with a
wall of sterile, stainless-steel drawers—this was rather like a still and
frigid hospital room: people covered with sheets waiting on parked
gurneys. But here they waited not with IVs, not for surgery, but with
toe tags, for a turn on the autopsy table.

After a particularly luckless weekend, the number of dead here
might range up to two dozen or more. Now the seven from Puente's
yard dominated this room, just as the pungent odor of decay would
dominate any competing smells in the building for several days. (Fresh
death has a lighter smell; burned flesh has a distinctively sweet stink;
but decomposed bodies reek so intensely that one's olfactory glands
almost ache.)

These withered corpses weighed little, indicating that each one had probably been dead for some time. Identifying such decomposed remains might take months, might even be impossible if the forensic team was working blind. But social workers had compiled a list of some twenty-five individuals who had roomed with Dorothea Puente and then turned up missing, and if any of them was among the hapless individuals extracted from her garden, he or she had a good chance of being identified. Police were scrambling to obtain any relevant records, so once the autopsies were completed and broad characteristics such as sex, age, race, and size had been determined, identification would be expedited by matching teeth with dental records, bones with X-rays, remaining tissue with known physical traits.

One of two forensic pathologists working for the coroner's office, Dr. Robert Anthony and Dr. Gary Stuart, would perform the autopsies on the seven corpses. These men, who seemed unaffected by the room's powerful odors, were charged with not only determining *who* these remains might be, but *how* their deaths had occurred. *When* was another question. "It's very difficult to determine time of death, despite popular misconceptions," according to the tall, slim Dr. Stuart.

The first body to be examined was the third unearthed, #88–3381, the one found in a quiet spot at the base of a newly planted tree. It was chosen because its size seemed to most closely resemble the description of Bert Montoya.

The gurney was rolled out to a nearby room where the remains were entrusted to Dr. Russel A. McFall, a man with long experience as a forensic radiologist. McFall expertly positioned and repeatedly X-rayed the wrapped corpse. Once the film was developed, he would begin comparisons with X-rays of former tenants of Puente's boardinghouse, noting first the gross anatomical structures, then the more minute features, such as joints and calcification.

If there was a match to be found, he was confident he would be able to make a positive identification—he's done so, when necessary, with a single bone. "No two bones are alike," he asserted, their patterns being "as distinct as fingerprints."

With the first set of X-rays complete, the bundled remains were sent to the autopsy room. Dr. Stuart put on his protective goggles and began the first physical autopsy at 1:00 P.M. on Wednesday, November 16. Start to finish, it would take eight hours. Of the select team assembled in the room, one member was forensic anthropologist

Rodger Heglar, Ph.D., no stranger to this lifeless bundle, having over-seen its excavation from the property on F Street. Dr. Stuart had also been at the site during the body's removal, and now these two started in with their examination of the remains.

There was no great hurry. No blood spattered the floor as the wrap-pings were slowly, carefully cut away and tagged with identifying num-bers: a green-colored blanket; several layers of clear plastic secured with duct tape; some blue, tarplike fabric secured with more duct tape; more plastic and a quilt. Beneath this, Dr. Stuart found some "white material, lime or lye." The obvious conclusion: The body had been dusted with this corrosive substance before being wrapped.

And the lime had done its work. An adult male stared back at them, ghastly in its decay.

Next, the rotting clothes were cut off. A light-colored T-shirt with "CANON" in orange print. Dark trousers. White socks. No identifica-tion, keys, or change in the pockets.

At each step the remains were photographed by a hovering police photographer, with knots in the covering fabrics given particular scru-tiny. Observations were logged, and the clothing and wrappings were tagged and bagged for closer examination at the crime lab. Such are the grisly minutia that become evidence.

The unwrapped remains were briefly wheeled back for more X-rays, then returned to the autopsy room.

Dr. Stuart could only estimate the time of death at perhaps weeks or months prior. (No studies have been conducted on how quickly lime will eat through a human corpse wrapped in cloth and plastic and buried underground.) He saw no obvious evidence of trauma. No knife or gunshot wounds.

His provisional determination was that "the deceased was a Cauca-sian male, 50 to 60 years old, 64 to 65 inches in height. Hair color was possibly light brown or blond." The remains weighed 128 pounds.

Now Dr. Stuart sliced open the body with a Y-shaped incision, cut-ting from each shoulder to the base of the chest bone, or sternum, then down past the navel. The rib cage was examined, and then using ordinary shears, Dr. Stuart cut through and removed several ribs, which Dr. Heglar inspected with interest.

Dr. Stuart found the viscera of the abdominal cavity, while markedly decomposed, still individually identifiable. He focused his attention on the major organs, which often chart the course of death's final pains. Heart, lungs, stomach, liver, spleen, kidneys—all were removed, then painstakingly probed, weighed, and studied in turn. There was some moderate hardening of the arteries and some enlargement of the liver, but no clues to the cause of death.

Next, the doctor examined the outside of the skull, noting some roughening of the nose bone, which suggested that it had once been broken. The brain would be of more interest. Using a Stryker saw— the same fine-toothed saw with which casts are removed—Dr. Stuart circumnavigated the crown of the head. He removed the protective bone and tissue like a cap, revealing the decomposed brain. It was carefully cut out, weighed, and inspected, the doctor noting that it was "small, soft, and discolored."

A portion of the brain was then sliced off with a dissecting blade and placed in a labeled jar of formaldehyde. Along with other specimens taken from the corpse, this was put into a refrigerated locker and preserved for microscopic examination. (James Beede, a toxicologist, would later take the specimens to the toxicology lab, where he would record their mute testimony.)

At length, Stuart and Heglar concluded their examination. The organs were returned to the abdominal cavity, the brain placed back into the skull. The examination complete, Dr. Stuart removed his surgical gloves, then scrubbed from his hands the sweat-soaked talcum powder that had kept the gloves from sticking.

Now it was late. The unnamed body was again covered with a sheet and left in the cold room, where it awaited the next step toward identification.

The cause of death for case #88–3381 remained "undetermined."

The next day Robert W. Wood, a registered nurse and a respected member of the forensic team, approached the sheeted body. He examined the hands, noting that the outer layers of the fingertips had deteriorated to the point that the coroner's lab wasn't equipped to identify the fingerprints. Selecting the least decomposed fingertips, he snipped off the digits at the first joint. These were sealed in small, individual jars of formaldehyde, then sent to the Department of Justice, where experts could examine the fingertips' deeper layers.*

Joe Sydnicki, the DOJ's latent print examiner, shortly took posses-

---

*Three of the seven bodies had fingertips removed and taken to the Department of Justice for identification.

sion of the jars. He unsealed the containers, removed the digits, then carefully cleaned and dried them. Finally, he injected them with fluid to rehydrate the tissue, dusted them with a black powder, and lifted the prints by making rolled impressions on a card.

Using a magnifying glass, Sydnicki would later compare the characteristic swirls and ridges of the prints on the card with the known prints of missing souls who had once roomed with Dorothea Puente . . . including those taken about a year earlier from Bert Montoya at the Department of Motor Vehicles.

CHAPTER 17

CAMERA LIGHTS GLINTED OFF THE WIRE-RIMMED GLASSES AND steely gray hair of Police Chief John P. Kearns as he fielded questions at a press conference on Wednesday, November 16. Looking every bit the flinty old cop despite his business suit, Kearns publicly acknowledged for the first time that Sacramento police had erred in their handling of the Puente case. For those who'd been following the case, a gratifying—if belated—admission.

First noting that he had been in L.A. at a California Police Chiefs Association conference on Saturday—the day Puente had walked—the police chief finally confirmed what most of the city had known all along: "The Sacramento Police Department made an error, and as a result of that we lost a suspect."

Still, Kearns hedged any public criticism of his force. He maintained that "there was not a weight of probable cause to make an arrest" the morning that Puente had strolled away in her purple pumps. "Of course, with a crystal ball of Monday-morning quarterbacking, the probable cause possibly could have been stretched, and there may have been an arrest made," he said.

After all, Puente had been extremely cooperative, he reiterated. "She'd been talked to by detectives and established a dialogue, and I feel that what occurred was that we possibly became too familiar with the suspect and too trusting," Kearns said. "Sometimes in law enforcement we find ourselves bending over a little bit too far to protect the rights of the suspects or individuals in criminal cases, and I feel that's what occurred here." He even went so far as to state she was "a prime suspect in a homicide case, and there isn't any excuse, as far as I'm concerned, why the suspect was not kept under surveillance." (For those who could read between the lines, this heralded some unexpected "reassignments" within the police force.)

Raising an ugly accusation, reporters asked why the police hadn't acted when they'd reportedly received a tip *last January* that Dorothea Puente was burying bodies in her yard. Kearns turned to Sergeant Bob Burns and, after a whispered exchange, swept this charge aside, explaining that there had been no real evidence. And besides, he said lamely, that case was "completely unrelated."

Whatever insights he had into the handling of the Puente case and the failings of his staff, Kearns could hardly have predicted that within the next twenty-four hours his police officers were going to commit yet another humiliating gaffe.

While the finger pointing and hand wringing continued in Sacramento, Dorothea Puente was preparing to leave her motel room in Los Angeles, about seven hundred miles south. After her smooth escape on Saturday, she'd checked into the Royal Viking Motel, a cheap, nondescript place, registering under the name Dorothea Johanson (a version of a former husband's last name), paying seventy-four dollars cash up front.

For the next three days, Dorothea Puente clung to her privacy in room 31. She was a paragon of inactivity, slowing to a torpid pace, dwelling within her dull, cramped little motel room. She wouldn't let the maid in to clean, only sticking her head out to ask for towels.

Perhaps she thought all the fuss in the media would eventually blow over if she just kept her head down, and then she could assume a new identity and vanish into this huge metropolis. She went out only for meals, walking to a nearby restaurant, the T&G Express, where she ordered everything from pancakes to chop suey, usually with beer, leaving generous tips.

But on Wednesday, Dorothea Puente became restless. That afternoon, she drew on her makeup, dabbed on perfume, and dressed to go out.

Once outside she hailed a cab and bluntly told the driver that she needed a drink. When he started to pull over at a beer tavern, she objected, "No, I have to have some hard liquor, not beer, because I couldn't sleep all night."

No problem. The taxi shortly pulled up in front of the Monte Carlo I, a seedy neighborhood bar on Third Street, less than two miles from the motel.

She seated herself right in the middle of the bar, next to one of the regular patrons, Charles Willgues. The thin, balding man could hardly help noticing this well-dressed, unaccompanied woman next to him. With a blond rinse on her hair and fine clothes, she appeared out of place in this dive.

The lady ordered a screwdriver, then sighed and dejectedly regarded the purple pumps she'd been wearing since skipping out of Sacramento. The heels had worn off, she complained. Looking at him, she shrugged and remarked, "I've been walking a lot, looking for a place to live."

Chuck Willgues to the rescue. He knew a place just across the street. "If you're willing to slip your shoes off, I'll take 'em over and get 'em fixed for you."

It was too kind an offer to pass up. She pulled off her pumps and handed them over.

"Enjoy your drink," he told her, popping out of his seat. "I'll be right back."

She sat dangling her stocking feet from her barstool while he carried her pumps to a nearby repair shop.

When Willgues returned with her shoes as good as new, Puente introduced herself as Donna Johanson, bought him a beer, and started concocting lies. She was recently widowed, she said with a sigh, and she'd just arrived from San Francisco two days ago.

Chuck Willgues, a widower himself, warmed to this good-looking, younger woman (she claimed she was fifty-five). She had style. And here she was a stranger, alone, in a town he knew well.

"Donna" took him into her confidence. She was trying to get over the death of her husband, so she'd decided to take a chance on L.A. Now she'd had all of her luggage stolen by an unscrupulous cabdriver, and she didn't know what to do. She had no choice but to stay in a cheap motel, and she was running short of cash.

Willgues wondered if there might be something he could do to help.

"Why don't we move down to the end of the bar so we can talk

127

privately?" she suggested. Sipping another vodka and orange juice, the charming widow bought Chuck another beer. She seemed to be curious about each of the patrons, and Chuck knew them all.

Then "Donna" turned the conversation to her new gentleman friend. Flattered, the retired handyman shared a few details of his situation: no family nearby; a few medical problems; a quiet lifestyle on a fixed income. "Donna" seemed to take a genuine interest in the pensioner's problems. She even suggested that she could help him increase his Social Security benefits, somehow seeming to know exactly how much disability he should receive for his back problems, tuberculosis, ulcer, and hernia. It made him momentarily uncomfortable.

But then she changed the subject. "I'm all alone too," she told him. No family. No friends. She was hoping for a fresh start in a new place and was looking for a job. If she could save enough, she thought she might eventually start a board-and-care business.

Willgues volunteered that he knew of a job at a nearby sandwich shop.

After ordering her third drink, "Donna" flashed him a smile and suggested, "Since you're alone and I'm alone, let's get together and I can cook Thanksgiving dinner."

Things were moving a bit fast for Chuck. He was even more surprised when she said she might even consider sharing an apartment with him. "Wait a minute," he said. "We'll talk about that later." But he was captivated.

Still, there was something about her, something he couldn't put his finger on. She was familiar, somehow. . . .

They talked on and on, and by the time their conversation came to an end, Chuck Willgues was quite smitten. Before putting her in a cab back to her motel, he made a date to pick her up and take her shopping the next morning.

But while he was walking home, the glow of their chat began to fade, replaced by "an ill feeling." Something just wasn't right.

Back at his apartment, he fixed himself dinner, but couldn't eat. He ran back through their conversation, trying to pinpoint the trouble, and suddenly realized that he was pacing the floor. He chided himself out loud, "Chuck, what the hell's wrong with you?"

He decided to watch some TV, but as soon as he touched the television set, it hit him: "Damn, that's the woman I saw on TV this morning!"

Or . . . was it?

Willgues again paced his tiny apartment. He could call the police, but what if he were wrong? "Donna" surely wouldn't want anything to do with him once he'd humiliated her with a visit from the boys in blue. But what if she really was Dorothea Puente? He could come right out and ask. . . . But if he'd made a mistake, she'd be insulted. And if he was right, she damn sure wasn't going to tell him. Wasn't there some other way to find out?

At length, he decided to contact not the police, but the L.A. bureau of CBS news. He placed a call, which was routed through to the assignment editor, Gene Silver.

At first, it sounded to Silver like "a typical viewer call," with Willgues asking a few questions about the Puente case. Then he asked if the TV station had a picture of the woman. Silver found a *Los Angeles Times* photo, got back on the phone, and described the photo to Willgues.

Willgues wasn't sure. He thought that he'd met Puente, but he said he needed to see a picture to help him decide.

Having already spent about twenty minutes with this strange caller, Silver was thinking, If he's a kook, he'll go away. If not, this could be big. By then it was nearly 8:00 P.M., so he suggested that Willgues wait for the upcoming newscast, adding, "Do you mind staying on the phone?"

Willgues held on, and the two men, separated by miles, watched the broadcast together. Indeed, there was a long story about Dorothea Puente, with some video footage of Sacramento, but not a single frame of Puente herself.

By now Silver was thinking that this could be the biggest scoop of his career. "I'll tell you what," he told Willgues, "I can bring the picture over and then you can decide for yourself whether this is really the woman you met." Silver jotted down the address and hung up.

When Silver pulled up in front of Willgues's dilapidated apartment building, some kids were doing crack in a doorway. Ol' Chuck was living in a pretty rough neighborhood, he thought.

Willgues was just hanging up the phone when Silver arrived. He and "Donna" had just firmed up arrangements to meet the next day, he said.

When Silver showed him the newspaper clipping, Willgues stared at Puente's photograph, "transfixed," but said nothing. The newsman asked questions, prodding him, but Willgues wouldn't say whether or not this was the woman he'd met in the bar.

Clearly, Chuck Willgues, a lonely man who'd seen better days, didn't want to believe that the enchanting woman he'd met that afternoon was Dorothea Puente. Finally, he said, "Well, you know, it looks a lot like her, but it's not the same dress. . . . I'd have to see a color picture."

Well, Silver suggested, how about watching the nine o'clock news? So the two men switched on the TV and settled down to watch, only to find that Lady Luck was being cagey: The newscast showed the same photograph—but in color.

Willgues leaned far forward and studied the image "like it was a test." When the screen flickered to other news, he sighed and dodged, "I just can't tell 'cause I can't see the rest of the dress."

Gene Silver could have strangled him. The guy had met the woman's twin in a bar, she'd told him some story about a taxi driver stealing her luggage, and then she'd asked about his disability checks! What difference did it make what dress she was wearing?

But Chuck Willgues was clearly reluctant to face the idea that he'd spent the afternoon with an accused murderess. Enraptured by the woman with "fire in her eyes," he didn't want to endanger this exciting new relationship. He tried explaining, "It's very important to realize that I'm going to pick her up tomorrow morning. . . ."

By now Silver was convinced that "Donna" was Dorothea. He continued quizzing Willgues, prodding and cajoling, assuring him that it would be handled very professionally by the police. If Chuck would give him the name of the place where she was staying, the police would simply go to her motel and ask for her ID. It would be painless.

Finally the two lapsed into a long silence, Willgues thinking, Silver hoping.

"Well, all right," Chuck said at last, "but just please don't go telling her that it was me who gave it to you."

A man with priorities, Gene Silver returned to his office and rallied a camera crew, then notified the police.

Detectives arrived shortly at Chuck Willgues's apartment. He told them what he knew, yet still seemed unable to believe that his charming, "very ladylike" friend could be as bad as they said. He even asked that they delay their arrest of Dorothea Puente for just one day. He'd made a date with her, after all, and he wanted to keep it.

But at 10:20 P.M., the police arrived at the Royal Viking Motel, knocked on the door of room 31, and waited.

She had no hope of shimmying out a window now. Slick as she'd been in the past, she just opened the door and walked straight into the arms of the law.

Seeing the officers, the camera crew, Puente stalled, identifying herself as Donna Johanson. But when the police asked for proper identification, a driver's license in her handbag revealed the name Dorothea Montalvo and her address, 1426 F Street.

Bingo!

Wearing handcuffs and the same pink dress and red coat she'd worn in her flight from Sacramento, Puente was led out to the patrol car. The waiting camera crew got it all.

CHAPTER 18

A$_{\text{T}}$ ABOUT 3:30 THURSDAY MORNING, JUST BEFORE LOADING A tired and frail-looking Dorothea Montalvo Puente into the waiting plane at Hollywood-Burbank Airport, Sacramento Police Sergeant Jim Jorgensen turned to reporters and observed, "In twenty-three years of law enforcement, [I've found that] nothing is beyond the realm of believability when you're dealing with human beings."

After Jorgensen read Puente her Miranda rights, they stepped aboard neither a police aircraft nor a commercial plane, but a Lear jet. Sitting next to Detective John Cabrera, handcuffed, her arms chained to her waist, Puente was not only in police custody, she was confined in the company of a Channel 3 reporter, a cameraman, and a newspaper photographer.

Dorothea Puente was more than just a prisoner, she was a media event.

When word had reached Sacramento that Puente had been appre-hended in Los Angeles, the local news media had scrambled to cover the story, but was frustrated to find that no commercial airline would be flying south from the city's small airport for several hours. Outmaneuvering the competition, KCRA-TV, Sacramento's NBC affiliate, and *The Sacramento Bee,* the city's largest paper, had chartered the jet and then invited the police to come along.

During the flight, Puente sipped coffee from a Styrofoam cup and submitted to a short interview. At one point, in response to a question by Channel 3 reporter Mike Boyd, Puente softly admitted, "I cashed checks, yes," but maintained, "I have not killed anyone." She also made the cryptic statement, "I used to be a very good person at one time." Then she clammed up.

A few hours later, Dorothea Puente was booked into the Sacramento County Jail. Police confiscated her purple leather purse containing a wallet, a California driver's license, a Seiko watch, a notepad, stamps, Tiffany cologne, miscellaneous cosmetics, two pairs of earrings, three rings with clear stones, a pack of Sweet'n Low, and one sealed plastic envelope containing $3,042.55.

She traded her nice red coat, pink dress, and purple pumps for a regulation orange jumpsuit with "Sacramento County Jail" stenciled across the back.

Later that morning, looking tired, pale, and bewildered, Dorothea was brought into the jammed courtroom of Judge John V. Stroud. She looked especially small standing between Assistant Public Defenders Peter Vlautin and Kevin Clymo, more like a victim than a culprit.

She spoke just once during the seven-minute arraignment. When the judge addressed her as "Dorothea Puente Montalvo" she softly corrected him, "It's Dorothea Montalvo Puente," and all the reporters took note, as if this would tell any of us who she really was.*

She nodded when the judge asked if she needed a public defender, uttering nothing that might dispel the mystery of how so many bodies had come to rest in the yard of such a sweet-looking old woman. She listened solemnly as she was arraigned on one count of murder—that of Bert Montoya—and ordered held without bail.

As soon as these somber proceedings concluded, an international assemblage of reporters elbowed in close to Puente's attorneys, hoping for quotes, and the public defenders were happy to oblige. It was highly improper to confine a suspect with the press at close quarters

---

*Up to this point, most reports had referred to her as Dorothea Montalvo.

for a long period, they declared. Puente's legal right to remain silent had been compromised. "It's unheard of to have a suspect transported with a reporter and cameras on the plane before she even has a chance to talk to an attorney," Peter Vlautin fumed. He accused the police of "enlisting the aid of the media to create a circus atmosphere in this trial," adding, "I'm surprised she wasn't on *Geraldo!* this morning."

(Geraldo would get his chance later.)

A deeply chagrined Police Chief Kearns meanwhile responded that he'd only just learned of the unorthodox travel arrangements, declining to comment further until he had more information.

While the cops squirmed about having committed yet another embarrassing blunder, the media seemed nothing short of delighted with its news coup. "Our job is to aggressively cover the news and to run after things when they happen. And frankly, I'm quite proud of what we did," crowed Bob Jordan, KCRA's news director. "We literally offered the police a ride. They accepted."

In a sense, Dorothea Puente had been apprehended by the media. She'd become a cause célèbre. The movie moguls were already making plans. Television or big screen? Mini-series or movie of the week? Whatever they would ultimately decide, the public-interest barometer clearly indicated it was time to prepare some contracts.*

Of course, Chuck Willgues had his photo splashed from coast to coast. In front-page headlines, the *Los Angeles Times* dubbed him the "Tipster" who had "Led Police to Death House Suspect." In one interview, Willgues summed up, "Everything happened so fast. The next thing I knew, I'd seen her on TV."†

Under the scrutiny of observers, Patty Casey's eyes teared up as she watched the noontime news and heard how her onetime friend had tried to con Chuck Willgues. The cabdriver who had been so taken in by Puente's guise said, "Bless her heart . . . It's ironic that she went back to the same environment, the same hustle."

Casey wasn't the only one who wept for Dorothea Puente.

"Sometimes she would have a heart of gold, sometimes she was

---

*Several people, including Judy Moise, Peggy Nickerson, Patty Casey, and others, eventually signed motion picture contracts with Robert Greenwald Productions.

†Willgues's sudden rise from obscurity had a happy result: He was reunited with his three children, whom he hadn't seen in thirty years, when a reporter passed along a letter from one of his daughters. After getting reacquainted by phone, Willgues moved back to Michigan to be close to his family.

the demon. She had many personalties," said one who should know, Dorothea's fourth husband, Pedro Montalvo, still residing in Stockton. Remembering his brief but passionate marriage to Dorothea, the old man's eyes spilled with tears. "Poor woman. The poor woman stole from innocents and gave to other people."

Montalvo sat very still, obviously affected by the woman he once loved. "One minute she is in this world, the next minute she is in another world. It is like a nightmare," he said.

But Montalvo didn't believe that the police had yet solved the case. "I don't doubt that she committed crimes . . . What I doubt is the manner in which she could drag them out and bury them. That is what I doubt. Some *bandido* must have helped her. Or two of them, or more *bandidos*."

Now that Dorothea Puente had been apprehended, law enforcement fell strangely silent about possible accomplices. Was it logical to believe she'd acted alone? Or was it possible, even with such suspicious circumstances, that she was actually innocent?

Now that Puente was locked up, Judy Moise felt safe enough to move back home, but she was still fearful that Puente's accomplices might be freely roaming the city. It seemed pretty darned unlikely to her that Puente had gone solo.

She'd given the police that inept letter written by "Michel Miguel Obregon," or someone named Don Anthony, yet they hadn't made any new arrests.

Meanwhile, Judy stubbornly clung to the hope that Bert might still be alive somewhere. Asleep or awake, she had visions of Bert smiling, laughing, walking toward her. Always inclined to look for a spiritual interpretation of dreams, she searched this recurring image for meaning . . . but conclusions eluded her.

She commiserated with Bill Johnson about the disappearance of their friend. They gingerly explored "should haves" and "if onlys," then gloomily discussed how these very public events had touched their private lives. "I told my five-year-old daughter that maybe Bert has died," Johnson said sadly. "She cried."

Judy's everyday life took on a surreal quality. Whenever she chanced by 1426 F Street, the house seemed shrouded in a sepulchral darkness, as if its once cheery blue paint had been tainted by the black events of the past days. And her job, long a source of pride and inspiration, now seemed sapped of meaning. She was only going through the motions, sleepwalking through the working day, tossing sleeplessly through the night.

Then the police called again asking about Bert's description, needling her about his height and weight, his hair color, and she was baffled by the conversation's edge of confusion. What was wrong? Had they identified him or not? And if they hadn't, where could he be? She pictured Bert again—his tousled salt-and-pepper hair, his nearly toothless grin—and this rekindled the illusion of Bert smiling, laughing, walking toward her. . . .

CHAPTER 19

A CHORUS OF VOICES DEMANDED TO KNOW WHETHER BERT Montoya's body had been retrieved from Puente's yard. But relatively little outcry followed the news that the coroner's office was trying to match the seven remains with any of twenty-five former tenants. Except for a few murmurings of concern, there was an uncanny silence regarding the identities of most of the others, as if no families remained behind to miss them, to wail in remorse, to demand answers. They seemed to have died in a void.

Who were these seven souls? Why had they died?

The coroner's office proceeded with their grim inquiry, autopsies filling the air with a putrid odor as they moved closer to identifying the victims, and, they hoped, to nailing the killer. In shifts, the two forensic pathologists cut, weighed, and observed, sprinkling their reports with a sort of morbid poetry.

Fragments of a jacket's metal zipper clung to "materials unraveled so badly so as to look like a necklace," according to Dr. Robert Anthony, who performed the autopsy on the first corpse unearthed from Puente's yard. Its disintegrating clothes suggested that it was female, the tattered shirt buttoning right over left. The bones of its feet shared the insides of its oxford-style shoes with insect larva, but the laces were still tied in bows.

Dr. Anthony found the corpse so mummified that it "resembled a large, parchment-like mass of beef jerky." With such advanced decomposition, he couldn't find much soft tissue. The internal organs, individually unidentifiable, were removed as a solid mass. The shrunken brain was "quite dried and had a putty-like consistency," yet he managed to send tissue samples of the brain upstairs for the crucial toxicology tests.

The other autopsies followed in rapid succession. While Dorothea Puente was being arraigned on November 17, Dr. Gary Stuart was conducting an autopsy on the second body found in her yard, #88–3374. The body was wrapped inside several layers of fabric, then plastic. Duct tape was strangely wrapped around the left wrist, binding the arm to the body, and twine was knotted around the legs. This adult female, markedly decomposed, was dressed in a long-sleeved blouse, beige slip, bra, stockings, panties, but there was no purse, wallet, or other ID. The body's toothless mouth said nothing about who this woman was, but the psoriasis of her liver spoke of alcoholism.

That afternoon, Dr. Anthony autopsied #88–3382: a white male adult wrapped in sheets of plastic, again sealed with duct tape. Clad in dark, short pants, boxer shorts and dark socks, he had been about five feet eight inches tall, forty to sixty years old, with brown hair, brown eyes, a mustache, and no teeth. Most telling were his four tattoos: a swastika on his left shoulder, "PSI" above his right knee, a dagger piercing a heart on his left elbow, and a small cross on his left forearm.

Criminalists live by the edict that criminals always leave behind a calling card—a rapist's pubic hair; a gunner's bullet; a burglar's footprint. During the slow, meticulous work on the autopsy table, a signature emerged. Each of these bodies had been wrapped and buried in essentially the same fashion. The materials differed somewhat, but the manner of burial—the knots, the duct tape, the twine—left little question that all were the handiwork of the same person.

For example, the fifth body found was wrapped in layers of fabric secured with red string; the sixth, wrapped in fabric and paper, was tied with twine. One was an adult male, the other female, and in life they may not have even known each other, but in death their fates were identical. Both were already beginning to skeletonize by the time they fell under the pathologist's knife. Dr. Stuart managed to identify major organs despite their extreme decomposition, and sent tissue exemplars up to the lab. Their burial clothes—including a woman's wristwatch that was still running—were individually tagged and added to the growing inventory of bagged evidence.

The seventh and last of the corpses found in Puente's yard, #88–3395, was autopsied by Dr. Anthony on November 22. Clad in a sleeveless flowered nightgown, this female was also markedly decomposed, and yielded a particularly ghastly surprise: Her head, hands and feet were missing. (When this particular gem hit the papers, those subscribing to theories of Satanism shuddered with gleeful horror.)

The three men and four women who had been uprooted from Puente's yard shared a macabre kinship in the means of their disposal. Wrapped in makeshift burial shrouds of plastic and cloth, each had been rotting in sad anonymity for a long period—estimated from weeks to months, even years.

But there were few clues to whatever had brought about the demise of these long-dead individuals. None showed any evidence of hemorrhaging, wounds, or trauma. No signs of violence. In every case, the cause of death remained "undetermined."

This was bad news for law enforcement. It's hard to prove someone was murdered when there's no evidence of how the person died. And without proof of cause of death, could the landlady get away with murder?

So far the autopsies left many vexing questions, but Coroner Charles Simmons was optimistic that toxicology tests would soon pinpoint the exact reasons for these fatalities. In a week or ten days, he predicted, "we might have some very conclusive ideas on what killed these people."

After all, forensic scientists can work wonders these days; that's what we've come to expect. From a few strands of his hair, they've even determined—more than 150 years after his death—that Napoleon Bonaparte was repeatedly poisoned with arsenic. From a nameless skull, it's even possible to reconstruct an individual's face.

But toxicologist James Beede, who would process the specimens of brain and liver tissue taken from the bodies, knew better than to make bold predictions; he knew the limits of his craft. Whether traces of poison could be found depended on the type; some poisons lingered, others degenerated. And the extreme decomposition of the bodies made his work harder. The magic of science could be thwarted by the complications of nature, and these bodies had been wrapped up and buried underground, where moisture, bacteria, and insects had long wrought their unseen destruction.

"If a lethal dose of poison was given, our chances are pretty good we'll detect it. But if a dose was given just to sedate," the toxicologist admitted, "we may never detect it."

Then, of course, there was always the problem of simple human error.

Identifying the bodies proved easier than saying how they died: Some still-distinctive patterns of dead fingertips finally yielded a match. The fourth body examined became the first one identified when, on November 21, the coroner's office announced a positive identification: Benjamin Fink.

This unhappy news came as no surprise to Ben's brother. As soon as Robert Fink had heard about the tattoos, it was obvious to him that his older brother was one of the ones in the morgue. The "PSI" tattooed above Ben's right knee stood for Preston School of Industry, where Ben had served in 1947. But the swastika on his left shoulder wasn't to be taken so literally. "It's kinda strange," Robert Fink conceded to the press. "We were Jewish, and he put that swastika on there like a dare: *You just don't mess with me.* That was his way of saying who he was."

After the long wait and all the worry, Robert Fink responded to the news of his brother's identification more with anger than with relief. "When the police showed up and told me, I just wanted to ask them, what are they going to do with her? What are they going to charge that woman with, now that they know?"

Law enforcement didn't have an answer yet for Mr. Fink.

Dorothea Puente was being held without bail. She wasn't going anywhere, so county prosecutors could afford to wait before filing additional charges. The DA's office wanted comprehensive facts, not just more of the speculation that was blowing about like autumn leaves.

But detectives were having a hard time with this case. Murder investigations can be labyrinthine, with leads both obvious and subtle being pursued in every direction. This case was worse than most, complicated by both time and numbers: Some two dozen missing people—elderly, transients, and others on fixed incomes—might be among those who'd rented rooms from Dorothea Puente and ended up paying with their lives.

Police detectives met with Social Security officials, tracking down payments made to missing persons who were once tenants at 1426 F Street. And they began searching Puente's bank accounts, tracking the money trail.

Meanwhile, video equipment was hefted along in renewed searches of the boardinghouse. Police found an assortment of papers, including information regarding funeral plots, photographs, mail and correspondence that they believed could "aid in identifying the bodies . . . and in determining motive."

They also confiscated duct tape, a blue tarp, and sections of blood-stained carpet.

While Clint Eastwood was striding down J Street, working on his latest film, *Pink Cadillac*, Sacramento's coroner was pondering the evidence unearthed from F Street. With all the autopsies now completed, it was troubling that none had been identified as Bert Montoya, who seemed a very likely victim. And Dorothea Puente had already been charged for his murder.

It was time for a reevaluation. Bert had weighed about two hundred pounds, yet all of the bodies recovered from the boardinghouse yard were believed to be too small to be him. On closer inspection, however, the coroner decided that the third body unearthed, the first autopsied, possibly matched Bert's description after all.

Fingerprints finally confirmed the ID.

An announcement came on Thanksgiving, and the news hit the papers the next day with a front-page headline, KEY IDENTIFICATION OF F STREET BODY, along with a photo of Bert.

Industrious reporters searching for grieving family located Bert's nephew, Henry Montoya, in New Orleans. "I heard that she [Puente] was so kind to my uncle and was good to him. She helped him so much with his self-esteem. For the tables to be turned so abruptly, it just leaves me spellbound," Montoya told the press. With dignity, he added, "I don't feel hatred. I feel the Lord will take judgment."

At the Volunteers of America headquarters, Judy Moise's boss, Leo

MacFarland, told reporters that "hearing the news was a shock." But Judy didn't feel that way. It was more a feeling of being overcome by an awful, undeniable truth. And, at bottom, a feeling of betrayal. Dorothea Puente had taken her in with an elaborate charade. That phony compassion. That little old lady act.

Had she conned them all from the very beginning, only pretending to care about Bert while all along planning to murder him? *Why?* Rumor had it that she'd done it for money—simple, base greed—but Bert was no Rockefeller, he was rock-bottom poor. And no matter how monstrous Dorothea now seemed, Judy just couldn't reconcile Bert's murder with a lingering belief that, at some level, Dorothea had genuinely cared about him. Killing him for his puny benefit checks just seemed inconceivable. There had to be some other reason, something less obvious. What could he have done that could have possibly motivated Dorothea to kill him? Had she begun to see him as some kind of threat? Had he learned something?

Suddenly Judy was jolted by a hideous thought. For days, she'd been wrestling with the unlikely image of little Dorothea dragging dead bodies out of her house and into the yard for burial. Now it seemed horribly clear that Dorothea had had help.

Bert.

Judy ran it through her mind, looking for flaws, but with closer examination it seemed all the more likely. Bert had adored Dorothea. He would have done nearly anything she'd asked. And Bert was so uncritical, he would have accepted any explanation Dorothea had given him. Maybe she'd told him that she couldn't afford proper funerals for these people, then asked him to bury them in the yard. Or maybe she hadn't even told him what the stinking bundles really were, just saying it was garbage that needed burying. In any case, Bert was so trusting and dim, he probably wouldn't have questioned her.

But suppose he had. Suppose it had bothered him. Suppose it had simply felt wrong. Suppose he'd seen something that scared him ...

It seemed instantly clear. That was why he'd suddenly appeared back at Detox, wanting to sleep in his old, familiar mat. He'd wanted to get away from her. He'd slipped back to Detox to escape.

And Dorothea had known it. She'd seen that he was afraid of her and realized that her pet tenant wasn't quite as dumb as she'd hoped. Fearing that he might spill whatever he knew, she'd decided she had to kill him. However she'd done it, whatever quiet method she'd used, she'd planned it out, snuck up on Bert, and coldly murdered him. Then she'd buried him in the yard and cooked up all those lies about Mexico, trying to cover her trail.

It all seemed to fit. Judy didn't want to believe it, but each chilling detail clinked into place. The whole scenario had an eerie roundness to it that made her shiver. . . . And as this icy notion gripped her, she was frozen by another thought: If Bert had helped Dorothea bury the others, *who had buried Bert?*

CHAPTER 20

ALMOST THREE YEARS HAD PASSED SINCE THAT NEW YEAR'S DAY when Detective Sergeant Wilbur Terry had skittered down the river embankment to investigate a makeshift coffin. Now he was a lieutenant, sitting with other Sutter County deputies, listening to the morning's briefing.

These days the homicide detectives were intrigued by reports coming out of neighboring Sacramento County about graves found in Dorothea Puente's yard. And today Lieutenant Terry, who had been out of the office for a few days, sat up and listened with interest.

"Whoa! Wait just a minute!" he burst out. "Some of these details are sounding awfully familiar." Lieutenant Terry bolted from the room and retrieved the old case file from his desk.

"Look here. Remember Uncle Harry, the ol' guy in the box down by the river?" he asked, his deep, smoker's voice filling the room. "Look at the way he was wrapped: bed sheets and plastic. It sounds like the work of the same person. I think we ought to give Sacramento a call."

Soon the Sacramento police and Sutter County deputies were comparing notes. "Things just clicked," in the words of Terry's colleague, Lieutenant Steve Sizelove. "The knots, the wrappings just matched our guy to a T."

Sacramento police supplied a list of missing persons, and the Sutter County Sheriff's Department set about looking for a match. One name caught their attention: Everson Gillmouth. The time of his disappearance and his overall description seemed to fit.

A positive ID would take some effort. Family members had to be contacted, medical records obtained. A frustrating search for existing fingerprints turned up nothing: Gillmouth's military records had been destroyed in a fire, and Oregon's Department of Motor Vehicles, unlike California's, did not register fingerprints.

But finally, they accumulated enough for an absolute identification. X-rays showed that, like their corpse in the box, Everson Gillmouth had lost the tip of his right thumb.

Reba Nicklous, up in Sweet Home, Oregon, now knew for certain that her brother was dead, though he hadn't been unearthed from Puente's yard as she'd suspected back in November when she'd phoned the Sacramento police. Still, she was now more convinced than ever that her brother had died by Dorothea Puente's hand. She remarked bitterly, "Everson said that Dorothea would take care of him. Well, she did."

Sacramento police ran Everson Gillmouth through their computers, and the DMV files coughed up a lead. Though Gillmouth's body had been found on January 1, 1986, records showed that his red Ford truck had been sold in July 1987. The name on the bill of sale was Ismael Florez.

Two detectives went to question Florez on December 9. Distinctly uncomfortable, Florez nervously ran his fingers through his thick hair and smoothed his black mustache. Yes, he knew Dorothea Puente; he'd once done some paneling at her house. He even admitted he'd bought a Ford truck from her in December 1985 but claimed to know nothing about Everson Gillmouth.

Finally it came out that Puente had once had him build a large wooden box. The next day, the police arrested him on charges of being an accessory to murder.

It was almost a fluke that forty-six-year-old Ismael Florez was apprehended as Dorothea Puente's accomplice. The trail connecting him to Puente was cold and nearly forgotten.

Still, no one was claiming that Florez had helped Puente bury any-one. And though his arrest fell years shy and miles short of linking him to the seven bodies found in her yard, it compounded the mystery: The body count had risen to eight.

Reporters and televisions crews swarmed around the courthouse as Florez was arraigned, and the media trumpeted the news that "Puente's assistant" had been arrested. "We have evidence and witnesses who saw the box being taken out of her house and his pickup driving away," Lieutenant Sizelove disclosed to an Oregon reporter. "We think this was probably her very first one; after that, she started burying 'em."

Dumbstruck, Dorothea Puente stared at the television as Ismael Florez was marched across the screen. The report apparently stunned her so that she forgot about the inmate sitting next to her, who had one eye on her and one on the news. Perhaps she was lost in rumina-tion . . . the letters Everson had written to her while she was in prison . . . their long-distance courtship . . . meeting him for the first time when he'd picked her up at the halfway house . . . their short time together . . . then that long, anxious wait after he disappeared. . . . Amazingly, no one back then had asked questions or raised suspicions. How was it that now, after all this time, the police had traced Everson back to her?

Dorothea leaned over and whispered to fellow inmate Michelle Crowl, "I'm shocked that they linked him to the others." She shook her head of white hair, adding, "He was the first one."

Dorothea had trouble resisting that lifelong urge to be the center of attention. Here at the rambling, one-story Rio Consumnes Correc-tional Center (where she was being temporarily held until the new jail was completed) she was a celebrity. And now—after years of si-lence—she apparently felt compelled to talk. "I was very close to him," she continued. "He wanted to marry me, but he had such a nasty jealous streak."

Michelle Crowl, a fresh-faced youngster doing time on drug charges, was a trusty here—a low-security inmate who brought others food and coffee—which gave her a fair opportunity to mingle. Sometimes watching television with other inmates, she noticed that Dorothea often got "frustrated" after watching news of her case, openly grousing about the report.

A few days later the two women were again watching television when newscasters reported that, just as suddenly as he'd been arrested, Ismael Florez was being released.

"Florez is getting a deal," Dorothea grumbled. That stunk as far as she was concerned. (Her intuition was dead-on: Florez had hired an attorney, and in exchange for immunity, he'd agreed to testify against her.)

Michelle Crowl repeatedly warned Dorothea about talking too much. Housed just one cell away, she couldn't help overhearing bits of conversation between Puente and the outspoken inmate housed between them, Paulina Pinson. "I let her know that in the evening she and Paulina could be heard talking," Crowl explained defensively. "I wasn't the only one who could hear her. . . ."

Regardless, Dorothea passed the nights whispering confidences from cell to cell, and unbidden voices buzzed in Crowl's ears.

CHAPTER 21

JERRY HOBBS'S "COLORFUL" MOTHER HAD ALWAYS BEEN UNPRE-
dictable, but she'd completely disappeared in October 1987. When
she'd failed to pick up the birthday gift he'd sent to Sacramento, he'd
come searching for her, but found nothing.

Now Jerry Hobbs placed a call from San Diego to the Sacramento
Police Department. All he knew was that his mother had supposedly
been "located" in connection with the Dorothea Puente case. He gave
her name, Vera Faye Martin, and waited anxiously for his call to be
transferred. Hobbs next heard some clicking on the line, then a voice
barked the crushing news: "Sacramento County Coroner's Office."

Usually, the families of possible murder victims are treated more
sensitively. But now the system was so intent on attaching names to
the numbers attached to the bodies from F Street, few realized these
names and number might have children.

Yet names were surfacing at last.

The remains of Hobbs's mother, sixty-three-year-old Vera Faye Martin, had been identified with medical X-rays. Next, a forty-hour fingerprint analysis yielded the positive identification of Dorothy Miller,

sixty-four. (Detective Cabrera would remember her name from the pill bottle he'd confiscated from Puente's bedroom.) On the heels of this news, X-rays confirmed the identification of sixty-three-year-old James Gallop.

How long had this been going on? Who else might have been killed? And why?

Amazingly, the alleged motive was money. Benefit checks, they said. Yet Dorothea Puente's tenants were mostly people who inhabited a world of shrinking horizons, their pockets a day from empty, their only extravagances memories. Why would anyone want to murder people barely on this side of homelessness?

It sounded ludicrous. The average Social Security payment, about $350 per month, seemed hardly enough to kill for. Still, if Puente had managed to collect this nominal sum for seven people the figure rose to $2,450 a month—hardly a fortune, but a healthy income. And that base figure of $29,400 a year would jump upward with each larger check*—all of it tax-free, of course.

With Puente's criminal record, it was hard to understand how she could have gotten away with this. If the allegations were true, this was a case of a documented sociopath quietly murdering society's outcasts, preying on those who fell through the cracks because she knew how hard they were to trace ... she'd fallen through the cracks herself.

So, as the dust settled from the calamity on F Street, as names were attached to the luckless deceased, the finger pointing and soul-searching began in earnest. Blame was in the air. After all, this wasn't just some sleepy little community, this was the capital—the fountain of state law!—and if there was a flaw in the system, it had to be found.

Virtually every organization that had had contact with Puente was doused with condemnation, sending ripples of activity through the white-paper ponds of government. Office typewriters hummed with explanations and denials; various agencies huffily traded accusations.

The police department's gaffes made it an easy mark,† but other agencies were scrutinized and scolded as well: The parole board had failed to keep an eye on the ex-con! The human services network had

---

*Some benefit checks, such as disability or SSI, reached over $700 per month.

†As the result of an Internal Affairs investigation, Lieutenant Joe Enloe and Sergeant Jim Jorgenson were reprimanded and reassigned.

neglected to check her background! The city had failed to detect an illegally operated boardinghouse! The Social Security system had allowed her to cash checks unlawfully!

A scorching editorial in *The Sacramento Bee*° expressed amazement that Puente's parole officers had visited her at the boardinghouse fifteen times, yet failed to detect that she was running a boardinghouse in violation of her parole. The parole board countered that they'd been led to believe that Puente was merely a tenant at 1426 F Street. They had no legal cause to investigate, and were forbidden by federal privacy statutes from checking to see if Puente was forging checks. Besides, "we never noticed anything about her lifestyle that led us to believe she was spending more money," protested federal probation officer Charles Varnon. "Usually, that's the mistake people make, but she didn't make it. She was crafty, very crafty."

Ah. It wasn't their fault. The wily old landlady had lied to them.

Of course, the Social Security Administration wasn't to blame either. It was simply routine that payees were named and checks issued. There was no cross-referencing to determine how many checks one payee might be cashing. And no one examined the backgrounds of those receiving the checks, not even the parole board. The Right to Privacy Act prohibited such "infringements."

To this chorus of "it's not my job," the Department of Health added a farcical note when a spokesperson explained why its investigation of an odor at Puente's property had revealed nothing: "Obviously, there was no problem. If there was any kind of problem, we would have given her a written notice of violation."

It was that simple: No notice, no problem.

Eventually, the bitter brouhaha boiled down to one issue: whether Puente's establishment should have been *licensed.* The argument went like this: If *care and supervision* were being provided, then Puente needed a license, which required fingerprints, which would have resulted in a criminal background check. (Rather than submit to this, Puente probably would have "simply evicted any individuals for whom we had determined she was providing care and supervision and continued to operate," as David Dodds, acting district manager of Community Care Licensing, pointed out. But this detail was disregarded.)

°"The Mistakes on F Street," November 25, 1988.

Besides handling her tenants' finances, Puente was overseeing their medications—certainly in Bert's case, and probably others—and this was deemed "care and supervision." So Michael Coonan, the county ombudsman for senior care, was emphatic that Puente's establishment "should [have been] licensed. There's no question about that. This [was] an unlicensed residential care facility, not a rooming house, as it has been portrayed." (Coonan went on to speculate, moreover, that as many as a thousand elderly and mentally disabled people in Sacramento County were living in similarly unlicensed establishments.)

Lest it be thought at fault, Community Care Licensing (CCL) promptly responded with indignation. "I believe, very clearly, that Licensing did not miss the boat here," protested Deputy Director Fred Miller. "This was a place that represented itself [as] a boarding home" which did not require a license.

No agency—not the police, not the parole board, not Social Security, not CCL—was willing to take responsibility for having overlooked the notorious landlady.

Individuals made easier targets.

The director of the Sacramento County Health Department launched an investigation into whether mental health and social service workers should have recognized that Puente was dangerous. (It was unclear exactly how these workers ought to have discerned this, especially since parole officers, familiar with Puente's criminal record and charged with keeping an eye on her, had not. But the thirst for fault-finding had yet to be slackened.)

Now Peggy Nickerson, the street counselor who faced daily the nigh-impossible task of finding housing for alcoholics and outcasts, became the scapegoat. With everyone so eager to assign blame, and with all parties so vigorously denying responsibility for whatever had gone wrong, it finally came down to the fact that Nickerson had lied. It was documented: Nickerson had misled the CCL investigator who'd inspected Puente's residence back in June. Never mind that she'd done it naïvely, with good intentions. Never mind that her little white lie would have made zero difference in the final balance.

Nickerson's colleagues described her as hardworking, compassionate, "one of the best people in the business." They especially praised her for having the courage to work "with hard-core people that other social workers had already written off." But none of this made the papers.

Instead, a local headline charged, WARNING ABOUT PUENTE IG-NORED, with the snide subtitle, "Social worker kept referring clients to landlady she thought was 'kind.' " The article read: "Peggy Nickerson, who placed 19 clients in Puente's care since 1986, said county officials warned her about the landlady's criminal past in June. She said she ignored the warning because she didn't trust its source and because she liked the work Puente was doing."

Worse, Nickerson ingenuously opened up to reporters. "I was trying to protect the clients," she explained with anguish to the *Los Angeles Times*. "At least they would have a place to stay. I don't like the idea of people being thrown out on the street."

But with the scent of blood in the water, the lawyers were soon circling. Ben Fink's brother filed suit against Nickerson, as did the children of Vera Faye Martin and Dorothy Miller.

In the end, Peggy Nickerson lost her job.

CHAPTER 22

J ANUARY 11, 1989, BLEW IN CLEAR, COLD, AND WINDY. ALVARO
"Bert" José Rafael Gonzáles Montoya was to be buried today in a
remote, unremarkable corner of Saint Mary's Cemetery.

A handful of people gathered for the graveside service. Bert's
nephew, Henry Montoya, had flown out from New Orleans with his
wife. He stood as the sole blood relation in attendance since Bert's
mother was not strong enough to make the trip to California. A good
number from the Volunteers of America had managed to come, including Judy Moise, Beth Valentine, Leo MacFarland, and Bert's longtime friend from Detox, Bill Johnson. Shifting from foot to foot in
the bright cold, pulling their overcoats tight around them, all were
recorded by news cameras, the media being another portion of those
in attendance.

The mourners finally settled into metal folding chairs, then strained
to catch the words of the reverend as they carried on the wind, beseeching God to take the soul of Bert Montoya up to "the perfection
and the company of the saints."

As he spoke, Lucy Yokota, the nurse who had come to know Bert through his weekly TB treatments, stared in dismay at his inelegant coffin. It was blue Styrofoam—standard for the derelicts buried here. It looked like an ice chest you'd use at a picnic, Lucy Yokota thought. She watched the flimsy container shudder in the wind, distressed that it seemed about to blow away.

Judy Moise was called upon to say a few words, and she stepped forward, gripping her notes and swallowing emotion, to speak of the kind, misunderstood fellow who had brought them here. "Despite his affliction, he was a warm and gentle man. Everybody liked him," she said. "Alvaro Montoya was not a man to be overlooked. We will all miss him."

To complete the service, Beth stepped forward, drew a deep breath, and delivered a stirring rendition of "Amazing Grace." Her golden a cappella tones suffused the wintery air, as beautiful as any elegy to even the wealthiest man.

When the final notes dissolved, the knot of attendees began to unwind. It was too blistery to linger, and after a few parting words they went to find their cars.

Inarticulate yet unforgettable, Bert had touched all of their lives, and long after the service was over memories of Bert Montoya lingered—particularly for Judy Moise, who was anticipating dinner with Henry and Laura Montoya and her boss, Leo MacFarland. That afternoon, she located the videotape of Bert and bundled it with some papers that she thought Bert's nephew might like to see.

The documents stirred memories of how fervently she and Beth had wished for Bert's identification, kneeling before Our Lady of Guadalupe, praying for assistance. She recalled how ecstatic they had been when Bert's official ID had finally arrived. She had really believed she'd delivered him from hopelessness. In fact, she thought gloomily, her efforts to "save" him had only sealed his fate.

At dinner that evening, Henry Montoya accepted the video with thanks and reviewed his uncle's papers with interest. But when Judy handed him the beautifully embossed birth certificate with its colorful stamps, he stopped her with an unexpected comment. "This isn't right," he said, staring at the parchment in his hands. "It says he was born in San Juan."

Judy was perplexed. "He wasn't born there?"

"No, he was actually born just outside of San Juan, in a little town called Guadalupe."

"Guadalupe?" The name was bittersweet. An image of Our Lady of Guadalupe swam before her eyes, and Judy was struck by an odd sensation of symmetry. With an ironic smile she thought, Wait until I tell Beth.

But by the time she got home from dinner, Judy's smiles had vanished. Grief weighed upon her. A comment from Bill Johnson came ringing in her ears: *Bert was like a sacrificial lamb. His death put a stop to the killing.* He'd offered this notion as a kind of solace.

Maybe it was true. If Bert hadn't been killed, how many more would have died? How long would it have been until Dorothea Puente would have been caught? Judy embraced the idea hopefully. But there was something else . . . something dismal lurking just behind this thought.

Bert had a premonition that an old woman would kill him. Again, she heard Bill Johnson's voice and realized that this had also come from him. He'd said that Bert once told him that he'd dreamed a white-haired grandmother would kill him.

She swallowed the painful realization that she had delivered Bert to his doom. With piercing clarity she realized they were all at fault—Bill Johnson, Beth Valentine, herself—everyone who had circled Dorothea Puente yet failed to sense deception and danger. "I'm sorry, Bert," she whispered. "I'm so sorry."

It was too much. The troubles of the day combined like an emotional cocktail, and Judy's fortitude dissolved. Sobs shook through her, and with each raw gasp she struggled to contain the hysteria of guilt.

Part IV
LIES AND POTIONS

Lies confuse. The evil are "the people of the lie," deceiving others as they also build layer upon layer of self-deception.

—M. SCOTT PECK, M.D.,
People of the Lie

"Well, Mortimer, for a gallon of elderberry wine I take a teaspoonful of arsenic, and add a half-teaspoonful of strychnine, and then just a pinch of cyanide."

—MARTHA BREWSTER in
Joseph Kesselring's
Arsenic and Old Lace

CHAPTER 23

Worry etched across his brow, toxicologist James Beede maneuvered through traffic, transporting his carefully packaged cargo to the Department of Justice. He just hoped this foul-up didn't get leaked to the press.

As supervisor of the coroner's toxicology lab, Beede was convinced that the fault lay with the DOJ lab, not his. But he couldn't prove it. After all, few people besides him had any opportunity to handle the tissue samples taken from the seven corpses. After the samples had been lifted at autopsy, they'd been locked inside a large, refrigerated cage at the morgue, safe from tampering. Beede himself had taken the tissue samples upstairs for processing.

Clad in a lab coat and wearing latex gloves, he'd weighed out twenty grams of tissue for each specimen, blending it with a measured amount of pure distilled water, then pouring it into a sterilized glass jar. For each, he'd carefully mixed two homogenates, one of liver tissue, one of brain tissue. (Except for Leona Carpenter, whose liver wasn't identifiable, and Betty Palmer, of course, since her head was never found.)

Beede had had to overcome a natural revulsion to the brain tissue, which looked to him "like cream of mushroom soup." And he couldn't get that awful stench out of his system; it seemed to cling to his olfactory glands. He'd wake up and smell it.

This case was anything but normal, and the putrefied state of the bodies had certainly complicated things. But Beede was sure—wasn't he?—that everything had been sterile, that the specimens had been processed according to standard procedure. The only thing that was clear in his mind was that someone had unwittingly contaminated two of the samples. And the buzz was that the Puente case hinged upon cause of death. Damn!

Now all of the specimens had to be resubmitted for testing. Beede wheeled into a parking space and hurried a new batch of specimens into the hulking Department of Justice building. Inside, he signed them over to the forensic toxicology lab, where William Phillips, a stocky, graying scientist, would again analyze the homogenates.

A murder case of this magnitude obviously demanded a precise accounting of whatever these seven victims had consumed before dying. But it would be particularly difficult to identify any ingested poisons in such decomposed bodies. Only the most sophisticated technology would be able to detect the trace amounts of chemicals that the forensic teams hoped to find, and the DOJ had exactly that: a $375,000 tandem mass spectrometer. This huge and complex piece of equipment was the only one of its type being used for forensic analysis outside of Quantico, Virginia, home of the FBI.

The problem with that first batch of samples had not been a failure of technology. No, the tandem mass spectrometer had hummed through its tests with amazing accuracy, striking molecules with an electron beam and identifying by molecular weight even infinitesimal amounts of an array of pharmaceuticals. Rather, the problem had been that expensive equipment cannot compensate for human blunders—a small spill, an unclean vial, a dirty fingertip . . .

A report showing contamination of any kind was bad enough, but this particular substance—which deteriorates much too quickly to be legitimately found in decomposed remains—had no business defiling specimens in a crime lab, of all places. Rumors flew and allegations simmered, yet no one came forward to confess how it happened that the specimens had become tainted with cocaine.

☼   ☼   ☼

Assistant Public Defender Kevin Clymo could hardly keep from chortling when he heard the news of the latest gaffe in the state's case against his client. Cocaine use in the crime lab! Oh, the jury was going to love watching the toxicologists squirm while trying to explain this one!

This case was looking up. The toxicology reports were ambiguous and now highly impeachable. Puente's comments aboard the media jet would be ruled inadmissable. And that Michelle Crowl character had retracted her statement about Puente's jailhouse outbursts. Good.

Clymo pulled one of his fat, new binders off the shelf and flipped open to the latest report. With his investigators working hard on the Puente case, the file was growing by about a binder a week. He'd found that Puente had "an astounding memory for a woman of her age," and each encounter with investigators sent them scurrying off in search of more information, more interviews, more reports to fill more binders.

Plenty had happened since that morning after Dorothea Puente's arrest. While driving to work that morning, Clymo had noticed that "the whole downtown was crazier than usual." The next thing he knew, his boss, Public Defender Ken Wells, was offering him not only his first death penalty case, but the biggest murder case in Sacramento history. Soon he was hurrying from the courthouse, swamped by "more reporters than I'd ever seen in my life," and the image of his bald pate shining above a sea of newspeople was being broadcast worldwide.

Such a high-profile case might have warranted a more experienced attorney, but Kevin Clymo was due for a major murder case, having already handled many less-serious murder cases—jokingly referred to around the office as "misdemeanor murders." Trying death penalty cases was voluntary, outside the ordinary rotation for major crimes, and Clymo could have turned it down. But he was ready and eager to accept. He'd almost felt this case coming, a visceral anticipation, a premonition in his bones. This was big. A career maker.

While the press had painted Puente as cool, calculating, and stoic, the woman Clymo had first met at the jail was "highly upset, emotional, crying, confused, frightened." He'd done his best to calm her down and explain what was happening. By now they'd established such a rapport that Clymo remarked breezily, "Dorothea is one of my favorite people."

Beyond the conventions of being a devoted father and an able attorney, Kevin Clymo was something of a character. He had an easy, unpretentious, down-to-earth manner, and a loose-jointed way of moving which led his foes in the DA's office to unkindly dub him "the man made entirely of spare body parts." Despite his tall, gangly stature, he had a gentle nature, his worldview having been shaped by the wide swath of experience he'd sampled as a young man. He'd had many jobs, but finally settled on a law career after growing bored with a job as a truck driver.

An odd mix of metaphysical and military terms peppered his speech: He might describe going to trial as a "multiyear war" requiring "guerrilla" tactics backed by a "defense arsenal," yet he spoke just as easily of philosophy, spirituality, or Karma. Apparently, this paradoxical blend was the linguistic residue of both his undergraduate major in psychology at Stanford and a stint in the Vietnam War.

Since California law allows a team of two attorneys to act as co-counsels in waging the defense in capital cases, the tall, bald, mustachioed Clymo was paired up with Peter Vlautin, his short, urbane colleague. Mutt and Jeff.

Vlautin, who often wore ties that coordinated with his fashionable, red-rimmed glasses, was cosmopolitan in dress and manner. Coming from a family of attorneys, he'd unswervingly pursued a law career, and now he could justly claim to have handled "more death penalty cases than just about anyone in the office." His walls were adorned with framed articles about clients he'd successfully defended, virtually lifting the noose from around their necks. He would point them out, saying, "These were 'hopeless' cases that in the end gave me the most joy."

Like many public defenders, both Clymo and Vlautin touted their work as a higher calling. Champions of the poor, defenders of the weak. "If there's a public defender archetype, I am one," Clymo declared. "It's who I am. It's what I do. Money has never motivated me."*

Now the slightly younger and decidedly shorter Vlautin was working closely with the less-experienced Clymo, who grinned and nicknamed him the "coach." Proving Dorothea Montalvo Puente innocent of murder became their common mission.

---

*Ironically, by the time Puente would finally come to trial, Kevin Clymo had launched his own private practice, heralded on classy, gold-embossed business cards.

For the most part, this mission stayed secret. Only a few investigators and experts were privy to the inner workings of their strategy. The most that Clymo would say was that there were "people that no one has any awareness of that we rely on every day. A case of this magnitude, by its very nature, is so complex it requires a lot of the defense team."

Part of their team was already knocking on doors, recording interviews, getting results. They wasted little time, for instance, in subpoenaing the medical records of the deceased. Without a cause of death, the DA was going to have a tough time proving murder, and Puente's attorneys were set on making it nigh impossible. For while public opinion had branded her guilty until proven innocent, every public defender knows that, in the courtroom, presumption of innocence is paramount.

And their client was not charged with illegal burial.

Reasonable doubt, reasonable doubt—this is a mantra in the religion of defense attorneys. No matter how small, how obscure, every doubt must be examined and amplified. Because, as every defense attorney knows, doubts can have hidden powers. With luck, they can even work miracles.

CHAPTER 24

"Besides defending the case," said Peter Vlautin, "you have to defend the person." His tried-and-true strategy was to "start from day one" and chronicle the defendant's life, tracking down former friends, family, and neighbors from decades past, while keeping an eye out for what he calls "outside influences."

So Clymo and Vlautin set their investigators on the trail of Dorothea Puente's long and decidedly tragic past. They quickly retained a private investigator who specialized in researching the social histories of defendants in death penalty cases. She was one of the few allowed to meet with Puente at the jail, asking personal questions, getting leads on distant family and forgotten friends, delving into Dorothea's childhood to try to discover the crosscurrents that had carried this orphaned child into adulthood, outside the law, and into the vortex of Sacramento's biggest murder case.

Clymo would only hint at some of the tragic events that his investigators had uncovered. Steepling the fingers of his big hands, he would just murmur, "I think she's remarkably interesting. She has endured a lifetime of trauma and adversity and upset, and has remained intact in spite of that."

Although he revealed about as much as a riverboat gambler, Clymo's team had already made real progress in answering the question that Judy Moise could never quite fathom: Who was Dorothea, this snowy-haired woman with the slippery personality? Was she the kind, generous, eccentric old landlady who went out of her way to make her guests comfortable, who treated Bert "like a son," who showered friends with gifts? Was she a pathetic old woman who lacked a firm grasp on reality, half believing her own outlandish stories? Was she a cold-blooded killer who planned the deaths of her tenants as coolly as one scheduled the removal of garbage? Or was she something else altogether?

Even on paper she was a chameleon. Her weight varied: She was 185, 135, 160, or 125 pounds. Her hair was white, or auburn, or dark, or blond. One probation report gave her height as a surprising five feet eight inches; others noted a more reasonable five two or five two and a half.

Her eyes, in any case, were blue. And she was born on January 9, 1929.

According to probation records, Dorothea's father, Jesus Sahagun, died when she was four, and her mother, Trudie Gray, when she was five. Dorothea had told her probation officer that she was the youngest of eighteen children, the only one of the surviving fourteen living in the United States, and that she was a primary means of support for her siblings in Mexico. On June 8, 1982, while in jail awaiting a hearing, she'd sent a pleading letter to the "Honrable Judge Warren," printing out her tragic history: "I'd like to tell you first off, I'm of Mexican decent. I look white tho. When I was 3 years old I had to start picking cotton, potatoes, cucumbers and chilies, then fruits . . ."

She wrote that she felt "so terrible for the poor people I did wrong to, and my brothers and sisters, they are the ones who are suffering. . . . Please, your honor, find compassion in your heart."

In adulthood, Dorothea had garnered accolades for donating both time and money to political fund-raisers, Mexican-American scholarships, and charities. She spoke Spanish, handed out homemade tamales, and talked lovingly of her family south of the border.

But despite her pretensions of Hispanic heritage, state records show that Dorothea Montalvo Puente was in fact plain ol' white-bread American, born in Redlands, California—far south of Sacramento, but still hundreds of miles shy of the Mexican homeland she claimed. She

165

was the sixth of seven children born to Jesse James Gray, a thirty-four-year-old World War I veteran from Missouri, and Trudie Mae Yates, twenty-seven, a housewife from Oklahoma.

The Grays were evidently unprepared for the daughter that struggled into the world at six o'clock that January morning; it wasn't until eight days later that they managed to officially name their baby girl Dorothea Helen Gray.* She was born at a difficult time, for while Dorothea's mother lay in the sweat and pain of childbirth, her father lay in his own hospital bed, racked by a terrible, chronic illness.

Jesse James Gray had seemed a fit young farmer when he married sixteen-year-old Trudie Yates. But by the time he was discharged from the Army in July 1919, Jesse Gray was bent by a strange, relentless fatigue. Mustard gas poisoning, they said. Thin, shaky, unable to walk more than a few yards, he found himself bedridden by the age of twenty-five.

With months of rest and nurturing, Jesse's health gradually improved. By the next spring, he thought he'd recovered. He got out of bed and farmed for a season, then the restless young man packed up his family and moved to the golden promise of Southern California.

For short periods in California, Jesse Gray would feel strong, take a job, and work for a while. But then another relapse would knock him flat, this one longer and move severe than the last, and times grew lean again. The family moved often in search of a better life—Texas, California, Oklahoma—and paychecks were as rare as rain in the Dust Bowl. Though he'd once earned fifteen hundred dollars a year as a farmer, Jesse could scarcely raise fifteen dollars a month for his family.

And Trudie and Jesse were a fertile pair; no matter what their circumstances, babies were always on the way. The first son, James Gloe, came in 1918; the first daughter, Jessie Wilma, in 1920; another daughter, Sylvia Geraldine in 1921.

In 1922, Jesse Gray thinned to 118 pounds and weakened so much that he had to check into a veterans hospital. Then he learned that he wasn't just suffering the lingering effects of mustard gas poisoning, or an especially pernicious flu. His lungs had become traitors: He had the dreaded TB.

Veterans compensation checks helped put food on the table, but by

---

*Her birth certificate shows that her given name was, in fact, Dorothea, but it was later legally changed to Dorothy.

the time Dorothea came along, the Grays already had five youngsters to provide for. Dorothea's earliest years were spent in a home full of hungry children in Redlands, California, with a mother unsuited to the burdens of caring for an ailing husband and managing a noisy household. The older children were frequently charged with taking care of little Dorothea, whose needs were often eclipsed by more urgent demands.

By the time she was five, the family had moved to the nearby town of Pomona, and a baby brother, Ray June, had been added to the fray.

By now, their mother chronically sought comfort in a bottle. Her father was also a drinker, but at least he stayed home. Dorothea's unruly mother was apt to take off. She was incarcerated more than once for being drunk and disorderly. Once the eldest son, Jim, even locked Mom in the pantry so she couldn't go out.

When Trudie landed in jail, the kids were with Jesse; when he was in the hospital, they were with her. Sometimes the elder siblings were in charge, sometimes no one was. The only consistency was upheaval: When the rent was past due, it was time to move.

As Dorothea got older, she sometimes took care of Daddy, who could no longer manage even sporadic employment. Advanced tuberculosis was eating away at his lungs, eating away at the time he could spend out of bed. Other families of the time sent TB patients to fancy sanitariums, but the Grays couldn't afford that. Sometimes, when his health deteriorated badly, Jesse would check into the nearest veterans hospital for a spell. The rest of the time he was at home—depressed, angry, and practically an invalid.

No one could reverse the steady sixteen-year progression of his disease. Finally, the painful, bloody coughing of chronic tuberculosis put Jesse Gray back in the hospital. Then, coupled with bronchopneumonia, it ended his life. On March 29, 1937, at age forty-two, he stopped breathing.

Dorothea was eight.

Did she stand at her father's bedside, watching him labor for breath? Did she watch the nurses come and go, giving him pills, administering injections? Did she wish there were some way she could help? What went through her little eight-year-old mind?

And what was she told after her father died? Did her mother stoop down and whisper that this was really the best thing, that now his suffering was over?

Probably not. With so many years of waiting for this inevitability, Jesse's death came as a relief to Dorothea's mother, who wasn't about to be hindered by widowhood. Even after seven children, Trudie Yates Gray still had her charms, and it wasn't long until she had moved in with a lover, George Coyne, at his Los Angeles address.

By now, some of the children had been shipped off to live with assorted relatives, and the three youngest, having attracted the attention of juvenile authorities, had been placed in an orphanage, The Church of Christ Home, in Ontario, California.

Released from the burdens of needy children and a sick husband, Trudie briefly enjoyed her new freedom, but soon veered recklessly toward calamity. She died in a motorcycle accident on December 27, 1938—two days after Christmas, and just two weeks shy of Dorothea's tenth birthday. Her body was cremated six days later.

It was a tragic enough beginning. What sort of person would feel compelled to embellish it?

CHAPTER 25

Dorothea Montalvo Puente. She was like a Russian babushka doll: open her up, and find another doll inside; open that up, and find another . . . Dorothea Helen Gray was buried deep inside a long series of personas.

What youthful experiences formed the woman who would become known as Dorothea Puente? The defense team was working tirelessly to solve the riddle of their client, but her versions of the truth were as changeable as her hair color.

Her own family had lost track of her early on. The orphaned Gray children were split up, and Dorothea was shifted from household to household. A sister living in Southern California disclosed, "The people that adopted me tried to take her, and she ran away from them."

When she was fifteen, she moved with her oldest brother and his wife to a modest house in Napa, a small, charming town in California's not-yet-famous wine country. James and Louise Gray took her in, and school records show that Dorothea transferred as a ninth grader to Napa Junior High midyear, November 6, 1944.

She made a big splash at her new school, telling everyone she was an exchange student from Portugal (Louise was Portuguese). English was difficult for her, she said, so she had to have her homework translated every night. But she was no dummy; she boasted that she was a math whiz, able to solve problems that stumped even Einstein.

This fascinating new pupil quickly caught the attention of the school newspaper.

School authorities read the article about their new "exchange student" with alarm, then called Louise to tell her that Dorothea needed counseling. But this suggestion fell on deaf ears, and soon Dorothea was gone. She left abruptly on January 22, 1945, less than three months after she had entered.

Back in Los Angeles, she stayed briefly with a sister's adoptive family and enrolled in Garfield High School, then switched to Whidney High School, which she attended until the next June. But Dorothea Helen Gray would never graduate, completing her education in much different ways.

At sixteen, Dorothea ran away and traveled north to Olympia, Washington. Part of the time she was scooping ice cream, calling herself Sherri. The rest of the time, she and a friend were sharing a motel room, working as prostitutes. (The defense team took note. Psychotherapists who specialize in treating criminals contend that women who turn to prostitution suffer from low self-esteem, usually precipitated by having been abused or molested as children.)

It wasn't long before this good-looking teenager caught the eye of Fred McFaul, a twenty-two-year-old soldier just back from the Philippines. Unperturbed by her profession, McFaul took her to Reno and married her on November 18, 1945. Never mind that she was underage; she said that she was thirty and widowed, then signed the register Sherriale A. Riscile. Aliases came to her early.

"She could pass for anyone she wanted to be by the way she acted," in McFaul's recollection. "Riscile? That was a name she made up, I think. I don't know where she'd come up with this shit, out of the clear blue sky."

The couple set up house in Gardnerville, Nevada. McFaul took a job as a bartender at the Golden Bubble Club. And his new bride "used to tell everybody that she was my nurse in the war in the Philippines."

Their first daughter, named Dianne Lorraine, was born September 6, 1946, shortly before their first anniversary. A second daughter, Melody Jean, arrived less than a year later, on August 4, 1947. But motherhood and domesticity didn't hold much interest for this young wife;

after the birth of her second daughter, she took off for Los Angeles, leaving her babies and husband behind.

Weeks later, when she just as suddenly reappeared, McFaul's elation quickly faded to disenchantment when he learned that his darling wife had come back pregnant.

She miscarried. He left her anyway.

Having experienced little parenting herself, Dorothea Helen Gray treated her daughters much as she had been treated: They were separated, placed in the care of others, and abandoned. One was raised by McFaul's mother, the other was adopted.

With arid Nevada, her inconvenient husband, and the dissatisfactions of their three-year marriage behind her, the shimmering blacktop carried Dorothea back to the familiar landscapes of Southern California, where she launched her career in crime.

In the spring of 1948, Dorothea earned her diploma from the school of hard knocks: the first entry on her criminal record. A larcenous shopping spree in Southern California yielded a hat, shoes, a purse, hose, and an arrest. She pleaded guilty to two counts of forgery, one of writing a fictitious check, and served four months in jail.

The doctor who interviewed her in jail at the time believed that her crimes were brought on by "a compelling need to buy clothes and re-establish her own self-esteem." The doctor determined that she was not a "true criminal," but rather a "situational offender." This being her first offense, Dorothea was given three years' probation.

Six months later, she skipped cleanly out of Riverside, leaving her probation officer with only a phony forwarding address.

The defense and the prosecution were grinding away at opposite ends of the time line. While the defense started with Puente's roots and worked forward, the prosecution started with her arrest and worked backward. The defense had the benefit of extensive personal interviews. But the prosecution relied on records, and the records, like Dorothea herself, lied. They were like a dog chasing its own tail.

For instance, while awaiting sentencing in 1982 (Dorothea had accepted a plea bargain, pleading guilty to four felonies*), she'd penciled that letter in her schoolgirl scrawl to Superior Court Judge Roger K.

---

*One count of forgery, two of grand theft, and one of administering a stupefying substance for the purpose of committing a felony.

Warren, claiming that her siblings in Mexico depended on her for support. Giving the judge a bit of personal history, Dorothea wrote, "I finally married when I was 13. He died after a few days. After working and marrying again I stayed married for 18 years, unable to have children who lived. . . ."

Dorothea Montalvo also told her probation officer that, after losing both parents by the age of five, she'd lived with a grandmother in Fresno, then went to Mexico to stay with an older brother. The probation officer wrote that she "returned to California at age 15½ and soon thereafter married Fred McFall [*sic*]. Her husband reportedly passed away two years later as a result of a heart attack. . . ."

(In Dorothea's revisions of her personal history, inconvenient characters simply died.)

But her probation officer, Tony Ruiz, wasn't taken in by Puente's piteous act. He saw that, brash and confident on her own, Puente had turned vulnerable and repentant only after being apprehended. In his report to Judge Warren, he wrote, "In this officer's opinion, her expression of remorse was diluted by her attempt to manipulate the interview."

At one point, Puente had interrupted him to point out that she was of Hispanic descent too. And though she'd "appeared distraught and tearful," it became obvious to Ruiz that she was reading his notes upside down from across the table.

She was sentenced to five years in prison.

About some things, the records were clear: Puente—or Montalvo, as she was then known—was sent to California's overcrowded maximum security unit at the Correctional Institute for Women (CIW) in Frontera. There, she proved to be such a quiet, obedient prisoner that she served only three of her five years' sentence and was released on parole in the fall of 1985.

Upon her release, a Department of Corrections psychological evaluation described her as "disturbed" and "dangerous" and recommended that "her living environment and/or employment should be closely monitored."

She'd had a few run-ins with the law—she was even called an ideal prisoner—but the Department of Corrections could not correct what was wrong with Dorothea Puente.

CHAPTER 26

Aꜰᴛᴇʀ ᴛɪʀᴇʟᴇssʟʏ ʜᴜᴅᴅʟɪɴɢ ᴛᴏɢᴇᴛʜᴇʀ ɪɴ ᴛʜᴇ ᴘᴜʙʟɪᴄ ᴅᴇ-
fender's office, trying to make sense of Dorothea's baffling past, Keven
Clymo and Peter Vlautin thought they'd finally discovered an essential
truth. "This is the key," Clymo said, grinning. "She's a multiple!"

It just made sense. All her fantastic personalities, fluxing like colorful
chips in a kaleidoscope, were just bits of a fractured psyche. She was
beyond schizophrenic, she was a multiple personality.

As a defense, this could be golden. Complicated, yes ... but so
was Dorothea.

They placed a call to one of the most well-respected psychiatrists
in this narrow field of specialization and explored their options. If she
were a true multiple, it would take time for him to establish trust and
get Dorothea to open up. Ultimately, they would need videotapes of
her slipping from one personality to the next so that they could convince a jury. All agreed it was a theory well worth testing. So arrangements were made for the psychiatrist to go to the jail and get to know
the woman called Dorothea.

❀   ❀   ❀

Flitting from group to group, changing names and stories as she went along, Dorothea had slid unobtrusively into adulthood. A fiery temper, a passionate streak, and an unbridled talent for fabrication marked her trail. Marriages, divorces, and a few arrests chronicled her progress.

She surfaced in San Francisco in 1952, at age twenty-three, where she married a twenty-five-year-old Swede named Axel Bernt Johansson. Inventing her most fabulous identity yet, she called herself Teya Singoalla Neyaarda, claiming that her father, Antony Neyaarda, was Egyptian, and her mother, Nazic Friad, was Israeli. And that she was Muslim. At first, even Johansson believed her.

Johansson was a merchant seaman at the time, and during his long absences Dorothea apparently pleased herself. Sometimes he returned from months at sea to find some new man living with his wife. Sometimes he found expensive merchandise of suspicious acquisition. Sometimes she took his money and gambled it away in Reno.

The neighbors weren't happy with Mrs. Johansson either. When Axel came home, they complained to him that taxis arrived at his doorstep hour after hour, dropping off strange men.

But in his line of work, away months at a time, it was hard to keep a tight rein on someone so untamed as Dorothea.

In April 1960, at thirty-one, she was arrested for "residing in a house of ill fame." Dorothea protested that she'd only been staying with a friend and hadn't realized she was in a brothel, but she was sentenced to ninety days.

In 1961, fed up with her running around, drinking, wild stories, and suicide attempts, Johansson had her briefly committed to DeWitt State Hospital in Stockton. Records there describe her as "very obese" and "infantile." She told them that she could speak Arabic, Greek, Spanish, and Swedish, and doctors there decided that she was a "pathological liar" suffering from an "unstable personality." They gave her prognosis as "guarded."

Despite their many, long separations—or perhaps because of them—the Johanssons were legally married for fourteen years.* Later, Dorothea would claim that she and Johansson divorced in 1960. It was really 1966. But for years after they separated, Dorothea continued using her husband's name.

---

*Now remarried, Johansson resides outside of Sacramento, in a house partly hidden from the street by a sentinel of cypress trees. He guards his privacy and refuses to discuss his ex-wife.

DISTURBED GROUND

Some knew her as Sharon Johansson.

A new name, a new personality. Yet there was nothing wildly criminal about Sharon Johansson. Just the opposite. She was a bighearted, heavy woman with her hair up in a French roll, a phone to her ear, and a hot line to the Seventh Day Adventist Church. She knew the needy families in her Broderick neighborhood, and with just a phone call she channeled food baskets and secondhand clothes to their front doors.

During this time, Mrs. Johansson established a reputation as a care giver. For several young girls, her home was a sanctuary from poverty and abuse. She welcomed hungry children and unwed mothers to her table, dishing out hot meals with plenty of free advice.

She gradually established a domain in Sacramento, and she would live there, at various addresses and using various names, almost without interruption until 1988.

On February 23, 1968, at age thirty-nine, the tempestuous Dorothea married a much younger man, twenty-three-year-old Roberto Jose Puente. Her ill-fated third marriage, commencing in Reno, was hardly an epic romance. Some said that Roberto married this older woman only for her money and American citizenship. (The little girls across the street whispered about "Mr. Gigolo.") But perhaps Dorothea simply couldn't dominate this young buck.

The two made a stab at domestic bliss, even buying an attractive, respectable-looking two-story house on Twenty-third Street in Sacramento, but had hardly settled in before they were screaming and throwing things. On July 5, 1969, after just sixteen and a half months, they separated.

Charging that young Roberto had treated her with "extreme cruelty" and had "wrongfully inflicted . . . grievous mental and physical suffering," Dorothea wasted no time in filing for divorce. She wanted their community property: the house on Twenty-third Street and a 1967 four-door Ford Galaxy. But Roberto took off for his native Mexico, frustrating her attempts to have him served with divorce papers.

Apparently, even finalizing the divorce on March 28, 1973, failed to extinguish their smoldering romance. It seems that Roberto hadn't had enough of his former bride, for in 1974 he was back, again living in her house. Attempts to rekindle the relationship obviously backfired, because in January 1975, when he refused to either leave or pay rent, Dorothea filed a restraining order against him.

175

The mismatched couple maintained contact into the next decade. In August 1982, Roberto Puente even wrote a letter to Judge Warren on her behalf, stating that he'd "known Dorothea Montalvo for the past many years," and that she'd been "very helpful to the Mexican-American community," giving "clothes and food to needy families and to people with alcoholic problems." He closed with, "Any consideration given to her well being will be greatly appreciated at this difficult time."

The young Roberto must have pleased Dorothea in some deep, enduring way, for despite everything, she would cling to his surname for more than twenty years.

For a time, Dorothea Puente ran a Sacramento halfway house for alcoholics, but it shortly went bust. Then she shifted her attention to running a huge, elegant, three-story boardinghouse at Twenty-first and F streets, the white "mansion" that she would boast about for years. She furnished the house with donated furniture from the Seventh Day Adventist Church, but she kept it spotless, with the floors always polished and the table always set. Even her tenants—down-and-out alcoholics and homeless mentally ill—were kept clean and tidy.

Everyone considered her a genuine resource to the community. She networked with all the agencies. She held AA meetings in her parlor. She steered the indigent toward Social Security benefits and away from alcohol. In the words of one who knew her at the time, "She knew how to get things done."

And she was always learning, especially when Dr. Carl Drake stopped by once a month to tend to her boarders. Dr. Drake found it convenient to make his diagnoses in her tidy kitchen, writing prescriptions at her table. Dorothea sat close by, watching, then daily placed each tenant's pills in little Dixie cups, which she arranged on a spotless tray.

The landlady was always cordial to Dr. Drake, but he couldn't help but notice her other side. Any breach of the rules brought a fit of cursing down on the head of the transgressor. It rarely happened twice, Dr. Drake noticed, "He was either out of there or else he changed his ways."

Her new enterprise flourished, as did her reputation, propelled along by serendipitous associations within Sacramento's Hispanic community. This identity as Dorothea Puente suited her emergence as something of a social butterfly. She befriended a big, charismatic man named Francisco Suarez (nicknamed *Muñeco de Oro*), and helped him launch his weekly Spanish-language newspaper, *la Semana News*. Soon she was rubbing elbows at Mexican-American fund-raisers, having her picture taken for the paper. She picked up some Spanish, dropped a lot of cash, and became known as *"la doctora."*

At the pinnacle of her fame and glory, Dorothea was like a junkie with a philanthropic habit. Charities, scholarships, radio programs, and assorted individuals all benefited from her sponsorship. If your daughter needed a wedding reception, ask Dorothea. If your cousin needed to pay his "coyote" for getting him across the border, ask Dorothea. Everyone dipped into her pot and benefited from her largess. And those who cautioned Dorothea that she was being taken advantage of were rebuffed. "I'm a wealthy woman," she told them. "I own this house, a house in Mexico, and a house in Spain."

She savored her renown and grew intoxicated by her own fantasy. At one point, she told her attorney, Donald Dorfman, that she was going into the hospital for surgery—cancer, of course—and she needed to draw up a will. Dorfman obliged, and was astonished by all the "adopted" children for whom Dorothea wished to provide, nearly a dozen, plus grandchildren (though she specifically dispossessed one). The benefactress to the end, she also left a large sum to a Catholic school.

At the time, Dorfman believed that Dorothea was a "highly respected and affluent member of the Hispanic community." Only later did he realize that she owned none of the assets she wished to bequeath.

At forty-seven, Dorothea set her sights on husband number four. Having soured on younger men, she was sweet on one of her tenants, a handsome fifty-one-year-old laborer from Puerto Rico named Pedro Angel Montalvo. "She told me she fell in love with me as soon as she saw me," Montalvo recalled years later. They were wed on August 28, 1976, in her favorite wedding spot, Reno, Nevada. Now she had thoroughly grasped her false Mexican identity, giving her father's name as Jesus Sahagun, and her mother's maiden name as Puente. (On the marriage certificate she also claimed this was her second marriage.)

Montalvo almost immediately started feeling uncomfortable with his beautiful, vain bride. Her free-spending ways and lying habits sparked distrust and resentment. "She was always lying. She never told the truth," he said. "She told me she was a doctor. Lies. She told me she owned property in Mexico. Lies. She told me she was Mexican, but she doesn't speak Mexican."

After just a week of marriage, he walked out. It would take months to get the marriage annulled, and even then, the two couldn't end it. They kept breaking up and then getting back together.

Montalvo recalls a relationship of destructive passion. "I had had enough. I said to myself, 'This will be the end.' I told her, 'You will destroy me.' I was a sick man. I wanted her to leave me alone, but she never did. We were on and off for a long time after we divorced. We would spend holidays together. She would call me up and say, 'Honey, come over.'"

Finally, Dorothea was through with marriage. She might have boyfriends now and then, but there would be no more husbands. She was on her own.

Using the name Dorothea Montalvo when it suited her, she continued with her exploits as *la doctora Dorotea Puente*. She lavished money on the Mexican-American Youth Association. At charity functions, she danced with Governor Jerry Brown, and had her picture taken with his successor, George Deukmejian. And she was so generous with various musical groups—including the well-known *Los Terricolas*—that she earned herself another nickname: *La Madrina de los Artistas*, the Godmother of the Artists.

Meanwhile, she ran her gorgeous and spacious boardinghouse. The residence was surely large enough to support a legitimate business, for sometimes she had as many as thirty boarders. But according to rumor, she pursued shady enterprises at this address. With her false reputation as a doctor, she supposedly administered black-market medical treatments, even giving injections. And one source claimed that her locked basement was "always full of wetbacks" whom she helped conceal from immigration officials.

Whatever else she may have been guilty of, Dorothea Montalvo was doubtless filching benefit checks intended for her tenants. She forged signatures, signing the checks over to herself, then depositing the money into her own accounts. Toward the end of 1978 she was caught and convicted. But apparently, illegally cashing thirty-four federal checks didn't impress the judge as especially serious. Her sentence was light: five years' probation and four thousand dollars' restitution.

When Pedro Montalvo, who still harbored tender feelings for his ex-wife, went to ask her about her crimes, she reportedly told him, "I did it because I wanted to be somebody."

"We are all somebody in this life," he replied. "Why do you have to steal?"

She looked at him and answered, "The way that I steal, I give to others."

Kevin Clymo sighed when he heard the psychiatrist's disappointing news. Dorothea Montalvo Puente was complex. She fit no simplistic categories. Unfortunately, neither did she fit the narrow criteria of a true multiple personality. There were no trancelike transformations from one distinct personality to another, no "blackouts" during which she "lost time."

Despite all the people who said, "The Dorothea I know could never have done this," Clymo would have to contend with the ink on her record, and with that first hint of blood on her hands.

CHAPTER 27

B IG AND BROAD-SHOULDERED, JOHN O'MARA HAD THE SHAPE of an ex-athelete, undisguised by his pin-striped suit and a few extra pounds. But he was years past calling any plays on a muddy field; now he coached a team on much dirtier turf: the DA's office, homicide. Every homicide case in Sacramento County landed on the desk of Assistant Chief Deputy District Attorney John O'Mara, head of the major crimes division, ruling monarch of the fourth floor of the DA's office. As homicide supervisor, he not only tried but assigned cases, usually giving death penalty trials to each deputy DA in turn so that no one prosecutor was overwhelmed.

O'Mara worked on the Puente case while it was breaking, advising the police to get a forensic anthropologist to oversee the exhumations, issuing search warrants. After filing the first murder count against Puente, O'Mara then handed the case over to Deputy DA Tim Frawley, a tall, lean man whose every sinewy inch was testament to a serious running regimen. In private, Frawley had a soft-spoken manner, so that he sometimes startled defense attorneys with his commanding presence in the courtroom.

O'Mara felt confident that Frawley would do an excellent job in bringing this case to trial. From now on, he thought, the Puente case would demand only slightly more of his attention than the usual media-grabbing, multimurder case.

He was wrong. The prosecution of Dorothea Montalvo Puente would demand far more than anyone anticipated, consuming time and energy in vast, unruly quantities, swelling and spreading like a feverish, misdiagnosed illness.

Despite a growing witness list, investigators were smacking up against a lot of dead ends. They questioned tenants and neighbors: Had they seen anything—struggles, suffocations, stranglings? Had they heard any strange sounds at night? Screams for help? Had anyone seen Puente mixing drugs or chemicals into food or drinks? Or giving injections? Had anyone seen her carrying or dragging or burying anything suspicious? They came back virtually empty-handed.

With fading hopes of finding any eyewitnesses, they shifted their focus to the paper trail, subpoenaing financial accounts and accumulating dozens of canceled checks. They studied pill bottles, located prescriptions, called on pharmacists, and queried doctors. Meanwhile, the crime scene investigators prepared scores and scores of detailed diagrams, as if the very layout of the house and garden could somehow convince a jury that Dorothea Puente was guilty of murder.

Some feared that the Puente case wasn't being pursued with much vigor or insight. But others thought, hell, they'd found seven bodies in that woman's yard—what else did they need to get a conviction?

The case continued to make headlines. The last two bodies at the morgue were identified: Leona Carpenter and Betty Palmer, both in their late seventies. Carpenter had been the first body discovered (the skeletonized leg bone, the dirty sneaker), and newspaper accounts reminded the reading public that Betty Palmer's identification had been complicated by the fact that she was missing her head, hands, and feet.

Who were these aged ladies? And why was Puente being charged with only *one count* of murder?

With allegations of octuple murders—seven bodies pulled from her yard and another found beside the river—the investigation had sprouted tentacles. That solitary murder charge was beginning to seem awfully lonely, yet weeks passed with little evident progress.

And the feds were getting hot about all the government checks

181

Puente had allegedly forged, wanting to charge her with federal charges of fraud and forgery. But O'Mara argued that this case was complicated enough without dragging in dozens, perhaps hundreds, of lesser charges. The jury was going to be overburdened as it was.

Since there was no statute of limitations on the federal charges, the feds agreed to back off; if Puente didn't go down for murder, they'd get her later. For now, the numerous checks would be used to prove motive.

Despite growing pressure, the DA's office didn't want to rush to file charges yet. Frawley and O'Mara agreed that a case like this demanded caution, thoroughness—especially since there was now another suspicious death, a 1982 "suicide" that looked an awful lot like murder.

One afternoon in late 1981, Dorothea Montalvo Puente clicked her high heels into one of her favorite drinking establishments, a place with a rounded exterior topped with a neon cocktail glass called the Round Corner Tavern. Inside, she spied Harold Munroe and his new wife, Ruth. Nice couple. They invited her to join them, so she pulled up a chair and nudged the wheels of fate into motion.

Ruth Munroe had been out of work since leaving the pharmacy at Gemco, she said, and the plump, sixty-one-year-old grandmother was ready to try something new.

Why, it just so happened that the owner of the Round Corner was interested in leasing out the restaurant portion of the tavern, Dorothea told her. "I've been thinking, this kind of opportunity may not come around again," she said, looking at Ruth, "but I sure could use a partner."

By leasing the restaurant, she and Ruth could launch their own business with minimal start-up costs. They would make a terrific team, Dorothea said. And Ruth wouldn't even have to cook; Dorothea would handle the kitchen. Since Ruth was the one with a car, she could handle supplies and transportation.

The venture seemed just about perfect, and after hours of discussion, they were sparked with enthusiasm. Ruth Munroe withdrew the capital for her share of the investment and handed it over to her new partner. They were in business.

Soon, Dorothea was working there in the kitchen nearly every day. And she was busy cooking up more than just hamburgers.

DISTURBED GROUND

The restaurant business was faltering, she told Ruth. They needed more capital just to keep the business afloat, and Dorothea was forced to ask Ruth for more and more money, either for the business or for personal loans. The bills kept mounting, Dorothea kept complaining, and thousands of Munroe's dollars were drained into the enterprise.

Meanwhile, Ruth Munroe had other things weighing on her mind. Her husband wasn't a well man, and since marrying him the previous year, Ruth had unfortunately found herself taking him to the veterans hospital with increasing frequency. Early in 1982, Mr. Munroe's doctors diagnosed terminal cancer. Finally, they decided he ought to stay in the hospital, and Ruth returned home alone.

In Ruth's time of need, her new friend stepped forward with a generous offer. It just so happened that one of her boarders was moving out, Dorothea told her. "Why don't you just move in with me? We get along so well. Besides, it would be less expensive than staying in that place all by yourself. I just thought that, with your husband in the hospital and all, we could help each other. . . ."

At her age, Ruth Munroe didn't much like living alone, and Dorothea's unselfish offer seemed just what she needed. So, on Easter Sunday, April 11, she moved into 1426 F Street, sharing the upstairs with Dorothea. Her sons helped her move, hefting furniture up to the bedroom off the kitchen, helping her arrange it.

Munroe had no way of knowing that the very next day, April 12, Dorothea was scheduled in court for a preliminary hearing for having drugged and robbed Malcolm McKenzie back in January. And as Dorothea was leaving the courtroom, she was arrested and temporarily held on a forgery warrant for having robbed Dorothy Gosling back in 1981.

But the key word here is *temporarily*. While her illegal activities were finally attracting some heat, Dorothea, slick character that she was, slid right back into action. Until now, she may have been just another petty crook, but she was about to move into the big leagues.

The quick theft and disappearing act wouldn't work with Ruth Munroe. This had become a long-term relationship, and something more was required. The risk was worth it, she decided, perhaps because Munroe offered not just loose change lifted from her pockets, but serious folding money.

Just two weeks after having moved into 1426 F Street, Ruth Munroe was abruptly stricken by a mysterious illness.

When her children came to visit, they were startled to find their ailing mother—who didn't drink—with a glass of crème de menthe in her hand. "Dorothea gave this to me to calm my nerves," she explained.

They were concerned that their mother looked so tired and pale, but Dorothea ushered them out, assuring them that she would take care of her new roommate. "After all," she reminded them, "I used to be a nurse."

With no idea what could be wrong with their mother, they put their faith in Dorothea, and in their mother's healthy constitution.

But very early the morning of April 28, the phone rang. It was Dorothea, with staggering news: Their mother had suddenly died. They rushed to the house and found that it was true.

Grief-stricken, the family was at first too upset to analyze the circumstances surrounding Ruth Munroe's death. But later, when they received a copy of the coroner's report, they were shocked to see that their mother had died of an overdose of codeine and acetaminophen, and her death had been judged a suicide!

Horror, then anger began to stain the edges of their grief, and then they began to reconsider how Dorothea, the former "nurse," had "taken care of" their mother. Their suspicions darkened when they found that Munroe's bank accounts had been cleaned out, and much of her jewelry was missing. Dorothea protested innocence, claiming that Ruth had owed her a lot of money.

Exactly three weeks to the day after Ruth Munroe's death, Dorothea Montalvo Puente was arrested. (Police found a ticket to Mexico in her purse.) She was charged with six felony counts, including robbery, forgery, grand theft, and administering stupefying drugs, and she was ordered held without bail.

Murder was not among the charges, and Ruth Munroe's name was not listed among Puente's victims. Munroe's family didn't even know that Dorothea Puente had been arrested. In fact, it wasn't until reading in the paper that Puente had been sentenced that her children were compelled to contact law enforcement and request an investigation into the possibility that their mother had been murdered. But the investigation floundered, and no murder charge was filed.

This time around, Ruth Munroe's children, named Clausen from her first marriage, weren't going to make the mistake of being too complacent. They handed over everything they had about their mother's suspicious death in 1982, and the DA's office reopened a case that it had long considered closed.

On the surface, this murder charge looked awfully promising. It had just what this case needed: a solid autopsy, motive, and grieving children, all the elements that make a trial attorney's palms itch.

But underneath were some legal problems that Clymo would doubtless milk for every advantage. Deputy DA Frawley consulted with John O'Mara, and the two agreed this wasn't going to be pretty. They could almost hear the jurors arguing in the deliberation room: If the Munroe case looked so solid in 1989, why hadn't it been prosecuted back in 1982?

CHAPTER 28

Trees that had been shedding their leaves at the time of Puente's capture were budding out with fresh spring foliage as the DA's office finally filed additional murder charges against her. On March 29, 1989, the DA's office fulfilled (perhaps even exceeded) public expectations when Tim Frawley, the prosecutor ostensibly in charge of the case, increased the number of murder charges from one to nine.

The counts against her included the murders of the seven individuals unearthed from her yard: Bert Montoya, Leona Carpenter, Betty Palmer, Dorothy Miller, Vera Faye Martin, James Gallop, and Benjamin Fink. Puente was also charged with two murders more remote in time: those of Everson Gillmouth, whose body had been found in a wooden box by the side of the river on New Year's Day, 1986; and Ruth Munroe, who had overdosed in Puente's home in April 1982.

Nine murder counts. Now Dorothea Puente had officially joined the unlikely fellowship of alleged serial killers—rare company for her age, rarer still for her gender. There was virtually no one else in her category. Across the country, FBI profilers and criminal psychologists

186

raised their eyebrows, then penciled the little old lady's name on a
very short list.

Those who believed they'd lost a friend or relative to murder now
suffered the ordeal of waiting, the absolute futility of trying to will
the legal apparatus into motion, waiting impotently by the phone,
hoping first for some news of justice, then lowering expectations and
hoping for news, any news, any movement. But the DA's office did
not revolve around the Puente case, and news was slow in coming.

In fact, the DA's office was in the throes of change, and for now
the pursuit of justice would have to take a backseat to office politics
and career ambitions. When District Attorney John Dougherty unexpectedly resigned to go into private practice, he left the office in
turmoil. The board of supervisors scrambled to find a replacement,
and speculation over Dougherty's replacement buzzed through the
corridors. But many were disappointed when, rather than promote
from the more than a hundred attorneys working within the DA's
office, the board settled on an outsider, Steve White, chief assistant
with the attorney general's office.

As anyone who has ever worked in an office knows, realignments of
power are disruptive. And new bosses, particularly those brought in
from outside, are likely to be at least controversial, even unpopular.

The newly appointed DA, green to the workings of his new post,
needed an insider to help him take charge, and shortly selected Timo-
thy Frawley as chief deputy, his second-in-command. Frawley was a
disciplined attorney with a solid track record, but in trying to juggle
his new responsibilities, he soon realized that he would have to find
someone else to help with his caseload, particularly that troublesome
Puente case.

And the state's investigation, which had yet to match strides with
the defense, continued to be plagued by mishaps.

Senior Document Examiner David Moore bent over his hand-held
magnifier and stared at the handwriting exemplars he'd been given.
This was his job with the California DOJ Bureau of Forensic Services
to try to find truth in loops and slants, scrutinizing scrawls of pencil
and ink, studying *i* dots and *t* crossings, comparing pressure, propor-
tion, and "baseline habits." He sighed, wishing that the photocopies
he'd been given were originals. These machine-made images rendered

signatures two-dimensional, eliminating signs of pressure and making them harder to compare to the handwriting exemplars scribbled by Dorothea Puente back in December.

It was Tuesday, April 11, and Moore had only just become involved in the Puente investigation. Using a stereoscopic binocular microscope, he looked again at the "questioned documents," mostly photocopied signatures on the backs of checks. He had hundreds of signatures to examine,* but so far he'd concluded only that the writer had tried to disguise his or her handwriting while signing these checks. In his experience, signatures that were written vertically or left of vertically were usually fraudulent.

Now Moore regarded the handwriting exemplars spread across his desk with disdain. It was obvious to him that these were woefully insufficient. There weren't enough of them, for one thing. And there wasn't enough variation in writing styles, which indicated to Moore that all of these signatures had been collected from Puente during a single session, without much direction.

Switching to the video spectral comparator (VSC-1), which allowed him to see the inks under different lighting, Moore again sighed at the inadequacy of the exemplars. What he saw here was not a well-planned collection of writing samples, but the criminal wrapping her hand around the pen and signing various names in an unvarying fashion.

He pushed the exemplars away in exasperation. This was pointless, he decided. Puente hadn't been instructed to write vertically or slanted left, so the exemplars were too homogeneous to compare with the signatures on the backs of the checks. The handwriting exemplars, like the toxicology reports, would have to be redone.

It was already April. With a haphazard investigation and no one really at the helm, how likely was it that they'd be ready for Dorothea Puente's preliminary hearing, now scheduled for September?

The blistering month of July was just ending when George Williamson returned from prosecuting an organized crime case in Fresno and stepped back into the air-conditioned hubbub of the Sacramento County District Attorney's Office. Around the office, Deputy DA Wil-

---

*David Moore would spend over 125 hours on this case.

liamson was regarded as a top prosecutor, even a troubleshooter. As one attorney put it, "If you see Williamson's name on a file, you know it's a problem case."

The *People* v. *Dorothea Puente* fell into that category. So it was no surprise when Tim Frawley, the new chief deputy, popped into Williamson's office and asked him to take over his caseload. Williamson accepted instantly, but once the paperwork was shifted into his office, he found the files in disarray, haphazardly stashed in boxes. Apparently, the Puente case had been sitting on the back burner.

It would take time to get this complex case cooking again, and Williamson had several cases to handle first. So, in a routine procedure, Dorothea Puente's preliminary hearing was rescheduled for February 20, 1990. But finally, nearly nine months after Puente's arrest, it appeared that the DA's office had at last found its prosecutor.

George Williamson was a man in his prime. Despite his cigarette habit, he was fit, sturdy, and fast-paced. He sated his penchant for the outdoors with a winter ski cabin in Tahoe and all the equipment needed for an array of sports, including handball, tennis, golf, and waterskiing. He preferred standing to sitting. Even his words were rapid-fire, with a vocabulary displaying obvious erudition and intellect. When he wanted to, Williamson could play down his education, assuming the salty speech and low-key manner that put less sophisticated people at ease. In the courtroom, he was razor-sharp, thorough, and pugnacious. His tenacity as a prosecutor had even earned him a nickname around the police station: the Bull Dog.

With his background, Williamson could have easily ended up on the other side of the law. His mother died when he was fourteen, he couldn't tolerate his father, and he was on his own at sixteen. But instead of succumbing to baser temptations, Williamson put himself through college, then law school, and ended up in the Sacramento DA's office.

While most new attorneys could expect months or years of trying misdemeanors before graduating to felony prelims and then felony trials, Williamson was trying his first murder within eight months. Eventually, he became the youngest supervisor of any task force in the office, heading up what he casually referred to as "major dope." Some might call him a star prosecutor, but Williamson would demur, conceding only that he'd been "lucky in office progression."

Deft at deflecting praise, Williamson happily turned nearly any conversation to the achievements of his seventeen-year-old son, Tyler. The boy excelled in athletics, and after work Williamson, the canny attorney, became just another proud father in the bleachers, cheering when Tyler got a hit. Any hint of bitterness over an ill-fated teenage marriage was eclipsed by pride in his son. He boasted that Tyler, a talented golfer, had a handicap of only three, adding with a chuckle, "I've caddied for him more than once."

Everyone knows that attorneys in private practice can earn truckloads more than county prosecutors. Raising even one teenager can empty one's bank accounts, and Williamson also had an adopted daughter, Diana, in college. Still, private practice didn't suit his temperament. He'd tried working civil cases for a while and was bored silly. "There were no surprises, the lawyers were only interested in billable hours, even the juries didn't care who won or lost," he complained. He was back in criminal law in five months.

Not everyone has the constitution to be a prosecutor, but George Williamson thrived on it. He was swift and sure in the courtroom, and it was no problem for him to be up at dawn, reading police reports or writing closing arguments. (Luckily, his new wife understood; Jean was a deputy DA herself.)

So here he was, cracking files and referencing case law, trying to marshal Tim Frawley's relinquished caseload into some kind of order. But reading through the Puente file, Williamson saw a lot of problems with this landmark, nine murder count case. Big problems.

The second set of toxicology reports had been completed, and though he was relieved to see they'd come back clean—no cocaine contamination this time—the reports still made him wince.

That Puente was a smart old bird. By artifice or accident, she'd apparently chosen an almost perfect poison. Early on, reporters had tagged this the "Arsenic and Old Lace Murders." Williamson shrugged; he should be so lucky. Arsenic is an ugly poison that wrenches through the guts, etching its painful history into fingernails, hair, and bones. Even years later, its telltale trace remains unmistakable to anyone trained to look for heavy metals. But Puente hadn't used arsenic, or any other easily traced toxin. Despite exhaustive studies of all the bodies unearthed from her yard, the coroner couldn't determine the cause of death for even one.

He pondered what they'd discovered, and the elements of the crime began to solidify in his mind: the motive, apparently, was money; the

MO was harder, since no one could determine a clear cause of death. But while sifting through the autopsy reports, the whole scenario began to clear. She'd drugged them, he guessed, serving up dinner and drinks laced with hidden ingredients. And she'd probably smiled as she'd done so, smiling her little old lady smile, ambiguous as Mona Lisa's, a mask to her intent. . . . But no one was alive to tell that tale.

Already, Williamson could sense the shape of Puente's defense. He popped out of his chair and paced around his desk. If only Michelle Crowl hadn't retracted her story. He'd read the reports, and to his way of thinking, Crowl had no motive to concoct lies about Puente. She'd only casually mentioned Puente's conversations to a jailhouse deputy, who'd quietly written up a report. But then Clymo and Vlautin had sent that investigator to check out Crowl's story, and he'd leaked Crowl's name to other inmates. The f——ing investigator could have anticipated the consequences: Crowl was instantly branded a "snitch" and threatened. No surprise, she'd recanted.

So what did he have?

The case was essentially circumstantial . . . not necessarily a bad thing, if he could build a strong enough argument. No cause of death . . . no material witnesses . . . except for that 1982 case. What was the woman's name? His finger slid to the bottom of the list: Munroe. Right. The problem case.

He checked his court calendar and found, as he knew he would, that his schedule was jammed as tight as the freeway at rush hour, with other cases demanding his attention before he could concentrate on Puente. He lit a cigarette and wondered how long it would take to wrap up the Yeoman trial.*

This was going to get complicated. Already, Williamson saw the witness list climbing toward three digits—and this was just for the prelim. Even if things moved quickly, he might be able to squeeze in only a month for preparation. He balanced his cigarette on the lip of an overflowing ashtray and began to flip through police reports and list witnesses, puzzling together testimonies so that he could convey his vision in the courtroom. . . .

---

*Williamson would also face off against Peter Vlautin in that death penalty case, slated just prior to Puente's preliminary hearing.

CHAPTER 29

THE DISTRICT ATTORNEY'S OFFICE, THE PUBLIC DEFENDER'S OF-
fice, the courthouse, and the jail all coexist within a small downtown
quadrant. Kitty-corner to the DA's office, the Sacramento County
Courthouse rises six floors above the sidewalk, a ponderous testament
to the "cement block" school of architecture, with its inelegant
"stacked-ice-cube-trays" motif.

Just around the corner from the courthouse, the new $100 million
Sacramento Main Jail dominates a full city block. Its eight-story sil-
houette weighs heavily against the skyline, yet—with the flow of its
curved lines and its dusty pink hue—it resembles a trendy office building more than a jail. Inside, cool marble tiles stretch across the floor,
sunlight filters through generous windows, and potted ficus trees reach
skyward. A huge aquarium tops a partition separating ordinary foot
traffic from jail business, with tropical fish gliding through a serene
$1000-per-month saltwater environment. (All this in a state that would
shortly hand out IOUs to its employees.)

Beyond the guards, beyond the heavy locked doors, the entryway's
airy stylishness falls away, replaced by the cool efficiency of modern

incarceration. Armed deputies carry out their duties, such as finger-printing and photographing the newly booked. Simple concrete hold-ing tanks house those unlucky ones in various stages of being "processed." And tireless video monitors oversee it all.

The sturdy elevator has no buttons to push. An unseen eye watches, a disembodied voice asks "What floor?" and a distant hand makes the selection. Then the elevator hums up to the west tower, seventh floor: the women's division.

As soon as the new jail opened in April, Dorothea Puente was trans-ferred here to be the first and only occupant of cell 10 in the 400 pod. Prior to this, she'd been housed at the aging Rio Consumnes Correctional Center. Now she lived in what could be called—with its well-designed "pods," each with an ample "dayroom" with a television plus an exercise room—a showcase institution.

Not that it was luxurious. Her padded bunk, stainless-steel toilet, and hard floor were standard. But since she was a high-profile inmate in protective custody, the top bunk had been removed: She had the cell to herself. Hers were the only feet pacing the floor. The walls and floor of her cell were a dull yellow. A small faux wood table offered a place to eat or write. Above her bunk, narrow horizontal windows afforded an outside view of other dark, narrow windows—a mirror image across the gap from tower to tower. And a speaker allowed those in the control room to eavesdrop at will.

Those brought here relinquished control over most aspects of their lives—eating, conversing, moving around. Their movements were watched, their contacts limited. Mail was read, contraband was con-fiscated. It was a hard adjustment for those accustomed to being in control.

Dorothea Puente, used to rising early, had little trouble with the 5:00 A.M. breakfast call. But now she wasn't the one who rose first, securing those dawning hours for her exclusive use. She wasn't the one selecting the menu and preparing the meals. She wasn't the one circling appointments, collecting the mail, making the rules.

Rather, three times a day, she exited her cell when the door elec-tronically clicked open, retrieved a tray from the dayroom, and re-turned to her cell for a quiet meal alone (plastic spoons; no forks or knives). And Dorothea Puente—formerly the dispenser of medica-tions—now had pills administered to her daily in disposable paper cups.

Day in and day out, it was the same routine. Hot breakfast at 5:00, cold sandwich at 11:00, hot dinner at 5:00, lights-out at 11:00. It was a monotony that made interruption welcome. The only way to reclaim any sort of control in this sort of environment was to refuse to eat, refuse to take medications, refuse to come out of your cell. Occasionally, that's exactly what Dorothea did.

"She's moody," one blond deputy put it. "She goes through phases."

Overall, Puente was a cooperative inmate. Not very talkative, but not troublesome either. Some of her jail mates found her downright charming—"a wonderful person," as one gushed—and found it hard to imagine that she could be guilty of murder. And, ever helpful, Puente stepped in "like a den mother," counseling the distraught, showing new inmates the ropes, sharing her sweets and supplies.

Within the jail, there was little change during this torpid period of Puente's life.

On one occasion the prosecutor, Puente's nemesis, had sent his emissaries to meet with her in compiling the case against her. These "fraud investigators" had come to take handwriting samples again. And it wasn't as easy as it had been the first time; now they were bossy, telling her to slant her writing this way or that. They took a break for lunch, but for three hours in the morning and another three in the afternoon, she'd courted writer's cramp by scratching out some five hundred signatures.

Other than the defense team, very few were permitted to visit or even correspond with Dorothea Puente. Clymo and Vlautin were keeping a close watch on their celebrity client, who sometimes sat across from them in the secure visitation room, discussing aspects of her case, passing confidential papers through the slot in the glass partition. Outside, others were investing considerable effort into learning about the paths that had brought her here. But locked in her cell, Puente remained an enigma. No public word came from her seventh-story concrete cocoon.

Perhaps her attorneys should have expected the unexpected. Dorothea had a rebellious streak. She didn't like having her actions dictated, her correspondence monitored. She began to complain that she was "too isolated."

No one—not even her own attorneys—could tell her what to do.

It was easy enough for her to place a call from the jail. A phone was available in the dayroom. The deputies in the control room could

A police officer stands guard in front of Puente's boardinghouse shortly
after the first body was discovered.

Investigators using shovels to unearth a body behind Puente's house

Sergeant Bob Burns struggling to explain why the
police let Puente escape

On November 18, 1988, Dorothea Puente is arraigned on one count
of murder.

Picture ID cards for Betty May Palmer
and Dorothea Puente Montalvo, all
with Puente's smiling photograph. The
middle card, dated 10-14-86, was surely
taken after Palmer's death.

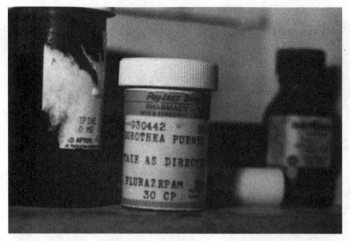

A bottle of the tranquilizer flurazepam, or Dalmane, seized at Puente's home

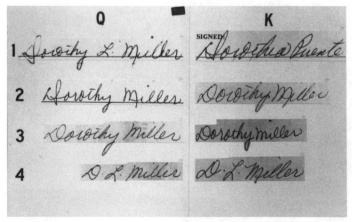

Handwriting samples presented at the trial. "Q" stands for questioned signatures taken from checks; "K" stands for "known" signatures signed by Dorothea Puente.

Bert Montoya, as he appeared in a videotape made by Judy Moise

Benjamin Fink, one Christmas shortly before his death

Dorothy Miller, during
better days

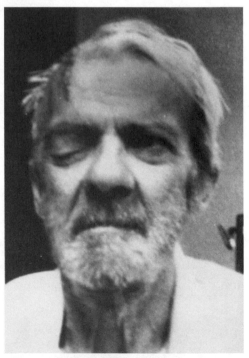

James Gallop, after brain surgery

Vera Faye Martin, who closely resembled this photograph, wasn't identified by a single witness.

Betty Palmer, smiling for the camera

Everson Gillmouth, who had hoped to marry
Dorothea Puente, was found in a box beside the
Sacramento River

Ruth Monroe with her grandson, Jason, in 1972

Judy Moise, who missed Bert and
contacted the police

GEORGE FARDELL

Prosecutor John O'Mara listening intently

CARLA NORTON

Bracketed by her attorneys, Puente sharing a joke with Kevin Clymo

CARLA NORTON

listen in, so there was no guarantee of privacy, but it was a simple matter for any inmate to wait until they were distracted by other duties, then place a collect call.

Did she call an old friend for solace? An ex-husband? A minister? A bartender?

No, she impulsively dialed an acquaintance who was writing a book about her case, Daniel Blackburn.* He was dashing out a manuscript and rushing his book to press. Never mind that Puente hadn't yet been to trial, hadn't even had a preliminary hearing to determine if there would be a trial. With a provisional nod from Kevin Clymo, who had dictated certain constraints, Blackburn had been granted permission to write to Dorothea in jail. Blackburn was no dummy; he'd included a phone number.

Now, with letter in hand, Dorothea secretly sought out a sympathetic ear. When he answered, she quickly established her ground rules: "Promise me you won't tell Kevin that I'm calling."

Headstrong Dorothea, brushing aside her attorney's admonitions, snuck three conversations with Blackburn over a month-long period. For the most part, the calls yielded few surprises, other than that she didn't especially like Peter Vlautin's halting manner of speech, and that she was in need of shampoo. But Dorothea soon revealed ulterior motives for phoning Blackburn.

It bothered her that others, in her perception, stood to make money from *her* story. She felt entitled to cash in on her celebrity, and she wanted Blackburn's help in lining up an entertainment attorney so she could explore marketing opportunities. She'd even given some thought to exact numbers. At one point, she said she wanted 70 or 75 percent of revenues. Another time, she declared that she wanted at least sixty thousand dollars before going to trial, claiming she wanted to make restitution: "It's what I need to pay back. It's what I stole—in the checks, you know."

Of course, Puente wasn't about to endanger her case by admitting to murder. She was willful, but she was no fool. In fact, she steadfastly maintained her innocence, declaring, "I didn't kill anyone. Those people were all my friends. How could anybody believe I'd harm them? I couldn't kill anybody."

---

*This Daniel J. Blackburn is not to be confused with Dan Blackburn, the CNN reporter, or others with the same name.

Later, Dorothea disclosed, "You know, all of those people were legally dead before, before they were, you know, buried. I wouldn't kill anyone."

What was she saying? That she would admit to illegal burial and theft, but that the individuals buried in her yard had all just happened to drop dead?

Blackburn rapidly scribbled notes, but also surreptitiously recorded two of their three conversations, which happens to be illegal in the state of California.

More than a year had passed since her arrest, but those who were getting antsy for Puente's preliminary hearing were disappointed when the February 20 date was also vacated and the prelim pushed back to April 25, 1990.

In the meantime, the institutional food apparently agreed with her. She gained so much weight that Assistant Public Defender Vlautin complained to reporters that she wasn't getting an adequate dose of thyroid medication. (He didn't mention, however, that she shunned the available exercise equipment.)

To relieve the tedium of jailhouse life, Dorothea regularly sat on her bunk with a stubby pencil and applied her nimble imagination to the writing of a manuscript—a Western, rumor had it, like her literature of choice. She wrote for hours, venturing out into the dayroom just long enough to sharpen her pencil. (No pens were allowed.) With her poor spelling and grammar, the finished manuscript was an undistinguished, amateurish attempt, giving Larry McMurtry no cause to worry. Puente's literary talents would bring her neither fame nor glory, but her name meanwhile stimulated the creative talents of others.

Sacramento had its share of clever pranksters: Humorous "calling cards," T-shirts, "gift certificates," and fliers were circulating the city. Most were simply passed hand to hand for a laugh, adding to Puente's notoriety. One flier, for example, advertised "Dorothea's Diner," suggesting that the recipient "dig in to these house favorites," including a menu of head cheese, elbow macaroni, liver and onions, kidney pie, and "cream of esophagus soup."

With the passage of time, one would think that Puente's name would be forgotten. Not so.

Halloween inspired a new round of parody. One shop sent out a black-and-orange flier boldly proclaiming "Horror on F Street" with "Dorothea Costumes." A few shop windows even featured such a costume: a red coat, white wig, pills, and a shovel.

All this doubtless entertained a large segment of the Sacramento populace. But beneath the snickering, there were unhappy grumblings about all this "disgusting, morbid humor."

Puente's defense team was not amused. It wasn't easy having a client who was the butt of jokes, particularly when pledged to the sacrosanct presumption of innocence. On top of this, with the prelim rapidly approaching, Kevin Clymo now learned that Blackburn had tape-recorded phone conversations with his client! Feeling stunned, vexed, and betrayed, he fumed that this was a violation not only of trust, but of the law.

Clymo considered filing charges, but it seemed pointless. This was only a misdemeanor, and besides, it was too late to stop publication. With perfectly awful timing, Blackburn's book was released in Sacramento just before Puente's preliminary hearing. Worse, the book, entitled *Human Harvest,* carried the inflammatory subtitle, "The Sacramento Murder Story." Puente hadn't even been tried yet, much less convicted, and once again her name was publicly linked with murder!

But the defense attorneys weren't just sitting on their hands. They would use this. Early on, Clymo and Vlautin had started keeping records of any public mention of their client, whether in print or on the air, so they could chart her exposure. Now their experts were analyzing all Puente's media coverage, preparing a surprise attack for the preliminary hearing, readying what Clymo termed their "defense arsenal."

Part V

GRAVE ACCUSATIONS

So many ways to die. Many of us do so under suspicious circumstances ... And just because death follows life as surely as ashes a
fire, we nonetheless demand an explanation whenever there is some
doubt as to the cause and manner of its coming.

—CHRISTOPHER JOYCE and ERIC STOVER,
Witnesses from the Grave

CHAPTER 30

In a whirlwind of preparation, George Williamson scrambled to rally witnesses who were dispersed across the country: former tenants, relatives, nurses, doctors, people from all walks of life. Important as this case was, he wouldn't have much time to spend with any of them.

He called Judy Moise in for routine preparation one afternoon to give her the rundown on what to expect in court.

"I'm really nervous," Judy told him. "I've never been on the witness stand before."

He leaned back and waved the notion aside. "Don't be nervous," he said. "You're a hero. Without you, there wouldn't even be a case."

Judy certainly didn't feel like a hero. She clasped her notes in her lap like a schoolgirl, afraid she'd confuse dates or forget something important. She was eager to help but felt that this meeting with Williamson was rushed.

It was. Williamson wished he had more time, but the Yeoman trial had squeezed his preparation time down to less than three weeks. Less than three weeks to organize a case spanning more than six years, a witness list of perhaps 120 people, and nine counts of murder.

For the preliminary hearing (the California equivalent of a grand jury), all he really had to do was prove that there was sufficient evidence to bind Dorothea Puente over to trial. But he knew that this might be his only chance to get some of these people on record. One witness, John Sharp, was due for heart surgery. Several others were aged or infirm. And former tenant Julius "Pat" Kelley had recently died—though not before both sides had rushed to his deathbed to videotape his testimony.

Time was running out.

After a quick review of Judy's testimony, Williamson was steering her out to the elevator. She suddenly realized that, with the preliminary hearing just days away, this was all the preparation she was going to get.

On the clear, cool morning of April 25, 1990, the media converged on the Sacramento courthouse with heady expectations. Sturdy men wearing power packs hefted video cameras; newspaper reporters paced the hall; radio news reporters double-checked tape recorders; television reporters with perfect hair reviewed their notes and bantered with cameramen; sketch artists compared expensive arsenals of pens. Finally, nearly a year and a half after her arrest, after being rescheduled three times, Dorothea Puente's preliminary hearing was about to commence. Now the court would decide whether to bring her to trial for murder. Nine counts. A death penalty case.

Carol Ivy, a San Francisco TV reporter who had been up at dawn to make the long drive to Sacramento, surveyed the scene and declared, "Everyone wants this story."

But if Puente's defense attorneys had their way, the entire preliminary hearing would be a nonevent. Even before the courtroom doors opened, the startling news had spread that the defense had filed a last-minute motion to exclude the press and the public. *A sham*, reporters scoffed, with varying tones of conviction.

When the courtroom finally opened, some of the media crush was vented into the empty jury box, and the bailiff still had to turn away disappointed spectators. The noise level rose and fell in waves of anticipation.

Puente was finally brought in, flanked by her attorneys. She clasped

Kevin Clymo's arm, which lent her an air of frailty. Once she was seated, Peter Vlautin poured her water in the deferential way one might serve an aged aunt. Despite a light touch of make-up, she looked extraordinarily pale. Her skin was milky and smooth, her features fine and even, and her white skirt and sweater made her snowy hair seem even whiter.

Off to one side, Deputy District Attorney George Williamson watched the proceedings coolly. Even physically, he and Kevin Clymo seemed virtual opposites. Williamson was clean-shaven, and had a full head of brown hair which lately he hadn't had time to have cut. Clymo's bald head gleamed within a ring of light brown hair, and he sported a large droopy mustache that earned him comparisons with the wrestler Hulk Hogan. In stature, George "the Bull Dog" Williamson was short and compact; Clymo's towering height was almost intimidating.

The bailiff intoned, "All rise," and Judge Gail D. Ohanesian, a petite woman with cropped dark hair and somber eyes, entered the court. With that, all the players were assembled.

The motion to exclude the press and public was the first order of business. In a bald attempt to catch the media flat-footed, this motion had been filed only the previous afternoon. Two attorneys representing various news media had scrambled to get here, and soon they were scrapping with the defense.

The prosecutor, who had witnesses waiting, listened impassively, his impatience scarcely breaking the surface.

The judge, meanwhile, seemed to be struggling to get a grasp on this unexpected turn of events. She quizzed both sides, yet appeared hesitant to give any response. The media began to buzz with consternation. Wasn't this odd? They'd expected the judge to promptly rule against the motion and get on with it. Maybe she was in over her head, they whispered.

Finally, Judge Ohanesian was persuaded that some of the arguments on this motion should be heard in camera, or in secret. The court was cleared and the doors shut.

Even Williamson was excluded. He came out in the hallway and told his witnesses—including an anxious Judy Moise—to go on home.

The whole of the next day, the attorneys argued behind closed doors. The defense called two expert witnesses who testified, using detailed graphs and charts, that the jury pool had already been polluted by protracted coverage, predicting dire problems with jury selection if coverage continued. (Ironically, these experts on the ill effects of media coverage were hit by the glare of TV cameras whenever they left the sanctity of the courtroom. Even when they went down the hall to the rest room, lights and video cameras followed.)

While arguing the motion to close the proceedings, the defense was fine-tuning an argument for a change of venue. Proving the extensive coverage to date, their exhibits included articles from *Newsweek*, *U.S. News & World Report*, and the *A.A.R.P. Journal*, as well as 252 newspaper articles, 711 broadcasts, Blackburn's premature book on the case, and even a Geraldo Rivera show called "The Murderer Next Door."*

Meanwhile, the press was left to loiter in the halls and debate whether this unpredictable judge might close the proceedings after all. With no other options open to them, resourceful artists took turns peering through the narrow crack between the closed double doors, sketching amazingly accurate renderings that were then dabbed with color in time to make the five o'clock news.

By 1:30 on Friday, Judge Ohanesian had heard all the defense's arguments. She acknowledged that the "nature and extent of coverage in this case has been unique," and that it had been "the talk of the country." But she concluded that an open preliminary hearing would not compromise the defendant's right to a fair trial. The prelim would be open.

The flag was up, and the prosecution would begin the proceedings. As his first witness, Deputy DA George Williamson called Judy Moise.

She entered looking poised, but in truth she had worried about this moment for weeks, reviewing her log and racking her brain in a fret over being correct about dates, times, and sequence. Her nervousness showed in a tendency to overanswer, to explain too much. Guided by Williamson's questions, she explained about her job, about Bert, about meeting Dorothea Puente, about how Bert had flourished while staying at her boardinghouse. She recalled Bert's disappearance, and how Dorothea had repeatedly assured her that Bert was in Mexico, promising his return.

She explained about the strange phone calls from a man claiming

---

*The neighbors of *convicted* murderers, such as John Wayne Gacy, were interviewed in the same program with Puente's; she was the only "murderer" who had *not* been convicted, an example of shoddy journalism.

to be Miguel Obregon, who'd slipped and called himself Don Anthony, and about the letter with the Reno, Nevada, postmark.

When Judy started off on a tangent, Williamson would cut in and put her back on track. He knew just where he wanted to go, and it was his style to focus on his point and move unswervingly toward it: the epitome of "direct examination."

The cross-examination wouldn't be quite so smooth. Clymo clearly wanted to discredit this witness. He attacked her credentials and slighted her job, since she wasn't a licensed social worker. He prodded her about her contract with the motion picture company, implying that she would profit from lying.

Judy hadn't expected this. She felt she was being alternately badgered and then cut off. Her testimony turned rocky.

At one point, Clymo stood just behind Puente and rested his big hands on her shoulders. Judy couldn't avoid making eye contact with the woman. Puente's stare was so unnerving, Judy shivered and looked away, vowing not to look at her again.

She was feeling uneasy and befuddled by the time Clymo got around to some provocative questions about Bert Montoya.

"Were you aware that he was a diabetic?"

Judy looked perplexed. "No."

"Are you aware that he took Micronase?"*

"No."

Clymo was making her seem uninformed. "You knew that he was schizophrenic?"

"Yes."

"Did you ever hear Bert talk to the spirits?"

"Yes," she replied, "he seemed as if he was admonishing them. He'd point to the sky."

"Didn't he tell you that the spirits told him to kill himself?"

Frowning, Judy said, "No." It was dawning on her, as on everyone else in the courtroom, exactly what strategy the defense would take.

It was no surprise that Clymo would argue that some of the victims unearthed at 1426 F Street—particularly oldsters like Palmer and Carpenter—had died of natural causes. But now it seemed that Puente's attorneys might make a case that even Bert Montoya, the youngest

---

*Micronase is an oral antidiabetic drug commonly prescribed for diabetes mellitus.

and arguably the healthiest of those discovered in Puente's yard, had been the victim of deadly disease, even suicide.

The argument began to crystallize: If Williamson couldn't establish the cause of these deaths, how could he prove murder?

By the time she stepped down from the stand on Tuesday, May 1, Judy was feeling wounded. (Clymo had given her such a hard time that he felt compelled to apologize, whispering as she left the stand, "I really don't have anything against you. It's just the way things are done.")

Williamson next called Donald Anthony to the stand.

A little guy in jeans and sneakers entered, and it hardly seemed possible that he could have caused Judy Moise any fearful, sleepless nights, or that his voice had once frightened her right out of her house. He was slight and wiry. Long brown hair spilled around a high forehead—which, his testimony would soon reveal, was no indication of elevated intelligence.

Anthony appeared nonthreatening, but he was no innocent. Williamson quickly established that he was a convicted felon seven times over: drug charges. And Anthony, who professed a genuine fondness for Dorothea, admitted he was on the stand only because he was under subpoena.

In short, lazy sentences, he grudgingly described how he'd met Dorothea Puente: In the interim between prison and freedom, Anthony had been working at a halfway house. "She called work furlough and needed cheap labor, so they called me, 'cuz I needed work." As part of the work crew, he'd dug trenches in four spots around Puente's yard, and had even helped pour cement. The landlady had told him that the trenches were "for pipes," but he admitted under questioning that he never actually saw any pipes.

After leaving the halfway house, Anthony briefly stayed at Puente's boardinghouse. There he did odd jobs and favors for her, including making phone calls to Judy Moise using the name of Miguel Obregon. "I just thought I was doin' it for a good cause," he claimed, "so Bert could stay in Mexico."

To Clymo's consternation, Anthony's testimony did more than just validate Judy's. He revealed that Dorothea had taken him to Reno "to gamble and to mail a letter." Moreover, she'd cautioned him to "have it wrapped in a paper towel so I didn't get fingerprints on it."

Having called only two witnesses, Williamson had shown that Puente had gone to elaborate ends to deceive Judy Moise about Bert's whereabouts, even camouflaging her own involvement. And from a legal standpoint, fabricating evidence is an indication of guilt.

*　　*　　*

Williamson's next witness was one of Puente's former tenants, John Sharp. The hawk-eyed, bony, retired cook looked as if his sixty-five years had not been easy, but his testimony was clear, concise, and articulate. (Scheduled for bypass surgery the next day, Sharp was unperturbed by the prospect of testifying. "I may be dead in a few weeks," he told Williamson. "This doesn't seem like such a big deal.")

Sharp related his strange tale of holes being dug in the yard, of disappearances, of foul odors. And he cast light on Puente's manipulations, including how she'd asked him to lie to the police when they came asking about Bert Montoya's whereabouts.

Anticipating that the defense would make a grand showing of Puente's kindness and generosity, Williamson tried to diffuse their argument by eliciting this testimony himself. Under questioning, Sharp confirmed that Puente had been an attentive care giver, especially concerning Bert Montoya, who, Sharp said, had improved "a thousand percent" while under Puente's care.

Still, when Williamson asked, "Were you afraid of her?" Sharp admitted, "Leery of her, yes."

In cross-examination, Clymo succeeded in getting Sharp to describe Bert as "basically a derelict." And while Sharp maintained that he'd never seen Bert drink, Clymo got him to admit that he "could smell it [alcohol] on him."

With the luxury of an abundance of evidence, testimony can be presented with both artistry and logic—the seeds of motivation, the climate of opportunity, the bedrock of hard fact—until the overall landscape of the crime appears. But Williamson lacked that luxury, and he privately admitted that presenting this care was like "pushing a tiny pebble up a large hill."

His evidence was circumstantial. No one had seen Puente strangling or poisoning tenants. No one had seen her dragging bodies into the yard or covering them with dirt. And there was not a shred of direct evidence—not a fingerprint, not a single strand of hair—linking her with the bodies unearthed from her yard.

So Williamson's approach would be "cumulative." If he had to, he would call a hundred witnesses—from cops to ex-cons, from bureaucrats to bartenders—to make his case against Dorothea Montalvo Puente.

CHAPTER 31

Hardly pausing for breath, asking questions rapid-fire and speaking so quickly that the judge had to call extra breaks so the court reporter could rest, Williamson called a string of experts, including David Moore, the senior document examiner at the Department of Justice. Moore—with the diligence of an entire army of ants—testified on hundreds of signatures (on pension, SSI, tax refund, and Social Security checks). In his expert opinion, they were virtually all signed by Dorothea Puente.

But, as the defense well knew, theft was one thing, murder was another.

Williamson also called deputy coroners, detectives, virtually everyone who'd been involved in the discovery and exhumation of the bodies. That included Detective John Cabrera, who testified about his role in apprehending Puente. (Afterward, he stopped to chat with reporters in the hall, confiding that complicated crimes of this nature "take a lot out of you." This same man who'd volunteered to escort Puente past police lines, who'd even agreed to stir her soup as she fled the scene, boasted—without the least hint of irony—about his

220

investigative instincts. "I had a gut feeling about this case," he declared.)

Next, Williamson advanced on the core of the case: cause of death. Grisly details emerged during the testimonies of the two tall, pale forensic pathologists who'd performed the autopsies. While Williamson displayed gruesome photographs of the bodies, first Dr. Robert Anthony and then Dr. Gary Stuart recited a macabre litany of decomposition and skeletonization. With the utmost thoroughness, the doctors verbally lay bare each individual's bones and organs, citing medical histories, tracing the maps of internal scars.

This dark subject turned illuminating when Williamson focused on the infinitesimal traces of drugs found in the bodies. Starting with the first body unearthed, Leona Carpenter, the court was about to get a crash course in pharmacology.

Dr. Anthony explained that found in Carpenter's brain tissues were traces of three drugs: Dalmane, Valium, and codeine. Of the benzodiazepine class of drugs, Valium (or diazepam) and Dalmane (or flurazepam) are both "sedative hypnotics," or sleeping pills, he said. Codeine is an opiate, a narcotic pain-killer.

A potent combination, obviously. And, the doctor noted, these drugs are "very liquid soluble."

"So they can be put in liquid rather easily—in water or alcohol?" Williamson asked.

"Yes, sir."

Visions of toxic cocktails floated through the courtroom.

Under questioning, the doctor explained the general effects of these drugs: "Sedative, muscle relaxant, hypnotic effect. In large quantities, stupor, coma, difficulties in operating."

"Could a large amount cause death?"

"Yes." Further, these drugs have a "synergistic effect," he explained, meaning the effects are even more powerful in combination, particularly for elderly people. And, he added, when added to alcohol, they can become "highly toxic."

Moving to a deeper level of complexity, Dr. Anthony explained that the sedative known as Dalmane, or the "parent" drug flurazepam, was quickly broken down by the body into metabolites, traces of which might linger in the body for two weeks or more. Since the metabolites were found in the tissues along with the parent drug, the body hadn't had time—probably less than twenty-four hours—to metabolize the drug prior to death. (For example, Leona Carpenter's tissues carried .04 milligrams per kilogram of flurazepam, the parent drug, and .84 and .13 milligrams of two metabolites.*)

As the testimony progressed, it became clear that all seven of the bodies unearthed from the yard had traces of both the parent drug and its metabolites. Damning as all this sounded, Williamson knew that his argument was flawed. He couldn't actually prove that any of these people had been killed with cocktails laced with drugs. Usually, when someone dies from a drug overdose, the autopsy is conducted promptly, and the cause of death is determined by a blood or urine analysis. Sometimes, other bodily fluids, such as bile or fluid from the eye can be tested. Unfortunately, the bodies in this case were so decimated that no bodily fluids remained, and instead, the decomposed tissue samples had been tested.

"The numbers can't be told with any degree of accuracy," Dr. Anthony was saying, because no one knows "when fluids leave the body whether drug levels go up or down."

Were the drugs *retained* in the tissues, thus *elevating* the numbers? Or were the drugs mostly *excreted* from the body with other fluids, thus *lowering* the numbers? And how many milligrams of flurazepam in extremely decomposed remains would indicate a fatal dose?

No one could say. Though these drugs could be identified and measured, no one could authoritatively state whether they were at toxic levels. No scientific tests could provide a scale.

Clymo was ready for this. In cross-examination, he got Dr. Anthony to admit that "because we're dealing with a dehydrated brain, the number is essentially meaningless."

What more could the defense want?

Further, Dr. Anthony said, "No studies have been performed to see where the drugs go when the body decomposes." (In a wry aside that delighted observers, he added, "It's very difficult to get a live patient to give up part of their brain.")

Clymo asked, "If I took five hundred capsules within two hours, my system would shut down?"

"Odds are," the doctor replied, "you would stop breathing, go into cardiac arrest, and die."

---

*See Appendix I, page 399.

"The metabolism stops?"

"Yes, sir."

"So no more of the drug is turned into metabolites?"

"Yes, sir."

"So, if that happened, there would be a very high amount of the parent drug and a very low amount of the metabolites?"

"Yes," the doctor answered. "What you'll see in acute overdose, generally, is a large amount of parent drug and a small amount of metabolites."

More points for the defense. Since these toxicology reports showed the reverse, Clymo had heaped doubt on the theory that Puente's tenants had died of drug overdoses. Underscoring this inconsistency, he went on to establish that someone with liver disease (such as many of these victims had) would metabolize the drug even more slowly.

Clymo pressed on, asking how many thirty-milligram capsules of Dalmane it would take to kill.

"That has not been established," Dr. Anthony admitted.

"Do you have an opinion as to whether or not it would take thousands of capsules?"

"I believe it would take a significant number of capsules to successfully lead to an overdose."

"Hundreds?"

"Yes."

"Maybe even a thousand?"

"Possibly."

Clymo continued, "I believe you testified that flurazepam is soluble in either alcohol or water, correct?"

"Yes, sir."

"The capsules of Dalmane, or generic flurazepam, also contain other material other than the raw drug, don't they?"

"That's correct."

"Well, can you give us an idea of how much powder you would end up with if you dumped out, oh, say, five hundred or a thousand capsules onto a piece of paper?"

"You'd have a significant pile of powder, probably the size of a softball."

Visions of toxic cocktails vanished. Who could possibly ingest such a quantity? (Clymo's colleagues at the public defender's office were so impressed with his gem that they created a "sculpture" of paper wadded up to the size of a softball, then presented it to him as a trophy.)

George Williamson may have inwardly cringed at the doctor's testimony, but this didn't show. The prosecutor, who seemed always in motion, was standing at the side of the courtroom. Typically, he paced, rarely sitting down even during cross-examinations, and he was always fidgeting with pens or paper clips. Intentionally or not, he distracted from Clymo's cross-examination by flipping a pen in the air and catching it.

But Clymo didn't seem to notice. He was busy making the point that such a large amount of powder would be virtually impossible to disguise in a glass of liquid.

Over and over, Clymo emphasized that the cause of death for each case was "undetermined." Then he ran through various possibilities for the cause of each person's death: Could the person have died from heart failure? From liver disease? From high blood pressure? Even, in one case, from syphilis?

Dr. Anthony had to repeatedly admit that there was no evidence that the person either had, or had not.

And so went the testimony of Dr. Gary Stuart, who next took the stand to testify about the rest of the autopsies, his testimony closely paralleling the first forensic pathologist's.

Through the month of May, Williamson called a parade of doctors to the stand to testify about the health of the various victims.

Again and again, Clymo asked the doctors whether it was "unusual" to see a person of this age and condition die a "sudden, unexpected death." And the doctors had to admit that, certainly, "it happens." Indeed, to the intense frustration of the prosecution, there was still no way to prove the cause of eight of the nine deaths.

Meanwhile, Dorothea Puente watched silently, sitting very still, looking remarkably like your grandmother, and not a bit like a serial killer.

Throughout the prelim, Williamson raced through his questions and battered the defense's cross-examinations with objections. Soon he was on to the forensic toxicologists: James Beede, of the coroner's office, and William Phillips, of the Department of Justice. They explained their work and testified about the levels of drugs found in the bodies. But finally, they had to face that vexing yet unavoidable topic: the cocaine contamination.

Cocaine, which is highly unstable and can not conceivably last in human tissues several hours—much less several months—was nonetheless found in Ben Fink's specimens. Yes, it seemed inexplicable. All their precautions, their careful procedures, had somehow been thwarted, and the tissue samples consequently had to be retested.

Clymo gleefully grilled these two witnesses, dragging each through a laborious analysis of the whole process, ostensibly searching for the possible source of contamination, yet hinting broadly at incompetence. The placid judge overruled Williamson's heated objections, and the toxicologists struggled to give cool, professional answers.

Would this prove to be the prosecution's Achilles' heel? During a cigarette break Williamson claimed unconcern, calling the whole cocaine contamination issue "a smoke screen."

In the end, the toxicology reports, while interesting, could hardly be called conclusive. Still, nothing could neutralize the coincidence that *all* of the bodies exhumed from 1426 F Street contained traces of Dalmane. And Dorothea, it turned out, had filled a surprising number of prescriptions for this particular sedative.[*]

Williamson put pharmacists on the stand to testify that, from late 1985 until just before her arrest in November 1988, Dorothea had endlessly refilled Dalmane prescriptions—thirty pills at a time—so that more than a thousand pills had passed through her hands.

Could she have possibly taken all those pills herself?

[*]See Appendix II, page 402.

CHAPTER 32

Ironically, after making a big stink about the extraordinary media coverage, Clymo and Vlautin often lingered to answer reporters' questions, being quoted and enduring bright TV lights, while Williamson's policy was to bolt from the courtroom, giving no comment. Clymo took these opportunities to publicly stress the fact that older people metabolize drugs more slowly, and that some of these tenants had been taking "sleepers" for years. Vlautin meanwhile intoned his misgivings about the "quality of the evidence," and made sure to point out, "We don't have the burden of proof."

Indeed, if you believed that Dorothea was a murderer, it was no great leap to believe that all these people had died by her hand. But if you couldn't make this initial assumption, it was a huge jump from forgery and illegal burial to murder. As Clymo cheerfully pointed out, no one could state under oath exactly what had killed the seven people buried in Puente's yard. Even top forensic scientists using the nation's most advanced technology had failed to produce a single unequivocal link between their deaths and Dorothea Puente.

But George "the Bulldog" Williamson was nothing if not tenacious. He just kept on calling witnesses. And he was about to liven things up.

A rather matronly woman wearing a blue dress entered with a humorous glint in her eyes: Dr. Ruth Lawrence. Presently with the U.C. Davis Medical School, the doctor stated that she'd been practicing at the VA clinic back in 1988.

Williamson asked, "On September 21, 1988, did you see a patient by the name of Dorothy Miller?"

"Yes," she answered, adding that the woman requested thyroid medication, a female hormone, and Dalmane.

September 1988. This was perplexing. Wasn't that about the same time Bert Montoya had disappeared? And hadn't Dorothy Miller's body been "markedly decomposed" when it was discovered in November 1988? How was it possible that she could have been buried *after* Bert?

Williamson continued, "You remember this patient fairly well, don't you?"

"Yes, because it's unusual to get female World War Two veterans."

"And is the woman you treated as Dorothy Miller here today in this courtroom?"

Clymo leapt to his feet in objection, Williamson countered, and they clashed over admissability. But Williamson was allowed to ask again, "Is the person who requested Dalmane and other drugs here in court today?"

"Yes," the doctor replied, and she nodded toward Dorothea Puente. Delight surged through the gallery as she described what the defendant was wearing.

Williamson was going to press this to the hilt. "When this woman came to you as a patient," he asked, "did you observe any scars on her neck?"

"Yes, the result of thyroid surgery."

Williamson asked Dr. Lawrence to approach the defendant to see whether she had such a scar.

The defense was appalled, but with their objections thwarted, the doctor walked over to Puente, gently tugged on her collar, and affirmed, "There's a very fine scar that runs across the lower neck."

It was a shining moment for the prosecution. But if this case went to trial, the defense wouldn't let it happen again.

❖　　❖　　❖

Williamson's "cumulative" approach had gained him some headway, but the defense had punched holes in the testimony of some of his witnesses. And the prosecutor still hadn't tied Puente directly to murder. He was circling, getting closer.

Now Williamson was astonished to learn that Michelle Crowl was ready to talk. At the lunch break, Williamson rushed over to the jail, surprised to see himself scrambling for the testimony of a "snitch." Informers are hardly the best witnesses: Criminals themselves, they're eminently impeachable under cross-examination. But when Williamson weighed risks against potential gains, this one seemed worth it.

Recently released from custody, Crowl had been free to keep her secrets to herself. But now, by the sheerest luck, she'd been rearrested, arraigned earlier in the day for felony drug possession. Her attorney sent word that she wanted to cut a deal: Crowl didn't want to go back to prison, so she would testify against Puente if, in exchange, she got released on probation.

Williamson deemed her testimony important enough to agree. The papers were drawn up, and he hurried back to the courthouse.

Still slightly flushed, he called Michelle Crowl to the stand. She came in wearing a Sacramento County Prisoner T-shirt, yet managing to look more like an ex-cheerleader than an ex-con. With her abundance of curly red hair, she appeared girlish and naïve—a long way from criminal stereotypes—the freshest face and youngest person yet to take the stand.

Williamson quickly established that a deal had been made. The straightforward approach. Then he got Crowl to explain how, as a low-security inmate, she'd had extra freedom to socialize, and sometimes watched television with Dorothea. Williamson asked whether she and Dorothea had watched a newscast about a body that had been found in a box next to the Sacramento River in January 1986.

Crowl confirmed this. "She told me that that was the first body that was killed."

Astonishment buzzed through the courtroom.

Under questioning, Crowl clarified, "She said she killed him, but Mr. Florez helped her." Dorothea was upset, she added, "that Florez was getting a deal."

This had the defense reeling. And this was just the beginning. Crowl said she couldn't help overhearing bits of conversation between Puente and the inmate with the "loud voice" who was housed between them, Paulina Pinson.

What had she heard?

That Dorothea had dispensed meds to her tenants, who were alcoholics. Sometimes she gave them "a little bit extra," not just Dalmane, but also amitriptyline, Crowl said.

"Did she explain why?"

"When she received them into the boarding home, they were already frail. She was the beneficiary of their Social Security checks. They relied on her," Crowl explained. "She was like a mom to them. . . . They trusted her."

"Did she tell you how they died?" Williamson asked.

"She said she'd give them meds with alcohol."

"What did she say about meds and alcohol?"

"She said it suppressed their breathing."

"Do you know what words she used?"

"Yes, 'cuz I never heard it before that: suppressed."

When Williamson asked about Bert Montoya, Crowl said she was positive she'd heard Dorothea tell Paulina that "Bert helped her bury the bodies."

Spectators gasped.

Here it was—too gruesome to be deception—chilling confirmation of Judy Moise's worst fear.

"She said he was retarded and he didn't know any better," Crowl continued, adding that Dorothea had admitted that she'd gotten "a little greedy."

Each word from her little cupid-bow mouth torpedoed the defense. But Williamson knew that any ex-con who recanted her story and then cut a deal was as easy to tear as perforated paper.

During cross-examination, he put up a shield of objections. Still, Clymo pounded away at Crowl's criminal background, slashed her credibility, and accused her of lying one way, then another.

Meanwhile, Vlautin scribbled notes. This witness put an admission of guilt into their client's mouth! But thank God for preliminary hearings. After this preview of the state's case, they'd work damn hard to make sure that nothing Michelle Crowl said would ever reach a jury.

Ex-cons weren't Williamson's first choice as witnesses, but he called two others to the stand. It cut both ways: These were impeachable sources, but since Puente was an ex-con herself, who else would she confide in? Who knew her better than her sisters in crime?

Joan Miller, a thin elderly woman with long stringy hair and a meek look, took the stand to say she'd been an inmate with Puente in Frontera during the mid-eighties. She claimed that Puente had told her that she'd used "over-the-counter medications, like eye drops, Visine, and she'd put it in people's foods . . . as a means of keeping people under control."

Visine? That colorless liquid that gives relief to "itchy, sticky, watery eyes"? Spectators scoffed. Reporters snickered. Even the attorneys seemed amused. During the next break, Peter Vlautin kidded with the press, joking about how much Visine would be needed to drug someone: "Three barrels? A bathtubful?"

Meanwhile, a young AP reporter used her time more wisely. She slipped down the hall and phoned the Poison Control Board . . .

Another ex-con, a slow-speaking, round, untidy woman named Brenda Trujillo, later took the stand. Trujillo, who admitted to being on methadone, said she'd met Puente "in a holding tank downtown in '82." She'd served time off and on until December 1986, and then had been paroled to Puente's boardinghouse.

Williamson asked, "Did you and the defendant have any conversations about the tattoos on your hand?"

She nodded. "She wanted me to go to the hospital and get the tattoos taken off" because they were too easy to ID, Trujillo explained.

"Why?" Williamson wanted to know.

"She wanted me to go to high-class restaurants to drug people and take their money."

Williamson asked what types of drugs Puente had suggested.

Dorothea had told her to put "a couple drops of Visine" in their drinks.

Here it was again.

Moreover, Trujillo added, Dorothea had boasted that "she could get any kind of drugs she wanted" from her psychiatrist, Dr. Doody. "Valium, codeine, Dalmane—all she had to do was pick up the phone."

Slow and unimpressive as Trujillo seemed, this was damning testimony, and Clymo was eager to launch his cross-examination. He shot out of his seat and berated her as a liar and a heroin addict.

Williamson did his best to protect this witness, but she seemed determined to sabotage her own testimony. Her memory was cloudy, her record stained, her answers lethargic—sometimes she even stopped in the middle of a sentence to confess that she forgot what she was saying.

Finally, this witness lumbered out of the courtroom.

During his next cigarette break, Williamson considered her testimony: "The only thing Trujillo has going for her is that she's too stupid to have made any of this up. How could she know that Joan was going to testify to Visine, too? How could she know that Dalmane was going to come up again and again?"

By then, the industrious AP reporter had returned with startling news from the Poison Control Board: Visine's active ingredient, tetrahydrozoline, can induce coma.

CHAPTER 33

Outside, may 15 was a sparkling spring day. inside, reba Nicklous sat in the hallway, weathering that piquant combination of nerves and boredom that is the province of those waiting to be called into court. Since the day Everson had been identified, she'd been steadily pulled toward this encounter, and now the day had arrived. She'd flown down from Oregon to confront the woman who, she was convinced, had killed her older brother.

Reba had never met Dorothea Puente before, but over time her belief that Puente was responsible for Everson's disappearance had congealed and hardened. She'd worn the idea smooth with years of reexamination, turning it over and over like worry beads, until now it had been polished to a lapidary certainty. Dorothea had killed him and put him in that box. It was true. She knew it.

Reba sighed, remembering Everson's kind, round face. He'd been too softhearted, she thought. He had courted disaster when he courted Dorothea Puente.

The bailiff came out and called Reba Nicklous to the stand. She entered the court and all eyes watched as she strode toward the witness stand. Despite her frosty hair, there was a sturdiness about her that defied those who might try to guess her age.

Her long face showed determination as Williamson guided her through the foundation of her testimony. In a strong, full voice, she told the court how her older brother, Everson Gillmouth, had left Baltimore after his wife's death and had come to settle in Oregon. For a few years, he had lived quietly with Reba and her husband, crafting elaborate wood carvings to fill his time.

Then, in the fall of 1985, he'd driven his red Ford truck down to California to meet Dorothea Puente, whom he planned to marry. When time passed and she hadn't heard from her brother, Reba grew concerned and contacted the Sacramento police, who went to Dorothea's house to check on him. Soon, her chagrined brother called and apologized for not having kept in touch. "That was the last time I heard his voice," she said, looking accusingly at Dorothea.

In mid-October 1985, Reba Nicklous received a handwritten letter from Dorothea, which Williamson entered into evidence. It was just a short, cheery note, with nothing particularly odd other than the line: "Said he did not want you to have the police out again."

It ended: "I'll try & drop you a line every couple weeks. We might get married in November."

If this seemed peculiar, the next letter, which arrived a couple of weeks later, was even more so. This longer, chattier letter brought the surprising news that the couple was planning "to go to Palm Springs next month so he can sell most of his carvings."

Shortly thereafter, Reba and her husband had received a strange telegram. Reba recalled that it said "that he was leaving Dorothea Puente and going south. And not to try to stop him."

"Was it ostensibly from your brother?" Williamson asked.

"I don't believe it was," she replied.

"Objection!" Clymo shot out. "Speculation."

Reba Nicklous glared at the defense attorney and shot back, "I *know* it wasn't."

Williamson's brisk questions continued, and Reba Nicklous explained that the family hadn't received any further word about her brother until April 1986. Then came a suspicious card from Sacramento, bringing a woman named "Irene" into the picture. On the outside, the card said "Thinking of You."

Spectators in the court leaned forward, quietly straining to catch every detail as Reba Nicklous opened the card and read its strange contents. Suddenly, Everson and "Irene" from Tulsa were planning a move to Canada. And Everson, who was quite dead in April 1986, had "lost about fifteen pounds and feels much better." The writer also assured them: "We go to church each week."

Though they had no idea what had happened to Everson, this card left the family feeling unnerved. It was signed Irene, but they suspected that it, too, had been written by Dorothea Puente. Not knowing what else to do, they'd called everyone named Puente in the Sacramento phone directory, but none professed to know anything. Then they called the police. A cop reportedly stopped by 1426 F Street, but later he phoned Reba to state that Dorothea Puente, whom he guessed to be about Everson's age, "looked innocent."

(Reba later scoffed: "How can you say that anybody *looks* innocent?")

Clymo sped through cross-examination and quickly got Reba Nicklous off the stand. She was crusty, difficult to impeach, highly sympathetic, and therefore truly dangerous to his client.

With her testimony, Williamson had established a pattern of criminal behavior. There were no jurors' faces to scrutinize for some hint of recognition (only the judge, who revealed nothing), but surely it was obvious: When Everson had disappeared and Puente wanted to cover her tracks, she'd sent a letter. And when Bert had disappeared years later, she'd done the same thing.

Those cheerful, clumsy letters. It had seemed to work the first time, so she'd just repeated the same old cover-up. Only now her attempt at cleverness had backfired.

Focusing on the discovery and identification of Everson Gillmouth's body, Williamson called several more witnesses. Then, almost as punctuation to their testimonies, he called Ismael Florez.

Puente sat placidly, but her stomach must have flopped when she saw her old friend enter the courtroom, his own attorney in tow.

Williamson started with the unassailable fact that Florez had possessed a red pickup truck that had once belonged to the deceased Everson Gillmouth. How had that happened?

In a soft voice, Florez explained that, late in 1985, he'd done some work for Dorothea, and the truck had been figured into his payment.

What sort of work?

Mostly paneling, he claimed.

"In addition to the paneling, did she ask you to build something else?"

"A storage box." It was about six feet by three feet, he said. "She told me the measurements."

In simple language, Florez, who didn't seem terribly bright, described how they'd gone together to buy the lumber. Then he'd constructed the box right in her living room, leaving the lid off, lying on the floor, he said.

"When was the next time you saw the box?"

"Three or four days later. Only now it was in the kitchen," he claimed. "And the lid was nailed on."

Dorothea asked him to take it to storage, he said, and he and another man used a dolly to load the heavy box into the pick-up. Then Dorothea had climbed in next to him, and he drove while she pointed directions. Finally, they'd ended up out of town, out by the river.

This would do, she'd told him.

He'd unloaded the box, rolling the dolly down the riverbank. "We left it near the river," he concluded. "She said it was just junk inside."

"Do you remember when this was?" Williamson asked.

"December. Before Christmas."

"Did you notice a smell?"

"No."

As soon as Williamson uttered "No further questions," Clymo was out of his seat and in front of the witness, pounding the point that he'd been granted immunity for his testimony, insinuating that he'd been offered a deal for his lies.

"Was it your decision to put two-by-fours in the bottom?"

"Yes."

"And it's reinforced?"

"Yes."

"With reinforced corners?"

"Yes."

"But you didn't know what would go in it?" Clymo exclaimed incredulously.

"No."

"Didn't Dorothea tell you that a man had had a heart attack and she needed it strong so she could put him in it?"

"I don't remember that."

A heart attack? Eyebrows went up around the courtroom.

Clymo hammered on, "You don't remember *what* she told you, do you?"

"I don't remember."

Clymo handed Florez a transcript of a detective's interview with him and asked him to read it. Slowly, painfully slowly, Florez read through, then looked up and said, "Yeah, I told that."

"Was that true?" Clymo demanded.

"No."

"You lied to him?"

He nodded, saying, "He lied to me, too."

"How was that?"

"He told me I wasn't gonna be arrested."

Either Ismael Florez was stupendously gullible, or he had a wide venal streak. In either case, this obtuse little man was no innocent. Clymo had amply suggested that he'd not only known about the body, but it had been his idea to build a very strong coffin.

Why wasn't he—or *anyone*—being charged as an accomplice?

CHAPTER 34

WILLIAMSON HAD SKETCHED THE ESSENTIALS OF EIGHT MURders. Count nine remained. The troublesome one. For both sides, this count was pivotal. Ruth Munroe, as the only victim autopsied at the time of death, could shed critical light on the manner in which the others had died.

Forensic pathologist Gwen Hall, the doctor who had performed the autopsy on April 28, 1982, testified to the fatal levels of codeine and acetaminophen (or Tylenol) in Munroe's system. Initially, her death was deemed a suicide, then reclassified as "undetermined."

Dr. Hall went on to describe a curious "green, minty substance" in Munroe's stomach. This seemed rather innocuous in itself, but an ominous tie to murder was pending.

While these legal proceedings unfolded inside, two men and a pretty blonde waited in the hall with shallow breathing and wet palms. Named Clausen from her first marriage, they were Ruth Munroe's children. A decade had passed since their mother breathed her last breath, but being here brought them fresh pain. They achingly realized that she could be alive today—playing with her grandchildren—if it weren't for Dorothea Puente!

The prosecutor called them one by one. And after the impartial testimonies of bureaucrats and experts, these flesh-and-blood relatives electrified the court.

Tall, wholesome, and good-looking, Allan Clausen took the stand, and Williamson led him through recollections of moving his mother into Dorothea Puente's F Street house on April 11, Easter Sunday, 1982. At that time, he said, his mother was strong and in good health.

They were a close family, and his mother, who was "spiritual" and "had the fear of God" did not believe in suicide, he said. "My mother always told me, if a person committed suicide, it would only hurt the family."

The prosecutor asked if she had been allergic to any medicines.

"Codeine and penicillin," came the answer, which would echo throughout the day.

When Williamson had no further questions, the court turned to the defense. But Clymo and Vlautin knew that Munroe's children were not the ones to attack. They had another strategy. Clymo said the witness was excused, subject to recall.

Next came William Clausen, the shorter, stockier older brother. He described Ruth Munroe as a loving grandmother who doted on her grandchildren. When she'd moved into Dorothea's house, he stated flatly, she was "healthy as a horse."

Then her health had quickly deteriorated. When William stopped by the house to see his mother about four days before she died, he said, "She looked nervous. She had a drink in her hand, which was out of character. She said Dorothea had given her a crème de menthe to calm her nerves." He shot Dorothea Puente a look of pure loathing, and everyone in court recalled the "green, minty substance" found in Munroe's stomach.

Williamson asked about the night before Munroe's death, and William Clausen spoke with a new edge to his voice. When he'd arrived, his mother was in bed, and Dorothea told him that the doctor, who had just left, had given her a shot. "The door was closed and she didn't want me to go in there." (He shot Dorothea another look.)

"Did you go into the room to see your mother?"

"Yes," he said tensely. He found his mother motionless, unable to speak. "Mom was lying there on her side, facing the wall. Her eyes were open, and I saw a tear come out of her eye."

The courtroom was utterly still, intent.

"I told her, 'It's okay. Dorothea will take care of you.' "

He swallowed, then bitterly explained that Dorothea Puente had told the family that she was a nurse. She'd asked Munroe's children to trust her, "to accept her in, like a grandmother."

Having established Dorothea Puente's duplicity, Williamson turned to the question of suicide.

"There's no way!" William snorted. "If she was gonna commit suicide, it would have been when my father died. She had to raise five kids by herself!"

On that note, Williamson ended his direct examination. Again, the defense waived cross-examination, reserving the right to recall the witness.

Next came Ruth Munroe's daughter, a lovely young woman named Rosemary Gibson, whose voice cracked with emotion from her very first words.

Williamson asked if she had a lot of contact with her mother.

"Very much so," she said. "We were very close." She described her mother as "overweight, but healthy."

"Did you see a change in her health?"

"Yes."

"When?"

"In the last week," she said, with tears in her eyes, "in the last three or four or five days."

"Did you see her with liquor?"

"I didn't."

"Was your mother a drinker?"

"No, she wasn't a drinker."

Munroe's daughter said she'd seen her mother the night before she died.

"Why didn't you call a doctor?" Williamson asked softly.

"Dorothea said she'd taken her to UC Davis, to emergency. She said that Mom was all stressed out, that they gave her a shot, and to leave her alone." Voice wavering, she went on, "Dorothea said, 'She's okay, I can take care of her, don't worry about it.'"

In obvious distress, Rosemary described going into her mother's room to check on her that last night, not realizing that she was on her deathbed. She'd found her mother "sleeping real heavy," which was unusual. She hadn't woken up.

Again, Clymo reserved the right to recall the witness, and Rosemary Gibson bolted from the courtroom.

Her family was waiting in the hall. So was the media. With tears in her eyes, she urged her brothers to hurry away from all the questions, and the family fled the courthouse.

The court promptly moved into closed session, the judge ordering the press and public expelled and the doors closed.

Ruth Munroe's family had brought the hearing to a dramatic peak, and for the defense, this was dangerous testimony, the sort that would make jurors weep. If the other eight counts were the rope with which to hang their client, count nine was the noose.

Acting on that old axiom that the best defense is a good offense, they launched their attack, arguing that count nine should be dropped.

And unfortunately, the court records allowed ample room for debate.

In May 1982, shortly after Munroe's death, Dorothea Puente had been arrested and held in the county jail. But her case never came to trial, because the deputy DA handling the case offered a plea bargain: In exchange for her plea of guilty to four felony counts, two counts were dropped, and a possible homicide dismissed. Puente snapped it up, and all investigation into the suspicious death ceased. But the records referred to the alleged homicide victim only as Puente's "friend and acquaintance." Missing from the records was any specific *name*.

It was outrageous but true.

Now this omission allowed Clymo and Vlautin to contend that the individual in question was Ruth Munroe. Their client could not be charged with Munroe's murder, they said, since the matter had been resolved in 1982!

Impossible, Williamson countered. The victim in question was a woman by the name of Esther Busby.* It couldn't have been Munroe, he said, because it wasn't until August that the DA's office had been alerted to the possibility that Munroe had been murdered, shortly after Puente had been sentenced, and *a month after the plea bargain*.

Judge Ohanesian listened to both sides, pondering the legal boundaries. Finally, she made a limited ruling, and the next day the doors were opened again.

With marked brevity, Williamson elicited testimony from former

---

*Esther Busby had been drugged and robbed by her "nurse's aide," Dorothea Montalvo, in 1981. There was little evidence connecting her later death to Puente.

Deputy DA William Wood, who had prosecuted Puente in 1982 and had arranged the controversial plea bargain. Wood had his testimony limited to the barest essentials, mostly case numbers and dates.

With that, Williamson felt he'd given it his best. There was no jury, no real reason to posture or elaborate; the judge knew the issues. The prosecution rested.

While the state was required to make its case, the defense had no such burden. Why tip their hand? The preliminary hearing allowed them to explore the state's case, to listen to the witnesses, find their weaknesses, and prepare for the battle that mattered: the trial. They weren't required to call a single witness, but the defense attorneys felt they had something to gain and little to lose.

First, with a handful of witnesses, they expunged the character of Brenda Trujillo . . . not a difficult task, considering her reputation as a liar and a drug addict.

Then, to counter the testimony of Michelle Crowl, they called Paulina Pinson, the jail mate to whom Dorothea Puente had allegedly confessed her crimes. Pinson spat out her contempt for Crowl, declaring that she'd never heard Puente utter any of the damning things Crowl had claimed.

(What would a jury think? "My ex-con is better than your ex-con?")

This was low-caliber fire; the real fight was still over count nine, which was too dangerous to ignore. The defense attorneys feared that Munroe's autopsy, coupled with the emotional testimonies of her children, might topple the other eight counts like dominoes.

They put former Deputy DA William Wood back on the stand, and Vlautin grilled him about the 1982 plea bargain. He essentially accused Wood of deliberately concealing the identity of the alleged homicide victim, even of purposely omitting the name when the plea was written up.

Williamson barked objections, but Wood had to stand up to these accusations. Seeming to brace himself in the witness box, Wood vehemently denied that Munroe had been named as the homicide. This was simply impossible, he declared, since Munroe's children had contacted him *after* the plea bargain, after seeing Puente's sentence written up in the newspaper. Wood even supplied dated memos to back him up.

Vlautin insinuated that Wood had fabricated these memos after the fact. To Wood, who'd spent plenty of time in court but didn't much care for being a witness, this was a slap in the face. By the time he stepped off the stand, he was red and fuming.

Yet Vlautin was still calm and controlled. And with his next witness, Puente's unimpressive defense attorney from 1982, Dennis Porter, he would try another approach.

Waving the 1982 file before him, Vlautin quizzed Dorothea's former attorney about what was in it. Like Wood, a writer, Porter had long since abandoned the confounding legal profession and had gone on to other business. Now, seeming positive about whatever it was he'd agreed to back in 1982, Porter gamely testified that the alleged homicide was Ruth Munroe.

Williamson exploded, snatching the file out of Vlautin's hand and beseeching the judge to read it herself. He knew Munroe's name was nowhere in Porter's file, and he blew up at Vlautin, whom he accused of unethically misleading his own witness.

All this heat and noise over count nine boiled down to fundamentally different beliefs. Williamson, a man attuned to fine legal distinctions and trained to avoid even a whisper of unethical conduct, was outraged that Vlautin had put Porter on the stand and, in his view, knowingly allowed him to give false testimony. "They'd pull my ticket [license] if I pulled that kind of thing," he growled.

But to the defense, it seemed the prosecutor had climbed up on his high horse for some unnecessary posturing. This was essential to their argument: Porter had failed to competently represent the plea bargain to his client. Even if the alleged homicide hadn't been Munroe, the other name, Esther Busby, hadn't penetrated Porter's brain, much less his file. So Dorothea Puente had *understood* that the deceased "friend and acquaintance" in question was Ruth Munroe, and to try her now for Munroe's murder was in violation of the 1982 plea bargain.

(Later, Williamson reluctantly gave them the benefit of the doubt, grumbling, "Maybe they don't see it as black-and-white as I do.")

For the rest of the prelim, the hostility between the attorneys hung in the air like a noxious vapor.

In a last-ditch effort to undermine count nine, the defense brusquely cross-examined Ruth Munroe's children, trying to shake their stories, particularly regarding timing. Indeed, each of them remembered the sequence of events a little differently. But the common theme was the newspaper article: After reading about Puente's sentencing, they'd talked to Wood.

And if there were minor discrepancies in their stories, didn't this only strengthen their credibility? If they had been coached, or had concocted a story, wouldn't they have ironed out differences?

But the defense wouldn't give up so easily. Just prior to summations, they again zeroed in on count nine to try to have it stricken. Vlautin launched the attack, quoting case law. Williamson rebutted him, point by point, and the courtroom air crackled with accusations.

Judge Ohanesian, who seemed to weigh everything as carefully as an anoretic on a Weight Watchers diet, finally ruled, "I'm satisfied that the death of Ruth Munroe was not part of the plea bargain."

In the back of the courtroom, William Clausen stage-whispered, "All right!"

George Williamson had submitted his summation in writing. He would stand by that.

Then Peter Vlautin rose to argue that, despite two months of testimony by some eighty witnesses, there was still no proof that any of these people had been murdered and "no reasonable inference of criminal agency." Case by case, he argued that each of these individuals had been chronically ill. He protested that various people's testimonies were "unreliable, incredulous." He accused the DA of having to stretch to make a case against his client. In conclusion, he asked the court to find insufficient evidence to bind his client over to trial.

After a short recess, Judge Ohanesian, who had exasperated everyone with her indecisive waffling over the past two months, resumed the bench and gave her final ruling. On June 19, 1990, she told the packed courtroom, "In this case I do find that there is ample evidence by reasonable inference to all nine counts." Dorothea Montalvo Puente would be tried on nine counts of murder.

Afterward, William Clausen was swept up in the spirit of relief and celebration. When the television cameras turned toward him, he stated that he had faith in Deputy DA Williamson, adding, "I believe we'll see justice done."

Clausen's wife later turned to Williamson and smirked. "Can I watch her fry?"

CHAPTER 35

PUENTE WAS IN JAIL AWAITING TRIAL, AND THE WELL-OILED wheels of justice should have been rolling along smoothly. But now came the wrench.

Blessed with brains and talent, Williamson had done a sterling job on Puente's preliminary hearing, even with precious little time to prepare. But though he may have seemed like the Golden Boy in the DA's office, he didn't see eye to eye with the new district attorney. "The killer for me," Williamson grumbled, "was when he waltzed the press into my office."

Williamson was a prosecutor who rarely gave interviews, and he zealously avoided the unwholesome practice of "trying a case in the media." District Attorney Steve White should have understood this. But one day the new DA unexpectedly came through the door of Williamson's office, reporters at his elbow. The press wanted a statement, White announced. They wanted to see the Puente file.

Williamson looked up, astounded, then jumped up out of his chair. He pulled a fat binder off his shelf, slapped it down on his desk, barked, "There it is," then bolted from the room, leaving them with mouths agape.

That may have been the beginning of the end.

Perhaps the rumblings of resentment toward the district attorney compelled him to make a move.* Or perhaps Williamson was simply too good to languish for long without a promotion. In any case, when the attorney general's office offered George Williamson a position as assistant chief deputy early in 1991, he snapped it up. (He was so eager to get started that he took up his new post just a few days after fracturing four vertebrae in a skiing accident. Never mind that his mobility was so limited that his wife had to tie his shoes.)

Now that Williamson had left the DA's office, the Puente case was in danger of slipping back into legal limbo. How long would this case languish before being brought to trial?

Maybe John O'Mara figured that after losing two prosecutors—first Tim Frawley and now George Williamson—he really had only one option: just go ahead and try the damn case himself.

It seemed natural enough. O'Mara and Williamson had been trying the toughest cases. And as head of major crimes, Assistant Chief Deputy John O'Mara had handled the case while Puente was on the run. But while O'Mara was bright, experienced, and well-respected, his caseload was approaching overload.

Lately, it seemed that nearly every high-profile case ended up on O'Mara's calender. Before Puente, Sacramento's most notorious murder case was the *People* v. *Morris Solomon,* and O'Mara was not only handling this seven murder count death penalty case, but also a host of other major cases. In fact, he was prosecuting so many of Sacramento's biggest cases that others in the office began to secretly grouse that he was becoming "a glory hound."

John O'Mara was a quick study, but at the very least, he was stretching himself awfully thin. "I'd be worried," he admitted, "except that George handled the prelim."

The news that George Williamson wouldn't be prosecuting Puente left Ruth Munroe's children feeling stung. William Clausen, in particular, felt victimized by the assembly-line judicial process, betrayed by the attorneys who had invited his confidence and then abandoned the case, passing his mother's file along to the next guy.

---

*Discontent in the DA's office reached such a pitch that *California Lawyer* magazine carried a February 1992 article entitled "The Trials of Steve White."

And he felt fresh aggravation over the botched investigation of 1982. Why hadn't Puente been tried for their mother's murder back then? They'd put their faith in Deputy DA William Wood, coming to him for justice. But Wood, who'd just finished prosecuting Puente on other charges and was wrapping up so he could leave the DA's office and start a writing career, wrote a few memos, passed the case along, and disappeared.

The investigation went nowhere, and it's clear that somebody dropped the ball. With bitterness, Bill Clausen grumbled, "I feel that the DA's office just didn't want to do anything."

Meanwhile, the change in prosecutors gave the defense team reason to grin. As Clymo saw it, O'Mara would be "less combative" than Williamson. Better yet, while they'd had more than two years to map strategy and gather information, the overburdened Mr. O'Mara was starting from scratch.

The legal machinery moves to its own rhythms—at times gliding with a sleek and awful beauty, at others, as slow and creaky as worn brakes. The Puente case, plagued with problems, would be an example of jurisprudence at its most sluggish. Delays and false starts would be its hallmark.

Puente's trial date was slated for March 13, 1991 . . . then rescheduled to June 15, 1991 . . . then Clymo was suggesting October or November as more realistic. And when O'Mara mentioned to Vlautin that they should try to finish pretrial motions before Christmas, Vlautin blinked at him and said, "How about starting everything *after* Christmas?" So it seemed Puente's trial might start early in 1992, more than three years after her arrest. Indeed, the case was rescheduled for January 15, 1992. But even that late date would prove overly optimistic.

One delay came as no surprise: a change of venue hearing.

On February 3, 1992, Clymo and Vlautin began a carefully choreographed presentation of charts and diagrams showing that Dorothea Puente's name and visage had never fully disappeared from the public eye. National coverage may have waned from time to time, but the local media's appetite for Dorothea Puente stories was never sated. She would never get a fair trial here, the defense said.

Beyond the normal helping of news, a good deal of peculiar humor had percolated through Sacramento, further contaminating the jury pool. To back their argument, they presented the humorous handbills and fliers they'd collected. Several blowups were submitted as evidence, including one large display of a widely circulated "gift certificate" touting "Dorothea Puente's Bed and Breakfast":

Come be our guest for an indefinite stay in one of
our luxury suites. (Social Security welcome.)
Everlasting tours of the beautiful gardens by
special arrangement. (Complimentary drinks!)
House sleeps 4; yard sleeps 7.

Peter Vlautin also presented a popular T-shirt showing Dorothea Puente standing with a pocketful of pills and a shovel (a takeoff on the famous painting, *American Gothic*), with body parts sticking out of the ground behind her, and "Sacramento: I Dig It" emblazoned across the front.

For much of the week-long hearing, the defense team relied on two expert witnesses (Edward Bronson, a California State University professor of public law, and Dr. Linda Meza, a litigation consultant), who provided persuasive testimony that Dorothea Montalvo Puente could not get a fair trial in Sacramento County. According to their surveys, for example, *98 percent* of the population in Sacramento County had heard of Dorothea Puente, and of those, over 75 percent believed she was guilty!

In his heart, John O'Mara was resigned to the judge granting a change of venue. He managed to shoot a few holes in his opponents' case, but in the end their evidence was overwhelming. The judge ruled that Dorothea Puente should be tried out of county.

Another delay.

The trial could be sent anywhere in the state, north or south. The problem would be finding a county able to accommodate such a mammoth trial. It would be a burden, tying up a courtroom for months, jamming up the local court calendar with an out-of-county headache.

"Nobody wants it," O'Mara admitted with a shrug.

Meanwhile, time seemed to be on Dorothea's side. For the defense, waiving Puente's right to a speedy trial may have been a strategical ace. With each delay, vigor was slowly drip, drip, dripping out of the prosecution's case like an old, leaky faucet. And with each passing year, their client had grown more sympathetic: older, paler, more grandmotherly. Serial killers were supposed to have tattoos and heavy beards; Dorothea Puente looked about as menacing as a slow-moving, fat old cat.

Boxes of files and binders of reports jammed the shelves climbing all four walls of John O'Mara's office, which wasn't any larger than others on the fourth floor of the DA's office, despite his title: Assistant Chief Deputy District Attorney, Major Crimes Division Supervisor. Sitting in the midst of this, O'Mara calmly sifted through piles of documents. His desk seemed a tiny island of calm, threatened by towering waves of white paper poised to crash down with horrific tales of murder and mayhem.

He was a paradox. Leaning back in his chair for a moment, O'Mara might look relaxed—in a snapshot, he might even appear serene or merry—yet he ran on nervous energy, fueled by the coffee that he gulped continuously from dawn till nearly midnight. He could be brusque and abrasive, bulldozing through ideas nonstop, words blasting out of him in the habit of courtroom oratory; or he could be wryly funny, turning his quick wit to the stress-releasing antics that often commenced at the end of the working day, dubbed the "four o'clock follies."

Irish Catholic and a dedicated family man, John O'Mara was intensely private about his personal life. He kept his office bare of any framed pictures of his family: his wife of twenty-two years, Pat, and their children, Molly, sixteen, and Conner, eleven. He strove to keep his personal and professional lives separate, preferring to arrive at the office at 5:00 A.M. rather than work late and miss his family's daily dramas. Still, while tending chores on his five-acre property, his profession would intrude. "That's when I have my best ideas," he said. "Things come to me when I'm shaving or mowing the lawn."

In the office, wearing natty suspenders with a conservative suit, O'Mara was hard to picture in a pastoral setting. He claimed that he had "never intended to be a prosecutor, never wanted to be a lawyer," yet he'd landed in the Sacramento DA's office in 1973, and had been prosecuting homicides almost ever since.

The secret to O'Mara's success as a prosecutor was his ability to single-mindedly obsess about a case. Problem was, while Kevin Clymo and Peter Vlautin had been studying Puente's case since day one, O'Mara was now utterly immersed in another murder trial, that of Morris Solomon.

Maybe it hadn't been the best idea for him to handle both Solomon and Puente himself. Even O'Mara conceded, "The fire that's about to burn you is the one you work on." And while the Solomon trial was scorching his heels, the Puente files lay cold. He had yet to do even a thorough review of the record. And it showed. Bottom line, whenever O'Mara was asked about Puente, he instead ended up answering about Solomon.

There were similarities, sure. Serial killer. Multiple buried bodies. Complex forensic studies. And except that he was African American, Morris Solomon fit fairly snugly into the serial killer profile, with his history of violence, with his victims being mostly prostitutes who hazarded across his path, and with the simple facts of his age and gender. Dorothea Puente was a whole 'nother animal.

(But both defendants were equally affected by the events of April 21, 1992. For the first time in twenty-five years, after a frantic volley of last-minute appeals, San Quentin's gas chamber was readied and California carried out a state-run execution. For a quarter of a century, California's death penalty had been given in name only. That changed as lethal cyanide fumes reached the nostrils of Robert Alton Harris. And every prisoner on death row, every defendant facing murder charges, felt the seismic jolt of California's legal apparatus. The road to San Quentin had just gotten shorter.)

It was hard not to see Solomon's death penalty trial as a dress rehearsal for Puente's, because opposing counsels in the Solomon case were both Puente's prosecutor, John O'Mara, and her defense attorney, Peter Vlautin.

A months-long trial eventually convicted Solomon on six of seven murder counts, but then the jury slammed all expectations: They were hung on the penalty phase.* This could mean a sentence of life without parole by default, but the DA's office deemed this case too big to let slip to a lesser sentence. The penalty phase would have to be retried, which put an ugly knot in the court calendar. Puente's trial was delayed again.

In the meantime, John O'Mara's amusing, satirical side vanished beneath a load of worry. What if the second jury was hung too? As

---

*In California, serious murder trials may have two phases. The first phase is to determine guilt or innocence. If the defendant is convicted, a second phase decides whether the sentence will be life without parole (L-WOP, in the vernacular) or death.

the retrial wound toward completion, he grew edgy and snappish. One colleague muttered, "It's like he has PMS."

On July 6, 1992, the second jury weighing the fate of Morris Solomon sentenced Solomon to death. Though the trial was finally over, this raised a vexing question: Could Puente's trial, too, end in a hung jury? After all, big mean Morris Solomon was a much scarier defendant than little old Grandma Puente.

Beyond trying to prove Dorothea Puente innocent, Clymo and Vlautin were also trying to limit the ways in which she might be found guilty, to shave off bits here and there. Their tool for this task? Pretrial motions.

The list was long and the files were thick. Two dozen motions were developed, word-processed, photocopied, and added to the fray. In every way imaginable, Clymo and Vlautin implored the judge to restrict the ways in which Dorothea Puente could be found guilty.

O'Mara scoured each motion for hints, trying to anticipate tactics. He felt handicapped by his embryonic understanding of the case. They'd had four years to investigate and refine, yet O'Mara was only beginning to dredge the files for nuggets of insight. They knew more about his case than he did.

In mid-September, Judge Michael J. Virga heard motions to strike, motions to dismiss, and motions to exclude. Some O'Mara conceded without a fight, others he railed against. The judge granted some, but denied most.

The defense also presented material for a questionnaire to be used in screening potential jurors. Reviewing this, O'Mara drew the conclusion that the defense would argue that Dorothea Puente was a victim of child abuse.

Psychology was not his strong suit.

Even at this late date, the prosecutor knew very little about the defendant he was trying to put to death. He was still so green to this case that he accepted the probation reports as gospel, even swallowing Puente's unlikely version of her history (that she was Mexican, the youngest of eighteen children, and so on).

One morning during these proceedings, O'Mara was confused when he overheard Clymo and Vlautin talking about "Dot." He finally broke in, "Who's Dot?"

Clymo grinned at him. "Dottie. Dorothea."

DISTURBED GROUND

❖   ❖   ❖

With just over a month until jury selection, John O'Mara was finally focusing his considerable mental wattage on the trial of Dorothea Montalvo Puente. He spoke with witnesses for the very first time, including Judy Moise, who wasn't thrilled to have this ghastly business haunting her again. So much time had passed, she'd begun to feel content with letting her memory fade.

To O'Mara's surprise, Ruth Munroe's children came in "with an attitude." He bristled at how they edged in to "audition" him, "to see if I was good enough to handle the case." He couldn't understand why the family hadn't bothered to come in before.

To his dismay, O'Mara now found dozens upon dozens of angles that needed to be followed up, yet the files had been lying fallow for all these years. And no one in the police department was eager to roll up his sleeves now. So O'Mara cranked up his own investigation, wearing the soles off the shoes of John Dacre and Frank Dale, criminal investigators with the DA's Office.

"The defense has more money to spend," O'Mara groused. "And they do spend it. Lavishly. We don't have the resources."

The years had eaten away at his case like battery acid. Records had been lost or destroyed. Witnesses were impossible to locate, had trouble remembering details, or had passed away. There was virtually no one left from the 1982 charges that O'Mara could call to the stand—Malcolm McKenzie, Dorothy Gosling, Esther Busby—they had all died.

Steeped in these files, O'Mara felt a fresh anxiety: Maybe George Williamson hadn't done as complete a job as he'd thought. Of course, Williamson couldn't have imagined that it would take so long to bring this case to trial. *But if I'd done the prelim,* O'Mara thought, *I'd have called more witnesses, especially the old people, to get their testimonies on record.*

Now O'Mara grappled with the elements of nine alleged murders— *Nine!*—wondering how to make all of the pieces fit, feeling like he was trying to put together a jigsaw puzzle in the dark.

How could she have accomplished these seven burials without a single witness, or without an accomplice? Who was lying? What if the jury couldn't tolerate the holes, the purely circumstantial evidence?

Dorothea Montalvo Puente. She was baffling, so far outside the ugly sweep of "common" killers, so far beyond the almost prosaic brutality of those he'd prosecuted before. Other serial killers attract attention with guns and blood, with the violence of their slayings. Yet she'd killed quietly, as women often do, and no one even noticed.

Female murderers were usually drug-crazed girlfriends, betrayed wives, crackhead mothers with hapless babies, or those infrequent "black widows" who kill their husbands. Yet, stealthfully disposing of her tenants, Dorothea Puente seemed to have had less in common with reality than with fiction, like both Brewster sisters of *Arsenic and Old Lace* rolled up into one.

One FBI adage goes: "Men kill in the bedroom, women kill in the kitchen." At least she fit that part of the profile, killing with poisons, the woman's weapon of choice. Nonconfrontational. Silent. And so easily mistaken for death by natural causes.

And what about the victims? O'Mara sipped his coffee and stared at the reports, wondering what these inky pages could possibly say about the last moments of their lives. Had she approached them with a slick routine, handing them cocktails, saying in a low, soothing voice, "Drink this, dear, it will make you feel better?" Had she watched them carefully, reading each flutter of the eyelids, waiting for her cue? Had she then gripped an elbow, cooing softly as she helped them off to bed, laying them down, tucking them in—just like a nurse, just like Mom? Had she stood over them, watching, hovering?

And had they looked up at her with gratitude, lulled into sweet repose, mistaking the warm embrace of false comfort? Had any of them—even dimly, even for an instant—realized that this was to be their final rest? Staring up into those ice-blue eyes, had they glimpsed the ultimate realization that she was their killer?

O'Mara took off his reading glasses and rubbed his eyes. There had to be something else . . . something elusive . . . something they had all missed. There had to be. There always was.

He wrestled again with trying to picture the scene. He tried to work out the steps, trying to get inside her head. He flipped through papers and photographs for the umpteenth time, hoping to spot some new pattern. . . .

A glimmer of an idea began to buzz around his head, like a mosquito just beyond his peripheral vision.

What was it? It buzzed past him. He looked harder.

And then he saw it. So simple. Like a child's prank, obvious and surprising at the same moment.

But was it too simple? Did it prove anything?

Maybe so. Maybe this could work. Besides, he didn't have much choice.

With little else to work with, O'Mara plunged into his task of crafting a convincing case out of raw circumstance. Details, details. He swam through them with Olympic speed. This was his strength, fashioning copious amounts of amorphous detail into something strong and sharp with which to pierce the armor of defense.

Photos of the crime scene were shuffled into order and enlarged. Diagrams of the house, of the yard, of the graves, were blown up and prepared for display. Witnesses were subpoenaed: one hundred-fifty, -sixty, -seventy, on toward two hundred and more. He would bludgeon the defense with bulk, he would confound them with sheer volume. And he would sabotage them with the utter finesse of his logic.

PART VI

TRUTH OR CONSEQUENCES

There is no such thing as justice—in or out of court.
—CLARENCE S. DARROW, 1936

Justice is not blind, nor is she evenhanded. The scales do not balance and they cannot be made to balance. Not, that is, until we are freed of our humanity and turned to demigods. And then justice will no longer be needed.
—H. L. MENCKEN, "Note on Justice"

CHAPTER 36

FROM THE CRASHING AZURE WAVES OF THE BAY TO THE EMERALD rows of strawberry plants in the rich soils of Salinas Valley, Monterey County is bathed by a luxuriant palette. It reaches up the foggy coast from Los Padres National Forest, past Big Sur, quaint Carmel and panoramic Seventeen-Mile Drive, beyond prolific artichoke fields, inland past pines and eucalyptus, into the sunny heartland and the rugged, amber hills around Soledad. The demographics range from the moneyed residents of opulent Pebble Beach, to overworked, underpaid, and often illegal farmworkers.

Sprinkled throughout, Puente's defense team noted with interest, was a large Mexican-American population. Would Hispanics tend to be more sympathetic to Dorothea Puente? Perhaps. Most were Catholic, after all, and as Clymo noted, "They at least have a pope who is opposed to the death penalty."

Monterey County was the chosen venue for Dorothea Puente's trial, which, in October, shifted its ponderous weight two hundred miles south. Kevin Clymo, after boxing up reams upon reams of paper, moved to a rented house in Carmel, joining Peter Vlautin, who had already found a house on the beach. Their legal aid rented an apartment, their investigators would be in town off and on. The judge, his clerk, and a court reporter also packed up and shifted operations. Lastly, John O'Mara, who had been too busy to personally scout for a rental, booked one through an agency; when he arrived he discovered that it was a tight squeeze just to move in.

The price of justice was up and running, with sixteen-hundred-dollars per month housing allowances for each of the attorneys and the judge, plus a per diem. All the expenses of Puente's trial would be paid by the county, of course, including the fees of expert witnesses, consultants, investigators, and staff. Many witnesses would have to be flown in, and virtually all would have to stay at least one night in a hotel. But weighty considerations of saving the taxpayers a chunk of money weren't permitted to even touch the scales of justice, much less tip them.

Meanwhile, taking a long ride in a motor vehicle for the first time in years, Dorothea Puente was secretly transported to her new accommodations in the Monterey County Jail in Salinas.

The potential jurors came in waves of more than a hundred, clutching the paper that had brought them to the courthouse, checking the summons twice, asking for the floor, then finding themselves among a jury pool that would climb to twelve hundred before the attorneys were through. Judge Michael J. Virga* graciously introduced himself, the attorneys, and the defendant, then explained to the restless crowd that this case would take many months. He asked whether this posed undue hardship for anyone, hastening to explain that "inconvenience" and "undue hardship" were not synonymous.

Some honestly could not leave their jobs, some lied, some were pregnant, illiterate, or in poor health. Those remaining were asked to fill out a hefty questionnaire and would be called again later. Exiting the courtroom, one man hoisted in his reluctant hands the fat pages of questions and grumbled, "This is a book we have to fill out!"

Two young women huddled together, whispering about what they'd heard about this case: "She buried all those people? That's *gross*."

Jury selection. Some attorneys consider it the most important part

---

*Adding to a sense of déjà vu, Judge Virga, who had presided over Solomon's trial, had volunteered to preside over the trial of Dorothea Montalvo Puente.

of our judicial process, claiming that a trial's outcome is determined the moment the jury is seated. Peter Vlautin certainly gave jury selection a lot of weight: "I always say, get the right twelve people, and you can sell them anything."

On November 2, 1992, the jury was a blank slate. Or more accurately, twelve empty seats. It would take many weeks of questioning before faces began to emerge as likely jurors, those dozen souls in whose palms would rest Dorothea Puente's fate.

The media converged on the story en masse. Everyone with a lens recorded as many images as he or she could. O'Mara shied away, muttering, "No comment." But the defense attorneys, always more comfortable with reporters, conceded to interviews in front of the courthouse. Kevin Clymo cautioned that they wouldn't discuss the evidence, but said that it was wonderful to finally get going, that his client was in good spirits.

Vlautin, immediately forgetting his co-counsel's caution, declared, "It's a circumstantial evidence case, and after four years the DA still doesn't have a cause of death." Further, he asserted, "The odds of someone dying from Dalmane are ten to none."

Apart from the cameras and journalists, O'Mara groused that jury selection was "boring" and nothing interesting was going to happen before trial. . . . But perhaps he protested too much.

Away from the prying eyes of the media, the prosecutor was about to shift tactics. Perhaps Dorothea Puente wouldn't have to go to trial after all.

On Monday, November 9, 1992, another judge from Sacramento presided over plea negotiations. O'Mara's offer was straight-forward: The state would remove the threat of the death penalty by striking the "special circumstances" allegations if Puente would plead guilty to nine counts of first-degree murder.

Clymo and Vlautin listened, appalled. That was it? Was he serious? Did the DA's office really imagine that their case was that weak? This was the hardest line the prosecution could take short of pressing for death. Why, they stood a good chance of winning far better than this from even the worst jury.

But O'Mara stuck with this niggardly offer, and after two hours of debate the hearing was adjourned without a settlement.

The defense would take their chances with a jury.

*   *   *

Up a winding road, surrounded by fragrant pine trees, the court-house where Dorothea Puente would be tried was both figuratively and literally a long way from Sacramento. Few people rushed up the steps into this modern, three-story structure, and no metal detectors buzzed those who forgot to shed car keys at the entryway. The halls were mostly quiet, the elevators rarely crowded.

Strange having such a celebrated case in such a little-known setting, but this sleepy, satellite courthouse offered a vacant courtroom. It was the only one on the third floor, and it was light-years from Hollywood courtrooms—no chandeliers, no ornately carved mahogany. Except for the churchlike wooden pews in the gallery (only the truly devout could bear to sit for long), it was mostly unremarkable.

Having sorted through stacks of jurors' questionnaires, the attorneys prepared for voir dire, the questioning of potential jurors. This would be done one juror at a time so that any quirky answers would not "contaminate" the entire panel. The goal, of course, was to seat a fair and impartial jury. But each side had a strategy for seating jurors who might be a bit *more* fair, from their perspective.

For the delicate selection process the defense hired a consultant, Dr. Linda Meza, who had proven her worth during the change of venue and preliminary hearings. A scholar of human behavior, literate in the language of crossed arms and posture, of voice inflection and word choice, she would advise Clymo and Vlautin throughout.

The defense team, a solid four (including Dorothea), sat squarely at one end of the long counsel table; John O'Mara sat stubbornly alone at the other.

O'Mara was having none of this pseudo-science. He just didn't be-lieve that "someone with a string of social science degrees" would necessarily fare any better than he would at choosing jurors. And he didn't want to even think about "the perfect juror," he said, "because you get yourself in a box" trying to match it. Besides, he insisted, "You can't know how people will process information." So the prose-cutor went solo, trusting his own instincts.

The citizens trooped in, one after another, to share their views on life, death, crime, work, family, and anything else they might be asked about. They were all ages, sizes, and shapes, a range of types pulled from the American mélange.

The defense did virtually all of the questioning. They'd already agreed on an approach: question them about alcoholism, child abuse, and our elderly. They'd scoured the questionnaires for hints of sympathy and compassion. They were looking for care givers, those who understood the tasks of "cleaning up after sick people who spill things and mess their pants." They wanted jurors who understood the financial and emotional costs of taking care of people who could be belligerent and demanding. Most of all, they hoped for jurors with "a heart and soul," Clymo said, people who could "identify with Dorothea."

As various potential jurors cleared their throats and answered questions, they stole glances at the defendant, who looked no more sinister than a little old dumpling of a grandma. After more than four years of confinement, she was so pale that her pasty skin and white hair made her appear almost luminous. She had pale delicate hands with well-manicured nails, and wore the classic, placid expression of the elderly. Who could believe she was accused of multiple murder?

Even law enforcement officers had trouble reconciling this docile lady with the heinous charges against her. Early on, a bailiff had approached Peter Vlautin to inquire whether Mrs. Puente was an escape risk. He'd grinned and quipped, "Not unless you drive her to the bus station and buy her a ticket."

Indeed, the elderly woman with the frosty hair and crinkled skin seemed so mild, so harmless, that on more than one occasion everyone seemed to forget about her. During breaks, the judge left the bench, the clerk left her desk, the attorneys wandered away, and the bailiff popped out for just a moment, leaving Dorothea Puente, alleged murderer of nine, alone and unattended. She sat quietly at the defense table, with nothing to do but wait.

Regardless of how prepared Clymo and Vlautin were, O'Mara's most formidable opponent might be Dorothea Puente herself.

Each side, of course, thought they were at a disadvantage. Anyone either strongly in favor or strongly opposed to the death penalty would not be seated. So, from the perspective of the defense, all the best jurors—those who opposed the death penalty—had already been excluded. And from the prosecution's standpoint, eliminating "all the really good people"—those who supported the death penalty, particularly in the case of nine premeditated murders—left a "skewed group."

With both sides dissatisfied, perhaps this would be close to fair.

Clymo and Vlautin were hoping for a team, not just people to "occupy a seat," but people who would stand up for their beliefs and inspire others to vote with them. And they needed only one person, just one stubborn holdout, to have a hung jury. (The Solomon case, with that particular jury hung by a Vietnam vet, was still fresh in the minds of both Vlautin and O'Mara.)

Now Peter Vlautin peered at a solidly built Army sergeant, noticing his gold chain. To Vlautin, this meant the Vietnam veteran was "unconventional." He speculated that this serviceman might be the "wild card that the DA won't be able to predict."

After questioning, the sergeant left the courthouse, climbed into his shiny red pickup truck, and drove away, leaving in his exhaust the receding image of his personalized license plate: XREMIST.

CHAPTER 37

JOHN O'MARA HUSTLED HIS BULKY DISPLAYS OUT OF HIS CAR'S trunk, through the rain, and into the courthouse. It was Monday, February 8, 1993, the day before opening statements. The attorneys were only meeting with Judge Virga to take care of last-minute details, so they hadn't expected the media to be here—sniffing out camera positions, laying down cables—as they spilled out of the elevator in decidedly unlawyerlike garb: Clymo in a sweater and a rakish "Indiana Jones" hat; O'Mara in long, baggy shorts, a T-shirt, and a baseball cap. Their outfits prompted some friendly joshing, a counterpoint to the somberness ahead.

Beneath the lighthearted banter, the attorneys kept eyeing each other like rival suitors. This was it. After all the years and man-hours of preparation, the trial was finally getting under way.

The next morning, they took their seats in the somber suits and ties that were their uniform. Clymo and Vlautin bracketed Dorothea Puente on the left, a trinity of varied hues: Clymo, sallow, mustachioed, with his shining dome; Vlautin, ruddy and bespectacled; Dorothea, paler than ivory, her white hair neatly coiffed, a deep blue shawl draped over her plump shoulders. The classic little old lady. On the right sat the solitary prosecutor, his graying temples and mustache contrasting sharply with his dark hair.

Press-pool cameras focused in from the back. A crowd of media people perched in the gallery. Reporters exchanged information, business cards, cynical jesting. Two British journalists snickered that Puente looked just like the landladies back home.

Someone wondered aloud, "Do you think she really did it?"

Another asked, "Do you think she'll take the stand?"

Then the jurors began to file into the jury box, looking squeaky-clean and serious, and all eyes turned to watch. Mainly in their thirties and forties, these jurors belied the myth that only retirees have the time and resources to sit for months of jury duty. All worked, putting on hold their jobs with Smucker's, Wells Fargo Bank, the post office, Pacific Bell, and Gallo. Two worked at Schilling, the spice company in Salinas, which realized too late that it had released two employees for the same lengthy trial. The oldest, Marjorie Simpson (mother of seven, none named Bart), had a good twenty years on most of the others, and at sixty-five she was a year older than Dorothea but looked an easy decade younger. Two were servicemen at Ford Ord, including the youngest, twenty-seven-year-old Earl Jimerson, an infantry squad leader, and forty-two-year-old Gary Frost, Army sergeant and self-proclaimed XREMIST.

"All rise," intoned the bailiff, and Judge Michael J. Virga swept in wearing black robes and a cordial expression. As he addressed the jurors in avuncular tones, his face seemed a wise, creased map of all he'd seen. Then he read the nine counts of murder charged against the defendant, one after another, and they tolled through the hushed courtroom like requiem bells through a valley.

It was time for the prosecution's opening statement, and John O'Mara popped out of his seat. "Good morning, Ladies and Gentlemen," he said as he began pacing off what would become miles of oratory.

"In the ordinary case," he explained, "the opening statement would be quite perfunctory." But this case was far from ordinary. This was like trying nine separate murder cases, and the jurors had to make a decision on each count. He had some 230 witnesses under subpoena, but he would try to limit testimony—since "the mind can only take in what the seat can endure"—and hoped to conclude 75 percent of his case before Easter.

DISTURBED GROUND

The jurors had been prepared for months away from their normal lives. If they resented this schedule, it didn't show on their faces.

O'Mara was worried less about time than about getting these well-scrubbed, hardworking, healthy jurors to identify with Dorothea Puente's down-and-out tenants. This had been the problem from the start. Alcoholic street people don't easily inspire empathy.

"Most of us lead a very patterned life," O'Mara began. "We leave the house at a certain period of time. We go to a certain location. Perhaps we go out to lunch. At the end of the day, we go home. The life we lead leaves a pattern, sort of like a fingerprint. One can look back and see where a person has been from day to day, moment to moment, hour to hour."

O'Mara looked into their faces. They were with him. "If you were to suddenly drop out of that pattern, it would be very easy to go back and find the last place you'd been, or the last person that had seen you."

Not Dorothea's victims. "These are not people that have established life patterns, that have jobs or immediate family they see on a regular basis. For the most part, their lives went on unnoticed. We can't be sure when they disappeared." O'Mara paused. "I call these people *shadow people*. They are shadow people in the sense that they're always there, but we don't see them."

Peter Vlautin could have groaned aloud. He'd heard this same shtick from O'Mara at the Solomon trial. Still, he couldn't risk tuning him out. He and Clymo listened carefully, intent on catching every nuance of their opponent's case, mentally preparing the counterattack.

Inexplicably, O'Mara veered away from his fine start and launched into a needlessly thorough explanation of Sacramento and of Puente's rough "Alkali Flats" neighborhood. He showed the jurors two amateurish videotapes (apparently done by creatively handicapped cops), one of the streets around Puente's boardinghouse, another of the exhumations.

Next, O'Mara showed them dozens of grisly photographs of the bodies. He marched these up and down in front of the jury box, eyes following him—back and forth, back and forth—in a kind of horrific hypnosis.

By the noon break, O'Mara's plodding pace had most of the media staring glassy-eyed toward their deadlines. No scintillating quotes. No eye-popping exposés. Even the British journalists—who knew this case would seize the imagination of a nation crammed with boarding-houses—were squirming impatiently.

They would have to make do with images of Puente's roses being fertilized by rotting corpses, for John O'Mara wasn't worried about steamy headlines, two-minute stories, or the short attention span of the media. After lunch, he trudged on, intent on educating the jury to the fundamentals of this complex case. Information flooded out of him. He explained the problems the decomposed remains presented to the forensic pathologists, outlined the intricacies of toxicological examinations, and defined the metabolites of Dalmane. Like a professor, he used a pointer with his diagrams, lecturing his class on Murder 101, handing them the tools of study.

A few nodded thoughtfully, several took notes.

Through most of O'Mara's remarks, Dorothea Puente watched impassively. Occasionally, she put a hand to a powdered cheek or gave a small shake of her head. She frequently wrote notes—pages and pages of notes—then passed them to Clymo, who nodded or wrote back.

O'Mara had prepared a placard on each of the nine victims, but by the end of the first day, he'd waded through the information on only one. No matter. The next day, rejuvenated, he plowed through the rest. For the first time, the jurors were being introduced to the seven tenants found buried in her yard—Leona Carpenter, Dorothy Miller, Bert Montoya, Benjamin Fink, James Gallop, Vera Faye Martin, and Betty Palmer—and to Everson Gillmouth, the man found in the box, and Ruth Munroe, who died of an overdose in Puente's home in 1982.

Explaining the medical histories of these nine, O'Mara subtly emphasized that these were not just names, but living, breathing people. Divorced, widowed, or abandoned, most were alone. He'd managed to round up a photograph—a family picture, a doctor's photo, even a mug shot, if necessary—for all but one. Leona Carpenter's placard remained sadly faceless.

O'Mara admitted their foibles. They were, for the most part, perpetual alcoholics; some were heavy smokers; some were mentally ill; most were not very good at following doctors' orders. And for each one O'Mara recited a litany of ailments, from arterial sclerosis to ulcers, noting that such diseases "can be troublesome, can be debilitating, or certainly can be fatal."

Spectators exchanged looks. Reporters frowned. Why was he putting so much emphasis on the abysmal medical histories of these people? True, the prosecution often defuses the defense's case by admitting its own weaknesses, but wasn't this overkill? O'Mara was making

Clymo's case for him: These were sick, aging folks who just dropped over dead!

But then the prosecutor began sowing the seeds of suspicion: the toxicology reports showing Dalmane in the victims' systems; Puente's copious prescriptions for the drug; the empty gel capsules found in her drawer, in halves, with Dalmane residue still inside.

The defense attorneys hardly stirred. They expected all of this. Dalmane they were ready for.

But now O'Mara was uttering something new: *"Asphyxiation,"* he said, and he could almost feel the defense attorneys staring at his back. There are two types of asphyxiation, he told the jury, strangulation and suffocation. "Even these decomposed bodies probably would have provided evidence of strangulation; none was found. But what about *suffocation?*"

Had the defense anticipated this? They should have, O'Mara thought. Williamson hadn't pursued this at the preliminary hearing, but the notion had jumped out at him while staring at those gruesome photographs.

"A pillow placed over the face," he was saying, "even a garbage bag over the head of a drugged, weakened victim, would have left no detectable trace. Did Dorothea sneak in, after her victims had collapsed into unconsciousness, to quietly extinguish them?"

Letting no alarm show on their faces, Clymo and Vlautin listened, immobile. He couldn't prove this, they told themselves. He was fishing.

"We're going to see a pattern of behavior," O'Mara continued, "that shows how she tried to cover up her crimes. Time and again, you're going to hear that after they've disappeared, they've gone mysteriously somewhere," he said, gesturing in the empty air. O'Mara recounted Puente's lies: that Bert had gone with his brother-in-law to Shreveport, Utah, "a place that doesn't exist"; that Leona Carpenter had gone "to the hospital to die"; that Ben Fink had gone "up north, to Marysville"; that James Gallop had gone "back to L.A."; and that Everson Gillmouth had gone "back to Oregon."

Such were her euphemisms for death.

O'Mara turned toward the money trail, itemizing the checks that Dorothea had stolen from her tenants, totaling upward of $58,000. (But he secretly wondered just how high that figure might go. The rekindled investigation was still turning up evidence.)

Everyone had assumed—with the checks, the lying, the forgery—

that the motive here was pure and simple greed. But now O'Mara threw another surprise punch: "You're going to see that she already had access to virtually all their money *before* they were dead. The motive is not getting their money," he declared. "There were a lot of forgeries while the decedents were still alive!"

What? Clymo and Vlautin could hardly believe their ears.

"Well then, what is the motive for murder?" O'Mara queried, and everyone waited for his interpretation.

"Dorothea Puente ran a very nice board-and-care facility. She took in some people that are very difficult. These are not people that the average board-and-care operators want to take. For the most part, they're people that have mental problems, substance abuse problems. They act out. They're not reliable. You can't really depend on them."

The problem with these people, O'Mara said, was that their health deteriorated to the point that they required extraordinary care. Rather than merely providing "a place to stay and a couple of meals," Puente found herself running a skilled nursing facility. "You've got a lot of people that are very, very sick, that require a lot of attention."

What was he saying? the defense wondered. That Dorothea killed them because they were too much trouble?

At the next break, Kevin Clymo puffed a cigarette, muttering, "For four years he's been telling the whole world that the motive was money, and now he says she did it because she's evil! I can't understand why he did that."

This threw a kink in their defense. As, of course, O'Mara hoped it would.

But was it enough? O'Mara still had to confront the defendant herself. He'd never had to prosecute a serial killer with such a sweet little old lady image.

"As you see her in court today," he said, gesturing toward Mrs. Puente, "the defendant looks somewhat delicate, an elderly woman." He smiled. "But in terms of personality, and in terms of her physical abilities, she is not an old woman. She's not Mary See at See's Candies."*

He cautioned them, "You're going to hear the defendant described as a very caring person, a person trying to help out unfortunates. And

---

*A California candy franchise, with a white-haired grandma as its trademark.

to some degree"—he shrugged—"that's true. But you're also going to hear a portrait of the defendant that's not nearly as flattering." He then described Dorothea Puente as extremely manipulative, a woman subject to very quick personality changes, who suffered "delusions of grandeur."

Dorothea Puente listened impassively, her face a mask of a million tiny wrinkles, slight tucks in her cheeks (the apparent result of a 1988 face-lift). Curious jurors glanced over at this pale enigma.

Stepping up to a chart of the F Street house, O'Mara pointed to the upstairs and said quietly, "She describes that as a haunted room."

All eyes went to the "haunted bedroom" off the kitchen.

Painting Dorothea Puente in sinister shades, he explained that "people died on her in there," that she was a deadly care giver.

"I'm going to take care of them," she would say, escorting some unsuspecting soul upstairs to that bedroom.

"Shortly thereafter," O'Mara intoned, "they would disappear. No one would see them again."

On this ominous note, O'Mara closed. He hoped it was enough, for even now he was playing catch-up. He'd found some flaws in his own case, and he'd tried to anticipate counter-arguments, but the defense had had four years to turn each small tear into a giant hole.

At times O'Mara had seemed awash in a sea of details, diagrams, and displays. Had the jurors resented this protracted stream of information? Had O'Mara dragged on so long that they begrudged him for it? Puente's attorneys certainly hoped so.

The next morning, defense attorney Kevin Clymo rose out of his seat to address the jury. "We are kind of at a disadvantage," Clymo began, playing the underdog. "You get used to that when you're a defense lawyer." He smiled at them. "You're not going to hear any of our arguments until midspring."

And after that, the prosecution would have a second chance to present evidence. "That's because," Clymo emphasized, "the prosecution has the *burden of proof*."

The tall, dome-topped defense attorney had a much different style than the prosecutor: slower, more measured, with broad gestures. The jurors shifted gears and listened.

"Now, I'm going to tell you some things that the prosecution didn't tell you. I suppose one of our jobs under our adversary system is to make sure that you guys, the true judges of the case, get a balanced view of the facts."

Clymo knew that, without a strong opening, they risked months of damning evidence piling up against their client. His imperative was to show that the state's evidence was open to interpretation. Yet, for defense attorneys, opening statements are a walk on a tightrope. Up until now the prosecutor—and the public—could only guess at how they might defend their client. Now, with each word to the jury, he clued the prosecution.

Clymo wheeled over a detailed, three-dimensional model of Puente's house, which looked like the elaborate dollhouse of an extremely spoiled child. He lifted off the roof and the jurors peered at the tiny furniture inside. "If, in fact, there was a 'haunted room,' you can see whether or not one of these rooms match that description," he said, his voice dripping sarcasm.

"I've got to tell you that I was a little bit surprised—for four years I've heard it suggested that Dorothea Puente killed people to steal their money. And what I heard yesterday was that Dorothea Puente killed people because she's a bad person. She's evil! And there is a haunted room in the haunted house! I went home and I scratched my head and I thought, *My God, how little progress we've made since the Salem witch trials.*"

Popping in his own amateurish videotape, Clymo went through a leisurely tour of Puente's home. "This is a normal house," he said. "This is not a wicked witch's haunted house!" Indeed, with bookcases filled with paperbacks, a pantry full of food, lace curtains on the windows, pillows and big knitted comforters on the beds, it looked remarkably ordinary. "All the rooms had televisions," Clymo noted as the camera wandered through the first floor, then upstairs. "That's one of the things that Dorothea Puente did. That's where some of the money went. Televisions, beds, mattresses, linens, food—lots of food."

This was a glimpse at their counterargument. Feeding a houseful of people over a period of three years would not be cheap. Was $58,000 an unreasonable sum? The defense didn't think so.

Their roles had reversed: While Clymo talked, O'Mara sat with pen in hand, plotting every turn of logic.

"We heard that the people at the house were 'shadow people.' They were people that, for the most part, were down and out. They were derelict. They were disabled. They were drunkards, the dregs of society, so to speak. They were people that didn't fit."

Emphasizing the services that Dorothea Puente had provided, and the stresses placed upon her, he continued, "Drinkers are the most belligerent. They are the most self-neglecting. They are people that don't take care of business, and they are the most difficult to place."

But Dorothea Puente would take people in, Clymo said, "when they didn't have anyplace else, when nobody would take them."

None of this struck O'Mara as surprising. The Mother Teresa bit, he thought.

Clymo moved to a more delicate area. "Someone said that Dorothea Puente has a touch of larceny in her heart. It may be true. I'm not going to stand here and tell you that she's a thief. But I'm not going to jump up and down and protest a whole lot about evidence that may suggest she had a touch of larceny in her heart. It doesn't make her a killer," he said, raising his eyebrows and adding in a mocking tone, "it doesn't make her an *evil* serial killer."

Now Clymo was saying, "She went to prison," and O'Mara listened closely. How much of Puente's record would Clymo reveal?

"I'm not going to hide that from you," Clymo went on. "I'll tell you from the get-go, she went to prison in 1982 after being convicted upon her plea of guilty to theft charges, writing and forging checks." Phrasing this carefully, he added, "She was also accused of administering a stupefying drug to an individual and liberating that individual of his property."

Clymo was giving this to him—and O'Mara would take it, he'd work it in whenever he could—but it was no error. It was a legal paradox in this tangled case that the prosecution would use it to establish guilt, while Clymo introduced it to fight for her innocence.

Clymo cast derision on circumstantial evidence, declaring, "Of nearly two hundred witnesses, not a single one will testify to having seen Dorothea Puente kill anyone! And not a single one will testify to having seen her bury anyone!"

O'Mara had expected this "failure of proof" defense.

But now Clymo made a surprising, if vague, concession: "After all you hear about this case, you will infer that Dorothea Montalvo Puente was connected with, somehow associated with, maybe even responsible for causing people to be buried in her yard. That's seven people in the yard. I'm sure you've already had that thought."

The jurors regarded him quizzically as he paused to remind them again of the presumption of innocence.

Then he held up a photo of the religious figurine standing over Betty Palmer's grave in front of the house. "Dorothea Montalvo Puente was the person who not only took care of these people, but remembered them in her own way. She took care of them when they were alive"—he glanced at the photo—"it looks like she took care of them after they were dead, too."

The reporters were loving it. This was something they could use! Spooky stuff! It made good copy.

But what did it say about Puente's defense? That even though she buried bodies in the yard, she still granted consent for the search? This was a strange way to argue for death by natural causes.

Clymo's interpretation of events suggested that it was the oppressive onslaught of the media, the crush of onlookers, the constant noise of the news vans that had compelled Puente to "rabbit" for Los Angeles. After all, she wasn't under arrest, so she hadn't really "escaped." "The only way to be unmolested by the media was to get the hell out of there. And she did," he said simply. "She did."

He pointed out that she had had over three thousand dollars in her purse and spoke Spanish. "She had the ability to duck into Mexico"—he opened his palms and shrugged—"she didn't do it."

And, just as the prosecution had humanized the victims, the defense humanized the accused. Clymo showed photographs of a younger Dorothea Puente holding a small child in her lap, standing in her immaculate house, and cradling her cat in her arms. The picture of innocence.

And with that image in her jurors' minds, Clymo reminded them again that in this case, with no cause of death, there was "no criminal agency." In other words, *"If you can't say how they died, then you can never establish unlawful killing."*

The evidence would show, he said, that tissues from Everson Gillmouth's body were saved and tested. Yet the toxicology exams showed nothing—no trace of Dalmane, or of any other drug. "The pathologist wasn't able to determine a cause of death, but it certainly wasn't due to a drug overdose."

That put a knot in the pattern.

Next, Clymo moved to that troublesome Ruth Munroe count. Of the nine, Munroe was the only one for whom there had been an immediate autopsy. Clearly, she had died from an overdose of codeine and Tylenol. Munroe's children had insisted that their mother wouldn't commit suicide, and that she was allergic to codeine. Now, with huge blowups of medical records, Clymo pointed out that Ruth Munroe, who was actually allergic to penicillin, was *prescribed codeine* by her own doctor!

In sympathetic tones, Clymo conceded that Munroe's children had been understandably confused and upset when their mother died. "They didn't want to believe she'd committed suicide." He paused. "But she wasn't murdered."

Looking into the jurors' faces, he asked softly, "That case wasn't prosecutable in 1982. Why now?"

This had to leave them wondering.

Further, Clymo went on, Dorothea Puente was the person who had called police when Ruth Munroe died. Yet she hadn't notified police when Everson Gillmouth died. Why not? What was different?

Some jurors leaned forward.

In 1982, Dorothea wasn't on parole. From 1985 on, she was. And as a condition of her parole, she was instructed "not to seek employment with elderly or mentally disabled people," or to handle government checks. If she lied about this, she could go back to prison. So, rather than alert the authorities when seventy-seven-year-old Everson Gillmouth died of old age, rather than risk questions, risk going back to prison, she'd quietly disposed of his body. And seven bodies after that.

Very tidy. But O'Mara's thoughts snagged on this neat little web of logic. There was a glaring inconsistency here. But would it be admissible?

The defense had prepared pie charts and graphs showing a kinder, gentler interpretation of the money trail. But since O'Mara had pre-empted this argument, Clymo kept it short. Given the daily costs of running a standard nursing facility, he asserted, Dorothea Puente didn't clear much profit in providing for her needy boarders.

Before turning the podium over to his co-counsel, Clymo laced together the fingers of his big hands and summed up their case: "We expect the evidence to show that eight of the nine died of natural causes, the ninth of suicide. And Dorothea Montalvo Puente is not guilty of these charges."

The jury was starting to fidget, but when Peter Vlautin began with a few humorous remarks, they chuckled. They were with him, their minds still open.

Vlautin hurried through a few important points of pharmacology. He explained that Dalmane was of the class of drugs known as benzodiazapines, developed in the seventies as a safer alternative to highly addictive barbiturates, such as Valium. "It's almost unheard of to have an overdose of Dalmane," he said.

Flourishing a red marker, Vlautin highlighted data on large blowups of the victims' medical records: Dalmane prescriptions, histories of drug and alcohol abuse, which would explain the Dalmane in their systems. And, with chart after chart, he showed these people to have been on the brink of death.

O'Mara had expected the defense to bring out "specters"—vague people who once threatened the life of this or that person—but he would have to fight something even more ephemeral: the general ill-health of these people.

Vlautin was being careful. He didn't want to alert the prosecutor to too much of their case. But now he declared, "I think the evidence suggests that alcohol and Dalmane played a role in the death of Bert Montoya."

But hadn't it been established at the prelim that Bert, the youngest and healthiest of the nine, was not a drinker? O'Mara scribbled notes on his legal pad.

Vlautin made a few parting shots at the testimonies of some of the ex-cons he expected to testify—particularly Michelle Crowl and Brenda Trujillo—and then, suddenly, he was done.

Judge Virga excused the jurors, who quickly spilled past reporters and out into the parking lot.

The paths of their normal lives had just taken a detour. For the next many months, this trial would roll forward, lurching along in fits and starts, carrying them on a life-and-death ride. They would bear witness to the passing of nine strangers who'd slipped away with scarcely a breath of notice.

But was it really possible to sit in a courtroom in 1993 and discern what had happened to nine people so many years ago? Wasn't this just the absurd hubris of our justice system? How close could even the most astute juror come to the truth? And how far could their hearts possibly travel from that sucking black hole of "reasonable doubt"?

CHAPTER 38

Testimony was set to begin after the President's day weekend, but when Peter Vlautin came in with tears in his eyes—not from emotion, but from a freak paper cut to the cornea—Judge Virga issued a delay. And John O'Mara, who had "witnesses stacked up like planes over Chicago," was thrown into a scheduling nightmare.

He put a busload of witnesses on hold and engaged in a logistical juggling act involving egos, employers, transportation, and hotel reservations. Hoping to open strong, he'd slated Judy Moise early, but she had to get back to work in Sacramento, so she repacked her rumpled clothes and headed home, leaving O'Mara to reshuffle his witness list. Vlautin's eye injury had been a cut to the opposition.

Instead, O'Mara began with five former employees of Lumberjack, a supply store, who testified to delivering gardening supplies and numerous bags of ready-mix concrete to 1426 F Street. Hardly the gripping start that prosecutors covet.

O'Mara soon shifted the focus to Bert Montoya, calling to the stand two of Bert's friends from Detox, J. D. Ridgley, still director of the facility, and soft-spoken, full-bearded Bill Johnson, who'd since left.

275

Both men spoke fondly of Bert, and during their testimonies, Bert seemed almost resurrected in the courtroom: his face, his mannerisms, his love of cigars, and his continual discourse with private spirits.

Despite all his years of Detox, both witnesses insisted, Bert wasn't a drinker. "Tobacco was his drug of choice," Johnson asserted. "He was not a public inebriate. There was no preoccupation with alcohol for Alberto at all."

Johnson stumbled over exact dates—this was nearly five years ago, he apologized—but he related his last encounters with Bert the best he could. He recalled the day that Bert had walked the four miles back to Detox to say that he was "very unhappy" at Dorothea's. They'd talked it over, he said, then Johnson had driven Bert back to the boardinghouse.

He'd asked Mrs. Puente "why she was giving Alberto this medication that he didn't like. She said that was not true, that he woke her up at 4:00 A.M. and asked her for the medication."

With regret breaking across his face, Johnson recalled how he'd convinced Bert to stay. Then he suddenly blurted, "I was wrong. I gotta live with this for the rest of my life."

Clymo objected instantly, and Judge Virga ordered the witness's statement stricken from the record. But there was no way to strike it from the jurors' minds.

The Sunday before she was to testify, Judy drove back down to Monterey with giddy dread her passenger. It unsettled her that there still seemed to be so much uncertainty surrounding the case against Dorothea Puente, that people still asked her, "Do you really think she did it?" She tried to anticipate questions and recall dates, picturing Kevin Clymo looming before her, assailing her with cross-examination. Loathing the idea of having to repeat that whole ordeal, she checked into the inn with dismal expectations.

But this time, the prosecutor had arranged to have his investigator bring Judy to his office, where he lavished time on her like a balm. He seemed candid, open, unhurried. He slaked her fears with a flow of conversation, and impressed her by being fluent in the particulars of her role in this case. He even surprised her by playing a clandestine tape recording made in Detective Cabrera's office back in November 1988. Judy sat listening to her own tremulous tones, startled by the intensity of her exchange with Beth Valentine as they whispered about Bert's mysterious disappearance.

DISTURBED GROUND

By the time she left O'Mara's office, Judy couldn't help but compare him favorably to George Williamson. He'd made time for her. He'd taken her comments and concerns seriously. He'd put her at ease. And he was so impressively sharp. . . . She even wondered idly if John O'Mara was married.

On Monday, February 22, the media converged on the courtroom, anticipating the testimony of "the social worker." Sketch artists chose perspectives and limbered their wrists. Reporters readied their pens. Then Judy Moise was called to the stand.

Stepping up to the witness box, Judy was vacillating between trembling inside and feeling almost comfortable. She raised her right hand, swore to tell the truth, and took her seat. Then she just had to hold on and race to keep up with O'Mara's questions.

He started in 1986 and sped forward, through an explanation of her job as a mental health worker with the Volunteers of America, past this co-worker and that, on to her relationship with Bert.

When she felt too nervous, Judy took deep breaths to steady herself, then plunged on. It was only when O'Mara asked if she would describe Bert as "slow" that Judy finally paused, scrunching her brow in reflection.

"No, I wouldn't call him slow. I'd just say that he didn't have the advantages that other people have."

A shadow of a smile crossed a few jurors' lips. They remembered that when O'Mara had asked Bill Johnson this same question, he'd replied, "I don't like the word *slow*. I like the word *innocent*." It was clear that these two people felt protective of Bert.

And, like Bert's two friends from Detox, Judy also insisted that Bert did not drink.

During her testimony, Judy was dying to get a look at Dorothea Puente. What a reversal from the preliminary hearing, she thought, when she had been dying *not* to. Now, finally, she rallied her nerve and glanced to O'Mara's left, past Peter Vlautin, to her old nemesis. She was almost startled by the pastel visage of this pale woman with her soft, white hair. Judy had expected her to be older, of course, but not so . . . changed.

While Judy was looking directly at her, Dorothea Puente shut her eyes.

Judy caught her breath. This was a defensive gesture—she was sure of it!—an admission of guilt. She glanced away quickly and answered O'Mara's next question, then looked back again.

Dorothea lowered her gaze and stared at the table.

There it was again!

Judy answered another question, and when she looked back, Dorothea Puente met her eye. They appraised each other for a long moment, with no measure of guilt or innocence, with no scorn, as if seeing each other objectively for the first time.

To Judy, it seemed an honest moment, and from it a fresh clarity spread across the scene. She suddenly felt in tune with everyone in the courtroom: aware of Clymo declining his head to ask Dorothea a question; of the judge sitting just a breath's distance above her; of the jury watching with a dozen pairs of eyes. Somehow, it seemed they were all here together, working for a common purpose.

Over the objections of the defense, O'Mara played for the jury an edited version of the old videotape that Judy had made of Bert so many years before, back when she was first working for the Volunteers of America. The tape was rough and jumpy, but Bert's character shined through, giving the jury a glimpse of this simple man who'd trusted the defendant and ended up dead.

To Judy, simply having Bert's image appear in the courtroom felt like a small triumph. She wanted the jurors to appreciate how special he was, she wanted the tape to affect them the way it affected her.

While the video was running, she glanced repeatedly at Dorothea Puente, hoping to catch some reaction. But she saw nothing there. No emotion. None.

For Judy Moise, testifying was an almost cathartic experience. Even the cross-examination, which she'd been dreading for weeks, transpired more civilly than she'd feared. Once or twice, she and Clymo even shared a joke, a truce of humor passing between them.

For others, testifying would be a decidedly less positive event.

Painfully aware of the suits pending against her, Peggy Nickerson had brought her own attorney to court with her. For this unlucky woman, opening Dorothea Puente's door had been like opening Pandora's box. And she didn't appear to have recovered. She answered O'Mara's questions clearly, but her tone was serious and subdued, and her soft features never once broke into a smile.

O'Mara skillfully extracted the information he needed, moving from item to item. Afterward, he thought her testimony had gone fairly well. But he couldn't understand why Peggy Nickerson—this church worker who'd labored at the impossible task of finding housing for the destitute; this scapegoat who'd caught the blame that rightfully belonged to the parole board; this social worker who'd lost her career; this altruist who'd been served the acid documents of litigation; this witness who felt so endangered that she'd paid to have her own attorney in court while she testified—O'Mara just couldn't understand why Peggy Nickerson couldn't relax.

Perhaps, as with many prosecutors, a blunt obsession with fact obscured more subtle insights into human emotion.

O'Mara filled the days with testimony from cops, deputy coroners, taxi drivers, and forensic anthropologists in a stream of collective consciousness that detailed the discovery of the bodies and Puente's smooth escape. Several men—some scruffy and coarse, others articulate and shining beneath wasted potential—took the stand to say that Dorothea Puente had hired them from the halfway house. They'd painted, hammered, raked, and dug.

The trenches, they'd been told, were for pipes—sewer pipes—but these were never quite located. Puente had told them where to dig, and John McCauley had stood, watched, and supervised. (John McCauley. John McCauley. That name kept resurfacing.) Almost no one could remember actually filling these holes back up, and no one had buried anything suspicious.

Except for one dark, good-looking young man, a felon named Bobby Mitchell. He remembered Puente telling him to fill up a hole one morning, saying that the stuff at the bottom—old carpet and such—was "just garbage." Also, Mitchell testified about an "odd smell" that had hit him when he was leveling the ground, preparing to lay cement. "I haven't smelled anything like it before," he said. "It was just a real foul odor."

On March 1 the exiled jury roamed the hallways while Clymo and Vlautin railed against the prosecution's latest surprise: a videotape of Detective John Cabrera's November 11, 1988, interview with Dorothea Puente, which O'Mara wanted to show in open court. They felt sabotaged.

For one thing, they complained to Judge Virga, they'd never even *seen* this tape until O'Mara had mentioned it to Vlautin the week before.

O'Mara could scarcely contain himself. He strangled his pen and glared at them. How could the tape have failed to be included in the tons of "discovery" materials the DA's office had turned over to them? They had the *transcript* of the interview, and "Transcript of a Video-tape" was stamped across page one! "I have no way of knowing what they don't have, Your Honor," he snapped.

Ever judicious, Judge Virga listened to both sides, then decided that this wasn't an issue of "deliberate withholding."

The defense tried another tack. They knew how incriminating this tape would be; they had to keep it out.

Clearly, they argued, Mrs. Puente had believed she was in custody, yet she'd never been Mirandized—never advised of her rights—so the tape was inadmissible. Legally, if Mrs. Puente even *believed* she was in custody, the interview couldn't be shown to the jury. And Mrs. Puente had every reason to believe that she was being forcibly held at the time, Clymo said. After all, police officers had been at her house since early morning, she'd been questioned at home, then Detective Cabrera had taken her to the Hall of Justice for interrogation. "The totality of circumstances would lead a reasonable person to conclude it was no longer a voluntary submission," Clymo insisted.

At one point, Puente had even asked, "Are you going to let me go, or do I have to stay here, or what?"

O'Mara wanted this tape shown as much as the defense wanted it excluded. It was perhaps his best chance to tarnish the munificent shine the defense kept trying to put on Puente's image. Since she didn't have to take the stand, he might never have an opportunity to cross-examine her. This could be as close to actual testimony as he'd ever get.

The judge decided to take the tape home and view it himself before making a ruling.

Meanwhile, Puente's former tenant, John Sharp, had his testimony repeatedly delayed. Suffering from an ulcer and having just undergone yet another operation, Sharp was keenly aware of the tenuousness of life. He chided O'Mara, "I'm living on Maalox—you'd better hurry and get me up there before it's too late!"

John Sharp was the first long-term boarder to take the stand. Older, balder, and thinner than he'd been at the preliminary hearing, he seemed every bit as alert. He testified about seeing other tenants come and go, about holes being dug and filled, about the note he'd passed to Officer Ewing saying "She wants me to lie to you." His credibility as a witness seemed to rise with each clipped answer.

Sharp noted that he and Dorothea used to converse about this and that. Once, she'd asked if he needed any help handling his finances. "I told her I didn't have any trouble spending money," he quipped, and several jurors grinned at him.

Asked about John McCauley, he answered crisply, "I didn't like him." But of course there was more to it than that.

Under further questioning, John Sharp recalled that the last time he'd seen Bert was in the downstairs living room, sitting on the couch. Later, "Dorothea told me she'd put him in a cab, to catch a bus, to go visit her relatives in Mexico."

O'Mara asked, "Are you able to tell us how much time went by from the time you last saw Bert until you had this conversation with Mrs. Puente?"

"Well, twelve hours."

Sharp also recalled that three or four weeks prior to this, Puente had mentioned her intention to send Bert to Mexico. "She told me she was going to send Bert down there to one of her relatives, where he would be able to speak Spanish with everybody and be able to live a lot better."

Were the jurors catching this? She'd planned Bert's euphemistic "trip to Mexico" weeks before he disappeared! Did the significance reach them? It was impossible to tell.

Unfortunately, Sharp also said that he'd seen Bert drunk. And under cross-examination, Vlautin coaxed from him the image of Bert staggering about, bottle in hand.

Vlautin further emphasized how Dorothea had cared for and comforted Bert. When he got upset about the voices he heard, "She'd tell him that Satan wasn't there and she'd calm him down," Sharp admitted. Their relationship was like "mother and son."

With Sharp on the stand, Vlautin reviewed all the niceties of Dorothea Puente's boardinghouse: the big meals, the clean laundry, the emergency loans, the special chair she'd bought for Sharp because of his bad back. It was going well.

Then Vlautin took a misstep: He asked about noises at night in the yard.

Sharp answered that he'd heard "nothing *outside*," his voice heavy with insinuation.

On redirect, O'Mara swiftly asked, "Were there disturbances that occurred in the evening or early-morning hours *inside*?"

"The early-morning hours one night there was."

"And what kind of disturbance do you recall?"

"About one-thirty in the morning, there was a lot of noise on the stairs above my room. Right over my bed. It was a bumping sound, like somebody falling down the stairs or something."

A chill passed through the courtroom.

"Were you asleep at the time this occurred or were you awake?"

"It woke me." But he hadn't gotten up to see what the noise was.

The next morning, Dorothea asked if he'd slept all right. He'd lied, saying, "Just fine."

CHAPTER 39

AT THE START OF THE FOURTH WEEK THE TRIAL STILL RE-
volved around Bert Montoya's mental and physical health. And since
he was only one of nine victims, the jury had to be wondering just
how long this would take. They'd sat through dozens of witnesses,
each sharing a tiny peek at some picture they couldn't yet see. It was
like trying to study at a cathedral through a keyhole.

Meanwhile, Dorothea Puente sat stoically between her two advo-
cates, watching silently, inscrutable as a sphinx. If the jurors had trouble reading her, this was about to change.

Gloom hung over the defense table the morning of March 9 as a
television was wheeled into place. The judge cautioned the jurors that
they should keep in mind that questions were not evidence, but Clymo
and Vlautin knew how damaging this videotape would be.

The bailiff loaded the VCR and a grainy image filled the screen. A
younger, thinner Dorothea Puente faced Detective Cabrera across
a table.

They heard the detective ask her basic questions about her residence, and now, for the first time, they heard the defendant's voice.

It was weak, plaintive, an old woman's timorous voice, spelling out her name, explaining that she didn't actually own the house.

And then they heard her lie: "Well, I mean I don't, I don't have the downstairs. I, I collect the rent for my nephew. . . ."

It was the first lie of many.

Cabrera pressed Mrs. Puente about the whereabouts of Bert Montoya, and she insisted she'd seen him the previous weekend, that he'd gone to Utah with his brother-in-law.

Everyone in the courtroom now knew, however, that Bert was then dead and buried in her side yard.

Clymo and Vlautin felt every lie stab through their case. How could they counter the negative impact of their client lying in the face of a police detective?

Next, Detective Cabrera was mentioning that John Sharp had said he hadn't seen Ben Fink in about three months. Recognizing Fink's name, the jury listened carefully.

"He was gone most of the time because he was always out drinking," Puente explained. "And he, he was on, ah, he had a bad leg, and he would go sell his blood every week."

"Down at the plasma center?"

"Right. And he said he was going to go back to Marysville."

"When did he say that?"

"When I told him he had to leave." She'd kicked him out, she said.

Cabrera put a diagram of the yard on the table between them, asking about trenches that had been dug, trees that had been planted, concrete that had been poured over sections of her yard.

The concrete was "to keep the weeds down," she explained. "I just don't want to have to pull up weeds. I don't care that much for yard work."

Cabrera kept pounding away, and Puente gamely offered up answers about sewer lines, about landscaping, about compost and garbage, all the while portraying herself as a woman who didn't have much energy for more than a few rosebushes and a vegetable garden. "I have a bad heart," she volunteered. "I can't lift anything heavy."

Exasperated, Cabrera told her, "I've got a man missing. Nothing seems—nothing fits, Dorothea, that's what I'm trying to say. Nothing fits."

Then Cabrera bluntly suggested, "Mr. Montoya is dead—"

"No, he's not," she retorted.

"—somewhere in that backyard," he went on.

She was indignant. "Sir, I have never killed anybody."

Alluding to her past arrests, Cabrera insinuated, "The similarities are there. The only thing that's different now is, rather than take something and let it go, you get rid of 'em and nothing's ever found."

The defense must have been sick.

Returning to Bert, Cabrera suggested that nobody cared about him. "Hey, when you're nobody, you're nobody. Nobody cares, so you disappear. You're a transient, or you're a bum, or you're an alcoholic—"

Dorothea stopped him. "I cared for him."

"A lot of people think nobody ever cares."

"I cared for him," she insisted. "I bought him clothes. I treated him very, very good."

Then the jury heard Cabrera lower his voice and whisper a bluff, "Dorothea, I know if we dig, we're going to find more. I know that."

"Well, I didn't put 'em there," the old woman retorted. "I couldn't drag a body any place."

The jury listened without reaction.

Cabrera's questioning seemed to go around in circles for a while. Then he asked, "Are there any other bodies—"

"No," she interjected.

"—in your backyard?"

"I didn't even know that one was there!"

"Did Mr. McCauley put any other bodies in the backyard?"

"You have to ask Mr. McCauley that."

"I intend to," the detective said earnestly, then continued, "Okay, I want you to be truthful—"

"Sir, I didn't even know that body was there," she repeated, adding, "If I had of, I would have said, 'No, don't search the yard,' you know. I had nothing to hide. I don't want to go back to prison."

The courtroom was hushed, the jury intent.

"I'm an old lady," she went on. "I'm trying to get off parole. I'm trying to get my life together."

Throughout the interview, Cabrera was clearly running on adrenaline, badgering her one moment, sympathizing the next. He kept goading her, then cutting her off, scarcely letting her finish a complete sentence. This is the sort of behavior that makes a defense attorney's pulse race. Clymo and Vlautin would grill Cabrera as soon as they had a chance to cross-examine. Now they stole glances at the jury, wondering how all this struck them.

Focusing on this bizarre discovery of bones in her yard, Cabrera demanded, "How do you explain that? Somebody snuck in your back-yard with a human body and buried it?"

Without flinching, Puente suggested that it must have been done by someone else. Then she turned the tables, asking the detective, "Do you really think I'm guilty?"

"I'm going to be real truthful with you, Dorothea," Cabrera said slowly. "I think somehow you're involved. And I think you are very, very frightened right now. I think you realize that whatever has been going on, is over. Because we are going to uncover that yard."

To the very end, Puente remained steadfast. "I haven't killed any-one," she repeated. "My conscience is not bothering me."

Finally, Cabrera was concluding. "Okay," he said, "do you have any problem with us digging, or—"

"No."

"None whatsoever?"

"No."

"Because you don't have to let us."

"Look, I want to get this over with."

In November 1988, after lying so boldly to Cabrera, Mrs. Puente had been taken back to 1426 F Street. The next morning, she'd put over three thousand dollars in her purse, and fled.

When the television was flipped off in 1993, the jurors were excused for a short break, taking with them whatever images continued to flicker in their minds.

Any dramatic effect the video had on the jury that morning was soon blunted by another onslaught of detail. O'Mara believed in hold-ing back nothing, so they sat through Detective Cabrera's seemingly interminable recitation of evidence seized, relevant or not, from empty gel caps in a drawer, to phone bills, to medications for Dorothea's cats. Seeming almost bouncy, the detective was clearly unaware that most of his testimony was about as flat and dry as west Texas.

Cabrera also conducted painstaking tours through multiple represen-tations of the house. By now the jury had seen scale models, photo-graphs, charts, diagrams, and videotapes of the house. Was it truly necessary that, as the people's exhibits passed a thousand, they had to view these repeated images of 1426 F Street? After all, it wasn't the house that was on trial here.

O'Mara knew this was hardly thrilling, but he feared that if he left out anything the defense would use it later to raise misgivings. He wanted to leave no questions unanswered. He wanted them to know he'd presented everything honestly, with no razzle-dazzle, no attempt to trick them.

If the jury still struggled with confusion, it involved not the floor plan of the house, but the landlady herself. They heard testimony that she was generous and warm, and that she was manipulative and cold; that she gave some people a second chance, and that she tossed others out on their ears. She was the queen of transmutations: the sweet matron, the manipulative ex-con, the generous retired doctor, the crabby old lady, the saintly landlady struggling with wayward tenants.

Chuck Willgues, the old gent who'd met "Donna" in a bar down in L.A., then ended up turning her in to authorities, recalled how she'd impressed him as "dignified . . . a lady of distinction."

The notary public who had documented the granting to Dorothea of power of attorney over Leona Carpenter's funds, said that Leona "was very grateful. . . . She was looking at Dorothea as if she were her savior."

Marshall Losano, a former friend, recalled how Dorothea had shown him the curved incision along her hairline, telling him that she'd had an operation and was undergoing chemotherapy for brain cancer.

And Puente seemed to have been everywhere at once. Some said she was always at the house, sitting on her porch, housekeeping, doing yard work. A few saw her mainly at charity organizations. Others saw her only in bars. To some, she was a toothless woman in curlers; to others, a fashionable, white-haired charmer.

Who was she?

Clearly, the old woman was a liar . . . but was she trying to protect someone? And who was this McCauley character they kept hearing about?

Sitting in court, the defendant looked so weary and old it was hard to imagine her even as a scam artist, much less a murderer.

But John O'Mara didn't care how old and kind Dorothea might appear to be, and he didn't care whether the defense uprooted every good deed she'd ever done and dragged it into the courtroom. This Mother Teresa bit didn't wash with him. She was a liar who liked to call herself "doctor" and a thief who stole from people who trusted her. And he was about to prove that she was a cold-blooded killer nine times over.

Carol Durning Westbrook, a former friend and tenant, described Dorothea as an aging barfly with a temper, and a busy landlady with a misplaced soft spot for hopeless cases. But most importantly, she'd lived in the house when Puente was taking care of a woman named "Betty."

This woman seemed so ill, Westbrook thought she should be in a hospital. She was "skeletal," she said, never left the couch, and "moaned and groaned constantly. She always yelled for Dorothea to bring her pills."

Then, suddenly, Betty was gone. "I noticed the silence," Westbrook recalled.

When she asked Dorothea about Betty, the landlady told her that Betty's daughter had come and picked her up. But later, when a woman identifying herself as Betty's daughter came asking for her mother, Puente revised her story, saying that Betty had gone to a nursing home.

To O'Mara, this was vintage Puente: a sudden disappearance, a vague story, then those inconvenient contradictions, followed by some hasty backpedaling. He wanted to ask the jury, "Do you see the pattern?" But all he could do was call another witness.

Robert French was a droll old cuss who lived in the boardinghouse in late 1987, and Dorothea glared at him while he testified. He ridiculed Puente, amused the jurors immensely, and shared two key views of life at 1426 F Street.

French remembered one of the victims, a "skinny little lady named Dorothy Miller," whom he described as "sorta dingy" and "about a hundred pounds soakin' wet." He recalled that when Miller had disappeared, Puente had explained that. "Dorothy got arrested downtown for shoplifting and she threw her out."

French also testified that Puente was far stronger than she looked. When six ninety-four-pound sacks of ready-mix concrete were delivered to the house, she'd wanted them put under the porch, he said. But French was recovering from a hernia operation, and another tenant, Homer Myers, "just turned down his hearing aid and pretended he didn't hear." With no one else to turn to, Puente had to move the heavy sacks herself.

Under cross-examination, Vlautin asked French to demonstrate, hoping he'd botch it. But French convincingly mimed how the landlady had turned each sack up on end, squatted down, wrapped her arms around it, then stood, lifting with her legs.

This was the tough old bird O'Mara wanted the jury to see, not the dough-soft grandma at the counsel table.

Another witness even accused the old woman of physical assault. An ex-con with a drinker's face and a smoker's voice, Joyce Peterson said she'd had a broken leg the month she'd stayed at the boarding-house. After being brusquely evicted, she'd returned for her things, struggling up the stairs with her leg in a cast. Then, Peterson declared, "I'm standing up on the very edge of the top step, and she just come at me—*brkkk!*—and pushed me down the stairs! I thought my leg was broken again, and she was just standing up there at the top of the stairs looking at me!"

Poor Joyce Peterson was hardly the most credible witness. The defense pointed out that, when Mrs. Puente called the police that morning, the officer had hauled Peterson off to Detox. She bore a grudge against Puente, and her testimony might be discounted. But a far friendlier witness sullied Puente's character without even realizing it.

Patty Casey, a stout, plain little woman, had done herself up nicely for her stint on the witness stand, with her dark hair combed back, a touch of lipstick, tasteful clothes, and lacquered-red nails. Under questioning, Casey recalled meeting Mrs. Puente in 1987. Gradually, Casey had become Puente's favorite cabdriver, taking her on shopping trips for groceries, gardening supplies, even carpeting. They'd grown closer in March 1988, when Dorothea had invited her into the house to give her a kitten, and later she'd visited the house several times. "I felt a friendship with her, and we had a communication going," she said earnestly. "I cared very much for her, yes I did."

Casey came to know some of Dorothea's tenants, including Bert, whom she described as "a very sweet, likable person. Very quiet, very shy."

"What did Dorothea tell you about Bert?" O'Mara asked.

"Basically, that he had brain damage. He had a very traumatic accident, and had been very severely injured." Casey stated this as if it were fact. (Even some of the press accepted this as true.)

"How did he act around Dorothea Puente?"

"He was very devoted to her. He'd refer to her as Mama, kind of like a son. He was very responsive if she told him to do something. He took good care of himself because she would tell him, you know, to straighten his hair, or fix his pants, or his belt, or something. And she made sure he was well cared for."

O'Mara asked if she'd ever seen Bert drink.

She had, she said, but only on two occasions. Joe's Corner Bar "was close by and safe," and so it was "prearranged with the bartender" that Bert could have two beers a day. "It was something he looked forward to every day," she explained. "Dorothea had mentioned that it was his way of having a little independence."

But sadly, Bert had gotten carried away, just as Dorothea had feared that he might. In late July, Dorothea told her that Bert, "in his naïveté," had poured out all of Dorothea's soda supply, then "took the cans and bought alcohol with the money. He became quite inebriated," Casey stated.

"What was Mrs. Puente's reaction?"

"She was quite distraught. It was difficult for her."

"Was she angry?"

"It bordered on anger. It disappointed her."

Clearly, Casey believed this story. But it was hard to reconcile this with the Bert Montoya who was so childlike that he had to be instructed at every turn, so honest that he'd turned in a large sum of money that he'd found at Detox. Bert hardly seemed cunning enough to view cans of soda as a ticket to the liquor store. Why would Dorothea even concoct such a story?

All during Casey's testimony, Dorothea Puente seemed agitated, nudging her attorneys, passing them notes, whispering in their ears.

In one apparently inconsequential exchange, O'Mara asked Casey whether Puente could drive. "Oh, she *could* drive," Casey replied, "but she didn't care to."

Later, when the jurors had been excused for a break and the courtroom was virtually empty, Dorothea burst out, "I don't know where these people get all the things they're saying about me!" Addressing her comments to Bailiff Bill Jackson, she complained, "I can't drive a car! I could never drive a car! I never even wanted to learn. I'm scared to death of driving."

Her voice low and contemptuous, she protested that Patty Casey had never been inside her house, not even when she'd given her the kitten. Further, the cabbie was in no position to know the least bit of what she was testifying to because "I stopped using her from June to September."

Puente seemed to think that this woman who'd called herself a friend had turned against her. And worse, in Puente's eyes, Casey was raking in fame and glory. "She was even on *Geraldo*," Dorothea griped. Then, making a startling leap, she added loudly, "And she's being paid by that lady back there."*

She went on, muttering, "Where do these people get all this shit they're saying about me? She never was inside my house, *never* was inside my house. . . ."

After her attorneys returned, the defendant resumed her nudging and whispering as Patty Casey's testimony continued.

O'Mara covered various things, then asked, "Was there a time when you no longer saw Bert?"

It was in early August, Casey said, when she "began to miss seeing him around the house."

"Did you discuss Bert's absence with Dorothea?"

"She said he had taken a trip to Mexico," Casey answered, recalling the day. "I picked her up and she said, 'Oh, I sent him off to Mexico.' And we joked about it because he got to go and she didn't."

O'Mara asked whether Casey had ever heard of Bert returning from Mexico.

She had. It was a Saturday in early November, she was sure, when Dorothea told her that Bert had returned for just a short time, and then someone had taken him away. "I believe she said it was a relative."

"No further questions, Your Honor."

The defense declined to question Patty Casey that day, and she was excused.

The plump cabdriver exited the courtroom, leaving behind the question of whether she ever fully realized that not just a few things, but virtually everything her friend Dorothea Puente had ever told her was a lie.

From the mouths of former friends, associates, and tenants came words of praise and scorn for Dorothea Puente, but their words also curiously linked her with one particular man: *John McCauley*.

First McCauley was supervising the guys on work furlough who dug here or poured concrete there. Next McCauley was riding some two dozen times in Patty Casey's cab, carrying supplies home from Lum-

---

*Author's note: As I was the only other person in the courtroom, this surprising news was clearly aimed at me.

berjack. Then McCauley was escorting Dorothea to Tiny's Bar on the day of her escape.

Robert French called him Puente's "majordomo."

And curiously, while many boarders had come and gone, he'd stayed on. And though most of the men had roomed downstairs, he'd lived upstairs, in a room near Dorothea's.

If they were lovers, it was a stormy affair. John Sharp recalled that the couple had battled and cursed, throwing a vacuum and even a small refrigerator down the stairs. Carol Durning Westbrook, hearing the two screaming at each other, said she'd rushed in to see McCauley punching Dorothea. And she described McCauley as "an antagonist. He constantly tried to start arguments with people, insulted people. A very mean person, I thought."

Others had been evicted for simple offenses, why not him?

Because they were lovers? Or because she'd needed his help? If she'd kicked him out, would he have told the cops what he knew?

Or might John McCauley be the murderer, she the accomplice?

If he wasn't an accomplice, what was he?

CHAPTER 40

No one could figure out this jury. A bit of kinship among jurors wasn't so unusual, especially once they'd become familiar and relaxed, finding avenues toward camaraderie. But they usually didn't get along so *well*.

At first, it was just good-natured kidding of a juror who arrived late or spilled a cup of water. It didn't matter that they joked and joshed during the breaks, or that this joviality sometimes carried into the courtroom. With such an extended, detailed trial, humor comes as relief.

The attorneys laughed along with them, and sometimes tossed out witty asides during questioning. Even the judge offered an occasional jest—(Peter Vlautin was wearing a particularly loud necktie one day when the power went off. In the sudden darkness came a long pause, and then Judge Virga's voice: "I told Mr. Vlautin not to wear that tie.")

And some of the witnesses were funny. When one former tenant griped about Dorothea's burritos, saying, "Let's face it, Dorothea's a lousy cook," even the attorneys broke up; Kevin Clymo laughed so hard he slapped the table.

But what had started as polite chuckles blossomed into open guf-faws. The jury got rowdy. A few whispered and pulled faces during testimony, with the XREMIST the most comedic of the group. Wear-ing bright "Jungle Training" or Harley-Davidson T-shirts, he fre-quently leaned forward and hung over the rail, behavior O'Mara had never seen. Strangest of all, some jurors made comments directly to the attorneys, and neither side knew how to respond. Certain that any impropriety would come back to haunt him, O'Mara tried to ignore them. Clymo, the most good-natured of the attorneys, fre-quently chuckled or offered a rejoinder. And Vlautin, literally and figuratively, was in the middle.

Anyway, it was jarring, in the midst of a multiple-murder trial, to have the jury suddenly burst out laughing. Even the court clerk wished they would "straighten up." But the dilemma was, who could chastise them without inviting hostility? The attorneys cer-tainly weren't going to risk offending the very people who sat in judgment. And the judge was reluctant to scold a group that, in performing its civic duty, would have to endure several months of testimony.

One could only wonder what the defendant thought of this merry bunch.

At the end of one long day of testimony, the attorneys were tired. Rather than have O'Mara call a witness to the stand to present yet another display—a map, this time—the defense stipulated that, yes, this was an accurate map of Sacramento, so O'Mara could present it to the jurors himself. He grabbed a pointer and, looking consummately professorial, indicated the yellow arrows showing 1426 F Street, Detox, and assorted other spots they'd heard about.

O'Mara wrapped up quickly, then Judge Virga adjourned for the day and stepped down from the bench.

Did the jurors file out meekly? Did they save their questions until the end of trial, when they could examine all the evidence at their leisure? No. In a raucous outburst, they started shouting questions at O'Mara: "Where's Tiny's Bar?" one demanded. "K Street Mall, K Street Mall," others chanted, standing.

Didn't they realize this was an incredible breach of decorum?

Apparently not. Out of blind curiosity, they forced the court back on record. The judge turned and resumed the bench. And the prosecutor, seeming flustered, took up the pointer and followed their commands, pointing out Tiny's Bar here, and—regaining his composure—the K Street Mall in this area. Satisfied, the jury was now prepared to release the reins of power, and court was again adjourned.

Nothing would tax the jury's collective attention span (and the strength of their stomachs) as much as the "tox and docs"—the toxicological and medical testimonies. Like it or not, they were about to become more intimate with nine strangers' medical conditions than with their own.

It began with autopsies. As tall, blond Dr. Robert Anthony took the stand in a conservative suit, it was hard to picture him in his greens, snapping off his surgical gloves, exiting the morgue with a *Worry, Be Sad* button on his lapel. Occasionally some black humor snuck into his testimony, but for the most part, he and fellow forensic pathologist Dr. Gary Stuart stuck to their morbid scripts.

Over a period of weeks, these two doctors were repeatedly called to the stand to share every odious detail of the autopsies, every Y-incision, every mushy organ, and some jurors couldn't help but blanch. For hours, images of decomposed, putrefied, even skeletonized remains sailed about the room.

By far the most macabre autopsy was that of the lady who had no head, Betty Palmer. Dr. Anthony testified that Palmer's head had been removed above the third vertebra, and several jurors visibly recoiled. "Both hands were removed at the wrists," he continued, "and both legs, from the level of the knees, were absent." Kneecaps were missing, too.

Under questioning, Dr. Anthony explained that the cutting had been done inexpertly at the "joint spaces," leaving "tool marks" on the bones. Judging from the sharp, smooth cuts and the flat faces on the bones at the ends of the arms, he surmised that the tool was "not an ordinary kitchen knife" but, more likely, "a saw, ax, cleaver, some heavy device. A machete. Something large and heavy."

A few jurors shook their heads. Others muttered, stealing glances at the accused.

O'Mara asked the witness if he could determine whether the cutting was done during life or after death. He could not. But Dr. Anthony also testified that *no blood* had been found on Betty Palmer's clothes or wrappings. Not a drop. And if the cutting had been done near the time of death, one would expect these to be saturated.

When questioned about the cause of death, the pathologist admitted, "Since we're dealing with less than a complete individual, I can't really rule out anything."

If Puente had mutilated Betty Palmer in hopes of hiding her identity, there was heavy irony in how she'd been ultimately identified. Palmer had broken her hip back in 1984, and the doctor had used a prosthetic device in repairing it. A photograph of her skeletonized hip clearly showed a metal plate with an imprinted number—the ultimate ID card.

Eventually, the heaps of details began to fall into patterns. With each autopsy came an inventory of how the body had been meticulously wrapped. O'Mara showed the jury grisly photos of the bodies as the layers were cut away, and the very images seemed to put out a stench. (At lunch, some jurors had trouble putting the "appetizing" images out of their minds.)

Typically, there were layers of plastic, then bed sheets and quilts. A few had absorbent, diaperlike Chux pads wrapped up with them. The strange bundles showed unmistakable similarities in the plastic held with duct tape, and particularly in the knots. Again and again, the jurors saw that the sheets had been distinctively knotted near the head or neck. A signature—even back to the 1985 wrappings of Everson Gillmouth.

Most of the time, Dorothea Puente sat immobile. But during Dr. Stuart's testimony she suffered a cold. While she listened, her pretty hands neatly folded tissues into smaller and smaller squares.

With the defense intent on proving death by natural causes and the prosecution intent on proving murder, lifestyles and medical histories were on trial. Doctor after doctor took the stand to recite the many ailments plaguing the alleged victims. Most had received haphazard medical treatment, chancing upon this clinic or that emergency room, leaving behind only sketchy records. Only James Gallop had been treated by anyone so specialized as a neurosurgeon.

Pompous, defensive, kind, or clinical, the doctors described patients who were mostly drinkers who abused and neglected themselves. Additionally, most had alarming maladies, fueling the battle over medical interpretations.

Bert Montoya had diabetes, and his blood-sugar count had tested abnormally high (464) on July 20, 1988, shortly before his death. The prosecution showed that his blood-sugar count had subsequently subsided (dropping to 50). But the defense elicited testimony that suggested a fatal diabetic coma.

To say that Ben Fink's alcoholism had undermined his health was understatement. It had taken him two years to recover from multiple leg fractures he suffered when he staggered out in front of an on-rushing car. His smoking and drinking didn't help his condition any, and the complications he suffered sounded as bad as his injuries. Further, the jurors heard that Fink had once been admitted to a hospital with a death-defying blood-alcohol level of 0.456. (In California, one is legally drunk at 0.08.) In Dr. Anthony's words, Fink "lived to drink."

Seventy-eight-year-old Leona Carpenter, who suffered a host of chronic ailments, was in and out of the hospital so much that it seemed amazing she hadn't dropped dead months before moving into Puente's boardinghouse. Most interesting, however, was the fact that she'd been treated for a Dalmane overdose after just a couple of days at Dorothea's. Was it self-administered? Or had Dorothea only nearly killed her that first time, succeeding later?

Vera Faye Martin, another alcoholic, had suffered the vagaries of the street, including being assaulted and raped, suffering a broken jaw and other injuries. Like Fink, this little, hundred-pound woman checked into emergency rooms with dangerously high blood-alcohol levels (0.34 and 0.32). Records also revealed that she had heart problems, including an 85 percent occlusion of one artery, which the defense highlighted as evidence that Martin had suffered a fatal heart attack.

Dorothy Miller's alcoholism had caused cirrhosis of the liver, and her smoking habit had contributed to cardiopulmonary disease. Additionally, she suffered from seizures and long-term mental problems, but no one seemed to know much about her.

Betty Palmer was certainly peculiar. Besides having heart problems, she complained about pain in her hip and pelvis area. She apparently had a real affection for pain pills, and a strange affection for doctors. She frequently demanded pelvic exams, and boasted about fictitious affairs with various physicians. One speculated from the witness stand that she suffered from "erotomania."

But of all these aging, ailing folks, James Gallop was the one with the most extraordinary illnesses. He suffered from a brain tumor, causing a "proptosis" or protrusion of his right eye. In January 1987 he underwent a craniotomy. The good news was that the tumor was benign; the bad news was that it was inoperable. Even radiation treatments had no effect on the nasty "schwannoma," and it would continue to grow, pressing against cranial nerves that controlled sight in his right eye and feeling in the right side of his face. But that wasn't all. Gallop had suffered a heart attack, had cardiopulmonary disease, and was about to undergo yet another operation to determine whether a growth in his intestine was cancerous.

Gallop's hospital records presented an especially prickly problem. One doctor had jotted, "Make last days as comfortable as possible." Apparently, the doctor had believed that Gallop had brain cancer. He was mistaken, but the defense stressed that Gallop's condition was so precarious that even a trained physician believed he might expire at any time.

And so it went. A parade of doctors marched into court to share information about the medical histories of the deceased, adding volumes of detail to the verbal tug-of-war between the attorneys. O'Mara elicited testimony that these people, if not 100 percent healthy, weren't knocking on death's door either. Then Clymo and Vlautin hammered home each ailment, getting doctors to admit that, indeed, some of these conditions could have proved deadly.

The jury learned that each of the seven bodies found in Puente's yard had tested positive for Dalmane, or flurazepam. Still, with the exception of Ruth Munroe—the only one promptly autopsied—there was no way to prove the cause of even one of these deaths. The question remained unanswered: Without a cause of death, could O'Mara prove murder?

Weeks went by and the jurors listened, with varying degrees of attention, to dozens and dozens of impersonal specialists who consulted their notes and talked of this or that victim, whom they couldn't clearly recall.

Except for lean and serious Robert Fink, who looked like the Marlboro Man when he came on March 10 to mourn the loss of his brother, Ben, the courtroom was strangely vacant of kin.

To O'Mara, this was one of the biggest problems with this case. At least Bert Montoya had been missed. But several of these "shadow people" had passed into the darkness alone and unnoticed. Without family to grieve them, their true identities seemed indistinct, nearly anonymous. It was hard to understand. Sure, some had never married, or had no children. But Dorothy Miller's family, who'd cared enough to get a lawyer and file suit against Peggy Nickerson and others, had never even bothered to contact O'Mara about testifying.

And Vera Faye Martin had seven children. How had this mother of so many become homeless? Was she so out of touch that she refused offers of normalcy and shelter? Was she such an irascible drunk that her own children had turned her out on the street?

On March 24, a tall, slender woman appeared briefly on the stand, then disappeared like an apparition. Her name was Edith Elaine Ehnisz, she said, and Vera Martin was her mother. Every year, she testified, her mother would call her on her birthday, October 19. But in 1987, this didn't happen. The last time she'd seen her mother, she said, was "probably 1982."

That was it. She knew so little about her mother's condition during the final five years of her life that O'Mara didn't question her further.

Whatever breach had arisen between mother and daughter was none of the court's business. And the defense wanted this potentially sympathetic witness off the stand as soon as possible; they excused Martin's daughter without a single question.

After six weeks of testimony and over sixty witnesses, Ehnisz was only the second family member to appear. A blink, and the woman's long, dark hair was vanishing out the door, leaving behind the unsettling question of how filial bonds can be so tenuous.

Throughout months of testimony, Dorothea Puente enigmatically read documents and passed notes to her attorneys. Jurors sometimes regarded her curiously, but she revealed nothing. At a break, one perplexed juror left muttering, "She never fidgets."

It was true. During court, the defendant was surprisingly placid. But when court was adjourned and the jury departed, Puente could stretch her legs and relax. She chatted with the bailiff about the scale models of the F Street house, pointing out this or that, complaining that they didn't truly show how many books she had, or the wedding dress she claimed she'd been sewing at the time of her arrest. Sometimes she even asked O'Mara about the pending trials of mutual "acquaintances."

One day the court reporter, Mary Corbitt, who had come down from Sacramento to work on the trial, was stunned to hear Puente ask, "How is your mother? I used to see her down at Frank's Meats. I always shopped there because they have the best quality."

Mary Corbitt smiled and mouthed something innocuous, but later she puzzled over this. She knew there was no way that Dorothea Puente could possibly know her mother. And it seemed very strange to her that Puente would concoct such a story. Eventually, she recalled that she'd once mentioned something about her mother and that particular butcher shop to the court clerk. Puente must have overheard. And then, apparently, she just couldn't help herself. Her reality was fluid, rushing in like the sea to fill any gap.

CHAPTER 41

Back from a long Easter break—stretched to three weeks by another trial Clymo was handling—the jurors came in on April 26 tanned and smiling. Peter Vlautin, who had run a 10K race the day before, seemed full of pep.

But not everyone was embraced by the sweet buoyancy of reunion. Dorothea Puente was still recovering from some minor surgery, having had a small abscess removed. Kevin Clymo was understandably fatigued, having squeezed one trial into his "vacation" from another. And John O'Mara, who'd spent the whole time bent over a desk, was volubly regretting that he hadn't brought down an assistant months before.

Usually, O'Mara knew a case backward and forward after handling the preliminary hearing. But now, lacking that experience, he was feeling overwhelmed. Despite random help from his investigators and whatever miracles the secretaries in Sacramento could fax down, he complained that "there just aren't enough hours in the day to get it all done." Sunk in a swamp of "to do" lists, O'Mara was biting back the sour realization that he needed full-time help, preferably another attorney. But it was office policy to work solo. Besides, now it was too late.

As usual, O'Mara had been overly optimistic in scheduling. A local hotel brimmed with waiting witnesses, including Dorothea Puente's mysterious friend and confidant, Mervin John McCauley.

McCauley had no idea how eagerly he was awaited. Whatever anticipations hummed around his name, he had more pressing concerns: He needed a drink. Never mind the hour, never mind the constraints, McCauley was a man with priorities. So, on the morning of April 26, while O'Mara was hoping to question him in court, McCauley was intent on consuming a pint of vodka.

By the end of the day McCauley was feeling not the least intimidated by the thought of testifying. In the hallway, he boozily joked, "This is the first time I've been in court when I'm not the defendant!"

O'Mara ruefully postponed McCauley's testimony until the next day, when some last-minute supervision managed to keep McCauley from downing more than "a couple shots of vodka" before being called to the stand Tuesday morning.

Thin and gray as a nail, he ambled into court, laying eyes on Dorothea Puente for the first time in four and a half years.

An unrepentant drunk, McCauley set the tone for his testimony when the court clerk asked him to raise his right hand and he responded, "Why?"

A bright blue baseball cap remained atop his head for a good hour of testimony, hiding even more of a face already concealed by large glasses and a bristly gray beard. When O'Mara spoke, he turned his good ear toward him, then cantankerously replied with a graveled voice, "I couldn't tell ya," or, "I have no idea." When O'Mara asked him to ID people in photographs, he tossed them aside with hardly a glance.

The jury couldn't help but snicker at McCauley's gall, and this seemed to set him at ease. Gradually, he warmed to his role. The cap came off, revealing a high, lined forehead and steel-gray hair slicked back in a straight plunge to his collar. The court reporter noticed that he smelled of alcohol.

He admitted doing some of the yard work at 1426 F Street. "Mostly, I supervised," he said, confirming the testimony of various ex-cons Puente had hired through work furlough. But, parroting the landlady, McCauley maintained that the concrete covering some of the graves was merely "to keep the weeds down." And he stubbornly denied knowledge of any digging, other than "planting, stuff like that."

McCauley also suffered convenient memory lapses, particularly when trying to remember any of the victims other than Leona Carpenter and Bert Montoya. Of Leona's disappearance, he said, "It just seemed to be general knowledge that she had to go to a nursing home." And he said that he and Bert used to drink together at Joe's Corner: "He'd put down a beer in three gulps."

Dismissing all others with a wave of his hand, McCauley said, "People come and people go."

By this time, McCauley was feeling quite comfortable on the stand, so comfortable that during one break, he called out to the defendant, "Dorothea, how the heck are ya?"

Defense attorney Vlautin hurried over and whispered some sort of reprimand.

"However, I am coherent," McCauley retorted loudly. "I'm a lucid alcoholic."

When the jury was again seated, O'Mara continued. Working from transcripts of multiple police interviews, he got McCauley to admit to his most damning act: digging a hole in front of the house, where Betty Palmer's truncated corpse had been buried beneath a religious shrine.

"How far in front of the shrine did you do this digging?"

"A foot. Or less."

"All right. And what kind of hole did you dig at that location?"

"About two by two."

"Do you remember when you did that digging?"

"Shortly after I moved in."

"Did someone ask you to dig, or did you do it on your own?"

"No, I did it on my own. I was asked to. Dorothea asked me to."

McCauley claimed the hole had been dug to plant some camellia bushes, but Ricardo Ordorica had asked him to fill the hole back up because it was too dangerous for Ordorica's small children. McCauley maintained that he'd buried nothing.

McCauley also volunteered the astonishing news that he was the one who'd built the shrine, and his motivation for this seemed oddly out of character. "I thought it'd be a nice gesture," the irascible old fellow said, "because I knew that Dorothea was kinda religious . . . A lot of people would come by and admire the garden. It seemed like a good spot."

When O'Mara pressed him for an explanation of where he'd come up with this idea, McCauley yielded only marginally: "I really can't tell you who put the incident in my head. But heck, I was glad to do it."

This religious shrine was an oddity. None of the other graves had any sort of marker. And none of the bodies other than Betty Palmer's had been mutilated. Earlier, another former tenant had testified that Dorothea had snapped at him one night because he'd accidentally switched off the light inside the shrine. Apparently, the landlady always kept a single, red Christmas light glowing inside it.

Whether or not McCauley knew more than he was saying, Dorothea was hardly in a position to accuse him of anything, or to contradict him when he announced, "I didn't know anybody was buried there."

If the jurors were wondering whether McCauley and Puente were lovers, if they were hoping that O'Mara might help dispel their curiosity, they would be disappointed. O'Mara would not ask, and McCauley wasn't saying. When O'Mara asked him about Puente, he shrugged. "We had good times, we had bad times. She had a quick temper, but it didn't last long."

Just how much did McCauley know? He seemed the most likely accomplice, and he'd surely seen more than he was letting on, yet the police had questioned him for days and the ornery old drunk had only frustrated them. Some jurors may have hoped that an accomplice would come forward to somehow exonerate Dorothea. But McCauley wasn't about to budge now that he was almost off the stand.

"Did you ever drag any bodies?" O'Mara asked.

"No, no."

That's about what O'Mara had expected. He took another approach, asking, "What were you arrested for?"

"Accessory after the fact."

"To the crime of murder?"

"It came as a heckuva surprise to me!" he retorted.

Then McCauley blurted out, "I also took a lie detector test." (McCauley had passed, but lie detector results are inadmissable in court. And some said that McCauley's "pickled brain" rendered those results meaningless.)

McCauley continued to insist he knew nothing, even though he'd escorted Dorothea away from the house, the two of them sharing a cab to Tiny's Bar in West Sacramento before her escape to L.A.

Now O'Mara asked, "Did you know she had over three thousand dollars?"

304

"No, I don't inquire into other people's finances," he responded primly.

If police detectives couldn't get more than this out of the old goat during long interrogations, O'Mara couldn't hope to do better now. He finally relented. "No further questions, Your Honor."

Clymo was surprised. He'd expected O'Mara to shake this witness like an angry guard dog. Leaving well enough alone, he waived cross-examination, and McCauley was excused.

He left with an almost theatrical flare, bowing and gesturing broadly, as if he'd just pulled off a fabulous interview on *David Letterman*. "Thank you individually, Ladies and Gentlemen, Mr. O'Mara, and"— looking at Dorothea—"I hope everything comes out all right."

Outside the courtroom, McCauley commented on his old buddy Dorothea, saying, "I thought highly of her." He paused. "Maybe a Jekyll and Hyde kinda thing, but you couldn't prove it by me," he said, claiming, "I wouldn't lie to save her."

Leaving the courthouse, he doubtless went to find himself another drink.

Sometimes, with a long trial like this, strange things arise. One afternoon, with the other jurors excused, an alternate juror informed the court that downstairs, on the wall by the phone, someone had scrawled messages, perhaps to try to influence the jury. The messages read "Free Dorothea Puente!" and "Go, Dorothea, go!"

The judge thanked the alternate for bringing this to the court's attention, and the messages were promptly removed.

One can only guess who might have written them.

If McCauley's testimony had jolted the courtroom, few outside felt its repercussions. Judge Virga had banned cameras, so—except for *Sacramento Bee* reporter Wayne Wilson, who came like clockwork— most of the media opted for only sporadic coverage; when some reporters popped in, they struggled like rank spectators to put testimony into context.

Meanwhile, curious about the notorious landlady, senior citizens huddled together and whispered in the gallery; jurors' relatives came to watch; groups of students sat in on assignment; courtroom groupies filtered in and out. And a wanna-be screenwriter from Southern California, a cheerful little butterball of a woman, scoured transcripts and

305

noted, "She looks like *The Bad Seed* all grown up, doesn't she? Did you see that movie?"

Figuring out Dorothea Montalvo Puente had become a spectator sport. Everyone wondered whether she really did it. And if she did do it, was she *crazy*, or truly *evil*?

The scales tipped toward crazy when testimony revealed that Puente had been receiving SSI benefit checks since 1978 based on a diagnosis of schizophrenia. Some wondered why she wasn't pleading not guilty by reason of insanity.

Why not? Because her attorneys were smarter than that.

For a time, schizophrenia had been a catchall diagnosis; it was almost fashionable. But if Puente were to plead insanity, her mental state would be fair game for courtroom argument. She would be reexamined, her psyche prodded and pushed. And psychologists today would come up with far different analyses.

More than this, the source of the schizophrenia diagnosis, Dr. Thomas Doody, was suspect.* The jurors had heard how easily Puente could get prescriptions from her favorite psychiatrist—Dalmane, Valium, whatever she wanted was just a phone call away.

Testimony revealed that Dorothea had helpfully suggested to friends that they, too, could get on SSI, if only they would go to Dr. Doody and "act crazy," in the words of one witness.

Puente's attorneys didn't want to make her alleged "schizophrenia" an issue. They'd invested heavily in mapping out the territory within Dorothea Puente's cranium and decided it was far better to wait, to save what they'd learned about her peculiar cognitive processes—if need be—for the penalty phase of the trial.

The ninety-ninth witness was even more controversial than John McCauley.

Puente's former friend Brenda Trujillo hadn't changed much since the preliminary hearing. Perhaps her long, straight hair was a brighter shade of red, but she was hardly a shade brighter. Getting her criminal history on record for the jury, O'Mara questioned Trujillo about arrests, paroles, and rearrests. Even though he'd prepared a "cheat sheet" of facts for her, she bungled dates, contradicted herself, and

---

* Dr. Thomas Doody was too ill to come to Monterey to testify, O'Mara was told.

came across as the same dim ex-con and former junkie who'd testified at the prelim.

Despite her disreputable history and weak answers, Trujillo knew another side of Puente's character. They'd been close, and Trujillo would put a new spin on the landlady's private moments. In fact, she said in her slow, soft voice, "She told people that I was her niece."

Trujillo had lived at 1426 F Street from September 1985 until September 1987 for short periods between arrests. And during that time she'd chanced to meet a few of Dorothea's doomed boarders. James Gallop, for one. She remembered the thin man with "a patch on his eye and a bandage on his head" who had come to live at the boarding-house. "He'd just got out of the hospital. I don't think he could walk, 'cuz he was sick," she recalled.

Trujillo had kept in close contact with Dorothea after being rearrested. And the landlady had mentioned Gallop to her in two phone conversations, Trujillo testified. The first time, Puente said that Gallop was so sick "all he wanted to do was lay on the couch and hold her hand." He was throwing up and had diarrhea, and looked "like he was gonna die."

In the next conversation, Trujillo said, her voice cracking, "She said he had died."

"Did you ask any questions about his death?" O'Mara asked.

"I asked if she knew where he was buried, because I wanted to go there."

"What did she tell you?"

"She said no, that she had his body cremated because he had no family."

The courtroom was as still as ice.

O'Mara pressed on. "Did Dorothea tell you about buried bodies?"

"Yes. When we was drinking, she would tell me that she had bodies down in the yard and not to go down there."

And this was only the beginning. O'Mara had more.

Trujillo remembered a man living with Dorothea back in 1985, and she identified a photo of Everson Gillmouth. Others had called him "Gill," but Dorothea's boyfriend was "Bill" in her recollection.

Later, held again at the county jail, Trujillo had a strange phone conversation with her friend Dorothea.

"What did she tell you about Bill, or Gill?" O'Mara prodded.

"She told me that he had a heart attack. She said that she couldn't afford to call the ambulance because he was dead, and she didn't want to go back to prison." In a whisper, Trujillo added that Dorothea asked "if I knew someone who can get rid of the body. She would pay them four thousand dollars. I told her that I would ask around."

"Did she say anything else about this person?"

"She told me that he was buried down in her garden."

Why would Dorothea have said this to Trujillo? Gillmouth had been found in a box at the side of the river, far from Dorothea's garden. Was this some kind of twisted boast? Or was Trujillo fabricating now, venting anger at Puente, whom she blamed for her last arrest?

Next Trujillo described a quiet evening at Puente's home. "Me and her were sitting in the living room drinking. And she left, and I went to see where she was at. And I walked in the kitchen, and she was leaning over the table, with a glass about that high"—she indicated a height with her hands—"and had fixed a Bloody Mary. And on the table was a napkin with some open pills. She was leaning over the table, and she was opening these pills and putting them in his drink. And I asked her what she was doing."

"You say she was opening these pills," O'Mara interrupted. "What did these pills look like?"

"They were pink capsules with white substance in them."

"And where were these pills?"

"She had them in her hand, and she was opening them and shaking them in the glass, and there was some empty ones on the napkin."

"You say you asked her what she was doing?"

"Yes."

"What did she say?"

"Fixing McCauley a drink. She said to knock him out."

O'Mara asked her to continue.

"I standed in the doorway and watched her take it to him." Then they returned to the living room, sat down, and continued talking, Trujillo said. "About thirty minutes later she went back in the kitchen. I was wondering what she was doing, so I went into the kitchen," she said softly, "and I called, and she wasn't there. I peeked my head around the corner, and she came out of John's room with his coat."

"What was she doing?"

"Going through his pockets."

"What did you see her do?"

"She pulled out some money."

"What happened then?"

"She offered me the money, but I didn't take it," she asserted. "And then she went back, because there was nothing else in the coat pocket, and started going through his pants pockets. He didn't have nothing, so we went back out."

Trujillo might be a liar and a junkie, but for a moment, her testimony was golden. After all the talk of Dalmane prescriptions, this witness had finally put capsules in Dorothea Puente's hands. Better yet, she'd presented an image of those hands opening capsules and emptying them into a drink.

Yet the defense had plenty to work with on cross-examination. Trujillo seemed confused and unreliable. Though now on methadone treatments, years of heroin and alcohol use had apparently dulled her brain. She equivocated. She mumbled. And she was especially slow to admit any wrongdoing of her own. Everything she said seemed suspect.

Peter Vlautin felt the jury was with him, scrutinizing her credibility, squinting at her with skeptical eyes. But now he pushed too hard. He stood and demanded, "Dorothea Puente never told you that she killed people, did she?"

After a weighty pause, Trujillo murmured, "Yes. She did."

Vlautin was incredulous. "She told you she killed these people?" he repeated.

"Yes," she quietly insisted. "She told me herself that she had killed people and that they were buried in her yard.'"

This was more than anyone had expected. Puente glared at her. O'Mara was nearly as stunned as Vlautin.

Vlautin continued to slash at Trujillo's credibility, getting her to admit that she'd never used the word *kill* before, despite numerous interviews with police. Still, he couldn't stop her soft words from settling across the room like dust.

After more than a hundred witnesses, the jury may have thought Mrs. Puente had an odd circle of friends, socializing with drunks and lowlifes like McCauley and Trujillo. Some probably wondered how she'd supposedly gotten away with these crimes for so long. She was an ex-con on parole, after all; hadn't her parole officers gotten suspicious when they saw her associating with junkies, ex-cons, and alcoholics?

Ah, but Dorothea Puente was, as Judy Moise once said, "Many things to many people." And O'Mara was about to prove that with a surprise witness.

Dressed in a fine three-piece suit, looking solid and upstanding, Mr. Gilbert Avila took the stand. He articulately described how he'd been introduced to Dorothea Puente in late 1979 or early 1980 when he was working as a special assistant to then Attorney General George Deukmejian (who later became governor of California). Puente had "purchased" a table at a charity dinner, and Mr. Avila had been invited to join her party. Throughout the evening, Mr. Avila believed that his charming hostess was a medical doctor who ran "some kind of rehabilitation facility or home for alcoholics."

Dorothea always had a way with men, and Mr. Avila was apparently as susceptible as any. This Mexican-American fund-raiser launched a two-year "friendship." And Avila explained that during their relationship (mostly "dinner dates"), he remained convinced that his well-heeled companion was a physician.

Strangely, Dorothea Puente had eventually asked Avila to become consignatory on one of her savings accounts, claiming, he recalled, that "she had cancer and didn't trust anyone but me."

Many things to many people, indeed.

CHAPTER 42

P OOR JAMES BEEDE. HE WAS JUST A MAN TRYING TO DO HIS JOB.
Sure, he'd made some mistakes in his career. And, yes, the cocaine
contamination that showed up in Ben Fink's specimens had posed
problems. But if anything, Beede had gone the extra mile for this
case, not only testing the tissue homogenates himself, but also sending
them out for testing by two other labs. He certainly hadn't expected
to end up in the hot seat for all his efforts.

But here he was. Since toxicology was an issue, James Beede was
an issue.

After determining in intensive closed-door sessions with Judge Virga
just how far they could press this witness, the defense was doing
exactly that. First, Clymo grilled Beede on the apparently lax protocol
at the crime lab. Then he zeroed in on the issue of contamination,
establishing that even an airborne microscopic speck of some drug
could contaminate an entire sample. "Isn't it true," he asked, "that
you were reprimanded in 1986 for having raw drugs in your work
area and at your desk without authorization?"

The jury perked up at this.

"Yes, that's correct," Beede said, explaining that he'd been doing "personal research with respect to cocaine" following the cocaine overdose of a local football star.

"In November 1990, you were again severely reprimanded?"

"Yes," Beede had to admit. "I was disciplined for conducting personal research with the compound sufentanil [citrate]."

Under questioning, Beede stated that sufentanil, a narcotic analgesic used in surgery, is one of the most potent painkillers known, "roughly a thousand times more potent and powerful than morphine."

"It's extremely toxic?"

"Yes."

"It can kill you?"

"Yes, it can."

Beede was compelled to explain that the substance is so dangerous that, even if wearing a full-body protective suit, one is supposed to be kept under observation for two hours after handling it. And Beede admitted that he hadn't worn a suit, not even goggles.

Clymo wasn't going to let him off easy. "You just cavalierly brought that into the lab one night, right? You just had it there on your desk?"

"Yes."

Judge Virga was listening carefully to how far Clymo was taking this. "You were suspended without pay for twenty days?"

"Yes, I was."

"The whole lab had to be decontaminated?"

Virga pounced. "Counsel, I'm going to restrict that."

But the jurors got the message.

Kevin Clymo scored big points with his cross-examination of this witness. Clearly, there had been lapses in Beede's work. Without question, there had been cocaine contamination of the Ben Fink homogenate.

But the issue here was Dalmane, and the Dalmane debate was hardly won. The attorneys were just warming up.

O'Mara again called Dr. Robert Anthony to the stand, establishing that, besides being a forensic pathologist, the doctor was a recognized expert in toxicology.

O'Mara hoped the jury was paying attention as Dr. Anthony explained that Dalmane, or flurazepam, has a half-life of one to three hours, so, after six or seven half-lives, this "parent drug" is eliminated from the body. Completely. It may take as few as six hours, or as many as twenty-one hours—to be conservative—for the drug to be fully broken down into its metabolites. Meaning that, in his expert opinion, *each of the individuals buried in the yard had ingested Dalmane less than twenty-four hours before death.*

This was not what the defense wanted the jury to hear.

Kevin Clymo edged into his cross-examination with a relaxed, casual tone, eventually asking, "Will sixty thirty-milligram tablets of Dalmane kill somebody?"

"I believe it will put them in a coma," Dr. Anthony replied. "I don't believe it will necessarily kill them."

"Dalmane has been reported as being one of the safest sedatives around, hasn't it?"

"That's its reputation."

"I believe at the prelim, you testified it would take hundreds of capsules to kill somebody."

"It could take as much as hundreds."

Here it was, the big punch for the jury.

"I asked how much that would be, if you poured out all of the white powder from the capsule and held it in your hands, and I believe you told me it would be the size of a softball, is that correct?"

"Yes, the amount of white fluffy powder you would end up with when you took a hundred or two hundred Dalmane and opened them all up, you would end up with a softball-size mass of powder."

Pleased with this victory, Clymo decided to push on. "Which is why, is it not, you told us that for all practical purposes, a massive overdose of drugs was ruled out in this case?"

The doctor saw his opportunity for clarification. "A massive dose of any *singular* drug was ruled out."

Clymo should have hoped the jury missed this distinction and moved on. Instead, he continued, "Ruled out because it would take such a huge quantity to kill somebody?"

"That's correct. But again, this is of any one substance. We are not talking about a combination of ingredients."

Belatedly, Clymo changed the subject.

The defense would later offer its own expert witness to refute Dr. Anthony's damaging opinions. But before letting him off the stand, Clymo extracted from Dr. Anthony another salient bit of testimony: When deprived of drink, alcoholics often turn to sedatives.

✿   ✿   ✿

With no discernible cause of death in this case, Dalmane was the "smoking gun," toxicologists the ballistics experts. Besides James Beede and Dr. Anthony, the prosecution called two additional toxicologists, William Phillips from the Department of Justice toxicology lab, and Dr. Michael Peat of Chem West. Like Beede, both had tested the tissue homogenates. The problem was that the experts had different findings.

Why was it that only Phillips, of the DOJ, had found Dalmane in each of the seven bodies unearthed from Puente's yard?

The obvious answer was that only the DOJ had the ultra-sensitive, $375,000 tandem mass spectrometer, which could most precisely distinguish any drugs from the "background noise" found in decomposed tissue.

More than this, Phillips quickly emerged as an impeccable scientist who ran his lab with ironclad protocol, leaving the defense no opportunity to attack him as they had Beede. But as Phillips discussed radioimmunoassay, ion capture, and gas chromatography, some of the jurors seemed painfully bored. Was this scientific minutiae becoming too obscure for ordinary citizens?

As O'Mara's exhibits marched on toward two thousand, the XREMIST nodded out. Spectators nudged one another. The court clerk sighed. The bailiff glared at him.

Finally, Judge Virga felt compelled to address this juror. After the others had been excused, Virga told him, "I've been concerned about your ability to pay proper attention," admonishing that both sides deserve an alert jury.

"I've got a lot of things weighing on me, Your Honor," Gary Frost apologized. "I'm sure you're aware of them."

With Fort Ord shutting down, Frost's company had been transferred to Fort Lewis, Washington. His commander had asked if Frost could be excused so that he could go too. But Virga could find no legal reason to do so, despite that six alternate jurors were waiting in the wings. Now, if Frost really wanted to go, all he had to do was state that he was unable to concentrate, and Virga would have to excuse him.

The defense hated the thought of losing their "wild card." The Solomon case had proven that a Vietnam Vet could stand up to other jurors. And though he was such a cutup, such an unpredictable sort, Clymo said they had their "fingers crossed" that the XREMIST would stay on. But Frost assured the judge that he felt competent to continue, and the defense attorneys breathed a sigh of relief.

It was now May, and after months of testimony and seemingly endless exhibits, everyone seemed weary. The joviality had diminished, occasional jokes seemed strained. The jury had been here since February, laboring to decipher accents, to grasp scientific terms, trying to give fair weight to the words of carpet cleaners and cardiologists, bankers and boozers.

During these months, the jurors, attorneys, even the judge and the defendant had come down with colds and flu. Birthdays and anniversaries had passed. At least one grandchild had been born. And Senior Bailiff Bill Jackson had passed away. (Jackson had been such an esteemed jazz musician that some four hundred people came to his memorial service, including numerous fellow musicians and a handful of jurors.)

By now, the jurors had every reason to feel overburdened by the load the justice system was putting on them, and to resent the fact that their "civic duty" had eaten up half the year. At breaks, most made ritual pilgrimages for coffee, and grumblings about trying to stay awake increased. But, except for the XREMIST, none dozed.

Despite months of testimony, the jury would never hear the whole story because reasons of law and strategy limited what reached their ears. For instance, deciding it wasn't relevant and would only complicate matters, John O'Mara wouldn't even mention Visine.

And he found himself in a quandary over Michelle Crowl. He knew she was a liar and a druggie, but he wanted to put her on the stand anyway. She had a great story to tell the jury, something no one else could say. But now he got wind of something rotten: The defense was ready to have Crowl's father testify that she was the biggest liar he'd ever met.

Brenda Trujillo was a liar and a junkie, too, but at least part of her story had corroboration. Not so Michelle Crowl. And O'Mara remembered one time that she'd come into his office so hopped up on drugs, he could almost hear her brain sizzling.

Finally, the prosecutor decided (to the great disappointment of the defense) that it was pointless to call her to the stand.

So, the jury would never hear about Puente's jailhouse chats. They would never hear that Puente had virtually confessed, saying that she was surprised "they linked Everson Gillmouth to the others," that she'd "suppressed their breathing" by putting drugs in their drinks, and that Bert Montoya "didn't know any better" than to help her bury bodies.

And, except for the scant references allowed by the court, O'Mara could scarcely squeeze in any mention of Puente's prior record. The victims of her 1981–1982 thefts were all dead, the testimonies of others precluded. Resigned, O'Mara said with a shrug, "It'll be very clean on appeal."

Even as the prosecution's case turned away from the seven bodies in the yard toward the two remaining counts—Ruth Munroe and Everson Gillmouth—even as O'Mara approached his last two dozen witnesses, testimonies were chopped to a minimum. And *hearsay* was the legal ax that cut them off.

A former friend of Munroe's, Nadine Nash, was too ill to come to court, so the attorneys agreed to have her testimony from the preliminary hearing read aloud—with significant deletions. The jury heard that Nash and Munroe had been friends for forty years, and that, a few weeks before her death, Munroe had stopped by Nash's home. They heard that during this visit Munroe had shown Nash "quite a lot" of money in her purse, saying it was $1,100 for the restaurant business she and Dorothea had started.

But the jury would not hear that Munroe had also said she had six thousand dollars in the trunk of her car—a stronger motive, perhaps, for murder.

Hearsay also cut short the testimony of little Dee Dee McKinnon. The jurors heard Dee Dee explain that she was Ruth Munroe's hairdresser, and that the Sunday before Munroe's death, she'd fixed Ruth's hair as usual. They heard that Munroe had looked pale. "She was sick. She didn't feel well," Dee Dee said, flying at the issue from every allowable angle. "She told me she felt awful. She didn't know why she was sick."

That was about all Dee Dee was permitted to say, and it bothered her that she couldn't share the significant fact that Munroe had also said, "Dorothea gave me a drink last night, and I don't remember anything else. I don't remember eating dinner, I don't remember going to bed."

To Dee Dee, Ruth had seemed shaken, bewildered. And after her appointment, the hairdresser had watched Ruth go downstairs and get into a car, where Dorothea Puente was waiting.

For Ruth's sake, she wished she'd been allowed to tell this to the jury. But who knows whether it would have seemed as important to them as it seemed to her.

But that final Sunday at the beauty shop was described in court by Camie Lombardo, another former friend of Munroe's. Camie had entered the shop just as Munroe was paying to leave, and she noticed immediately that Ruth looked drawn and pale. "She just looked ill," Camie told the jury. "She was kinda crying a little bit."

To Camie's friendly greeting, Munroe had responded with grim, prophetic words. "I can't talk to you now, Camie. I'm so sick, *I feel like I'm going to die.*"

Like Judy Moise, Ruth Munroe's children had been won over by John O'Mara. The Clausen family had been bitter about George Williamson abandoning this case after the prelim. But O'Mara wasn't just another attorney in the rotation, they discovered; he'd been Williamson's *boss.*

While the Clausen family was feeling more confident about O'Mara, he was feeling more disturbed about them. First, there was that whole codeine business, all of them *insisting* at the prelim that Munroe was allergic to it, when she was actually allergic to penicillin. And they'd all maintained that their mother would never have committed suicide—but if they'd been so sure about that, why hadn't they screamed bloody murder back in 1982?

To O'Mara, the Munroe case—the only one for which there had been a prompt autopsy—was looking shakier all the time. It hadn't been investigated properly in 1982, and, to his disgust, the reinvestigation in 1988 and 1989 had only muddied the waters. The defense had plenty to work with. So, when O'Mara called the Clausens to the stand, he kept their testimonies short and to the point.

William Clausen's hairline was beginning to retreat, but he still looked strong and feisty. When asked to identify Dorothea Puente, he shot her a look of complete distaste. He then described his mother's friendship with Puente, their budding restaurant business, and how he'd helped her move into 1426 F Street.

Her room? The bedroom off the kitchen—the one everyone now knew as the "haunted room."

"How would you describe her mental outlook when she first moved in?" O'Mara asked.

"Looking forward to a companion. She didn't want to live alone, that's why she moved in there."

When O'Mara asked if there had been some change in Munroe's demeanor, Clausen said that, about four days before her death, he'd noticed that "she looked tired." He added, "I checked on her every night before I went home from work."

On this occasion, "She had a drink in her hand. And that was odd. Mom was always energetic, and that day she was just sitting on the end of the couch with a drink. Well, I know my mom didn't drink, and I questioned her about it. She said it was just a drink that Dorothea had fixed her. Crème de menthe. And at that time, I didn't know that crème de menthe was alcohol." (That was easy to believe. He pronounced the drink "cream de mint.")

This was the only time that he'd seen his mother with a drink. But he saw her condition worsen.

Clausen's voice tightened as he turned to the night of the April 27, "when I saw her the last time."

"Where did you find her on that occasion?" O'Mara asked softly.

"In the bedroom."

"Was Dorothea at the house that evening?"

"Yes."

"What did she tell you?"

"She said that Mom was sick, and not to bother her. And I said, 'I want to see her.' And she said, 'The doctor was just here and gave her a shot. She's sleeping. Let her sleep.'"

"Did Dorothea tell you what type of illness your mother had?"

"No."

"Had Dorothea, in the past, ever said anything to you about medical training that she had?"

"Yes. She told me that she'd worked at a care home for the elderly as a nurse's aide."

The jury was intent. Even the defendant, who at first seemed to ignore this witness, set down her papers and listened.

"Did she say anything else?"

"Just that the doctor had been there, and she just kept trying to keep me from going into the room."

"Did you finally go into the room?"

"Yes."

"What did you see?"

"My mom was lying on the bed, facing the wall, on her side, and I went in and touched her and kind of moved her, rolled her over a little, and told her everything would be all right, Dorothea would take care of her, that I would be back the next night to check on her."

"Were you able to tell whether she was asleep or awake?"

"When I first went into the room, I couldn't tell. She looked like she was asleep." Voice thick, Clausen continued, "And when I rolled her over, her eyes were open and she just stared at me. She couldn't talk. She couldn't say anything. When I told her that Dorothea was going to take care of her and I'd be back to check on her the next evening, a tear come out of her eye."

"Why didn't you get any medical attention for your mother?"

"Because we trusted Dorothea," he said bleakly. "She had us believing that she would take care of Mom, she wouldn't let anything happen to her. And then when she said that the doctor had been there, I didn't know any different. As far as doctors coming to the house, I didn't think anything of it. I just figured, well, Dorothea will take care of her. I'll go home."

It had taken 114 witnesses, but O'Mara finally moved hearts with this bitter tableau.

With each of Munroe's children—William and Allan Clausen and Rosemary Gibson—the court heard the most heartrending testimony yet. But when O'Mara turned his witnesses over for cross-examination, the defense did their best to drain out all emotion, steamrolling Munroe's death to a flat, pointless suicide.

It was true that Harold Munroe, Ruth's new husband, had terminal cancer, and he'd run up a $7,000 medical bill. Yes, they'd been in the throes of divorce. And, yes, Ruth and Dorothea's restaurant business was going under.

Painting Munroe as broke and depressed, the defense carefully highlighted contradictions. Her kids had insisted that "she just didn't drink at all," yet she'd spent a lot of time with Harold in bars, and her autopsy showed an enlarged liver, which indicated a drinking problem. The children said they were close to their mother, yet they didn't know she'd recently been prescribed meprobamate, a mild tranquilizer. And they were wrong about her codeine allergy. The defense wanted the jury to wonder whether these kids knew their mother as well as they thought they did, for they had all maintained that she would never have committed suicide.

CHAPTER 43

Dᴇᴛᴇᴄᴛɪᴠᴇ ᴡɪʟʙᴜʀ ᴛᴇʀʀʏ ꜱᴛᴀʀᴇᴅ ᴜᴘ ᴀᴛ ᴛʜᴇ ᴄᴇɪʟɪɴɢ, ᴛʀʏɪɴɢ to recall the morning of New Year's Day, 1986. He had the rugged kind of face you'd expect to see up on horseback, under a cowboy hat. When he spoke, his voice was low and husky from years of smoking. "When I first got there, I was directed to the edge of the river," he said. "I saw a wooden box with the lid off, about three feet off the river. There was a body in the box."

O'Mara handed him a stack of photos, and Terry stroked a bushy mustache as he looked at them.

"Was the box up against a tree?" O'Mara asked.

"It appears to be, but as I recall it wasn't," he growled. "The body in the box was wrapped in clear plastic and a bed sheet. All I could see was the clear plastic at that point."

O'Mara asked if anything was used to fasten the plastic.

"Black electrical tape. And the sheet was tied in knots."

O'Mara asked about the box.

"It was plywood. Looked fairly new."

"Did you inspect the lid?"

"Yes. The lid had been nailed on all the way around." He speculated about how the lid had been pried off, noting, "The nails on the land side were straight, on the river side, they were all bent over. And they were rusty. All the nails were rusty."

"How was the body?"

"The body had slid down in the box, more or less in a fetal position. And the box was at quite an angle. . . . You could see enough to tell it was a body."

"Was there an odor?"

"Yes, it was deteriorating badly at this point."

If the jurors had any trouble getting the scene in mind, John O'Mara had more than pictures to help them. At the next break, he wrestled the box into place. When the jurors returned, it was standing on end in front of the jury box, tagged "Homicide."

Without seeing it, they took their seats, joking and good-humored as usual. As they all noticed the weathered and stained coffin, their faces hardened, gravity registering in their eyes.

Lieutenant Wilbur Terry resumed the stand, and O'Mara had him identify the box. While the jurors scrutinized this ugly evidence, he asked Terry a few summary questions. Finally, he handed this witness over to the defense.

Clymo said he had no questions and quickly removed the box to the back of the room. The defense had other tactics.

Sure, Everson Gillmouth had been found dead in a box by the side of the river, but that still didn't prove he was murdered. The man was seventy-seven years old, had phlebitis in his leg and a heart condition. He could have died of a stroke, a heart attack, any number of things. Dr. Hanf had testified that his autopsy showed nothing suspicious. Even his toxicology reports came back clean.

It was Ismael Florez, the builder of the box, that seemed dirty.

O'Mara got nothing more out of Florez than he'd learned from the preliminary hearing transcripts. Florez had built the box for Dorothea for "storage." He'd dumped it at her direction without asking a single question. And he'd bought Gillmouth's nearly new pickup truck for eight hundred dollars and a few days of work. Sure.

Peter Vlautin clearly wasn't buying any of this, and he struggled to get Florez to admit more on cross-examination. He asked, "Didn't Dorothea Puente tell you that Gillmouth had a heart attack and she needed a coffin?"

Florez denied this. He didn't know what was in the box. He'd just built it, then left it with the lid off.

Steering the witness over to the makeshift coffin, Vlautin asked, "You said Mrs. Puente told you she nailed the lid, right?"

"Yes."

"The nails on the lid all appear to be in a nice, straight line, don't they?"

"Yes."

Florez admitted that he was a pretty good carpenter, that he could hammer nails in straight, but then he balked.

"Anyone would be able to put in all these nails without hammer marks, is that what you're saying?" Vlautin demanded.

"Yes."

"I don't believe you," Vlautin muttered in disgust.

"You're arguing with the witness," Virga interjected.

Florez was excused, and he exited the courtroom, taking his secrets with him.

Reba Nicklous, Everson Gillmouth's sister from Oregon, came in with hair now as white as Dorothea's. She was a bit more halt of step, but just as clear of mind as she had been at the prelim.

Clymo remembered her as a dangerous witness. O'Mara had only just met her, but he knew that she—and the letters—were key.

Dressed up in purple, she looked so pretty and frail that it was almost a shock when she spoke in her strong, full voice, explaining how her brother had left Oregon in August 1985, intent on marrying Dorothea Puente. When she'd received no word from him, she got worried and asked the Sacramento police to check on him. Then she'd received a phone call from her chagrined older brother. "That was the last time I ever heard from him," she said.

She couldn't remember when, exactly, but she later received a phone call from Dorothea Puente. "She said they were planning on coming up around Thanksgiving time," Reba recalled. And Dorothea had wanted to know "would she be accepted. And I said, if everything was on the up and up, she would be."

Now O'Mara moved to the letters, those damning, duplicitous letters that the defense could do nothing about, that Puente was surely vexed were still in existence. (Even Reba was amazed that she'd kept them.) In a clear voice, she read the first one, dated October 14, 1985:

DISTURBED GROUND

Dear Reba,

Gill is staying at my home. He's got the trailer parked for now.

He asked me to write and let you know he's O.K.—said you know how much he hates to write.

Hes doing well with selling some of his carvings.

Said he did not want you to have the police out again.

I'll try & drop you a line every couple weeks. We might get married in November.

> Take care and God Bless,
> Dorothea Puente

Maybe it seemed innocent enough to the unenlightened, but to O'Mara's ear this sounded like a death notice. He had to wait until closing arguments to explain, so he hoped the jury was paying attention. Glancing over, he saw some of them taking notes.

The second letter, written on flowered stationary and dated October 22, was chatty and rambling. Reba Nicklous also read this one into the record:

Hello,

Gill's busy with his carving, getting ready to take some to Palm Springs to sell.

He sold five for a nice price. Hes made six redwood coffee tables real pretty odd shapes. made one for the living room—looks real nice. and matches nice with my furniture.

They turned him down at the Vets.

But when we get married next month he can get on my VA Insurance.

His leg been bothering him again, and hes having trouble driving a little.

He got new glasses so sees a little better.

We will get married on November 2nd.

He wanders around in my big flat. He sold his trailer 9 days ago. And is getting a patio room for the back yard to work in.

Hes fixed a lot of furniture for people and is making quite a bit extra money for himself.

We will go to Palm Springs next month so he can sell most of his carvings.

Hope this finds you and yours well.

> Write soon
> Dorothea & Gil [sic]

Gillmouth was surely dead when Puente wrote this—but Reba couldn't have known.

Next, O'Mara handed his witness a brief, disconcerting mailgram ostensibly from Everson. He specifically asked Reba the date, November 2, hoping the jury would notice the odd coincidence that this was the day that Everson and Dorothea were supposed to marry.

Reba now read for the jury:

LEAVING FOR PALM SPRINGS 11:30 A.M. TODAY. TRIED TO CALL BUT LINE WAS BUSY. DECIDED TO GO ON. YOU'D TRY TO STOP ME. WILL RETURN TO DOROTHEA'S FOR THANKS-GIVING BUT WILL BE IN TOUCH WITH YOU BEFORE. PLEASE DON'T WORRY.

                                                        EVERSON

As soon as she'd finished reading, O'Mara asked incredulously, "Did you ever in your life try to stop Everson from doing anything?"

Clymo promptly objected but was overruled. Reba told the court that, no, she'd never tried to stop her brother from doing anything. Clearly, she didn't believe this mailgram had been sent by Everson.

A final, audacious correspondence had come to the family in April 1986—four months after Everson Gillmouth's body had been found alongside the river. The outside of the card said "Thinking of You," and Reba also read this into the record:

Hello,

We came to Sacramento to pick up the rest of Eversons things from storage. they told us you had been worried & had the police over. We are O.K. he had a small stroke in January. he can't drive any more. he sold his trailer & truck—But we have a new car—I got it in Dec.

We love the desert and the warm and dry weather.

We are going to Canada in August so will stop and see you. Everson wrote to you in Feb.

When we get the phone in in June we will call.

Hes lost about 15 lbs. and feels much better.

We are both health nuts so we are doing O.K.

And I also work so our Income is pretty good.

We go to church each week.

It was 90 all week. he did not care for Tulsa at all—But guess we'll buy a small home with the money from my home.

Take care.
Irene   &
Everson

Irene?

The handwriting was familiar, the postmark was Sacramento, even the pacing sounded the same. From the word choice to the short paragraphs, these letters were obviously—even blatantly—written by Dorothea Puente. (And the jury heard a handwriting expert confirm that Dorothea and "Irene" were one and the same.)

After locking horns with Clymo at the preliminary hearing, Reba Nicklous had steeled herself for a rough cross-examination. But to her surprise, the defense passed. "No questions," Clymo said softly, and she was excused.

When O'Mara came out into the hall to bid her good-bye a few minutes later, Reba asked why they'd let her off so easy.

"They wanted to get you out of the courtroom," O'Mara explained, chuckling. "You're like a hand grenade: With every question you blow up and hurt them." Reba smiled at this.

"You're one of the few *real* people I've had in this trial," he continued. "There have been scientists, toxicologists, criminalists, but not many flesh-and-blood relatives."

"Well, I hope I helped you some."

"You helped me," he assured her, shaking her hand. "You helped me a great deal."

He only wished he had more witnesses like her.

The question of whether or not Dorothea Puente would testify seemed moot as witness after witness revealed facets of her character. She was nothing if not skilled. She played the system like a musical instrument, coaxing from it the familiar music of lucre. Social Security and SSI checks were only what attracted the most attention—the high notes, so to speak. There were also checks from pensions, General Assistance, tax refunds, Renter's Assistance, and more. Federal, state, and county agencies played to her tune.

Senior Document Examiner David Moore attested to Dorothea Puente's forged signatures on seemingly endless checks and forms.

Clearly, the woman had devoted terrific energy to orchestrating this complex and clever larceny.

Her applications for the Heat and Energy Assistance Program (HEAP) displayed true virtuosity. Under this program, as the name suggests, low-income households can apply for a bit of help in paying the heating bills. One household, one check. So legitimately, 1426 F Street could receive only a single, puny payment. Instead, the landlady had filled out applications for assorted boarders, assigning each one an apartment number—Bert in Apt. 12, Ben Fink in Apt. 3, Brenda Trujillo in Apt. 4, for example, while Dorothea Puente occupied Apt. 1 and Dorothea Montalvo was in Apt. 35.

And one needn't die to have funds pilfered. Short-term boarders were fair game, as long as the landlady could come down off her porch and snag the check out of the mailbox. Even her loyal friend John McCauley had been ripped off (but apparently he'd been too drunk to realize this).

The postman also brought mail-order catalogues from which she ordered shoes, clothes, linens, even Giorgio perfume. In payment, she merely signed over this or that government check.

And that was just some of the money. With a handful of forged checks, Dorothea would pop over to Joe's Corner Bar, which she used as Joe's Corner Bank. The proprietor, Mr. Vogeli, sheepishly testified that when she brought over checks at the first of the month, he would make a special trip to the bank to cash them for her, returning with three or four thousand dollars.

In early June, O'Mara finally called Puente's long-awaited landlord and "nephew" to the stand. He came as a big surprise in a small package. Surely none of the jurors had anticipated that the owner of the F Street house, Ricardo Ordorica, would enter the court so sad-faced and short, standing just shy of four and a half feet.

The man who had funneled so many of the dead tenants' checks through his accounts struggled earnestly with his heavily accented English, mostly forgoing the interpreter, who stood ready to come to his aid. On two consecutive days, Ordorica labored through his lilting explanations of how his highly incriminating signatures had come to be on the backs of so many U.S. Treasury checks.* "Mrs. Puente would give them to me to pay the rent," he explained.

---

* Ordorica had been given immunity from prosecution regarding these forged checks.

"Did she give you a receipt?" O'Mara asked.

"No." Usually, she would bring him two signed Social Security checks to make up the seven-hundred-dollar rent. (Ordorica had previously testified that the rent was six hundred dollars; now he said that was a mistake.) "She gave me two checks, from Dorothy Miller,* or sometimes a check with a different name."

"Treasury checks?"

"These kinds of checks," he said, indicating the stack of Treasury checks before him.

Working to catch O'Mara's racing questions, he further explained, "Sometimes Mrs. Puente told me, 'Ricardo, can you cash this check?' And I say, 'Okay,' and I go to the bank and I give her the money."

It was an arrangement that Ordorica scarcely questioned. He did it, he said, "to make a favor to her."

Some tenants he had met, some he had not. He explained he scarcely spoke with them except at chance encounters while visiting Mrs. Puente. "I just, hi, hi," he said, waving his child-sized hand in greeting.

O'Mara took special care with the largest check, a $9,980 tax refund that had been sent to Julius Kelley, the now-deceased tenant who had testified via videotape that he'd known nothing of it. O'Mara asked Ordorica if he'd ever received this check, and Ordorica unhesitatingly said he had.

Supplementing his weak vocabulary with body language, he explained with choppy sentences and fluttering hands. "Okay, she went to the place I work and she told me, 'Ricardo, can you cash this check?' And she told me, 'Take three months' rent, deposit some, and give me the rest of the money. Because I'm afraid that the owner of the check, he drink a lot, and I am afraid that if he went to Joe's Corner, people can stealing his money.' "

O'Mara clarified, "Is this something that Mrs. Puente told you, or is this something that you knew about the person?"

"Mrs. Puente told me."

O'Mara urged him to continue.

"I told her, 'This is a lot of money, I don't know if the bank cash the check or not.' I went to the bank, and they know me very well. When they saw the check, 'You're not Julius, Ricardo,' the teller told

---

* At Puente's urging, he had become Dorothy Miller's payee.

me. And then she told me this check needed to be endorsed. Next day, she [Puente] gave me again the check, and I took some money and I gave to Mrs. Puente the rest of the money."

If his unquestioning faith in Dorothea Puente seemed suspiciously convenient, Ordorica deflated skepticism with a spontaneous testament to her kindness: "I make all the time favors to her because she was like part of my family."

O'Mara asked, "You would sometimes refer to her as your aunt, or *tía*?

"Yes."

"Was she, in fact, your aunt?"

"No."

"You were just close?"

"Very close. That's why I cash this check for her when the owner of Joe's Corner don't have money or wasn't there, she went to me, and I go to the bank ... I make a favor to her, because she was like my aunt, like my mother, like *tía*, you know, very close. We are like family because she was living upstairs, and we was living downstairs [prior to 1987]. And we was like one family."

When Dorothea was in state prison from 1982 to 1985, Ordorica had power of attorney to deposit her SSI checks into an account for her. He explained this so unabashedly that it seemed he was unaware that it was illegal for her to continue receiving this money while incarcerated. He seemed most eager to explain that he did not use this money for himself. "I can cash her checks. I send to her a lot of things—boxes of food, perfume, colognes, a lot of things—every month, I send to her with her money."

Clearly, little Ricardo Ordorica would have preferred to have been a defense witness.

Leaving the stand at the lunch break, he did the unthinkable: While the jurors were exiting the jury box and the bailiff's back was turned, he crossed over to where his old friend was seated, whispered in her ear, and kissed her on the cheek!

During Peter Vlautin's cross-examination, Ordorica gave his most exonerating testimony. Ordorica had testified that the last time he'd seen Everson Gillmouth, he'd had "some pain in his face."

Vlautin asked for clarification, and with the help of the interpreter, Ordorica explained, "When I saw him, in his face, it seemed like some sort of pain in his chest. And he was limping somewhat when he walked. And I saw him take a pill from his pocket and put it in his mouth."

"Could you show us?" Vlautin urged.

The little man stood, grimacing, his tiny hands clutching at his chest.

Had seventy-seven-year-old Everson Gillmouth died of natural causes? Or was Dorothea's loyal little pal lying for her?

As Vlautin reviewed each element with Ordorica, O'Mara was watching intently, the end of a pen clamped between his teeth.

Leaning forward in her seat, Dorothea Puente was also riveted.

Now Vlautin gave the witness full opportunity to vouch for his friend. "You mentioned this morning that you consider Mrs. Puente part of your family?"

"That's corrrrect," Ordorica replied, trilling his r's.

"And why was it that you considered her part of your family?"

Ordorica seemed relieved to be able to convey some important information to the jury. "Okay," he said eagerly, "when we met Mrs. Puente, we start talking, and we saw picture with big personality, for example, the Bishop Quinn."

"The Catholic bishop of Sacramento?"

"That's corrrrect. And with Governor Deukmejian. And we saw, he sent to her flowers. And we saw letters from the Vatican, the secretary of the Vatican. And we saw letters from Shaw of Iran Two," he said, holding up two fingers and urgently repeating, "Shaw of Iran Two. And we saw pictures of the babies of King Jordan, the king sent to her. And, and, we saw her with the sheriff, the chief of police, and she was political relationship with."

"She was involved with the Mexican-American community?"

"That's corrrrect, sí. And, but, um, my children saw in her their grandmother who they never have. When they get home from school, they would run up the stairs—"

"You say she was like a grandmother?"

"Like an aunt, like a grandma, like a mother take care for us our children. She took my children to San Francisco, to Marine World, that's why we consider her our family, too. Because she told us the first day that she doesn't have family, only ours."

Veering back to self-justification, Ordorica added, "That's why, when I saw all those things, when she asked me favors to cash the checks, I did. For part of the rent."

To get off the subject of money, Vlautin prompted, "You had referred to Dorothea Puente as tía?"

"Yes. Because emotionally," he said, choking out the words, "in our heart, emotionally, she is still part of our family."

"In your heart?"

"In our heart, in our lips, in our thought." Voice thick, Ordorica added, "My daughters dream of her, they wake up crying for her."

Defense attorney Vlautin thanked the witness and sat down. Dorothea Puente blew her nose as little Ricardo Ordorica left the courtroom wiping tears from his eyes.

O'Mara had devoted nearly every waking hour to this case since February, trying to work in evidence as it continued to trickle in, handing to the jury every piece of the puzzle he could manage. Now, on June 7, 1993, after 136 witnesses, the prosecution rested.

CHAPTER 44

On the morning of June 15, Puente's attorneys looked particularly telegenic, and Kevin Clymo appeared relaxed and upbeat as he shared a joke with his client, who sat beside him in a blue-and-white print dress. Her skin seemed so milky and translucent, one observer whispered, "She looks like a porcelain doll."

Speculation about Puente's defense simmered. After the prosecution's marathon case, what could they hope to present besides smoke and mirrors?

News vans with microwave dishes hummed out in the parking lot, ready for reports of Dorothea Puente's defense. A fresh flock of spectators peered and murmured. Reporters made room for sketch artists, who readied pencils and paints.

Most important, the jury appeared rested. Several were tanned. All seemed ready and alert.

The defense called their first witness, a retired social worker who spoke in bureaucratese about the clean, respectable, and openly unlicensed room-and-board establishment Mrs. Puente had run back in the seventies.

A backdoor character witness. O'Mara felt no need even to cross-examine this one.

But the next witness was different.

Plenty of behind-the-scenes wrangling preceded the testimony of longtime criminal Raul Hernandez. The defense argued that their witness, who happened to be a convict, ought to be afforded the same courtesies as others. But certain considerations mitigated against absolute parity. Hernandez was a violent felon and known escape risk; the judge had understandable misgivings about allowing him to sit, unshackled, just a few feet away. Finally, Judge Virga ruled that the prisoner would wear a leg brace. Hernandez would be brought in and seated during a break. Since the brace couldn't be seen beneath his trousers, the jury would not be unduly influenced.

Wearing the penal system's de rigueur orange jumpsuit, Hernandez shuffled in and sat in the witness box. With his big, bullet-shaped head, droopy mustache, and blunt features, he looked inherently menacing. A watchful armed deputy stayed close by.

With the jury again seated, Peter Vlautin carefully established the criminal's record, his heroin addiction, and the fact that he was now serving twelve years for armed robbery. Then he turned to the man's relationship with Brenda Trujillo.

It had to be done. Though Trujillo's testimony may have seemed lost in the prosecution's massive case, hers was singular. Only Trujillo claimed to have seen Dorothea emptying capsules into a drink. Only she had claimed that Dorothea had killed people. Trujillo's credibility had to be destroyed, and Hernandez was The Terminator.

Hernandez explained that he and Trujillo had grown up together in the same low-income projects. As children, they'd played together. As adults, they'd drunk beer and shot heroin. In his quiet, calm voice, Hernandez described junkies relaxing with their drugs at the end of a long day.

Trujillo lied compulsively, Hernandez told the jury. In particular, he recalled Trujillo laughing and boasting about some story she'd cooked up about Dorothea Puente forcibly drugging her so that her urine test was "dirty" and she had to go back to prison.

"I told her that was wrong," Hernandez stated. "She said she just wanted to stay out of prison, and that was the best excuse she could think of."

He was here today, he said, to set the record straight. Trujillo lied so much that she offended even drug-addicted felons.

Vlautin turned the witness over to the prosecution, and all eyes turned toward O'Mara. For months, the jury had watched him question his own witnesses. How would he cross-examine?

First, O'Mara asked a few questions, laid a few traps. Then, at the first discrepancy, he flew at the witness, shouting out questions between snide remarks.

"He's badgering the witness, Your Honor," Vlautin objected.

The judge sustained.

But O'Mara's in-your-face assault continued. "You don't like being here, do you Mr. Hernandez?" O'Mara sneered.

More combative questions, more objections, and soon the judge was trying to calm the hostility between the attorneys, like a parent caught between squabbling children.

The jurors tittered and exchanged looks.

Meanwhile, the witness struggled to explain, "As far as dates, sir, like I said before, I can't remember the dates. Honestly, I can't."

Finally, O'Mara muttered that he had no more questions.

Vlautin was immediately on his feet. Seeing his opening, he asked Hernandez why he'd mentioned being uncomfortable, and that opened the floodgates. Hernandez's rock-hard features crumbled. "My wife is expecting a baby. And right now, my life is in danger." The big man's voice wavered and turned to sobs.

Everyone stared in amazement.

"If any of this [testimony] gets twisted just a little bit," he whimpered, "my life is in danger. I'm in for twelve years. And there wouldn't be nothing for me to be up here lying about."

Hernandez looked suddenly vulnerable and small. Clearly, if his buddies back in prison mistook him for a snitch, he'd be in for a world of hurt.

"You said your situation has changed," Vlautin prompted gently. "What did you mean?"

Regaining his composure, the witness replied, "I'm a born-again Christian. That's another thing. I can't lie. I have nothin' to gain from this! Nothin'!"

Now it appeared that the criminal was the victim, O'Mara the bully. Scanning the jurors' faces, one wondered whether O'Mara had made a strategical blunder.

Over the next few days, the defense continued their onslaught against Brenda Trujillo. And they weren't just taking potshots, they were engaged in full-blown character assassination. They called former boyfriends, cell mates, junkies, even a special agent with the Department of Health and Human Services, who, among other things, pointed out that Trujillo had once made the outlandish claim that Puente had used Visine—*Visine, of all things!*—to drug people.

There was little O'Mara could say. There was no point bickering about the Visine issue now.

Being more circumspect in his cross-examinations, often forgoing questions altogether, O'Mara just hoped that the jury remembered that Trujillo had gone to the police months before Puente's arrest, saying that she had bodies buried in her yard. About that, at least, she had told the absolute truth.

The defense bulldozed forward, employing the oldest of strategies: blame the victims. They set out to prove that it was ill health, not Dorothea Puente, that had caused these deaths. And in this case, attacking the health and lifestyles of the victims was child's play.

The next several witnesses portrayed Bert Montoya as a down-and-out drunk. A former boardinghouse operator named Lloyd Lambert recalled that when Montoya had been a tenant at his place in the early seventies, Bert had consumed alcohol "anytime he could get a bottle." Puente's neighbor, Alice Mansuetti, testified that she frequently saw Bert sitting in the shade, drinking from a bottle in a paper bag. And a fellow who had worked at Puente's house said that one day Bert was so "snockered" he could hardly walk, so he'd helped him back to the house.

Some of the prosecution's witnesses had even described Bert gulping down beers faster than anyone they'd ever seen. Coupled with previous medical testimony, this fit in nicely with the defense's scenario that Bert had suffered a fatal diabetic coma.

To illustrate this scene, they called Mark Anthony, Don Anthony's brother. More law-abiding and better-looking than his weasely brother, Mark Anthony described a day in the summer of 1988 when he'd given his brother a lift to 1426 F Street. As he was about to drive away, he said, his brother had come back to the car and asked if he'd give him a hand because, "one of the boarders was unconscious over at the bar across the street." Anthony described rushing over to find Bert passed out on the floor. "We shook him and called out his name, tried to bring him into consciousness."

"Were you able to arouse him?" Vlautin asked.

"No."

"Were there signs of breathing?"

"Not heavy," Anthony said. "He was blowing bubbles out of his mouth."

The men had tried to lift Bert off the floor. Finding him too heavy, the Anthony brothers and another tenant, Pat Kelley, had finally hoisted him under the arms, letting his feet drag as they hauled him across the street, through the gate, and into his room. Then they'd laid Bert on his bed and loosened his clothing.

Mark Anthony soon had to leave for work, he said, and as he was leaving, "Dorothea showed up. Seemed like she got out of a taxi on Fifteenth Street. My brother tried to introduce me to her, but she seemed pretty concerned about what was happening to Bert. It seemed like she was already informed. Seemed like she was asking questions—where he was and everything. She walked toward the boardinghouse."

That was it, plain and ugly. Bert Montoya had collapsed one morning in Joe's Corner Bar. Had he been poisoned? Or had his blood-sugar level zoomed out of control, sending his metabolism into a terminal tailspin?

After a brief cross-examination, Judge Virga called the noon recess, giving the jurors time to ruminate on the awful image of Bert Montoya lying unconscious and blowing bubbles.

As June waned, the defense continued to slowly undermine O'Mara's case. The prosecutor had called more witnesses and had taken more time, but they were intent on weakening the foundation of his case. Grain by grain, they were draining the sand from beneath his pillars of reasoning. And now, with a surprise witness, Ruth Munroe's death was cast in a much different light.

Dean Fesler, former husband to Munroe's daughter, Rosemary, described Munroe as "a chronic complainer" who popped pills like candy. The court had already heard that Munroe had once worked in a pharmacy. With Fesler on the stand, they also heard that she'd hoarded manufacturers' samples of both prescription and over-the-counter drugs, stashing them in a large cardboard box. "Each time she had aches or pains," Fesler said, "she'd reach into her box and take something."

Fesler described Munroe keeping "between eight and twelve bottles of pills" on the nightstand beside her bed. "She was always getting a glass of water and taking one of these pills," he said.

When Clymo asked Fesler what he knew about Ruth Munroe's death, he said, "My information was that she died of pills," underscoring the impression that—whether accidentally or intentionally—Munroe had self-administered the lethal dose of codeine and Tylenol.

With another witness, Carol Durning Westbrook, who was recalled to the stand, the defense drew multiple benefits. James Gallop was described as looking like "death warmed over." Brenda Trujillo was described as a lying, ungrateful bitch who responded to Dorothea's help by giving only pain and disappointment in return. And Dorothea was again portrayed as Super-Landlady, cooking and cleaning for her tenants, even lending them money.

Plenty of time was lavished on Puente's role as the operator of a boardinghouse of last resort for the truly down-and-out. Boarders such as Ben Fink, Vera Martin, Betty Palmer, and Dorothy Miller were portrayed as so foulmouthed, offensive, unmanageable—even deranged—that other landlords had turned them out on the street.

Kindhearted Dorothea Puente had stooped to accept even the lowliest clientele. How could she be held responsible for their alcoholic, pill-popping habits?

Additionally, Puente was exonerated as a hardworking woman who, despite some illicit pilferage, never showed much profit.

Running a boardinghouse was a tough business, as two former operators could attest. There were plenty of bills to pay, yet those paying rent were about as reliable as the weather. For most, a bottle was more important than a bed, regardless of debts outstanding. So, to make sure tenants paid, plenty of landlords collected the mail, deducting room and board from Social Security checks, then handing over the rest . . . just like Dorothea Puente.

One operator said he even had to put a lock on the mailbox.

This same man testified about a young, apparently healthy tenant who'd died suddenly. "He was an alcoholic. He got some pills"—the man didn't know where—"and drank too much. He swallowed his tongue and choked to death."

Sudden, unexpected death. Not murder.

Witness by witness, they were sowing the seeds of doubt, underscoring the possibility that these people had passed on without being pushed.

And the jurors—despite months of fatiguing testimony—seemed to absorb it all, jotting notes and revealing little.

The defense now turned to diffusing the money issue, calling Carl Curtis. With his meaty face, close-cropped hair, and nice suit, it wasn't hard to believe that Curtis had spent twenty years as a special agent with the FBI, covering white-collar crimes. Currently he ran his own private investigations business.

Clymo reviewed the man's ample experience, then offered him as an expert in fraud investigations.

Curtis testified that the defense had handed over all of their information, everything they'd received under "discovery," then asked him to independently arrive at "a conclusion about whether Mrs. Puente committed murder for profit." The message to the jury: Curtis was objective, his conclusions untainted by coercion or bias.

Using pie charts and comparison studies, Curtis undertook a detailed explanation of why Dorothea Puente's chronic larceny never brought in much profit. Most of the money was eaten up in simply maintaining her business (which was, in his estimation, a "long-term care facility"). Food, laundry, utilities, rent—it all added up. At minimum, Curtis said, Puente's cost would be $13.20 per day per "patient." And even if Puente had filched every dime from checks totaling some $77,739 (based on the handwriting expert's figures), she just couldn't have made much profit over a three-year period. Curtis figured her break-even point, given an average of five patients, at $55,536.

Further, since Puente had purloined funds from people both living and dead, Curtis concluded, *"There is nothing that would suggest there was any reason to cause the demise of anybody."*

The press took note.

In fact, Curtis asserted, there was *more* money traceable to those still living then to those deceased.

The defense was sticking fast to their contention that Puente stole, but did not murder.

But John O'Mara wasn't greatly impressed by this expert, or by his figures. He derided the comparison between a long-term care facility and Puente's boardinghouse, which he snidely characterized as "three hots and a cot," or "a mom-and-pop operation without the pop." In a three-day brawl, O'Mara thundered through the numbers, questioning the investigator's "universe" of funds, and forcing Curtis to back down on several points.

❀   ❀   ❀

Naturally, the defense had saved the big gun for last. They called Dr. Randall Baselt, a man with such extensive credentials that it took Kevin Clymo nearly an hour to admiringly list them all before offering the toxicologist as an expert witness. He was a writer of multivolume texts, founder of the *Journal of Analytical Toxicology*, esteemed member of myriad professional organizations, an expert among experts. And he looked every bit the part: the angular academic, wearing a serious, furrowed brow behind his spectacles.

Clymo was as pumped for this as a point guard in the NBA playoffs. Over and over, he passed the ball to his witness, who then took his shot.

"Given all the material you've reviewed for this case, Doctor," Clymo asked, "have you been able to arrive at any conclusions?"

"I've concluded that I cannot make a determination of the significance of the presence of flurazepam and its metabolites at these levels."

Clymo paced and waved, ready to clinch the game. "Do you have an opinion as to whether or not Dalmane was taken within twenty-four hours of death?"

"I have not been able to draw that conclusion. Whether or not tissue parallels drug levels in blood or plasma, we don't really know. I wouldn't be prepared to make that assumption. And if you did," he stated ominously, "you'd be in very dangerous territory."

Swish.

Jurors exchanged looks and jotted notes. O'Mara furiously scribbled on a legal pad. Clymo gestured and queried, joking casually with the jury as his witness impassively deflated the conclusions of all the toxicologists who had testified before him. Dr. Anthony, Mr. Phillips, Mr. Beede, Dr. Peat—all were given a respectful nod before having their "unreasonable" opinions lanced like irksome blisters.

Next, Dr. Baselt compared the dehydration of human tissue to evaporation working on a glass of salt water. In the end, the doctor said, "the drugs are like salt. They don't evaporate."

O'Mara had expected this particular shtick. But it got worse.

The toxicologist tossed up three obstacles that, he said, prevented drawing *any* conclusions from the toxicology results. First, there was no blood to test, and blood, as every juror knew by now, was the "gold standard" of toxicology. Second, the toxicology tests were based on decomposed, putrefied tissue, for which there was no standard whatsoever. And third, the drug levels ultimately detected were extremely low.

Amazingly, the defense somehow managed to turn the pride of the DOJ toxicology lab—that finely tuned marvel, the $375,000 tandem mass spectrometer—into a handicap. Why, its sensitivity levels were *too* low, the doctor suggested, so low that it actually took science into uncharted territory. James Beede's tests hadn't come close to the DOJ results; Dr. Peat's lab also failed to approach them. So, if the DOJ readings were *so infinitesimal,* who could possibly say what they meant?

It seemed to Dr. Baselt that these low readings could indicate some *residue* lingering in the body from past exposures. After all, he reasoned, Dalmane is fat soluble, so might be retained in "fairly fatty tissue" like the brain and liver. "It may be," Dr. Baselt concluded, "that every time you test anyone who has taken Dalmane in the past week, it would show up" on the DOJ's hypersensitive equipment.

How could John O'Mara hope to combat this pedigreed Ph.D. from hell? He loaded his arms full of scientific tomes and headed to his office for a long night of preparation.

The next morning, O'Mara was ready to take on this intellectual ace. He began slowly, courteously, citing first one scientific study, then another, discussing half-lives, fat solubility, and dosing regimens. But soon the debate heated, O'Mara's tone sharpened, and they clashed over fine points of interpretation.

It became a match of minds. And as technical terms were smacked from one end of court to the other—
"pharmacokinetics,"
"dynamic equilibrium,"
"receptor occupancy,"
"electrophilic attraction"
—the jurors watched, their heads pivoting like spectators at Wimbledon.

O'Mara even managed to score a couple of points. Though Dr. Baselt had given the opinion that the seven individuals exhumed from the yard had taken Dalmane within *three days* of their deaths (clearing Dorothea Puente of blame), he now conceded that he wouldn't exclude the *possibility* that the drug had been ingested within twenty-four hours.

And O'Mara got the doctor to admit that even though he believed that Dalmane was retained in tissues, such as brain and liver, at levels many times higher than in the bloodstream, he could cite only anecdotal evidence to support this; there were no published studies.

Yet, as charged as the air had become, the jurors were drifting. It was an uncommonly hot day, the scientific jargon was hard to follow, and now this esoteric debate was straining the concentration of even the best among them. After all, what did it mean when experts disagreed? Didn't they just cancel each other out? Some jurors began to fidget. The XREMIST dozed.

Finally, on the afternoon of June 24, the defense was wrapping up. A last forensic toxicologist took a few parting shots at the prosecution. A few stipulations were read into the record. Then the defense rested.

Save for a single certified document, O'Mara offered no rebuttal.

The attorneys would need time to prepare final arguments, so Judge Virga freed the jurors for a week's vacation. They exited cheerfully into the sunshine, without the faintest idea that they'd left Dorothea Puente fuming in the courtroom.

This trial had been a long, unpleasant ordeal for her, and with the attorneys momentarily out of the courtroom, she chose this moment to act out. Glancing about, she spied Wayne Wilson, *The Sacramento Bee* reporter. Then someone mentioned Channel 3 reporter Mike Boyd* and that apparently set her off. "The *Bee* and Channel Three, those guys! The *Bee* and Channel Three have not been very kind to me," she announced loudly. "That's two I'd never give an interview to."

The bailiff hurried over, gesturing at Wilson, trying to get her to hush.

"I know he's sitting there," Puente declared, "that's why I said it. All this shit they're writing about me! I've never killed anyone, I've said so since the day I was arrested. If I get the death penalty, I'll make damn sure they don't get to be there!"

After this stunning outburst, and still she fired a parting shot: "It's pretty bad when you have to make a living off somebody else's misery."

Coming from her, Wilson found this supremely ironic.

---

*Mike Boyd had flown with Puente back to Sacramento when she was apprehended in Los Angeles in November 1988.

CHAPTER 45

TUESDAY, JULY 6, 1993, THE JURORS SEEMED EAGER AND UPBEAT as they took their seats. Moments from closing arguments, days from deliberations, their ultimate role was nearly upon them.

Judge Virga solemnly assumed the bench. As he read each of the murder charges against Dorothea Montalvo Puente, Kevin Clymo scanned the jurors for clues to their mind-sets.

Then Judge Virga called on O'Mara, who gathered his thoughts and stood.

Now thirty pounds lighter, down to fighting trim, he was ready to wrestle this case to the finish. It was massive. It was complex. And Dorothea Puente was the most unlikely killer he had ever prosecuted. She'd left an unruly trail of purely circumstantial evidence, and now he had to weave together threads from a thousand sources, some reaching back more than eleven years, to convey to them the truth of her crimes.

If he could convince each one of them, he believed they would convict. But he had to reach all twelve, even the most reticent, even the most remote.

Pacing the length of the jury box, O'Mara cautioned the jury not to be fooled by the visual and logical contradiction presented by the white-haired, little old lady accused of serial murder. Though she appeared to be a "grandmotherly figure," he said, she was actually a "cold, calculating" killer. And he quickly zeroed in on two counts that revealed her criminal nature.

He reminded them that the body of Everson Gillmouth, the Oregon man who'd hoped to marry Dorothea Puente when she was released from prison in September 1985, was found beside the river in a make-shift coffin on January 1, 1986. "This is a man that she was going to *marry*. This is a man that supposedly she had some feeling or affection for," he said with amazement. "What happened to Mr. Gillmouth? He was unceremoniously dumped beside the Sacramento River! Most of you even treat your pets better than that! You don't just abandon them behind the highway, you don't just drive off and leave them."

The jurors were rapt. How many remembered burying a pet?

O'Mara was just warming up. He stopped pacing and announced, "The most compelling fact which demonstrates the cold, calculating nature of Dorothea Puente is what happened to Betty Palmer."

Everyone recalled the dismembered corpse of Betty Mae Palmer, found beneath a religious shrine in Puente's front yard.

O'Mara drew a distinction between Palmer's mutilation and the un-pleasant task of a hunter. "We're not talking about taking off a duck's head, or gutting an animal. We're talking about cutting a human head off! We're talking about cutting the arms off somebody! And we're talking about cutting the bottom parts of their legs off!" Slicing with his hands, O'Mara had unleashed a dramatic streak they'd never seen.

"I don't care whether a person has been dead five minutes or five years," he declared, "that kind of an act is a very *cold, cold* thing to do."

He scoffed at the defense's contention that Puente had quietly bur-ied her tenants because she didn't want to get caught running a board-inghouse in violation of her parole. "That head, those legs, those arms have never been found," he cried. "She's worried about going back to prison on a technical parole violation? *What do you think the cops are going to say if they see you walking down the street with a garbage bag with a human head, a pair of arms, and a pair of legs?*"

He let this powerful image hang.

Then, holding up a picture ID card—with Betty Palmer's name and

Dorothea Puente's own smiling photograph—O'Mara pointed out that Puente had used this card to cash Palmer's checks. "You wouldn't take the chance to get a card like this in someone else's name, and cash their checks, if they were still in existence."

How, then, to explain a discrepancy: The card was dated October 14, 1986, yet a witness had described a woman called "Betty" lying on the couch, "moaning and groaning" and begging for pain pills *four months later*, in February 1987. O'Mara had wrestled with this for many nights before the simple answer had finally dawned him. "Ladies and Gentlemen," he announced, "that was not Betty Palmer. That was Leona Carpenter!"

Jurors blinked.

In O'Mara's startling scenario, Betty Palmer, the first tenant buried in the yard, had caused Dorothea Puente such extreme anxiety that she'd gone to elaborate ends to conceal her disappearance. Palmer's mutilation—to hide her identity—showed just how paranoid Puente felt.

When Leona Carpenter moved in, Puente came up with some "Hollywood idea" of a cover-up, and told other tenants that Leona's name was "Betty." The woman was so ill that she never left the couch, couldn't converse, and would never contradict this. No one heard anything but moans from "Betty" until the day she disappeared, and there was suddenly silence.

But Dorothea got away with murdering both Betty *and* Leona, and decided her troublesome precautions were unnecessary. Decapitation was rejected. She would simply bury them.

Clymo and Vlautin furiously scrawled notes while O'Mara raced ahead.

Characterizing this as "the mother of all circumstantial evidence cases," O'Mara implored the jury not to harbor prejudice against the term *circumstantial*. Though no one had seen Puente burying bodies, he urged them to look at the facts and draw their own conclusions. "Our common sense, our reason, our logic tells us there's a lot going on here."

He propped up a placard quoting Henry David Thoreau: "Some circumstantial evidence is very strong, as when you find a trout in the milk."

Quizzical looks passed through the jury box. It was a peculiar phrase, but ... didn't it convey an obvious truth? Trout in the milk, bodies in the yard, circumstances too bizarre to overlook.

But behind O'Mara's back, Peter Vlautin smiled to himself and jotted a note.

O'Mara turned to points of law, presenting boldly titled definitions, laboriously explaining each one. But the more he explained, the more convoluted the laws sounded. As the afternoon wore on, he seemed to wilt inside his nice suit. The hair at the nape of his neck grew wet.

Admitting fatigue, he decided to wheel out the television and let the VCR do his talking for him. He popped in the November 11, 1988, videotape of Detective John Cabrera's questioning of Dorothea Puente. It had been a long time since the jury had watched this back in March. Now that they knew the case, every lie jumped out at them.

When it was over, O'Mara resumed his pacing and explaining. He pointed out subtle contradictions they may have missed, saying, "She lies from her very first words."

Puente had even supplied her motive for getting rid of Ben Fink, he said, when she told Cabrera that she'd kicked him out of the house. "I couldn't take his drinking anymore, he was always falling-down drunk," O'Mara quoted. "That's the only honest thing she said in the whole tape!"

Puente wanted people who had a steady income but no family, who did what they were told, who were, in O'Mara's words "easy keepers." But Ben Fink was not an easy keeper.

He reminded the jury that Puente said she would take care of Ben, taking him upstairs to make him feel better. "Mother Teresa over there took care of him, all right," he said scornfully. "She planted him out in the side yard."

The defense teamed frowned and added ammunition to their notes.

The next morning, O'Mara intoned that "the most troubling of all the cases" was the 1982 death of Ruth Munroe. "That's the system's fault," he said, shaking his head. "The system did a terrible job of investigating this case eleven years ago."

Munroe's death hadn't appeared to be a homicide. The assumption at the time was that the sixty-one-year-old, 179-pound woman had died of a heart attack, so police undertook only the barest investigation.

Two weeks later, toxicology reports showed that Munroe had died of an overdose of codeine and acetaminophen, probably Tylenol #3. Strangely, she'd also taken a small, therapeutic dose of a mild tranquillizer, meprobamate. Only a single prescription bottle for meprobamate had been found at her bedside. And in retrospect, this seemed ludicrous. "If Ruth Munroe committed suicide, wouldn't we find some Tylenol Number Three pill bottles?"

O'Mara challenged the jury to imagine Munroe gulping down a fatal dose of pills, carefully disposing of evidence of her suicide, then taking a single dose of tranquillizer before going to bed. "Did she decide," he asked caustically, "I'll take a little meprobamate so I'll be calm before I die?"

Heaping fresh scorn on the suicide theory, he highlighted other suspicious inconsistencies. Puente claimed to have checked on Munroe at 4:00 A.M., finding her alive, but authorities arriving on the scene just two hours later found Munroe's body already in full rigor mortis. And the forensic pathologist who conducted the autopsy estimated Munroe's time of death as midnight, give or take a couple of hours. O'Mara also reminded them that Puente had shooed Munroe's children away on the eve of her death, claiming that a fictitious doctor had just been there, and Ruth needed to rest.

O'Mara clutched a batch of letters Munroe had written to her husband just a couple of weeks before she died. Reading through them, he noted all the positive aspects. "This is a woman who's in control of her life," he concluded. "This is not a woman who's on the ragged edge of suicide."

He leaned toward them and dropped his voice ominously, "You have two choices, Ladies and Gentlemen. Either she took her own life, or someone took her life."

A massive overdose left no other option.

"Who is the person that spent the most time with her before her death? Right here, Ladies and Gentlemen." He swung around and pointed at Dorothea Puente. "They were together all the time! They got up together! They had breakfast together! They had a business together! This person was with her all the time! The evidence does not suggest that Munroe committed suicide," he declared, *"it proves that she was poisoned!"*

Of the nine victims, frail Leona Carpenter had been closest to death's door. O'Mara suggested that, of all the cases, this might fit

345

into the category of involuntary manslaughter.° "But," he alerted the jury, "there's a catch at the end."

He started quietly. "This is a person who needs a *lot of care*. She was emaciated, and had a decreased level of mental functioning."

O'Mara recounted all the efforts to place Leona in a skilled nursing facility, which Leona had resisted. According to hospital records, Puente had initially declined to take Leona, then finally agreed she would be able to care for her. Leona was released into Puente's care shortly before Christmas, but just three days later she was back in the hospital, where she stayed for more than a month until being released to Puente's care again in February 1987.

"What happened," O'Mara explained, "is that Dorothea Puente got power of attorney" over Leona's funds. Electronic deposits started January 1, 1987. "You don't even have to go to the mailbox to get this one. This is a freebie! You don't even have to go to the bank," he said sarcastically.

"Now, if she had her there just one day and she died, maybe we would have involuntary manslaughter. Maybe she undertook to provide care, and as a result of negligence, Leona died."

But that wasn't the case. Instead, Leona Carpenter stayed at 1426 F Street for two to four weeks. "She was waiting for her to die!" Leona didn't go to another convalescent hospital, as Puente had claimed, "she went out in the side yard! That's not involuntary manslaughter, that's first-degree murder!"

Now came the catch.

"What drugs did we find in her system? Flurazepam and codeine." His eyebrows rose with surprise. "This lady couldn't get up. Carol Durning Westbrook said she never got off the couch the whole time. They had to physically take her to the bathroom! So how did this lady wander around the house and find the Dalmane and codeine that got into her system? Did she have a miraculous recovery one afternoon, go and take those, and then die? How did the drugs get into her system? The only reasonable explanation is that somebody gave them to her. And the only person that took care of this lady was *Dorothea Puente*," he said, swinging around to accuse the defendant.

°Added by the defense at the last minute, this option gave the jury an out. If they had problems with first- or second-degree murder, they might compromise on the lesser charge of involuntary manslaughter, or criminal negligence.

"So if this lady got drugs, there's only one person that gave her those drugs. It wasn't Mr. McCauley. It wasn't any of the other people living there. It was that lady over there!"

With all eyes on her and accusations ringing in the air, Dorothea Puente didn't even look up.

It was the end of the day, the jury was excused, and they filed out in grim silence.

The next day, shifting gears, O'Mara narrowed the window of time when each individual had disappeared. He put up chart after chart, citing dates when they were last seen, noting when Puente's forgeries had begun. "Follow the money," O'Mara said. "When you find the money, you'll find Dorothea Puente."

He focused on count two, Everson Gillmouth's death, and finally, he could explain.

Referring to the cards and letters written to Everson's sister, Reba Nicklous, O'Mara asked, "Does anyone think for a moment that Mr. Gillmouth actually left town and went to Palm Springs on November 2, 1985?"

He stared at them and announced, "Mr. Gillmouth is dead long before November 2, when he's supposed to get married."

O'Mara knew in his bones that this made perfect sense. He laid out the paper trail, showing how the character of Gillmouth's banking transactions had abruptly changed on October 2. Suddenly, Gillmouth wasn't just paying bills; his checks were being cashed at bars, usually in increments of twenty dollars, sometimes several times a day. And over the next many weeks, Everson Gillmouth's checking account had been steadily exhausted.

"Follow the money," O'Mara said again, "and you'll find Dorothea Puente."

One juror turned his eyes on Puente and stroked his chin in contemplation.

Covering ground like a storm front, O'Mara showed how Puente had looted the accounts of her tenants, not only the victims, but other, short-term boarders. Federal, state, and county benefit checks were all funneled through her hands, ranging from Julius "Pat" Kelley's tax refund of nearly $10,000 to Everson Gillmouth's pension checks of $42.50.

According to O'Mara's handwriting expert, Puente had forged signatures on hundreds of checks totaling some $85,000 (the amount to date; checks were still coming in).

Flipping through Puente's check stubs, he spotted a three-hundred-dollar check for "shoes for Leona." That showed how cynically Puente had written these checks, he said. "Three hundred dollars for shoes for Leona, huh? So she'll have some nice shoes to wear while she's over there in the side yard?"

The money trail showed that Vera Faye Martin, who had come to Puente's boardinghouse on October 2, 1987, had been murdered almost immediately. Puente was already forging her signature three days later, on October 5. And even the most reliable witnesses couldn't remember ever laying eyes on Vera Martin.

Dorothy Miller disappeared just a month or so later. She'd been described as "the goofy lady" who Puente had forcibly kept in her room upstairs (the infamous bedroom off the kitchen). Sometimes Miller would sneak downstairs, then scurry back up. And when one tenant noticed that she wasn't around anymore, Puente told him, "She got arrested for petty theft, and I had to throw her out."

Tracing dates and events, O'Mara sometimes relied on Puente's scrawled notes on her calendars, which he waved in front of the jury box. Yet he pointed out that certain entries, all written in the same color ink, were distinctly self-serving in tone. For example, on Sunday, November 7, 1988, when the mythical brother-in-law had supposedly taken Bert to Utah, she'd written, "Bert left while I was at church."

O'Mara couldn't resist a wisecrack: "We have to bring God into this somehow, because we know He wouldn't be involved if this weren't true."

But perhaps O'Mara was alienating the very people he was trying to convince. (The jury remained unfathomable. Media types buzzed about how curiously cheerful and boisterous some were. One day, as a joke, the XREMIST and some of his cohorts came in wearing sunglasses. Others were steadfastly impassive.)

Later, O'Mara addressed the subject of poor Jim Gallop, the man with the brain tumor. Reviewing Gallop's medical records, O'Mara noted, "He's certainly got a serious condition, but it's worlds apart from a malignant tumor."

The records also noted that Gallop was living with a woman he'd met in a bar. "He thought it was Mother Teresa," O'Mara said snidely, "but it wasn't!"

The defense attorneys squinted at him and jotted notes.

Noting that Vera Martin had been raped and beaten, that all of these people had been in and out of emergency rooms, O'Mara intoned, "These people had wretched lives. They made it through all kinds of things. They survived." He paused. "Then they go to this island of peace—this oasis!—this woman who takes in homeless and gives them new lives. They make it there, and most of them don't live out the month! Isn't it kind of ironic? They go to this warm, grandmotherly place, and they're history!"

Watching the jurors' faces, O'Mara spied the occasional nod, the knowing smile that told him they, too, thought Puente's guilt was obvious. He was sure he was reaching them, sure he was winning convictions.

Later, he would wonder how he could have been so wrong.

The morning of Friday, July 9, the defense moved for a mistrial, charging prosecutorial misconduct. By evoking God and making references to Mother Teresa and Christian conduct, they said, O'Mara's argument was prejudicial and inflammatory, and was not fair comment on the evidence.

Judge Virga quickly ruled that O'Mara had not exceeded the bounds of proper argument.

Next, the defense moved that the jury be given an additional instruction for count seven, the alleged murder of Ben Fink. According to the prosecution, they said, Puente felt so outraged by Fink's drunken behavior that "she just lost it" and killed him. That sort of "heat of passion" killing required an instruction for voluntary manslaughter.

Judge Virga agreed. And once the jury was again seated, they were instructed that, for count seven only, they had this additional option.

And the more options, the more possibility for friction. Such was Clymo's logic.

Back on his feet, O'Mara promptly put responsibility for the morning's delay in the lap of the defense. He hadn't meant to imply that Ben Fink had been murdered in a fit of anger, he said, cluing them to the fact that the additional instruction had come from the other side.

O'Mara had plenty to cover, so now he pulled out more charts and warned, "We're going to talk about something boring—the famous Dalmane Wars," and several jurors smirked.

He summarized the toxicological findings, stressing the strange coincidence that all the bodies showed traces of Dalmane. And he enumerated Puente's ceaseless refills for the drug. All the while, he attacked the defense experts and commended his own.

The defense expected nothing less.

Finally, he was coming to things he had saved for last. Some bits of evidence had been numbered and entered into the record with hardly a comment. Found on Puente's dining room table, for instance, was a scrap of paper torn from a spiral notebook. "This is a very interesting piece of paper," O'Mara said, showing them a huge blowup of a scrawled tally:

Jim	657
V	637
B	637
B	637
L	500
D	600
J	700
	5,058

A glance brought a slap of realization. O'Mara hardly needed to explain, but he did. Jim was Jim Gallop, V was Vera Martin, the two B's were Betty Palmer and Ben Fink, L was Leona Carpenter, D was Dorothy Miller, and J, he said, was either John Sharp or John McCauley. "What she's figuring out is how much money she can expect every month. She's computing her income."

What else could one conclude? Her addition was off, but this closely reflected what each person received from Social Security, SSI, and other sources.

"I suggest that this was before Bert Montoya was killed," O'Mara said grimly. "Otherwise, there would be three B's."

Why had she murdered these people. For the money, mainly, but not *only* for the money, he explained. For the prestige, for the lifestyle, for the respect that money can buy.

O'Mara picked up a box of Christmas cards, explaining that they'd also been found on Puente's dining room table in November 1988, and passed one to the jury.

Flipping it open, they saw festive, preprinted Season's Greetings from "Dr. Dorothea Puente."

The woman had more than a lifestyle to support. She had an image to maintain.

He put away the cards and mused, "I'm sure she rationalized in her mind, 'They're better off dead. They're going to be dead soon anyway, what's the difference? I'm really doing them a favor.' "

But the prosecutor didn't believe she'd done them any favors. Now he snatched up the photographs that showed her simple, final solution. One by one, he marched them past the jury box, announcing them name by name: "Everson Gillmouth, wrapped with garbage bags about the face. Betty Palmer, with garbage bags on the torso. Dorothy Miller, with a Chux pad on her face and duct tape to hold her arm in place. Ben Fink also has a Chux pad over his face. And Mr. Montoya—the man she treated like a son!—Mr. Montoya has a garbage bag over his face."

"Do you notice the similarities?" he shouted. "Suffocation couldn't have been detected twenty-five minutes after death. *Why are these objects over their faces?*"

He set aside these dreadful images. "Whether you believe they were poisoned to death, whether you believe they were smothered to death, does it really matter?"

Square in front of the jury box, he made his final plea: "Don't buy this story that they all died of natural causes. She murdered each one of them. She did it *willfully*, she did it *deliberately*, she did it with *premeditation*. And if there's any doubt in your mind as to whether she did it in that fashion, think about after she did the first one. If there isn't deliberation on the first one, there sure as heck is by the time you get to number two! *And when you get to three, four, five, six, seven, eight, and NINE, what do you think is going through your mind?*"

O'Mara silently folded into his chair, his question reverberating through the paralyzed court.

The jurors went home to rest over the weekend. Kevin Clymo would work on his closing argument. And Peter Vlautin was cooking up a little "payback."

During the Solomon case, Vlautin had somehow misquoted Robert Louis Stevenson, and O'Mara had made him pay for the error during closing arguments. So, Vlautin had someone check up on O'Mara's quote from Thoreau, just to see what might come of it.

Now he had a response from their researcher. A note reading "Can't find 11/11/1850 passage in *Journal,* but see attached re circumstantial evidence," was clipped to a short piece from *Thoreau's World.*

Vlautin read it gleefully, then approached his co-counsel.

Eyeing the story, Clymo protested, "Peter, I told you, I don't do quotes."

But after reading it, he changed his mind.

Part VII

SYMPATHY FOR THE DEVIL

Some call her the devil incarnate, others call her an angel.
—KEVIN CLYMO, defense attorney

She had many personalities. At one moment she is the virgin. At other times she is the devil.
—PEDRO MONTALVO, Dorothea's fourth husband

I can tell when Mom drinks because she gets so mean I can smell it.
—DOROTHEA HELEN GRAY, age seven and a half

CHAPTER 46

H ER SHORT CURLS INTENSELY WHITE AGAINST THE MIDNIGHT blue of her sweater, her small hands folded before her, Dorothea Puente looked especially grandmotherly and proper on Monday morning as she watched the jury box fill. In the gallery, two elderly women peered over reporters' shoulders, guessing her age at perhaps seventy-five. "She's so pasty," one whispered, "her skin matches her hair."

Judge Virga swept his black robes into court, assumed the bench, then announced, "Mr. Clymo, you may proceed."

The defense attorney rose to his full height.

After O'Mara's heart-stopping summation, expectations for the defense were not high. Clymo was expected to finish this same afternoon. After all, observers wondered, what could he possibly say?

Clymo wasted no time. "If you believe all that the prosecutor *testified* to last week"—said with heavy cynicism—"if you believe all he's told you, you'll probably convict Dorothea Puente on nine counts of murder," he began simply. "The passion, the anger, the prejudice that were directed at you . . ." he spread his hands helplessly. "The plea was very, very powerful."

He smiled. "At one point, I looked up at the jury and I thought, Oh my God, they're not only going to convict Dorothea, they're going to convict us for sitting beside her!"

But then he realized, he said, that these very sensible jurors would not let their "passions dictate."

Good-humored and unpretentious, Clymo spoke to them in confidential tones. "I agree with Mr. O'Mara about one thing," he said, "this truly is the mother of all circumstantial evidence cases. It's a difficult case, difficult for the prosecution, difficult for the defense."

He reminded them that the change of venue was necessary because emotions ran so high in Sacramento that Puente couldn't get a fair trial there. They'd been selected, after months of interviews with hundreds of prospective jurors, because they could weigh both sides fairly.

As an aside, Clymo grinned and said, "I almost wore my fish tie today," flipping his necktie. "A trout in the milk is very strong circumstantial evidence—*but of what?*"

Serious again, he continued, "It's a tough case, and it will take a truly *courageous* jury to ignore that passion and to apply the law objectively."

Gently, gently, he began defusing the prosecution's argument.

"Your reason, not your passion, will convince you," Clymo stated, that O'Mara's version of the truth was "at times slanted, at times fudged, at times manipulated. If you believe everything the prosecutor has said, you will convict her. But if you test it against the truth," he intoned, lacing his big fingers together like a preacher, "you will see where it's slanted. And after you go through that process, it is our expectation that you will reject what was told you last week."

Clymo had initiated his first tactic: attack the prosecution.

"You were bombarded by one of the strongest emotional pleas that I've ever heard from a prosecutor. Every nerve ending was assaulted! The name of Christianity was invoked! Mother Teresa's name was used to inflame you! Does this situation call for that kind of sarcasm?"

Clymo first suggested that O'Mara had committed blasphemy and insulted their intelligence. Next, acknowledging that some of them had military counterintelligence training, Clymo asked, "Do you recall the classes you had in interrogation techniques? Do you remember all the stuff that we learned as a country after the Korean War? If you want to control somebody's thinking, if you want to implant an attitude, you put them in a situation where you have absolute control of them, in the sense that they can't get away from your diatribe."

Clymo was actually comparing the prosecutor's marathon argument to mind control techniques.

"You hammer it incessantly," he continued, "you tire them, you wear them down, you fatigue them, and you slant the facts. Gradually, slowly, during the fatiguing process, you slant the facts. But," he warned, "don't let that happen to you. Recognize the process."

Having disparaged the prosecution's style, Clymo now went after substance.

He thought it was ridiculous to suggest that the woman identified as "Betty" might actually have been Leona Carpenter. "Why in the world would Dorothea Puente tell anybody that this woman's name was Betty? That doesn't make a whole lot of sense," he said, shaking his head.

"Carol Durning Westbrook told you that Dorothea Montalvo Puente fed this woman. That she would go out on the couch, lift her, feed her soup, even when she didn't want to eat, when all she wanted was her pain pills. She would bathe her, wipe her behind like a baby. Dorothea Montalvo Puente did that. Now, that's not some story that she told Detective Cabrera and is therefore to be discredited and disbelieved. That's from a witness that the prosecution told you was one of the few you could believe."

In soft, reasonable tones, he went on, "There was nobody taking care of Betty except Dorothea Montalvo Puente. Does that make her Mother Teresa? No. Is Dorothea Montalvo Puenta a crazed serial killer, preying upon the helpless, looting people beyond the grave? She's neither. She's neither saint nor demon. She's like all of us, a little bit good, a little bit bad," he said, spreading his upraised palms, as if balancing her two sides. "Half this case has been devoted to proving to you that she's a thief. So be it. She is. That doesn't make her a killer."

Clymo suggested that Dorothea had been a good friend to all of these people. She'd known Leona Carpenter, for instance, for twenty-seven years. And her friend Betty Palmer knew she was "going downhill," so she'd simply agreed that if Dorothea would take care of her, the landlady could receive "her trust" of Social Security checks.

Then, perhaps drawing on his study of psychology at Stanford, Clymo held before the jurors a well-known black-and-white image, a perception test. "Some people look at this and see a chalice. Others see two faces that are facing each other," he said, walking the image past the jury box. "What it fairly graphically represents is that there are frequently two ways of viewing things. I would suggest to you that if you have it in your mind what it is you are going to see, you will see it. Each view eliminates the other."

It was an ingenious move, illustrative of the task before them, subtly persuasive.

To make his next point, Clymo popped in the videotape of newsclips from November 11, 1988, that the jurors had seen months before. The courtroom grew still while sounds and images from that fateful day filled the room. "And topping our news tonight, a gruesome mystery . . ." ". . . uncovered the remains of a dead body . . ." "This is the house of Dorothea Puente . . ."

Clymo ridiculed the prosecution for failing to present substantially more than the suspicions voiced that very first day. "Did you hear on the video, from day one, in essence what you heard in the prosecutor's final argument? Bodies buried! Suspected poisoning! Dorothea Montalvo Puente has a prior! Checks were cashed! People missing! From day one, that was the view of the case.

"What has really been proved to you in the six, seven months, whatever it's been, that we've taken evidence on this case?

"Not much.

"You know, from day one they've been trying to prove that Dorothea Montalvo Puente poisoned people. Has that been *proved* to you?" he asked skeptically. "Has that been proved to you beyond a reasonable doubt and to a moral certainty?"

He let the question hang for a moment.

Clymo next turned to the subject of flight, claiming that the defense had never denied that Puente had fled. "What significance does it have, that's the question before you," he said. "Hell, she didn't have to run away. They *escorted* her through the crowd!"

(Detective Cabrera had handed him this one.)

"Does that prove she's conscious of having committed murder? Or does that just mean that, yes, she knows she's been ripping off the government for a long time, that she's been snagging Social Security checks after people die because, as we've heard, it doesn't take a rocket scientist to figure out that Social Security is pretty easy to rip off."

Clymo conceded that, on the face of it, seven bodies buried in the yard was very powerful evidence. "But of *what*?" he asked. "Of a *graveyard!* It doesn't say anything about how people died!"

With that, he began flourishing medical charts regarding the questionable health of each of the individuals Puente was alleged to have murdered. He recounted the dire medical problems they faced. And over and over, for each of these counts, Clymo reminded the jurors, "What do we know as to cause of death? Nothing. Nothing! It's *undetermined.*"

Clymo's fundamental tactic was to raise questions, raise doubts. It wasn't his job to supply answers, but to raise those little worries and concerns that add up to something short of "beyond a moral certainty."

"You've heard a lot about the smell of death. How could there be a smell of death if nine people were killed premeditatedly? It takes two, three days before a body starts to smell. If these were premeditated, deliberated murders, why was there always the smell of death? Why were bodies around long enough to start the decomposition process? How do you explain that?"

And why would someone go to the trouble to wrap the bodies so meticulously, he asked, reminding them of the quilts, the sheets, some of them stitched like a shroud. "Why not get them out into the hole as quickly as you could and get them covered? Once they're in the hole, they've disappeared."

In softer tones, he suggested, "Bizarre as it may seem, didn't the body wrappings represent some crude form of trying to provide at least a measure of dignity to these people, to provide some barrier between them and the dirt?"

At one point, Clymo listed all the former tenants who had testified at the trial. Clearly, they weren't dead. Why hadn't Puente killed them, too, if she were such a crazed killer?

Subtly yet unmistakably, Clymo was making progress, raising doubts.

Clymo saved his best argument for the end of the day. He popped in the videotaped interview of former tenant Julius "Pat" Kelley, turned to the jurors, and asked, "If Dorothea Puente hadn't been arrested in November 1988, what would have happened if Julius Kelley had remained at the house, if Julius Kelley had died there of lung cancer? I just ask you to think about that as you watch the video."

The image of a shrunken and feeble man filled the screen, the digital date, 4/20/90, stamped in a bottom corner. The jurors remembered seeing this video months before, but now Puente's former ten-

359

ant seemed frailer than ever. They heard George Williamson and Kevin Clymo question the old man in turn, and they heard him respond in a barely intelligible rasp. On the tape, Kelley said he'd repeatedly asked Dorothea for Dalmane to help him sleep. At first she'd refused, but finally gave him a couple of pills.

Kelley recounted life at 1426 F Street, but what he said was less important than how sick he looked. Though only sixty-three, the man appeared as fragile as ancient parchment.

After half an hour of Kelley's sickly image, Clymo stopped the tape and again addressed the jury. "Just consider," he said thoughtfully, "if the cancer ran its course, as we know it did, and Julius Kelley was found buried in the yard, don't you think he would be *count ten*?"

The jurors sat up straighter. Clymo's logic seemed undeniably sound. A sick old guy with a regular check dies, and Dorothea makes a space for him in her own private cemetery.

Clymo continued in this vein, "When the toxicological testing was done, wouldn't they also find Dalmane in his system? He asked for it to help him sleep, but he didn't have a prescription for it."

If Kelley had died at the boardinghouse, if he'd indeed become count ten, "Dr. Anthony would have been in court testifying to the autopsy results, testifying to the toxicological findings, and you would have heard that Julius Kelley had Dalmane in his tissue, in his liver and his brain, and he had no prescription for it!"

"How often," he asked rhetorically, "had that scenario played out?"

Clymo invited the jury to remember some of the earliest testimony about Bert. "Remember Bill Johnson? With the big beard? Remember how emotional he got talking about Bert? Bert was his buddy, he checked up on Bert." Clymo smiled. "One thing that Bill Johnson knew about Bert Montoya was that he had this peculiarity, he was *nocturnal.* He would walk around at night, and he would do his talking to his spirits at night. He didn't sleep. When everyone else would sleep, he would be up all night."

Johnson had indeed said this.

"Isn't it just as reasonable to conclude that that's why Dorothea Puente sent him over to Dr. Doody with a note: *He doesn't sleep, give him some Dalmane?*"

Could this be true? Had Dorothea Puente only handed out a couple of pills now and then to help her tenants sleep?

At the start of the day no one thought Kevin Clymo had a chance to save his client. But now, with the gravely ill visage of Julius "Pat" Kelley, he'd done the impossible: He'd raised the nagging concern, the active worry, that Dorothea Puente might actually be innocent.

The next morning, characterizing the prosecution as desperate for a cause of death, Clymo launched a scathing attack on the "incredibly exceptional" handling of the tissue homogenates, and on James Beede. He pointed out discrepancies in the results found by the three labs that had tested the samples. And he claimed that, having failed to find a cause of death, the prosecution had shopped from lab to lab until they'd received the findings they were hoping for.

Further, he suggested that James Beede was responsible for the Dalmane that registered in the DOJ's high-tech analyses. "We're not talking false reading," Clymo said ominously. "We're talking contamination. *Proven, known contamination.* Somehow, cocaine ends up in Ben Fink's tissue sample. Bill Phillips [of the DOJ] proved for me that the samples that were prepared by James Beede were contaminated.

"What do you do with it? I don't know. You consider it.

"I cannot prove to you that all of these samples got contaminated with Dalmane, but I know that it has been proved to you that they possibly could have been.

"And bingo," he said sarcastically, "we got a cause of death."

He pitted Dr. Baselt against Dr. Anthony, stating that his expert had broader experience and greater credibility. But, even granting that Dr. Anthony was an expert in his field, Clymo asked, "How many times did you hear him tell you, when you are talking about decomposed tissue, everything goes out the window?"

And that was the sticking point. Through all the hours of toxicological debate, no one could ever make an informed statement about how the process of decomposition affected Dalmane. This was the Achilles' heel of the prosecution's case, and Clymo meant to cripple O'Mara with it.

"When decomposition occurs, dehydration follows. Dehydration is like that glass of water with the salt in it. When the water evaporates, the salt is still there."

Then, snatching up a copy of the court transcript, Clymo read his exchange with Dr. Anthony about the amount of Dalmane that it might take to kill someone. Striding and gesturing, he greatly emphasized his personal favorite, the softball analogy—"When you took a hundred or two hundred Dalmane and opened them all up, you would end up with a softball-size mass of powder"—but he carefully omitted Dr. Anthony's clarification that, in combination with other drugs, a much smaller dose could prove fatal.

Did the jurors notice this? Clymo certainly hoped not.

Again and again, he returned to the issue of reasonable doubt. "It's not my job to prove to you that Dorothea Montalvo Puente is not guilty," he declared. Rather, it was the prosecutor's job to prove beyond a reasonable doubt and to a moral certainty that she was.

Clymo explained away the fact that Ben Fink and others had no prescriptions for the drugs found in their systems, citing testimony that alcoholics, when deprived of alcohol, will resort to pills.

Recounting the many ailments that afflicted these people, Clymo suggested that the only pattern to emerge in this case came from the checked box on the autopsy forms: "Cause of death? Undetermined. Undetermined. Undetermined. Undetermined. Undetermined. Undetermined. Undetermined."

Clymo waved multiple charts to argue his case, charts about "moral certainty," homicide, jury instructions, and the law. "If you follow the law," he argued, *"you can't convict Dorothea Puente of murdering eight people unless you can prove that they did not die of natural causes!"*

And the ninth, he insisted, was suicide. Citing all the troubles in Ruth Munroe's life—her husband's diagnosis of cancer, mounting medical bills, and the failure of the restaurant business on top of her divorce—Clymo made it seem likely that Munroe had been terminally depressed.

Reminding the jury that O'Mara had called this the most troublesome of all the counts, Clymo declared, "I'm not supposed to have to stand up here and convince you that she's not guilty. This is America! If there is doubt, if it is troublesome, it's not supposed to be prosecuted!"

Finally, after two and a half days, Clymo was about to conclude. He picked up some papers that co-counsel Vlautin had prepared for him and started to read.

It was a tale about following fox tracks in the snow, leading to rabbit tracks, leading to where a rabbit "has been killed and apparently devoured." The writer, seeing the bloody, trampled snow and tufts of fur, is convinced the fox killed the rabbit.

Farther on, the writer spies the remains of the rabbit, "but here there is no distinct track of any creature, only a few scratches and marks where some great bird of prey—a hawk or owl—has struck the snow. . . ."

Everyone could guess the author as Clymo continued reading: "The circumstantial evidence against that fox was very strong, for the deed was done since the snow fell and I saw no other tracks but his at the first places. Any jury would have convicted him, and he would have been hung, if he could have been caught."

Clymo looked up at the jury. He could almost see the doubt clouding above their heads.

This story, he told them, was entitled "Murder Mystery: Rabbit, Fox, Owl" and was written by Henry David Thoreau the year before he died, "ten years after he told us about the trout."

Softly, Kevin Clymo implored the jury, "Keep in mind that things are not always what they seem. Thank you."

Ending the longest closing argument of his career, Clymo sat down. And Peter Vlautin, grinning to himself, thought, *payback.*

Because of the burden of proof, the prosecution gets a second shot at summation: rebuttal.

O'Mara was itching to argue. He'd filled pages and pages with notes. Clymo had presented the side of Dorothea Puente that was all sweetness and light; he was ready to counter with the side that was sinister and dark.

He rose and began. Urging the jurors to "step back and see the big picture," he derided Clymo's argument as absurd. The defense suggested that Puente had quietly buried the bodies because she couldn't risk shutting off "the big computer in the sky." But, he demanded, "What risk did she run with Everson Gillmouth? None at all!"

She could have easily reported his death to authorities. After all, her "fiancé" only received a small pension of $42.50 a month. But instead, after Gill picked her up from prison, she'd looted his bank accounts and dumped him beside the river. "She's been out of the joint less than a month!" O'Mara exclaimed. "The ink hasn't even dried on her discharge papers, and she's back to her old tricks!"

Just minutes into his rebuttal, O'Mara was already erasing the traces of reasonable doubt that Clymo had so carefully written across this case.

He went on, "Kevin Clymo says it wouldn't surprise anyone if a seventy-seven-year-old man died of natural causes." He shook his head. "What is surprising is that a man who died of natural causes would be *disposed of* in this way."

O'Mara cast contempt on Ricardo Ordorica's claim that he'd seen Gillmouth in mid-December 1985, and mocked his pantomime of Everson Gillmouth's heart attack. "It's not that he's wrong, it's that he's lying to you!"

Ismael Florez was also lying about building the box sometime in December, O'Mara said, because of "the same kind of mindless loyalty" to Dorothea that they'd seen in McCauley and Ordorica.

O'Mara sped on. "Mr. Clymo didn't say much about Betty Palmer because there isn't a lot to say. What would be an explanation for why someone would cut her head off, cut her hands off, and cut her legs off? The only reason that makes any sense at all is to hide her identity. If she died of natural causes, why the heck would you cut those parts off? *Why?* There's no reason! Clymo had also suggested that someone else may have dismembered Palmer's corpse, but O'Mara derided this with heavy sarcasm: "Is she gonna ask someone else to do that? It's pretty hard to bring up at Joe's Corner."

Switching quickly to the Munroe case, O'Mara said again that "the problem is that it was never investigated properly, that's the problem." But he attributed this sloppy investigation to the manipulations of Dorothea Puente, who told the police that Munroe had been complaining of chest pains, leading them to believe she'd had a heart attack. Consequently, the police hadn't recognized this as a potential murder, and lost the opportunity to inspect the scene.

O'Mara reminded the jurors what Munroe had said at the hairdressers just three days before her death. "She doesn't say, *I'm so depressed.* She says, *I'm so sick, I feel like I'm gonna die!*"

His words came down like a sledgehammer.

Deriding Clymo's list of the many tenants who were still alive and well, who had come to court and testified, O'Mara said, "She didn't kill all of them, so she didn't kill any of them? Does that make sense to you?"

Consciously letting someone die is first-degree murder, and now he attacked Puente for not having called for help for any of these nine victims. "Why didn't she call the ambulance for Leona, if she had a friendship with her for twenty-seven years? Did she do anything for

Jim Gallop, does she call for Mr. Gallop to save his life? No! The only phone call she makes is to say he can't make his doctor's appointment because he went to L.A. This is the same person that says Ben went to Marysville, that Dorothy Miller went to the VA hospital, that Bert goes to Mexico. This is the same person that sent the letter to Reba. It's sophomoric, admittedly, but that's her way to stop the trail.

"More important," he went on, "if you cared at all about these people, wouldn't you have called *before* they needed a coroner?"

(A voice in the gallery whispered, "He's good.")

O'Mara knew he had to confront the damage wrought by the videotaped image of frail and dying Mr. Kelley. Clymo had suggested that Julius "Pat" Kelley could have easily ended up being count ten against Dorothea Puente. But, he pointed out, "Mr. Kelley told you himself why he wouldn't be a victim."

Eyebrows arched curiously.

"The problem with Mr. Kelley," O'Mara exclaimed, "is that he had *family*. When Peggy Nickerson interviews him, he arrives with his *niece*. You couldn't get rid of Mr. Kelley without somebody asking questions!"

Abruptly shifting gears, O'Mara said, "Let's talk about drugs. We're not talking about a massive overdose, we're talking about a fatal *mixture* of drugs, but it's not massive. And we all know that when you add alcohol you have a time bomb."

Responding to Clymo's criticism of the inconsistent findings of the three toxicology labs, O'Mara's voice was again pitched with sarcasm. "They say this is so *unusual*—but you all know this isn't the usual case. When you go to the trouble to use the most sophisticated equipment available, you're doing something wrong?"

He turned again. "The salt analogy. It's not the levels that count, it's its *presence* that counts. It shouldn't be there *at all*."

Zipping from point to point, O'Mara gradually lost focus, going over material the jury had already heard. His delivery was coming in tones of harangue, and the jurors were looking restless.

At day's end, Vlautin remarked that the prosecutor's long-windedness was good for the defense. "Let him keep talking."

Meanwhile, Dorothea Puente seemed pleased, smiling at her attorneys and joking with the bailiff. Noticing this, reporter Wayne Wilson asked Vlautin if Puente would like to make a statement about how she was feeling at this point.

Before leaving with the bailiff, she laughed and told her attorney, "Tell Wayne he can kiss my ass! I'm not giving any interviews to those vultures of the media."

The next day, O'Mara knew he couldn't afford to talk much longer. The jury would revolt. He had a few points to make about Bert Montoya, and then he had to stop himself and let them start deliberations.

Standing before them again, he said, "I know there's an imaginary headline going through your heads: O'MARA CONTINUES TO HOLD JURY HOSTAGE." They laughed, and then he was racing through his closing points, speaking even faster than usual, then turning to the subject of Bert Montoya.

Dorothea Puente's boardinghouse should have been the "best of all possible worlds" for Bert, and Judy Moise and Beth Valentine were gleeful when they'd finally placed Bert in her home. The mother/son bond between the landlady and Bert "appears to be this perfect relationship," O'Mara said. And yet, on at least two occasions, Bert had fled back to Detox. "There's something going on that disturbs him," he said ominously.

Again waving one of Dorothea's famous calendars before them, O'Mara pointed out that, on September 8, the day Bert would have turned fifty-two, Mrs. Puente had written his name. "But we never hear anything about his birthday, because Bert isn't around to celebrate his birthday," he declared. "Bert is gone before his birthday ever arrives."

And there it was. With all her love of fanfare, of balloon bouquets and cards and presents, would Dorothea Puente have let Bert's birthday pass unnoticed?

No. Bert died before turning fifty-two.

Finally, O'Mara was ready to demonstrate the utter absurdity of Puente's defense. "Let's indulge this fantasy to the ultimate degree," he said dryly. "Let's assume they all died as suggested by Mr. Clymo. They all died of these various diseases, conditions they built up from abusing their bodies over time."

He started slowly, gathering speed. "Ruth Monroe overdoses, commits suicide right in front of her. Everson Gillmouth, the man that she was thinking about marrying, he goes and has a heart attack, and he dies. Then Betty Palmer, who arrives on her doorstep, she dies unexpectedly. Then Leona Carpenter, her friend of twenty-seven years, she dies unexpectedly. Then James Gallop, a man that she meets in a bar, he dies unexpectedly. Vera Martin arrives at her doorstep, she's only there five minutes, she has this occlusive condition of the heart, and she dies unexpectedly. Then Dorothy Miller, she's there for a short period of time, she dies unexpectedly. Ben Fink—the drunk—she tries to deal with Ben Fink, but because of his repeated alcohol abuse for all of these years, he dies unexpectedly. And now her *son*, the man that she treats like a son, that she buys a Spanish-language Bible for, gets a new pair of shoes, rubs medicine into his head to take care of his psoriasis, she does all of these things for him, and now *her son is sick.*

"Three people—Mark Anthony, Don Anthony, and Pat Kelley—had to carry him back to the house. He's unconscious. He's blowing bubbles. We can't rouse him. He's unresponsive.

"And who's the last person to be with Bert Montoya?

"Dorothea Puente!"

A chilling moment.

"Now," O'Mara continued, his voice sharp, "if we assume all of that is true, did she make any attempt to get medical aid for Mr. Montoya? Did she call nine one one? Did she do *anything? No!"*

Eyes turned toward her, but Mrs. Puente resolutely ignored everyone.

O'Mara resumed pacing, the jury watching him closely. "When Mr. Clymo closed yesterday, to use a little double entendre, he outfoxed me with his Thoreau tale—the fox and the rabbit, huh? The fox is falsely accused. The circumstantial evidence was strong. Any jury in the world would have convicted the fox if they could have caught him.

"Well, Ladies and Gentlemen, there is no fox. The tracks in the snow do not mislead you, do not trick you. Kevin Clymo misleads and tricks you!"

Clymo objected instantly, and the judge instructed the jurors to disregard O'Mara's comment.

But O'Mara returned to his analogy. "We have nine rabbits that are dead. The tracks in the snow are clear: an unassuming, seemingly innocent old lady—the visual and logical contradiction—in front of the old Victorian house with the lush landscape. It's almost inconceivable in anyone's mind that this could happen. And yet it did.

"Dorothea Puente murdered nine people."

367

CHAPTER 47

FOR MONTHS, THE JURORS HAD TALKED ABOUT MOVIES, WEATHER, politics, vacations, and family—anything and everything except this trial. Now, finally, they could open the floodgates. Filing out for deliberations on July 15, 1993, they gave no clue to what images had left the greatest impressions, which witnesses had swayed them.

Could it be John Sharp telling of the thumping, bumping down the stairs in the middle of the night? Brenda Trujillo's description of Dorothea "leaning over the table and breaking open capsules" into a drink? The angry, grief-stricken children of Ruth Munroe? The headless, truncated, blood-drained corpse of Betty Palmer?

Or would they, instead, recall the doctors testifying, again and again, to the lung, heart and liver diseases that plagued most of these people? Would they suspect that James Beede had somehow bungled the toxicology tests so that all the results were questionable? Would the toxicology experts cancel each other out? And would they remember, above all else, how Dorothea Puente had cleaned and cared for society's castoffs?

They had to sift through some 3,500 pieces of evidence, the testimonies of 153 witnesses, months and months of impressions, ultimately distilling the facts down to an essential question: Was Dorothea Puente a kindly but unbalanced old woman caught in an unfortunate web of circumstance? Or was she a cunning, manipulative, murderous old crone?

Even if they supposed she was somehow responsible for these deaths, did they feel they had enough evidence to *convict*? Could they find enough evidence in aging documents and faulty memories to find *beyond a reasonable doubt* that these people had been murdered with premeditation?

Or, might they decide this was a case of criminal negligence and opt for the lesser charge of involuntary manslaughter?

At this same time, Dr. Kevorkian was hitting the news with more "assisted suicides" in Michigan, and the Netherlands had just broken new ground by legalizing euthanasia. With these people so weak and ill, had Dorothea really done anything so terrible? They were already living on the edge; hadn't she just nudged them off?

By the end of the first afternoon, it seemed clear that the jury was working fast. Michael Esplin—the sole member to come to court each day in a necktie, who had listened with notably acute attention—was selected jury foreman. Their first request was to hear what Dorothea Puente had told the police about Ruth Munroe's death in 1982.

Next, they wanted to hear the testimony of John Sharp, which touched on a number of issues, especially the disappearances of Bert Montoya and Ben Fink.

After that, the only request from the jury room was for some labeling stickers, which, observers agreed, indicated that they were being methodical.

While summer fog clung to the coast of Monterey, there was apparently no fog of confusion in the jury room. At breaks, they seemed just as cheery and good-natured as ever—a good sign.

Four news vans remained parked outside the courthouse, waiting for a verdict, and reporters and cameramen speculated on how long the jury might be out. A week? Two? More? A betting pool went up. But a week passed and the most impatient were quickly disappointed.

As the next week commenced the all-male television crews awaited a verdict like expectant fathers, querying everyone, seeking reassurance over the progress of something over which they had no control.

369

Another week went by with hardly a peep of news, so they dug up news of their own.

"The trial has cost one and a half million?° Where did you get that figure?" one asked.

"That's the old figure updated," came the answer. "All the costs of the defense, prosecution estimates, witnesses, jury selection, and staff."

Meanwhile, the loitering media started casting the movie, which all agreed should be out soon. For Dorothea, who better than Olympia Dukakis? For Judge Virga, Anthony Quinn. Terry Bradshaw would be well cast as Kevin Clymo. And it wasn't perfect, but Michael J. Fox could play Vlautin. O'Mara was tough, but Robert Duvall would do. And, in a bit of whimsy, Cindy Crawford was cast as Mary Corbitt, the attractive court reporter.

July expired, and there was still nothing to do but wait.

Then, on the afternoon of August 2, came the first whisper of activity. The attorneys were summoned, and while they huddled in Virga's chambers, the media swarmed like bees around a disturbed hive.

Rumors and questions buzzed through the air. "It's a hung jury! I hear they're deadlocked!"

Reporters perched in the gallery, preparing stories and comparing notes. A voice said, "What do you think the split is?"

"Ten to two," one guessed.

"Eleven to one," another joked. "And Frost's the holdout."

The truth was no one knew. It could be six to six, any combination.

The attorneys spilled into court and speculation ceased. Dorothea Puente came in dressed in pastel pink and lavender, looking thinner and seeming lighter of step. Vlautin was impassive, but Clymo looked pleased. O'Mara came in grim and tight-lipped.

Judge Virga went on record only long enough to read the jury's note:

We are deadlocked on all nine counts.
We would like further instructions.

Virga stated gravely that he would instruct the jury the next morning. Exiting the courtroom, he muttered, "It's going to be a long night."

°According to a FOX-TV reporter who later obtained sealed documents, this figure was closer to $3 million.

O'Mara promptly disappeared, but Puente and her attorneys lingered. Clymo winked at her and gave her a hug, and she slumped against him in apparent relief. Now, after these many, arduous months, some good news. Some hope.

The defense attorneys couldn't even get out of the courtroom before being besieged by reporters. "We're encouraged," Vlautin said. "For all we know, it's leaning toward not guilty. If the jury's hung, the ball will be in the prosecution's court."

Asked about Dorothea's state of mind, Clymo said she was too emotional for words, responding with tears. "She's obviously happy," he said. "The whole world predicted for five years that she'd be convicted in five minutes, and that hasn't happened."

Grinning, Peter Vlautin shared a fortuitous little story. Friday night, up in Sacramento, he'd eaten at a Chinese restaurant. "My fortune cookie said 'Good news will come to you from far away.' I think I got it." With unintentional irony, he added, "We just hope the jurors hang in there."

Later, back at their office, Clymo and Vlautin called upon their minions, who left Sacramento and hurried down to Monterey.

Moments later, the news was blistering through the airwaves, and people were calling Judy Moise in Sacramento. "I can't believe it," she cried. "Oh, my God, I'm shocked! I just can't get over it. I'm just really, really shocked." Almost wistfully, she recalled, "It looked like such a sharp jury. It really looked like they would be able to come up with a verdict."

Social Worker Mary Ellen Howard had a similar reaction. "It just blows my mind that they could spend that much money and not put that lady away!"

And Mildred Ballenger, who remembered what a slippery character Puente was in 1982, reminded her friends, "I predicted that this would happen."

Meanwhile, the rumormongers were quick to castigate O'Mara for imagined failures, even concocting conspiracy theories around Puente's supposed political connections. But what could he have done differently? Were the toxicology reports too tedious? Had it been a mistake not to call Michelle Crowl to the stand? Did the jurors think John McCauley was the real culprit? Had O'Mara lost them during closing arguments?

371

Ever self-critical, O'Mara was asking himself just these sorts of questions.

Perhaps it just came down to a juror or two who *could not be convinced*. In legal circles, there's an adage that a case is decided from the moment the jury is seated. And at jury selection, the defense had the benefit of Dr. Linda Meza, who had apparently perceived something about these jurors that the prosecutor had not.

The next morning, Judge Virga swept in looking edgy. He quickly spurned a defense motion for a mistrial, offered by an almost giddy defense.

The jurors entered looking uncharacteristically downcast, features stamped with worry, dismay, disgust. One juror sharply angled her chair toward the back of the room, turning her back on spectators. In the gallery, a juror's wife whispered that her husband had been so stressed that he hadn't been able to sleep and was taking stomach medication. Eleven days of dissension had changed them.

"Ladies and Gentlemen of the jury." Judge Virga's voice filled the room. "It has been my experience on more than one occasion that a jury which initially reported it was deadlocked was ultimately able to arrive at verdicts on one or more of the counts before it. . . . Both the evidence and the issues presented are complex. It is not unexpected, therefore, that it would be a difficult, time-consuming task for you to arrive at verdicts. . . ." His words came in an even stream of reason, chastening them, encouraging them, urging them to try once again.

"As I have previously instructed you, you have absolute discretion to conduct your deliberations in any way you deem appropriate. May I suggest, however, that since you have not been able to arrive at verdicts using the methods you have chosen, you consider changing the methods, at least temporarily."

Judge Virga suggested new leaders, reverse role playing, and a re-reading of certain instructions, then ordered them to resume deliberations. "If you have not arrived at verdicts on any or all of the nine counts by tomorrow afternoon at 4:00 P.M., I will reconvene court at that time and inquire whether or not you have made any progress. The answer you give me will determine what further action I will take, if any."

The jurors stood and filed out, exchanging small courtesies, the crowd in the gallery scrutinizing every gesture.

Dorothea Puente, former "Queen of the Bars," now emerged as Queen of the Court, beaming up at her attorneys, accepting congratulations from assembled members of the defense team.

Afterward, Clymo and Vlautin strode out to the waiting barrage of cameras, talking of a mistrial, a hung jury, even acquittal.

But John O'Mara was nowhere to be found.

Rather than fret and do nothing, he threw himself into his car and sped toward home and family—something that had been distinctly absent from his life during the past many months. His twelve-year-old son, Conner, was angry that his father had "chosen" to take on this marathon, out-of-county trial. His daughter, at seventeen, seemed less affected. Still, his wife pointedly opined that the only way he'd pay attention to his children was if they got arrested.

O'Mara knew his workaholism was a problem, so he was trying to reform. He was shedding cases like he was shedding pounds, delegating trials to other attorneys.

But . . . a hung jury.

He blamed himself completely. He replayed every mistake, every strategical misstep, every poorly turned phrase. He rethought things he'd brought out, things he hadn't. . . . "Well O'Mara," he chided himself, "you spent all that money, one and a half million taxpayer dollars, and you didn't get a conviction."

If he lost, he knew it wasn't because Kevin Clymo had done such a great job, but because he'd failed to meet the burden of proof. She was guilty. He knew it. It seemed obvious. But for some reason, he hadn't been able to reach all of the jurors. He'd picked them, he liked them all, but somehow he'd failed to connect.

And worse, even though this would hand the advantage to Clymo, he couldn't retry this case himself. He just couldn't do that to his family. "There are other Dorothea Puentes out there," he thought, "but I only have one son."

He hated to do this to another attorney. It was a complex, burdensome case, which was part of the reason he'd taken it on himself after Williamson left. This wasn't a case that he could just assign to anyone. It was, at bottom, a hardship assignment. It had cost him plenty of sleepless nights, and nearly a year away from his family.

And for what? *A jury deadlocked on all nine counts!*

CHAPTER 48

SATELLITE TRUCKS HUMMED OUTSIDE THE COURTHOUSE, LIGHTS and cameras staked out positions on the steps, and reporters roamed the hallways. On August 4, any glimpse of the jurors fueled speculation. How did they look? What if they were still deadlocked? Would the judge declare a mistrial? Questions ticked steadily toward 4:00 P.M.

The attorneys began to arrive, and reporters crowded into the courtroom. Dorothea Puente was brought in, looking cool as ever. The defense team calmly took their places, and O'Mara burst in looking—resigned?

Judge Virga appeared and made a polite joke, dispelling tension. Directing his words to jury foreman Michael Esplin, the judge first cautioned, "Please don't tell me how the jury is split in any way," then asked, "Has there been any progress since yesterday morning?"

All held their breath.

Esplin answered, "Yes, Your Honor, there's been quite a bit of progress."

A wave of silent congratulations surged toward them. Not just progress, but *"quite a bit of progress."*

The judge instructed them to resume deliberations the next morning at 9:30, and the courtroom emptied.

The defense contingent remained optimistic. "I'm encouraged that the energy seems to have returned to the jurors," Clymo said. "I do not believe this jury is looking for reasons to convict Dorothea Puente."

And a clearly relieved John O'Mara remarked that *any* verdict would be better than a mistrial. Even if Puente got only second-degree murder (which would put her safely beyond the reach of the death penalty), Judge Virga would impose a stiff sentence and "bury her into the next century."

The wait resumed, and the bloom of progress was soon buried beneath the steady progression of time. Another week passed without any indication of a verdict. Then another. Not a word, not a request, not a hiccup of change slipped from the jury room.

The media folk grew restless, trying to satisfy their editors' demands for news. They toured the austere holding cell where Puente stayed every afternoon. They pestered the court clerk and interviewed janitors. They filed brief, desperate stories, and kidded and complained about each other.

But still, no verdict. No news.

On August 15, when a full month of jury deliberations had passed, everyone was well past cranky. The judge, the attorneys, and Puente's unofficial entourage anxiously marked the days. Everyone wondered whether the jury's prolonged and ominous silence meant their next note would echo their last: "deadlocked."

"What *can* they be doing in there?" O'Mara groaned.

One juror got the flu. Another came down with pneumonia, further delaying deliberations.

"Stress," the watchers agreed.

The jury tied, then passed, the longest murder trial deliberations in California history. Not an especially happy landmark for anyone.

Finally, on the afternoon of August 25, the jury sent Judge Virga a two-line note. It wasn't a verdict, but it was something.

The note was kept secret as the judge huddled with the attorneys in his chambers, crafting a proper response.

The next morning, Judge Virga responded to their questions about "what clearly constitutes poison," and how the various charges could be considered in relation to one another.

Whatever else this meant, it was progress.

At noon came another note, this time asking for additional verdict forms. Definitely progress.

At an afternoon break, a cluster of jurors seemed anxious, saying little but virtually bouncing on the balls of their feet.

Finally, another note: *verdicts*.

Word went out over the airwaves, and the tiny courtroom noisily filled to standing room only. Spectators conferred: "I thought she'd go scot-free." "People in Sacramento's social services thought she was the best thing around." "The guy in the box—that's a murder conviction for sure."

The attorneys took their seats, all business. The defendant was brought in looking ghostly pale. She accepted brief assurances from Clymo and Vlautin.

The bailiff announced Judge Virga, and the courtroom froze with anticipation as he assumed the bench. Virga turned toward jury foreman Michael Esplin and said he had received their note, reading, "We have reached the verdicts we will be able to reach."

He then asked, "Mr. Esplin, on how many counts?"

"Three, Your Honor."

The crowd murmured with surprise.

With a calm that was surely felt by no one else, Virga asked the breakdown of the votes on the other six.

Esplin said that four counts were hung eleven-one. The other two were split eight-two-two, and three-six-three.

Virga declared a mistrial on those six counts: Ruth Munroe, Everson Gillmouth, Bert Montoya, James Gallop, Vera Faye Martin, and Betty Palmer.

Shock breathed through the courtroom. How could they fail to convict her of murdering Bert? Or Ruth Munroe? Or Betty Palmer?

The remaining verdict forms were handed to court clerk Barbara Beddow, who read their findings in a clear voice:

"Guilty of the crime of murder in the second degree of Leona Carpenter. . . ."

"Guilty of the crime of murder in the first degree of Dorothy Miller. . . ."

"Guilty of the crime of murder in the first degree of Ben Fink. . . ."

"Special circumstances allegations: Dorothea Montalvo Puente did commit multiple murder."

She could get the death penalty.

Dorothea Puente briefly clasped Peter Vlautin's hand but showed little emotion until court was adjourned. As she stood to leave, Kevin Clymo put an arm around her and whispered close to her ear. Later, she cried.

Although John O'Mara was relieved simply to get guilty verdicts, plenty of people were less than thrilled with the trial's outcome.

How could the jury possibly believe that Puente had murdered three of the people buried in her yard, but not the others? It made absolutely no sense! And why those three? Ben Fink, okay, there was strong evidence she murdered Ben Fink. But how about Dorothy Miller and Leona Carpenter? Nobody knew anything about those two! Why did they convict on two that no one could remember a thing about, yet didn't convict on Bert Montoya! Or Betty Palmer, the lady with no head! Or Ruth Munroe, who said, "I'm so sick, I feel like I'm going to die!"

Some fumed, some rejoiced, some simply sighed with relief.

When Judy Moise got the news, her first reaction was: "I think it's absolutely wonderful. At least they got convictions!" Yet she was keenly disappointed about Bert, since she'd believed that convicting Puente of Bert's murder was key.

John Sharp concurred. "I can't see how they split on Bert," he said. "His was the most perfectly planned!" He recalled that Puente had said she was going to send Bert to Mexico, and then, a couple of weeks later, she said he'd gone. Still, Sharp said, "I wouldn't wish the death penalty on her."

When news of the verdict reached Reba Nicklous up in Oregon, she was at first shocked and "quite emotional." But on reflection, she said, "It doesn't bother me she wasn't convicted of Everson's death. I know she did it, and I can't see any sense in a retrial as long as she gets life without parole. A retrial isn't going to bring any of them back, and it's a waste of taxpayers' money. None of us will gain anything by having it rehashed over again. I want to put it behind me."

Not everyone was so sanguine.

Ruth Munroe's son, William Clausen, felt hurt, shocked, and angry. "The jury, I feel, was not educated enough in murder trials. They weren't even listening. What do they call it—blind justice? They're the ones that had blinders on! They didn't see anything! It's so irritating. [District Attorney] Steve White was on the news last night saying that he's satisfied. I'm not. I won't be satisfied. They can't just leave these other six hanging. *Undetermined.* That's bullshit! I need to finalize this. I need to get this taken care of. In my heart, I need it."

And Vera Faye Martin's son, Jerry Hobbs, added his voice to the chorus of frustration. Having learned from O'Mara that his mother had arrived at Dorothea's on October 2, 1987, her check forged just three days later, on October 5, Hobbs was convinced his mother had been murdered. "My mother would never have relinquished her check to anyone. Ever. Period. She was absolutely fanatical about her check. Her check was never out of her sight. I can say with certainty that she wouldn't have given her check to a perfect stranger."

Hobbs believed that his mother had simply accepted a drug-laced drink from Puente. "She went in there like a lamb to slaughter."

The prospect of Puente getting life in prison did nothing to mollify his anger. "She will adapt. That lady will live fine in prison," he said bitterly. "She's very popular."

Unable to move the criminal justice system, Hobbs would try the civil route. He decided he and his brother should proceed with their suit against Puente's longtime friend Ricardo Ordorica.* "He's either a total idiot, or he's dirty as hell," he said. "You don't let someone hand you these sorts of checks knowing their record. I don't buy it that honest people let this happen. Their dishonesty is what she fed on."

But no civil action would ever resolve this for Vera Faye Martin's family. Unlike the other victims, she was buried fully clothed, which left Jerry Hobbs worrying over a horrific possibility: "Was she buried alive?"

---

*Vera Faye Martin's family was inclined to drop their suit against Peggy Nickerson.

CHAPTER 49

ALMOST EVERYONE THOUGHT THAT CLYMO AND VLAUTIN HAD done an incredible job. Despite that any fool in Sacramento knew that their client was guilty nine times over, despite John O'Mara's months of witnesses and mountains of evidence, they'd managed to get Puente off on six of nine counts. Half a dozen times, they'd heard the word: *mistrial*. It was phenomenal. As one astonished observer put it, "They made something out of nothing."

But Clymo and Vlautin were devastated. Six of nine wasn't good enough. Whoever the holdout was, he or she had buckled when it came to Ben Fink, Dorothy Miller, and Leona Carpenter. And for those three, Dorothea Puente might get the ultimate penalty. She was marked a serial killer, and the state would try to execute her.

Much as they'd prayed they would never reach this point, they'd prepared mightily for it. They'd investigated every ugly little secret, every tiny act of virtue stretching from Dorothea Montalvo Puente all the way back to Dorothea Helen Gray. "The only way a jury is going to spare anyone's life is, they have to understand them and feel compassion," Vlautin explained.

379

Clymo and Vlautin had long ago retained experts to chart the mysterious evolution of Dorothea Puente. She was not a multiple personality, and she was far too organized and controlled to be legally insane. Yet these experts would hold up the lens through which to view her, and now her disorders would be inspected, her tragedies laid bare, her life subjected to a most intense voyeurism.

Much as she may dislike the process, a heartrending appeal by her attorneys might actually save her life.

On September 21, 1993, the jurors locked their eyes on Judge Virga and listened as he instructed them that, after this portion of the trial, they must decide whether Dorothea Puente would be sentenced to life imprisonment without parole, or death. With that, the whole legal apparatus swung away from whether she'd committed murder, to why; from the question of the crime, to the question of the criminal.

As always, the prosecution went first, but the law placed strict limits on the aggravating factors he was permitted to present. So O'Mara's case was kept to a minimum: one prop—a large chart of crimes, dates, victims, and locations—and a transcript of Malcolm McKenzie's 1982 testimony against Puente. (What more could he do? Call to the stand orphaned children who had become upstanding citizens? Call Dorothea's siblings and ask, "You had the same awful childhood, but you've never murdered anyone, have you?")

The law gave great leeway to the defense in this phase of trial, however, and they had some powerfully mitigating factors in store. As their first witness, they called Linda Bloom.

A graceful woman entered wearing a tailored teal suit. She raised a well-manicured hand, swore to tell the truth, and sat down.

"How do you know Dorothea Puente?" Vlautin asked.

"She's my mother."

The room snapped to attention.

The resemblance was unmistakable. Smoothly styled blonde hair framed a face that—with China-blue eyes, broad cheeks, and small nose—was a younger, prettier version of Dorothea Puente.

Linda Bloom explained the circumstances of her adoption as she understood them, and as she spoke in clear, dignified tones, her mother plucked out a tissue and dabbed her eyes. "I was born with pneumonia," Bloom was saying. "At the time, pneumonia in children was not something all that common. Shots had to be flown in from

St. Louis." It was expensive, Bloom said, adding that she'd been told that Dorothea had gotten in "some trouble for writing bad checks to take care of me."*

In Bloom's understanding, eighteen-year-old Dorothea, pressured by her family, had reluctantly relinquished her baby girl to parents who were more able to handle the medical bills and provide a nurturing, loving home. "My mother always told me that my [biological] mother was a very sweet, concerned person," Bloom said. "She'd stressed how important it was that I receive a college education. That struck my mother as odd at the time." (Daughters didn't often go to college in those days).

Under questioning, Bloom explained that she had indeed gone to college, earning a master's degree in economics.

Vlautin asked how she'd become reunited with her biological mother.

A phone call from Dorothea's eldest brother, James Gray, had come out of the blue in 1982. Bloom then corresponded with various members of the Gray family, but they'd claimed not to know where Dorothea might be. (She was in prison from 1982 to 1985). Later, Bloom said, her voice cracking, she'd learned that her uncle had lied to her; he'd been in contact with Dorothea all along.

Dorothea plucked another tissue from the box.

In 1987, Dorothea had phoned. "She was very warm," Bloom recalled. But when her mother told her that she was a doctor, Bloom knew this couldn't be true, and felt "that maybe she needed to impress me."

After months of phone calls, letters, and Dorothea's characteristic gifts, the two finally met in 1988 when Bloom stopped by with her husband and young son for a visit. (Dorothea Puente, ever the actress, had greeted her in a fancy pink chiffon dress, welcoming her into her home at 1426 F Street on an August day when the weather was warm and the yard was crowded with graves.)

Linda Bloom hardly knew her biological mother, yet the forty-six-year-old had flown up from L.A. to plead for her life. "I know that she had a horrendous childhood, was neglected and let down every

---

*This was a distortion of the truth. Bloom's birth (as Melody Jean McFaul) was registered August 4, 1947, and she was adopted three months later. Puente pleaded guilty to forgery charges five months after that, on April 28, 1948.

step of her life," she said, looking stricken, "and I'm asking the jury to consider life without parole rather than the death penalty."

As Linda Bloom stepped from the witness stand, she and her mother—virtual strangers bound by genetics—both wept.

It was an emotional start to what would be the most tear-stained portion of Puente's trial.

Having carefully plotted the course of testimony, the defense planned to present the puzzle of Dorothea Puente bit by bit—the impoverished child, the confused teenager, the ill-equipped mother, the reckless hooker, the compulsive care giver, the battered wife, the Hispanic philanthropist, the disturbed adult—assembling their argument that her life should be spared.

Next, they called Dr. Mindy Rosenberg, a clinical psychologist from Sausalito, California, the designated expert on Dorothea Puente's childhood. As Dr. Rosenberg spoke to the jury in mellow, serious tones, the murderess before them melted away, replaced by sad, skinny little Dorothy Helen Gray,* a bewildered child in a chaotic household.

It was an ugly scene, a homelife that went from bad to worse, with a father terminally ill and a mother hell-bent on drinking herself to oblivion. They fought constantly, screaming about booze and money and men. Besides being a drunk, Mom was a hooker.

In the mid-1930s, Jesse James Gray, increasingly incapacitated by TB, nearly succumbed to suicidal depression. One night he climbed a water tower and threatened to jump off. More than once he put a gun to his head while the children pleaded, "Don't do it, Daddy, don't do it!"

With their mother in and out of jail and their father in and out of the hospital, the eldest children tried to fill the parental void, with uneven success. The two littlest ones, Dorothy and her brother Ray, were frequently unsupervised, always starved for attention.

In 1936, an aunt finally called the juvenile authorities, who came to investigate. They took statements from all seven children, including Dorothy, who said, "I'm seven and a half. I'm in the first grade and go to San Antonio School. I want to live with Daddy, and if I can't live with him, I want to live with my sister. I don't want to live with Mama, she gets drunk."

---

*Although she was named Dorothea Helen Gray at birth, Dr. Rosenberg referred to her as Dorothy, her legally changed name.

The authorities wrote: "These are exceptionally fine youngsters who are sadly in need of a mother's care." The American Red Cross called the situation "pathetic."

But this was a time when government was loath to take children from their own parents, and they were subsequently returned to their mother's custody.

Meanwhile, each time Jesse Gray's health took a downturn, the family bade farewell and braced for his death. When it finally came, Trudie Gray's alcoholism spun out of control. She would simply disappear, leaving the children to fend for themselves. They scavenged for bottles to turn in for coins, emptied the cupboards and existed on catsup sandwiches, or begged in front of the bakery shop.

When Trudie Gray was home, it was worse. If Dorothy told anyone that her mother had left them alone, she got whipped.

And then there were the men, drunken strangers, traipsing in and out of the house at all hours. When a man arrived, whatever the weather, the children were often sent out to ride the trolley cars to nowhere. Or they would lie in bed and listen to the sounds of brawling and copulation coming from the next room.

The kids remember their mother riding off on motorcycles. They remember her coming in with two black eyes. They remember cleaning up her vomit.

One weekend when Dorothy was nine, her siblings were sent to stay with various relatives, but she somehow was left behind. Forgotten.

On Monday, discovery of this solitary, sobbing child finally prompted action. Juvenile authorities snatched the three youngest children from their neglectful mother and placed Audrey, Dorothy, and Ray in the Church of Christ Home in Ontario, California, in February 1938. At registration, Dorothy was described as very thin, with the beginnings of a potbelly, a sign of malnutrition.

Though the Gray children were in an orphanage, they weren't *real* orphans, they told the others, because their mother was still alive. Maybe she would get sober. Maybe she would get a home and come for them.

But months later, just after Christmas, a car full of relatives came to take the youngsters to "a service." They rode along without explanation. Then, when the car pulled up in front of a funeral parlor, they were told that their mother was dead. Little Audrey screamed hysterically. The eldest daughter, Wilma, fainted. (A little more than a year later, she, too, would die in a motorcycle accident.)

After the funeral, the three youngest kids were brought back to the orphanage and dropped off as if nothing had happened . . . except that the Gray children were teased because now they were truly orphans.

The orphanage was hardly idyllic. The older kids sometimes took the younger ones down to the basement, where they sexually abused them. Ray recounted such an incident; he recalled seeing Dorothy down there too. She was naked.

More than once, Dorothy ran away. Early on, she became a thief. And she was always, *always* telling wild stories.

For a time, Audrey and Dorothy were sent to live with their maternal grandmother, a nasty old woman who left them with more emotional scars. She made sure they felt unwelcome. And she always told fair, blue-eyed Dorothy that she was illegitimate, born of one of her mother's customers. (Jesse Gray was of darker coloring.)

Her older sister Audrey, who was eventually adopted, said their childhood was "like living in hell," adding, "I always thought there was something wrong with Dorothy."

Off and on, Dorothy and her little brother Ray lived with their eldest brother, James, and his wife, Louise. The Grays were Seventh Day Adventists of varying conviction, meaning that Dorothy and Ray might be punished today for something that was permitted yesterday. And there was later some suspicion that James had sexually molested his littler sister.

Dr. Rosenberg talked of the damage wrought by pervasive neglect, multiple losses, overwhelming deprivation, and psychological maltreatment. She also explained that, surrounded by so much chaos, by fluctuating rules and an ever-changing cast of characters, Dorothy had had trouble forming a strong sense of who she was. She'd lacked the feedback needed to develop a solid identity.

Small children often go through a period of fantasizing or "magical thinking," Dr. Rosenberg said. Extremely deprived children might fantasize, for example, that they're adopted, that their "real" family is wealthy, loving, and kind. In this psychologist's view, due to the emotional shocks of losing both parents and a sister at such a young age, Dorothy "got stuck" in this stage. She had a deep-rooted compulsion to distort, an overwhelming need to impress others. The truth, Dr. Rosenberg said, was too painful.

In fact, Dorothea Puente had even lied in her interviews with Dr. Rosenberg, so the psychologist testified only to information that she'd been able to substantiate.*

While Dorothea's life was a pastiche of larceny and deception, it was also laced with unselfishness and generosity. She'd become, Dr. Rosenberg said, a "compulsive care giver." And witnesses were soon streaming into court to testify to the warm, compassionate side of Dorothea Puente.

One young woman wept continuously as she recalled how Dorothy Johansson had taken her and her sisters under her wing. She told a touching story of impoverished kids dazzled by the kindhearted gestures of a heavy but "beautiful" neighbor. Dorothy had made sure that charity food baskets and clothes were delivered to her family. She'd taught them how to dress, even taking them to restaurants and teaching them manners. At eleven, this little girl had seen her first Santa Claus. "We didn't know Christmas until we knew Dorothy," she sobbed.

And Dorothea Puente, the cold-blooded killer, wept too. Several now-adult women spoke lovingly of a kind but "lonely" woman who had made a difference in their lives. Still, it was hard to keep all of Dorothea Puente's identities straight. One well-dressed young woman, describing her own chaotic upbringing and how Dorothea had stepped in to offer calm, guidance, and "sanctuary," declared, "I hate to think where I'd be today if it weren't for Sharon Johansson."

Others spoke just as passionately of "la doctora" Dorothea Puente. An entourage from Sacramento's Mexican-American community marched through the courtroom to recount the good works of la doctora— scholarships, sponsorships, donations—and to declare their enduring affection for the woman they knew as generous and kind. Ricardo Ordorica's brother-in-law recalled how they'd sat on her front porch while she taught him English. A radio announcer who owed his first job to Dorothea admitted he still kept a picture of her on his wall. And a Sacramento TV reporter, Rosie Gaytan, recalled a charity dance when Governor Jerry Brown had crossed the room to kiss Puente's cheek, then danced with each of them.

---

*Family members agreed to speak to Dr. Rosenberg on the condition that they wouldn't have to testify (which presented legal problems for John O'Mara). Their childhood was too awful to talk about, they said, and they didn't care to be publicly linked to their serial killer sister.

At about this same time, Puente was dating Mr. Avila, of the attorney general's office, and writing up a generous will to bequeath all kinds of things that she did not own. Her attorney, Don Dorfman, recalled that she would bring in young women (usually "adopted daughters") in need of legal services, and she would pay the fees.

Many who knew *la doctora* during this period could not accept that she'd been convicted of multiple murder. One Mexican-American man hotly declared outside court, "We know the real story. We know the real Dorothea."

Perhaps. But more likely, they knew just one version, a public persona subsidized by secrets.

What had happened? What had made this maven of good works turn from the light to the shadows?

Answers flowed from a forensic psychiatrist with sterling credentials (a graduate of Harvard Law School and University of Southern California Medical School), Dr. William Vicary. Having studied Puente's massive file, having administered psychological tests, having scanned for brain damage, Dr. Vicary concluded that Dorothea Puente was a woman of normal IQ, with normal brain function, who suffered from "antisocial personality disorder."

In less polite terms, she was a sociopath.

Speaking compassionately of Mrs. Puente's predicament, Dr. Vicary said, "She's in a very bad situation here. She's a very sick lady. She's got one foot on a banana peel and the other in the gas chamber."

Citing some of her more outrageous stories—that she was a doctor of psychiatry, had a villa in Mexico, was on a committee formed by Governor Brown—Dr. Vicary called her lies "symptoms" of a "sad person that has a lot of pain inside. They make up a reality in which they're special. They invent a wonderful, dreamlike world, and others are fascinated."*

In Dr. Vicary's view, Dorothea's problems were rooted in a childhood that was nasty, brutish, and short.

He interpreted her nurturing of little girls as an attempt not only to right the wrong in her own upbringing, but as an expression of remorse over having given up her own daughters. Further, he said, it was no accident that she'd ended up taking care of alcoholics, just as

---

*Even the Rorschach or "ink blot," test, now computerized and considered objective, revealed "impulsiveness," "disorganization under stress," and a "self-image based on imaginary rather than real experience."

she'd taken care of her own parents. These were the types of people she was accustomed to, the types she'd cleaned up after, even the types she'd married.

Anyone remotely familiar with psychology could spot Dorothea Puente's repetitive attempts to resolve the problems within her own past. But she wasn't just another adult child of alcoholics in need of a twelve-step program. The psychiatrist observed, "Over time, she seems to be getting worse, not better."

Defense attorney Vlautin asked the pivotal question, "How can someone like Dorothea Puente do so much good, yet stand convicted of these crimes?"

"In a way, her greatest strength turned out to be her greatest weakness," Dr. Vicary replied. "She had some empathy, some positive feelings, [a talent for] taking people quite broken and trying to fix them. She had a need to help. On the other side of that, there's a lot of pain, resentment, hostility, even hatred."

In Dr. Vicary's view, the tenants at 1426 F Street were a step down from the boarders at 2100 F Street. And dealing with these skid-row alcoholics put her in such a stressful situation that she "unraveled." As he put it, "Who are the people who are missing? Very difficult, exasperating people. And inside this woman is a lot of anger and pain against these people—just like the people who abused and neglected her."

He continued, his voice dramatically low, "Inside, there's this thing that's eating her. It festered, and festered, and finally erupted. It had to come out somewhere. It came out with all these missing people. That is the bridge between her traumatic past and these horrible crimes."

John O'Mara had declined the opportunity to cross-examine most of the witnesses—there was nothing to be gained by arguing over Puente's childhood or belittling her good deeds—but Dr. Vicary had voiced opinions on her criminal nature, and this, in O'Mara's view, demanded some response.

In a trial, psychiatrists are the ultimate spin doctors. Now, under questioning by O'Mara, the jury would get a slightly different spin on Puente's past.

For instance, while all of her husbands had been painted as abusive drunks who took advantage of kindhearted Dorothea, the jury now learned that Pedro Montalvo, her fourth husband, had come through for her when she was arrested for forgery in 1978. He'd posted a bond to get his former wife out of jail. And a hefty portion of the more than four thousand dollars she was ordered to pay in restitution came from a thousand-dollar Social Security check made out to him.

Dr. Vicary had suggested that the tenants at 1426 F Street were so unruly that they'd somehow ignited Puente's smoldering hatred, but O'Mara pointed out that this paradigm didn't hold true for either her friend and business partner Ruth Munroe, or for her fiancé Everson Gillmouth.

O'Mara asked about his euphemistic use of the term *missing*, and Dr. Vicary made a surprising admission: "I guess that's one way of saying people were being murdered. . . . I assume—with all due respect to the jury—that all the people that were missing were murdered."

(The defense cringed at this bit of candor from their expert. "Their faces fell like cakes in an oven," a juror noted.)

The psychiatrist also admitted that Dorothea Puente was conscious of her actions and knew the difference between right and wrong. She did not kill in a blind, murderous rage; she did not hear voices; she was not psychotic. Dorothea Puente was in control.

Finally, Dr. Vicary had virtually guaranteed Puente a mouthpiece in the courtroom, having told her that everything she told him would be funneled into court; there was no confidentiality, no doctor/patient privilege. So, asked about each of the nine victims, she'd claimed to have known this one since the seventies, that one since the sixties . . . they were all longtime friends.

Yet she hadn't the faintest idea how these dear old friends, about whom she cared so deeply, had ended up buried in her yard. Of course, they had plenty of health problems, she told him, which she ticked off one by one, including Ruth Monroe's "fatty liver." Clearly, she'd been paying attention during her trial.

Dorothea had also hastened to point out that she'd *always* had trouble sleeping. She rarely slept more than four hours a night, even after swallowing a double dose of Dalmane. That's *two* thirty-milligram tablets, she noted, in case the doctor might miss it.

Dr. Vicary dutifully testified to each transparent embellishment, each classic bit of Puente fabrication. To the end, she just didn't understand that she couldn't lie her way out of this one, that in trying to shield herself, she only revealed herself.

✿   ✿   ✿

It seemed unlikely that Dorothea Puente would get the death penalty. Not in the state of California. After all, there was no pain: Whether with pills or pillows, she was killing them softly.

But prosecutor John O'Mara had other criteria for the death penalty. By his moral standards, Puente had earned the highest possible sentence. So, on October 6, 1993, he stood—bearded now, and angry—with righteousness blasting through him. Paraphrasing Robert Louis Stevenson, he said, "Eventually, everyone sits down to a banquet of consequences," then paused, letting his theme sink in.

Either sentence—life without parole or the death penalty—would protect society, he pointed out, so this was a "nonissue." But, he asked, "Is that the end of the inquiry? Isn't there some measure of justice? Isn't there some question of accountability, some responsibility that lies at the foot of this woman?"

Voice rising, he went on, "That's what this trial is all about. She killed three people! Some of you think she killed seven people, some of you think she killed all nine of them! *How high does the body count have to be?*"

His question boomed through the room.

O'Mara brushed aside Puente's traumatic past. "She's not twenty years old, still suffering the ravages of an abused childhood. She wasn't some teenager, she was on the advent of her sixth decade! This woman was fifty-eight years old when she killed Leona. She was fifty-nine years old when she killed Mr. Fink."

Returning to his theme, he demanded, "Does anyone ever become responsible for their conduct in this world? Shall we dismiss this person because she had an abused childhood?" Dr. Vicary had said, "Sick people make sick choices." But, O'Mara asked, "Isn't that a way to minimize her culpability?"

He found Dr. Vicary's explanation of Dorothea Puente's festering anger and exploding rage simply fatuous. "Is she symbolically killing her mother? Is she symbolically killing her father? That would be convenient," he scoffed.

"If she had a thing about abusive drunks, why didn't she kill John McCauley? He was the most abusive of them all! If this is inevitable, why didn't she kill Pat Kelley? Was she able to control that rage?"

And if she'd been so emotionally brittle, so angry inside, why had she been able to make so many friends over the years? Why had so many people come to testify for her? And why hadn't her friends—or even her psychiatrist, Dr. Doody—observed that she was on the brink? How had she been able to conceal her uncontrollable acts? "If this was an explosion that occurred over time, how was it that she was so lucky that she could commit three, seven, *nine* murders, *and nobody saw or heard anything?*"

In O'Mara's view, Puente hadn't been irrepressibly compelled, but rather, had coldly *elected* to kill these people. She'd had three years in prison to ruminate on the fact that those who had lived had filed charges against her in 1982, while Ruth Munroe lay silent in her grave.

Clearly, the dead caused fewer problems.

"Antisocial personality disorder," he said, waving *DSM-III*,* the "Bible" of psychiatry, "is characterized by lying, cheating, stealing. No conscience. What is the ultimate antisocial act? *Murder.*"

O'Mara was indignant, his voice rising in emotional cadences. "They were human beings! They had a right to live! What did they have? They didn't have cars—they had their little Social Security checks and their lives. *She took their checks away, she took their lives, and then they didn't have anything!*"

He recalled that, in a juror's questionnaire filled out nearly a year ago, one of them had written, "The punishment should fit the crime." Now it was time, he declared, for Dorothea Puente to "sit down to the banquet." Scoffing at the defense's appeal for mercy, he declared. "She should be afforded the same mercy she showed to Leona Carpenter, Dorothy Miller, and Ben Fink!"

Abruptly, he lowered his voice and said, "I've yelled at you enough. I apologize. And whatever your decision, the People of the State of California thank you."

After his thunderous speech, the jury exited looking pale and shaken.

Next, Kevin Clymo stood and evoked Dorothea the child, Dorothea the caregiver, unfolding the facets of her personality that the jury might weigh in her favor.

Finally, Peter Vlautin addressed the jury in confidential tones. Intentionally contrasting with O'Mara, in a voice so low it was almost a

---

*American Psychiatric Association: Diagnostic and Statistical Manual of Mental Disorders, third edition, revised.

whisper, he began, "We are here today to determine one thing: What is the value of Dorothea Puente's life? That is the question. Does it have value? Does she have to be killed?"

Vlautin spoke gently about Puente's childhood, touching upon the traumatic aspects that had shaped her, urging them to try to see the world through her eyes. "You have heard about the despair which was the foundation of her life, the anger, and the resentment . . . If anyone says that what Dorothea Puente went through wasn't that bad, ask them, would you want that to have happened to yourself? Would you want that to happen to one of your children?"

Vlautin spoke almost poetically of mitigating factors, and of the people who had come to testify on Puente's behalf. "I am led to believe that, if there is any reason for any of us to be living here on this earth, it is to somehow enhance one another's humanity, to love, to touch each other, to know that you have made even just one life breathe easier because you have lived. And I submit to you that is why these people came, because Dorothea Puente made their lives easier."

He continued in hushed tones, saying, "I think you can only truly understand why this unprecedented array of people came to Monterey if you have ever been lost in this world. If any of you have ever fallen down and stumbled on the road of life, and had somebody pick you up, give you comfort, give you love, show you the way. Then you will understand why those people came in here and testified. Because that is what Dorothea Puente did for them. That is mitigating. That is a human quality that deserves to be preserved. It is a flame of humanity that has burned inside her since she was young," he concluded quietly, "and that is reason to give Dorothea Puente life without possibility of parole."

On October 7, 1993, the jury began deciding whether Dorothea Puente would join the four other women waiting on California's death row.

She'd proved a most paradoxical killer. She could be argued convincingly from either side because she was so strongly two-sided. Not schizophrenic. Not insane. And never what she seemed. She was an enigma for the jury to try to fathom.

So now, her web unraveled, her beauty faded, she waited to hear her sentence.

❖　　❖　　❖

391

On October 13, 1993, *Oprah* was interrupted for breaking news from Monterey: Dorothea Puente's jury had deadlocked in the penalty phase.

Judge Michael J. Virga was declaring a mistrial, and the DA's office had decided not to retry the penalty phase. Puente would get life without parole by default.

"Dorothea is relieved; we're all relieved," said an ebullient Peter Vlautin. Kevin Clymo nodded, saying, "Thank God it's over."

That sentiment was echoed by the jury. They'd hung seven-five in favor of life without parole, but they were unanimous in their expressions of relief.

It had been a long, frustrating ordeal. Eleven of them were firmly convinced that Puente had murdered not just three, but seven, eight, or all nine of the victims. A single person had them deadlocked, nearly causing a mistrial on all counts. In the end, they'd felt lucky to convict on even three.

Asked why the jury hadn't convicted Puente for murdering Bert Montoya, postal worker Joseph Martin shook his head with regret. "Bert was a real obvious one to me," he said, adding dismally, "I argued about Bert for hours and hours."

Asked about the holdout, Sergeant Gary Frost, the XREMIST, shrugged and said, "I can't get inside his head," adding, "I don't see, as a reasonable human being, how you could ignore what was presented to us."

At times the jury room had been filled with heat and noise. Eleven of the jurors had argued feverishly about other hung counts—Ruth Munroe, Vera Faye Martin, James Gallop—but nothing could persuade that single juror. (Strangely, the vote on Betty Palmer had split three for first-degree murder, six for second-degree, three for acquittal. On Everson Gillmouth, the split was eight for second-degree, two for manslaughter, two for acquittal.)

During their record-breaking deliberations, they'd examined the evidence from all sides—the sequence of events, the credibility of witnesses, the toxicology results, the money trail—until they knew the case cold. Each juror had brought to deliberations some distinct talent or keenness of mind that dovetailed neatly with the others . . . except for that solitary holdout.

He'd insisted there wasn't enough evidence. And he'd balked at the idea that pharmaceutical drugs could be synonymous with poison.

Only after Judge Virga had urged them to try reverse role playing had he been convinced that Ben Fink, Dorothy Miller, and Leona Carpenter had been murdered. But only those three.

"We had eleven frustrated jurors," one said, adding sadly that the families of the victims "were never forgotten."

Citing reasons for the three convictions, jurors recalled that Dorothy Miller had been forcibly kept in her room by a hired man who said she had a "phenobarbital drool," though Puente had told him she was drunk; that after Puente had taken Ben Fink upstairs to "make him feel better," workers burying "garbage" found maggots in the yard where Fink was later unearthed; that the evidence completely supported O'Mara's argument that "Betty" was actually Leona Carpenter, a woman too sick to have ingested anything without help. A couple of jurors, having scrutinized Puente for months, commented on her cold façade, her lack of remorse. Much as they'd tried, they said, they couldn't summon any compassion for the woman.

Jury foreman Michael Esplin even shared a short poem he'd penned about the case:

> *One by the river,*
> *One in the bed,*
> *Seven in the ground,*
> *One with no head,*
> *All dead.*

Lastly, a Catholic member of the jury noted that the religious figurine in the shrine over poor headless Betty Palmer's corpse was not Saint Francis, as it was often called, but Saint Anthony, the patron saint of missing things. And Saint Dorothea, she recalled, is the patron saint of gardening.

EPILOGUE

It's a little seedy now, but the blue-and-white Victorian at 1426 F Street is still being rented by Ricardo Ordorica. Before the trial, news crews stopped by the house on two separate occasions to interview the renters. And both times, from two sets of tenants, they were told that Dorothea Puente's former home was haunted. They'd wakened to strange sounds, to inexplicable moaning. Crossing themselves, they'd hung rosaries on the walls.

After Puente's convictions, another news team visited her former boardinghouse, and a fresh set of tenants told them that the house was normal and quiet.

Perhaps now, with some measure of justice served, the spirits can rest.

The vagrants of Sacramento still wander from place to place, sleeping on cold concrete, waking in city shadows, mining dumpsters for some worthwhile refuse. These vulnerable souls, often unable to take care of themselves, make easy victims. They always will.

But, as one result of this strange case, the Social Security Administration has tightened controls on the representative payee program. Still, there are loopholes and budget cutbacks. The system is far from perfect.

Judy Moise still works in the mental health field, but has left her stressful job with the Volunteers of America. She can finally speak of Bert Montoya without tearing up, having "let go of the guilt" she felt for trusting Dorothea Puente, and feels satisfied with her role in launching the investigation. Meanwhile, her lovely daughter studies acting and appears in TV commercials. And her son is finally responding to treatment for his schizophrenia, thanks to a breakthrough drug, Closiril.

John O'Mara, who lost some thirty pounds during Puente's arduous trial, has returned to his family, to his five acres, and to his fourth-floor office, where he plows ahead in typical workaholic fashion. Though still heading up the homicide division, he has promised his family that he won't prosecute any more out-of-county cases.

Peter Vlautin has decided to forgo any more capital cases for a while, handling other serious crimes, such as serial rape. After the Puente trial, he says, "It will be like working drunk-driving cases."

Kevin Clymo has returned to his private practice in Sacramento, where buttons and stickers on his walls proclaim "Death-defying" and "DON'T KILL FOR ME, I oppose the death penalty." He's looking forward to a quieter life, out of the limelight. A little sailing would be nice, he says.

He probably doesn't remember it, but during an interview in 1992, Clymo made a cryptic comment about Dorothea Puente. "She has an identity problem," he said, not knowing that Judy Moise had made this exact comment about Bert Montoya long before.

In some ways, Bert and Dorothea were two sides of the same coin: deprived children, fully grown; one trusting, one untrustworthy. Like Dorothea, Bert wandered a tragic trail, from a bruised childhood in Costa Rica with an abusive father, to a psychotic adolescence in New Orleans with his distraught mother, to a rootless adulthood that eventually brought him and his voices to Sacramento.

It would have been easy enough for Bert to have turned mean. But he was an honest, goodhearted man who never lifted a hand in anger to anyone. There was something deeply appealing about Bert Montoya, something timid and inarticulate that tended to draw out one's best impulses. Maybe people loved this simple man because of what he let them discover in themselves.

Many wondered how Dorothea Puente, this apparently caring old woman, could have been so cold-blooded . . . especially in the case of Bert, for whom she appeared to have a genuine fondness. But Puente is a sociopath, and it's probably a mistake to think she had any true feelings for anyone. Egocentric, motivated purely by self-interest, sociopaths cannot form relationships in the usual sense. Her victims were a means to an end. Convenient. Disposable. Her affection for Bert was a ruse.

Unlike male serial killers, who kill random strangers, Puente killed those who trusted her, who ate at her table. Most likely, every boarder she met was sized up first as a possible donor to her coffers. Some victims surely stood and watched as the digging went on, never guessing that they were the intended occupants.

Some believe there may be other bodies yet to be found. John O'Mara investigated two other missing people, but had too little evidence to press charges. With a shrug, he says, "There are some things we may never know."

Dorothea Puente will probably live out her days without confessing to the nine murders that bear her signature. Serving out her life sentence, she is surely shepherding her "nieces" within the confines of the women's prison at Chowchilla, playing the godmother. At least she won't be shanking guards and shimmying out air vents.

One can only wonder why painful childhoods beget both gentle souls and heartless killers. Are we born tabula rasa? Or with distinct personalities, good and evil? Decades of doctoral theses, of clinical studies, of philosophical speculation have brought us no closer to an answer than to an effective way to stop dogs from howling through the night.

But if we give much heed to theories of behavioral patterning, to the subliminal influences of even the most neglectful parents, there remains a little nugget from Dorothea's past that may explain some imprinting that even she can't recall. Typed on her mother's death certificate is a telling detail, Trudie Gray's final lie: her occupation, she claimed, was *practical nurse*.

❀   ❀   ❀

Epilogue

Dorothea Puente is extremely calculating, a master manipulator, a beguiling liar. She's played many roles. But with all her aliases and all her stories, the woman born Dorothea Helen Gray never developed into a whole person.

Who is she, in the end, but some sad, vast lie? She's devoid of feeling. Hollow. Empty as an open grave.

APPENDIX I

Trace amounts of drugs found in the bodies' tissues, given in milligrams per kilogram. Any asterisk indicates prescribed drugs. "<" is the sign for "less than."

#88–3372: LEONA CARPENTER, 78, approx. 100 lbs., 5'2"

Drugs	Brain
flurazepam*	0.04
metabolite 1	0.13
metabolite 2	0.84
diazepam	0.74
codeine	0.50

#88–3374: DOROTHY MILLER, 65, 120 lbs., 5'7"

Drugs	Brain	Liver
flurazepam	0.03	0.07
metabolite 1	0.06	0.09
metabolite 2	0.97	0.83
carbamazepine	54.0	68.0

#88–3381: BERT MONTOYA, 52, 180 lbs., 5'5"

Drugs	Brain	Liver
flurazepam*	0.95	0.88
metabolite 1	0.09	0.06
metabolite 2	0.41	0.35

diphenhydramine	<0.5	1.5
loxapine	<2.5	<7.7
amitriptyline	0.10	0.49
carbamazepine	<3.0	<5.0

#88–3382: BENJAMIN FINK, 55, 155 lbs., 5'8"

Drugs	Brain	Liver
flurazepam	0.0	0.04
metabolite 1	0.2	1.30
metabolite 2	1.8	0.66
loxapine	5.3	15.5
amitriptyline	3.8	21.6
nortriptyline	7.7	22.0

#88–3384: JAMES GALLOP, 64, 132 lbs., 5'10"

Drugs	Brain	Liver
flurazepam*	0.29	0.36
metabolite 1	0.19	7.73
metabolite 2	0.90	5.97
phenytoin*	8.5	13.5
amitriptyline	<0.5	1.1
nortriptyline	0.5	0.7

#88–3394: VERA FAYE MARTIN, 65, 100 lbs., 5'2"

Drugs	Brain	Liver
flurazepam	0.15	1.6
metabolite 1	0.35	0.75
metabolite 2	1.60	0.13

#88–3395: BETTY MAE PALMER, 79, 100 lbs., 5'1½"

Drugs	Liver
flurazepam	1.5
metabolite 1	3.31
metabolite 2	1.28
haloperidol*	2.17
doxylamine	<1.0

Amitriptyline, an antidepressant, is commonly sold as Elavail.

Carbamazepine, an anticonvulsant, is commonly sold as Tegretol.

Codeine, a narcotic, is often combined in other medications.

Diazepam, a tranquilizer, is commonly sold as Valium.

Diphenhydramine, an antihistamine and depressant, is a common ingredient in medications such as Benadryl and Sominex.

Doxylamine, an antihistamine and hypnotic, is an ingredient in Unisom and other medications.

Flurazepam, a sedative, is commonly sold as Dalmane; its two metabolites are N_1-hydroxethyl-flurazepam and N_1-desalkyl-flurazepam.

Haloperidol, an antipsychotic, is commonly sold as Haldol.

Loxapine, an antipsychotic, is commonly sold as Loxitane.

Nortriptyline, an antidepressant, is commonly sold as Aventyl.

Phenytoin, an anticonvulsant, is commonly sold as Dilantin.

APPENDIX II

PRESCRIPTIONS FOR DALMANE (FLURAZEPAM)
AVAILABLE TO DOROTHEA MONTALVO PUENTE
(30 pills, 30 mg unless otherwise noted)

Date	Pharmacy	Doctor	Patient
10-29-85	McAnaw's	Herrera*	Dorothy Montalvo
12-16-85	McAnaw's	Herrera	Dorothy Montalvo
1-24-86	McAnaw's	Herrera	Dorothy Montalvo
2-20-86	McAnaw's	Herrera	Dorothy Montalvo
2-26-86	McAnaw's		Leona Carpenter
4-11-86	McAnaw's	Herrera	Dorothy Montalvo
6-09-86	McAnaw's	Doody†	Dorothea Puente
7-02-86	Payless	Doody	Dorothea Puente
7-24-86	McAnaw's	Doody	Dorothea Puente
8-22-86	McAnaw's	Doody	Dorothea Puente
9-08-86	Payless	Doody	Dorothea Puente
9-19-86	McAnaw's	Herrera	Dorothea Puente
9-19-86	McAnaw's		Leona Carpenter
11-10-86	McAnaw's	Herrera	Dorothea Puente

*Dr. Jose Herrera has stopped practicing medicine.
†Dr. Thomas Doody's attorney said he was too ill to testify at Puente's trial.

Appendix II

Date	Pharmacy	Doctor	Patient
11-28-86	Payless	Doody	Dorothea Puente
12-29-86	McAnaw's	Herrera	Dorothy Montalvo
1-24-87	Payless	Doody	Dorothea Puente
2-13-87	Payless	Doody	Dorothea Puente
2-19-87	McAnaw's	Herrera	Dorothy Montalvo
3-25-87	Payless	Doody	Dorothea Puente
4-20-87	McAnaw's	Herrera	Dorothy Montalvo
5-20-87	McAnaw's	Mesic	James Gallop (15 mg)
6-15-87	McAnaw's	Doody	Dorothea Puente
7-15-87	Payless	Doody	Dorothea Puente
8-12-87	Payless	Doody	Dorothea Puente
9-01-87	McAnaw's	Doody	Dorothea Puente
9-25-87	Payless	Doody	Dorothea Puente
10-29-87	Payless	Doody	Dorothea Puente
12-01-87	Payless	Doody	Dorothea Puente
1-22-88	Payless	Doody	Dorothea Puente
3-15-88	Payless	Doody	Dorothea Puente
4-13-88	Payless	Doody	Dorothea Puente
5-24-88	McAnaw's	Doody	Dorothea Puente
6-28-88	McAnaw's	Doody	Dorothea Puente
7-11-88	McAnaw's	Doody	Bert Montoya
7-27-88	McAnaw's	Doody	Dorothea Puente
8-24-88	Payless	Doody	Dorothea Puente
9-26-88	Payless	Doody	Dorothea Puente
11-01-88	Payless	Doody	Dorothea Puente

INDEX

Index

Index

Index

Index

Index

413